EVIDENCE
NO ONE COULD EVER
IMAGINE

A Memoir

FRANK CLAY JR.

Copyright © 2023 Frank Clay Jr.
Special Editing (Monticello) Omar Falay
Book cover design by FourStage Marketing

All rights reserved. No part of this book may be reproduced, stored, or transmitted by any means—whether auditory, graphic, mechanical, or electronic—without written permission of both publisher and author, except in the case of brief excerpts used in critical articles and reviews. Unauthorized reproduction of any part of this work is illegal and is punishable by law.

This book is a work of non-fiction. Unless otherwise noted in a reference, the author in conjunction with the publisher make no straightforward guarantees as to the specific accuracy of the information found in this book. In some cases, names of people, companies, and places have been altered to protect their privacy or secrecy.

Scriptures marked KJV are taken from the KING JAMES VERSION (KJV): KING JAMES VERSION, public domain.

Scripture quotations marked NKJV are taken from the New King James Version. Copyright © 1982 by Thomas Nelson, Inc. Used by permission. All rights reserved.

Scripture quotations marked (NIV) are taken from the Holy Bible, New International Version®, NIV®. Copyright © 1973, 1978, 1984, 2011 by Biblica, Inc.™ Used by permission of Zondervan. All rights reserved worldwide. www.zondervan.com The "NIV" and "New International Version" are trademarks registered in the United States Patent and Trademark Office by Biblica, Inc.™

ISBN: 979-8-88640-448-7 (sc)
ISBN: 979-8-88640-449-4 (hc)
ISBN: 979-8-88640-450-0 (e)

Because of the dynamic nature of the Internet, any web addresses or links contained in this book may have changed since publication and may no longer be valid. The views expressed in this work are solely those of the author and do not necessarily reflect the views of the publisher, and the publisher hereby disclaims any responsibility for them.

One Galleria Blvd., Suite 1900, Metairie, LA 70001
1-888-421-2397

ACKNOWLEDGEMENTS

To my all my grandchildren and their children.

In honor of my ancestors and family, who paved a way for me to be who I am today. THANK YOU!

To future generations of African Americans… let my story be apart of your proud history in America. I made it and so can you. Stay free as you are!

CONTENTS

Author's Note vii
Chapter 1   When I Was a Child 1
Chapter 2   Fighting Back 28
Chapter 3   Moving Away for Better 36
Chapter 4   Why Me? Why Not Me? 43
Chapter 5   Choosing to Go Forward 54
Chapter 6   College Escapades 64
Chapter 7   I've Only Just Begun 83
Chapter 8   Working Things Out 92
Chapter 9   Paying Uncle Sam His Due 97
Chapter 10   More than Just About Us 112
Chapter 11   Here We Go 128
Chapter 12   A Fork in the Road 141
Chapter 13   Taking Charge after My Discharge 148
Chapter 14   Real Challenges to Overcome 175
Chapter 15   You Can Only Go So Far 194
Chapter 16   To the Motherland 213
Chapter 17   New Ways to Share 224
Chapter 18   Politically Correct 241
Chapter 19   The ClayGroup 260
Chapter 20   Defining What It Will Take 275
Chapter 21   Hard to Do without You 287
Chapter 22   Knowing When 303
Chapter 23   A Lot to Be Thankful For 312
Chapter 24   The Joy of It All 334
Chapter 25   Monticello 345
Appendix 393
About the Author 400

AUTHOR'S NOTE

Please accept my gratitude for joining my life journey, as I have written about the **EVIDENCE – No One Could Image** that has formed me into the person I am today. When I wrote the first edition of my memoir, it was mainly for the purpose of telling my life story so that one day my grandson would come know what it took for me to become a successful African American man in this country. The challenges that men like myself face from time to time are unavoidable… **no one could ever image,** but so are the successful and amazing stories we have enjoyed that are rarely told in a book for others to read about.

If you go to a bookstore or library, there are very few memoirs or autobiographies on the shelves about how an average African American man, with good character and values, is able to find success in life despite the worldly challenges and in spite of their own personal flaws and shortcomings. I was not a celebrity, President, or some historical figure. I was just a young boy from Philadelphia, trying to navigate life to find good, better and… the best of what life had to offer. I wanted to know more about my roots and make the connection for future generations of African American to somehow appreciate how "slavery and civil rights" plays a part in what we see and witness happening today.

While society misleads and debates concepts like Critical Race Theory and as schools seek to band books about "Black life," writing this second edition of my memoir has helped me to gain a greater meaning of the many struggles of the past. My memoir is not a history book, it is an authentic account of my life's story from the 1960's that hopefully provides guidance, wisdom, and practical advice to anyone who reads these pages. It is a passing down of knowledge. It's a story that should be told. I want any reader to be aware, inspired, enriched and to gain a deeper understanding about what it takes to be a successful African American. It is an opportunity to explore the legacy of success that I have achieved in many ways **no one could image.**

In writing **EVIDENCE - No One Could Image,** I wanted the narrative to be that if you can conceive it, you can find a way to believe it… and if you have the faith to believe it, you can achieve anything in life to a certain degree (good, better, or best). Distractions and Discrimination are a given in the life of any African American, but you handle the mess, past the tests and move on with grace to a better place. So much can be learned from your own history about your family and ancestors: both good and bad. The legacy I wish to promote by writing my memoir is to never give up and never give into the negative… alway seek the positive as you journey toward success and the best of everything that life has to offer.

What I learned by writing memoir was that through it all… I made it through by the grace of God. I realized I was blessed in this life… I am the **EVIDENCE - No One Could Image!**

Thank you for investing your time and resources into purchasing and reading my latest book. Enjoy the read and let me know your thoughts!

Frank Clay Jr.

CHAPTER 1

When I Was a Child

With the life I've been blessed to live all these years, it is interesting that I can remember only a few landmarks from my early youth since my birth in Philadelphia on February 23, 1955. For instance, I recall that at my elementary school—which was six blocks away from our house on East Woodlawn Street—we had to stand in line and hold hands as we walked into our classrooms as little ones. I was always positioned at the end of the line—not because of the color of my skin but because I was tall for my age and tall kids had to stand in back. I guess that could be called height discrimination, which I have suffered all my life. I desperately wanted to be the first kid in the front of the line, but that never happened at my elementary school. If lines were necessary, maybe the teachers should have lined us up from the tallest to the smallest sometimes to make things more fair.

Our schoolyard where we all assembled had no grass, which made it a perfect place for kickball, which I was good at. We used a bouncy red ball. It was fun to play with, especially when it came to dodgeball. I was particularly good at dodgeball because I was quick and skinny. In fact, I had the nickname Sticks because I was as skinny as a stick. If I was being picked on, my grandmother knew it was either because of my last name, Clay, or because I was skinny. She would say to me, "Sticks and stones might break your bones, but names will never hurt you." That little reminder helped me deal with the bullying, stay out of trouble, and avoid retaliation with those who were calling me names.

A block away from our row house was a corner store that had all my favorite candies and bubble gum. I would have done anything for a Kit Kat, Good and Plenty, a Tootsie Roll, a Three Musketeers bar, Wise potato chips, or the Philadelphia original, lemon Tastykake pie. You could get a piece of candy for one or two cents back then. For that reason, I stayed alert at all times for any copper one-cent Lincoln coins on the ground, especially around the baseball park right across the street from our house. A tall, pointed black iron fence surrounded the baseball field and the East Germantown Recreation Center.

I learned the value of a penny early on. I was also attuned to places where coins were dropped or left behind. I routinely checked the telephone booth at the gas station at the end of the block and looked through the sawdust on the floor of our neighborhood butcher shop. In school, we learned of Benjamin Franklin's quote "A penny saved is a penny earned," and I instinctively realized that you needed a penny in your hand to save it. Benjamin Franklin was one of the heroes of my youth because he had flown kites and discovered electricity. I loved to fly kites made of paper, utilizing a ball of string to get them high in the air. I only wished I had learned about and admired other African American scientists like Benjamin Banneker and others.

In a way, I had it all right near me—everything I needed to do keep busy as a kid. The recreation center and baseball field in front of our house were surrounded by grass a full block long in each direction. My favorite time to run around in the field was when all the dandelion weeds were in full bloom and yellow flowers were everywhere. It would be awhile before I was told they were weeds and to stop bringing them into the house. I'd slip through a hole in the fence, and I would run and run until I heard my name: "Junior!" I knew my mother's voice from a mile away, and I came running when I heard it from anywhere.

The iron fence around the recreation center and baseball park has had a lasting impression on my memory. One day, while I was still in school, I saw each section of iron fencing go flying by during a bad storm in the fall. I found myself clenched closely inside the coat my mother was wearing when she came to get me from school. My right ear was against her heart as she held me tightly in her arms and ran quickly to get us home after picking me up from school. The wind and leaves twirled all around her as she rushed home to get back to my brother and sister. It is a fine memory because I never felt that type of closeness to her again. That recollection of a loving mom sacrificing herself to protect her child has stuck with me all my life. I knew my mom cared for me deeply and would have done anything for me to ensure I grew up to be the man I ultimately became—even if she ended up doing some things I never understood the reason for. I loved my mommy, as I called her in my youth. I could always count on my mom to come rescue me.

At the East Germantown Recreation Center, I reigned as the best at playing checkers, which I loved to do. Checkers was my grandfather Clay's favorite board game. I kept an eye on how he mastered a winning checkers strategy from start to finish during our annual family get-together in Fairmount Park in Philadelphia. I studied Grandfather Clay's every move and watched him beat everyone in the family over and over again. I observed how he set someone up for double and triple jumps. He would even jump backward and then call the game "Spanish checkers" to legitimize the move. I never understood the Spanish connotation, nor did I know any Spanish-speaking people at the time. One day, my opportunity to play Grandfather Clay came and we were sitting alone under a tree. I was quick to respond to each move he made. Somehow, I knew what his next moves would be. With me having the only king on the table, I knew I had a sure win if I could maintain control of the Mason Dixon Line—and I did.

The first time I beat Grandfather Clay—or Dear Heart, as we called him—it was as if I had broken his heart. My grandfather was not happy about losing in that moment of final defeat. I could see the disgust on his face. On top of being disappointed about losing in general, he was disappointed that he had lost to the son of one of his least favorite sons, my dad. In his quest to prevent defeat, he made a brilliant move to sucker me into losing my king, but I did not fall for it and I won. After his defeat, he quickly set the checkerboard up again and challenged me to a rematch, motioning firmly for me to make the first move. It was a lesson well learned that Clays are not happy losers. I was a hard person to beat at checkers, and like my grandfather, I did not like losing either. Losing drove me to be more observant and calculative to win, not only in checkers but also in life.

WOODLAWN

On Woodlawn Street, we lived right in the middle of multiple two-story row houses up and down the street. Each had a little patch of grass in front. The patch of grass was so meager that you could cut it with a big pair of scissors. Unfortunately, we lived in front of a drainage sewer, which caused us major problems when it rained, as the street drains would clog up with leaves and trash. That situation would bring out the rats—big rats! They would come into our basement and try to eat their way from the basement door to the kitchen, where they could smell the lingering aromas from my mom's excellent cooking. Because of my experiences growing up, I never liked the cat-and-mouse stories popularized in cartoons and the like. The real cats in the alleys behind us were big and aggressive—they were not the pet type. Likewise, the real rats they looked for were scary. I hated having to go downstairs to get things for my mom at night—particularly in the basement. She would not go, nor would anyone else in my family. I was the one always tasked with doing it, and I hated it with a passion. In the basement, I would swing along the cold water pipes to get what my mom had requested—usually some clothes or a toy for my brother. I hardly ever touched the ground if I had to go into the basement at night. If I had to go to the kitchen, I would line up the chairs so I could leap from one to another to get to the countertop that surrounded our kitchen area. I especially went to those lengths when I could hear rats carving into the basement door to make a hole in it during the night. I just knew those rats were trying to get me, but they never did. My dad would set a trap or put poison down. It was my job to—reluctantly—scoop up the dead bodies with a shovel and throw them in the trash or the garbage can that we kept outside.

Lurking behind our house were narrow alleys where big dogs barked from behind nearby fences. Gangs took shortcuts through the alleys to multiple streets nearby without detection. Like the rats, the dogs and gang members presented an ongoing danger to me. As the first son in a family of five at the time, I was frequently called upon to run to the store for this and that. As part of the mission, my mother would add, "return safely" to whatever she had on the list. The dogs were usually behind the fence, but some were known to jump the fence and get loose—and they were not nice dogs. A few of them chased me and almost bit me. My dodgeball quickness paid off in those incidences. I would leap over a fence as if I were in a track meet if I saw a loose dog coming.

Now, the gangs were different. They wanted either what I had in the brown bag or my money; by instinct, I learned to avoid them on the streets by using the alleys behind the houses as well. Sometimes it was better to go the long way, three or four blocks out of the way, to avoid trouble. When I did, I had to run fast because getting home late and facing my mom in the doorway was not a wise option. Why, you might ask? Because if I took too long, a good beating would be waiting for me!

It was not a good feeling to be robbed by a gang member. Sadly, I had my money and the goods I purchased from the store, taken from me a few times. However, at that age, getting taken advantage of was expected, and the best defense was avoidance of both gang members and dogs. I became good at avoiding both.

On the bright side, while living on Woodlawn Street, I enjoyed watching the evening local baseball games that took place right across the street from our house. I liked baseball, or so I thought. I had never played it officially, even though I had watched it many times. I also don't remember ever having someone to play with who knew the logistics of the game, let alone the proper equipment. Even so, you could find me standing behind the home-plate fence, right behind the umpire. At my age, I was not supposed to cross the street alone, where all the cursing grown men were, but the sound of the ball smashing into the catcher's glove and the umpire saying, "Strike!" drew me. As I clung against the batter's-cage fence, I excitedly anticipated foul balls hitting near where I stood. I longed to feel the vibration of the fence through my clenched fingers. I got my fingers stung a few times, but that did not keep me from standing behind the home-plate fence—that is, until my mom or dad called me home. "Get over here!" they'd yell in the distance. I'd scurry home until the next game. I definitely was going back. The park was where all the action was in my life, and I enjoyed it.

One day I hung around the park after it was locked. I slipped through my usual bent section of the fence and found a glove left behind with a beat-up hardball. I took it home and then brought it back to the park the next day when the teams were playing, and no one claimed it. After my attempted inquiries, a man gestured that it was mine to keep. What a day that was! After that, there by myself, I would try to throw the ball across the plate with my skinny frame. I tried to throw like the pitchers I had observed. Into the dirt my fastballs would go, with no catcher there to receive them. Pretending to my heart's content, I would play all the positions. I even ran the imaginary bases I had carved out in the dirt. That was baseball to me. I never played on a team there or even put on a uniform. Nonetheless, the open field and my imagination provided a great experience for me.

MY PARENTS

My dad worked multiple jobs with the government and worked as a choir director and a nighttime Yellow Cab driver. We saw him at dinnertime or for a few moments before he went to his next job. My mom, who was a stay-at-home mom back then, would give him a brown paper bag with his food wrapped in wax paper. When calling us to dinner, my mom would sound like a bell if we were all outside or upstairs, yelling, "Time to eat!" and we all would come running. Fried chicken with mashed potatoes and peas was my favorite. My mom made golden fried chicken that was to die for, and everyone who knew her wanted her to cook it. I took food my mom cooked to friends, church members, and neighbors when we had plenty to eat. Sharing food was something my mom loved to do. In our home, there were three of us at first—and then four and then five.

On Sundays, we attended church all day. We attended two to three services on any given Sunday. They were long days, but the good news was that somewhere along the way, we would be offered something to eat, and desserts would be guaranteed. In my mind, there was nothing like church cake, which usually was pound cake baked by a church member. I loved that flaky, buttery lemon flavor and usually found a way to get at least two pieces by being a good boy in someone's eyes. It seemed we were the perfect churchgoing family. My dad was the organist or pianist as choirs marched in to the music: "Walk in the light, beautiful light. Jesus, the light of the world." When it was hot, the church opened the windows, and the womenfolk waved hand fans, sweating rivers down their faces with their colorful hats and full wigs on as they praised God while sitting on those long wooden pews. I thought it was funny that my dad was up there on the keys of the church piano or organ, knowing he probably had a beer or two before he got there, along with a few Camel cigarettes at some point. It seemed no one ever knew because he had his mints nearby. I knew, but I kept my mouth shut about it.

My dad's first love was Ballantine beer. He would call me to get him a cold one from wherever he stored them while traveling or at home. Honestly, at times, I knew he had too many beers for his own good, and others knew it too, but no one would ever have known by the way he played the piano and organ. He was the best at playing the piano and organ, no matter his condition. His command of the choirs he directed was inspiring, and I usually had a firsthand view of it all.

At an early age, I was confused while listening to the preachers of the many churches we attended speak condemnation about those who sinfully drank alcohol and got drunk. Often, the message was "You are going to hell if you keep drinking and smoking." I did not want that to happen to my dad, and I was always afraid he would die because of his drinking in particular. We knew my dad drank all the time and was intoxicated on many occasions, as were many of his close friends he hung around with. At my young age, I never questioned him about it. My mom did a good job of putting him in check. Still, I always wondered about our Christian way of living, particularly because I knew what wrongs my mom was involved in as well. My dad and mom rarely prayed openly around us, and they were not disciplined to routinely open the Bible and teach us, as some of our cousins were accustomed to. The most consistent act of religion we participated in was praying at the dinner table, where we all gathered for family meals. Dinnertime was my favorite part of the day. I loved it when my dad would say, "Junior, say grace." I would put my hands together in all sincerity and say, "God is great, God is good, and we thank him for our food. Amen!"

DELIVERY BOY

One day my mom asked me to take a package of food in a brown grocery bag across the recreation center field to a man in a Yellow Cab. It seemed okay until I approached him, and he called me Junie or something like that. My mom told me to run over, give the guy the brown bag, and then run back. She would be standing at the front door to send me off and wait for me to return. That request from my mom became more frequent, and I later learned that the man's name was C.J. As time went on, I took not only packages but also handwritten notes, and I sometimes returned to my mom with a sealed plain envelope. After a while, I became concerned because I could see that boys in the gangs were taking notice, and others probably were as well. My trips to C.J.'s car were becoming more frequent and obvious as many times his was the only car on the street. Here I was, this little boy dropping off these obscure brown bags to this grown man.

One day my mother, my siblings, and I all walked across the field and got into C. J.'s private car, which was long and wide enough for all of us to fit in the backseat. He drove to the expressway; pulled off the Lincoln Highway; and took us to a high-rise building on Ridge Avenue, along the Schuylkill River. He parked his car in a parking lot near the railroad tracks nearby. We all got out and went up in an elevator. As we walked into his place, my mom told my brother to go out onto the cage-like enclosed balcony to play, and I followed to look outside and see the Schuylkill River below, where rowboats headed toward downtown. Directly below us was a playground area. My mom told me to go there alone, and I left everyone else—my sister and my two youngest siblings—inside, where the TV and music were on. While going down in the elevator by myself, I wondered what was happening. Why was I being sent downstairs by myself? What was going on? Why had my mom brought us to that place?

When the elevator hit ground level, I went to the playground. I could barely see my brother as I looked at the building way up in the sky. Nearby I noticed boys assembling like the gangs in my neighborhood did near the recreation center. Instinctively, I sensed that I was in the wrong place at the wrong time. Hearing a train go by in the direction opposite the river, I ran toward the train. The railroad tracks were at the top of the hill, near the parking lot where C. J.'s car was. I positioned myself on the opposite side of the railroad tracks, where I could see everything approaching me—particularly the movements of the boys, who I'd concluded were junior gang members. I knew I was in their territory—North Philly—and I didn't know anyone. I had heard about gangs from there. As a boy, I'd learned at an early age to respect those in the territory I was in. Like in the tale of Goldilocks, I'd learned in the city to never travel into a new territory alone—and there I was alone. Not good.

I stayed in position across the railroad tracks and watched many commuter trains go by one after another until I saw my mom and siblings come out to the parking area with C. J., looking all around for me. I came across the railroad tracks, only to be scolded by C. J. for crossing the tracks: "Junie, it's dangerous to do that!" I simply said, "Yes, sir," and quickly got into the car, eyeing the boys from a distance. They still had an eye on me as well. It was dangerous for me to be left alone in a playground area in another gang's territory. Worse, I still didn't understand what had taken place that day, nor did I want to know. I asked my mom not to take me back there, and she never did.

One day, while I was taking a package to C. J. across the field by the recreation center, my dad intercepted me and asked me questions about what I was doing that I could not answer. I don't know what I said to him, but he was madder than hell. My mom saw us coming, and the next thing I knew, a nasty argument broke out between my mom and dad. It was terrible. Things got crazy and even got physical between them, and my dad eventually stormed out of the house. When he left, my mom started crying and questioning me while yelling: "What did you tell him? What did you tell your father?" To this day, I do not remember anything I said other than "I don't know." In my eyes, I had done nothing wrong—I'd done only what my mom had told me to, but I do remember feeling very bad and so alone. However, I knew from my dad's enraged comments that something was wrong, and I was in the middle of all the blame. It was tough to be my dad's first son and be put in that position. My dad was distant with me for a long time after that incident.

What happened that day was a turning point for me. I began to question everything my mom had ever said, done, or asked me to do. When we went shopping, my mom would take us to the dressing room and tell me to put on clothes on top of what I was already wearing. Later, in retrospect, I realized we should not have been doing that. I would have done anything my mom asked me to do up until the day my dad questioned me about what I was doing. He had no idea, and neither did I. I wanted to tell him all I knew, but I also knew instinctively that would not be a good thing for my mom, so I kept silent and hoped we would be father and son again.

One day I was in the store with my siblings, and we were all charged with stealing by the store manager. Ironically, on that day, I was not shoplifting. Somehow, when the store manager communicated to my mom who had taken, I then became the scapegoat as he pointed to me. I did not understand why my mom was so outraged at what I was accused of, knowing what she had taught us to do. In fact, I was not sure if any of us had ever stolen anything from that store, but the store manager wanted us out all the same. If his aim was to keep me out of the store, he succeeded; I never returned.

My unfair punishment was unbelievable. My mom held both of my hands over a fully lit gas stove to make sure I would never steal again. Both hands were burned and turned black and blue as I screamed crazily, "Mommy, please!" in the worst pain ever. My mom kept my hands over the flames until she could smell the burning of my flesh. Suddenly, she snapped over what she had done and started crying and panicking. I could have killed her right there, but my hands had no feeling other than pain. It was child abuse for sure, and it happened over something I did not even do. I also wondered why I was the only one being punished to such an extent when all three of us got kicked out of the store together.

Before I knew it, I was in a state of shock, stepping up onto a public bus with both hands in the air extended outward as if I were blind. We got off of the bus, and I headed into the emergency room at the nearest hospital. They rushed me into a room where I was treated and gently bandaged up with white gauze and tape. My mom made up a story about how my hands had gotten burned. It wasn't the truth, but I did not dwell on the matter. I just wanted the pain to stop.

After being treated and given pain medicine, I walked out of the hospital, and guess what I saw? A Yellow Cab waiting for us— and it was not my father's. It was C. J. I never had been so glad to see him. I did not want to be seen going home on a public bus, which, to me, was so embarrassing. I did not understand why my dad had not come to see me at the hospital. C. J. took us near the field by the recreation center, and I thanked him as my mom and I exited his cab to walk home. My mom paid him to make it look legitimate. It didn't matter at that point what was going on. We needed a ride home, and I needed all the help I could get to forgive my mom for what she had done to me.

THE VILLAGE

It has been said that it takes a village to raise a child and raising me was no different. My mom knew I needed to be exposed to something different, so she took me to her biological dad. Spending time with my grandpa Thomas, who lived in Woodbine, New Jersey, was key to my development as a young man. He was a big dark-skinned man known by everyone in town as Cornel Thomas. I remember when he put me into his big car for the first time. There I was, right beside him, as he went down the road with his Al Capone–style hat. He reached under the seat, grabbed his flask of liquor, and took a big swig on that sunny day as we traveled down Dehirsch Avenue, which ran parallel to the railroad tracks. As if it were normal for a grandfather to offer his underage grandson liquor, Grandpa Thomas handed the flask to me, and I knocked down a little swig for myself. It was my first taste of hard liquor. He closed the flask, put it back under the seat, and turned the music up, and we laughed and sang together.

As we entered town, he showed me Clay Street to make me feel like there was a street that had my name. He then dropped me off in the center of the neighborhood, on a dirt road that led to the ice cream parlor; gave me two quarters; and told me to buy ice cream for everyone in the neighborhood who was my age—and I did. All the girls loved me from that point on, and I loved them too. I was the boy everyone wanted to be with, and my grandpa had set me up.

I needed that validation and time with him. I needed to be propped up by a man of my grandpa's stature. I wanted to be around my grandpa Thomas as much as I could. I remember him putting me on a horse and walking me through the fields of corn behind his house. Being from the city and looking at the tall corn stalks was like looking at tall buildings but much more enjoyable. I enjoyed going to Woodbine and crabbing around there with my dad and brother. Sadly, my time with Grandpa Thomas was cut short due to his early death. Sometimes a young man can learn a lot by just hanging out and doing simple things with no agenda and no restrictions—just taking it easy.

Now, my grandparents on the Clay side were strict and virtually no fun at all when I was growing up. Grandfather Clay was a highly respected preacher in Philadelphia and a highly decorated Lieutenant Colonel and Chaplain (LTC) in the US Army; although those facts had little meaning to a young boy like me growing up in Philadelphia. The few times we went over to Grandfather and Grandmother Clay's house, I had to sit still for the whole visit, which was hard for me. Maybe that was payback for my beating him in checkers. I often saw Grandfather Clay sitting in his office, which was behind a curtain. He sat with a naked lightbulb and a magnifying glass. He never called me by name; rather, he called me "boy" all the time: "Boy, come here. Boy, sit down. Boy, go get your father. Boy, take this." He had a deep voice, and I felt he always wanted and demanded respect the few times I was in his presence, and I gave it to him. This would mean that I sat down and listened, giving him my full attention. I was also always amazed at how he could preach a storm by reading off of his folded-up notes. I wish I could of known him much better. No doubt he was to be admired for his achievements as an African American man during his time.

My grandmother Clay—or Mother Clay, as she was called— called me Junior in her high-pitched voice, and I loved to hear her call for me, because it usually meant I was getting some food. She always went right into the kitchen to find me something to eat, saying, "Junior is hungry, and he needs something to eat"—no doubt she said this because of my skinniness. As soon as she said that, I would follow her into the kitchen, and she would break out the big black iron fryer and throw some lard in it. Then she would get a bowl and throw in some flour and seasoning. Her dark hands would grab and toss some chicken in the flour mixture, and then into the hot, bubbling fryer those chicken pieces would go. Quickly, she made her famous punch, and there you had it: hot golden fried chicken with some juicy leftover potato salad.

She always vouched for me: "Dear Heart, let the boy look at TV or listen to the radio." Mother Clay was a smart woman, and she was encouraging to me. If something was wrong, she would say, "Well, that's all right. You keep going on!" I wish I had more to say about our relationship, but we did not do much together. I wish it had not been that way.

WHAT CAN MAKE A DIFFERENCE

My maternal grandmother lived with my step grandfather, and life was different at their place. She was my greatest teacher of the Bible and life. She wanted me to conduct myself as a fine young man, or "good boy," and she was intentional about everything she did for me. She taught me about work and character and how to eat properly, dress, and speak. She saw that I kept my head up while walking. She would make me walk from one end of the room to the other with a book on the top of my head, and I could not let it fall without being reprimanded. I learned how to be a gentleman and a good man. I learned about sterling silverware and how to clean and take care of it. I was exposed to poetry and had to memorize scriptures from the Bible. She was vested in my development.

I knew her better than any of my grandparents, and I saw her work hard and make a nice home to live in. I tried to do everything right for her. She was nice and nurturing to me, as if she always knew what I was going through. One thing is for sure: Grandma loved my mom. When I was a teenager, we discussed their mother-daughter relationship, which allowed me to accept the fact that as a man, there were some things I would never know or understand. She was right.

My step grandfather, whom I called, Pop-Pop, was my grandma's husband and, of course, my mom's stepfather. He was sharp and well dressed. He rode a motorcycle and routinely played at the tennis club at the park, but like my dad, he drank a little too much. In fact, his drinking was the reason no real love existed between my mom and him. His bouts with alcohol usually ended in some sort of abusive act toward my grandmother. I did not like that, and he knew it. We constantly eyed each other with respect.

All in all, I will always respect him because he knew what I was missing as a boy growing up in the streets. On my tenth birthday, in 1965, he took me to a sports store in South Philly. I had no good sneakers at the time, and he became my hero when he bought me my first pair of white Converse basketball sneakers, a pair of high-top socks, and my first brand-new Volt basketball. I loved him greatly for that gesture of giving and I thanked him sincerely for making that sacrifice for me. After leaving the store, man, was I living in hog heaven! I took to the court, flashing my new gear, and my basketball game improved significantly. Just having a completely round ball to practice with made all the difference.

When the other boys saw my new shoes, they all stepped on them to get them dirty. It wasn't a bad thing. It was just something boys did to show some love when someone had something new. The act also had a hidden message: you can't really have anything good in the hood. We were all in that mess together. Still, later in my life, that lesson had an even deeper meaning. It was proof that being envious or jealous of the good that comes to another in his or her moment of gain only thwarts personal advancement and success.

In the summertime, my siblings and I would work in my Grandmother Richardson's immaculate block-long garden behind her house. She was the best gardener I had ever seen. Her garden had every flower known to man, it seemed, and she particularly loved roses and marigolds. I came to love them too. We planted marigolds from the seeds each year and watched them grow. When they withered, we broke them off and let them dry out in a jar for next year—a practice known as deadheading. At the end of our summer days' work, after we memorized our scriptures or a poem, we were allowed to go to the five-and-dime store. There we would pick out any toy we wanted as long as we could afford it with the money we'd earned by tending to the garden. If we got bonus money, we could go to the movie theater, which was something we never did with our parents. They always took us to the Pennsauken Drive-In Theater, which was across the bridge from Philadelphia. All of us would jump into the station wagon, and we'd pull up and put our speaker in the window. However, it was not the same as going to an actual movie theater with Grandmother. There I watched boys and girls hold hands, eat popcorn, and maybe even kiss when it was dark.

Grandma insisted I read and go see the movie *Pinocchio*. I saw it twice and learn two key things. First, I learned not to keep telling a lie. My grandmother would say, "You can fool some of the people some of the time and most of the people most of the time, but you can't fool all of the people all of the time. Sooner or later, you will get caught in your lie." Those words of wisdom have stayed with me all my life. The other thing I learned from watching *Pinocchio* was that I too could dream. I hoped my dreams for change in the things I was dealing with at home and in the streets would one day come true. The Disney song "When You Wish upon a Star" brought tears to my eyes because it had so much meaning for me, especially the lyrics at the end:

> When you wish upon a star, makes no difference who
> you are. Anything your heart desires will come to you.

Each year, Grandma took us to Atlantic City with the church on a bus. We would make peanut butter and jelly sandwiches and tuna sandwiches, which always seemed to leak excess mayonnaise, and we'd take her cold fried chicken and potato salad—which was best eaten on the way there. We would have a ball. I remember seeing *The Dick Clark Show* near the Steel Pier, and I always wanted to see Mr. Peanut and the White Diving Horse. Watching that horse climb up to the top with the woman rider in a bathing suit who would jump into the pool below was the biggest thrill. My grandmother took us to the nicest places to eat on the boardwalk. We had fun on the beach, playing in the sand and swimming in the water. The Atlantic Ocean was much cleaner back then. The biggest challenge we had was the walk from where the buses were parked. Those trips were quality time spent together, and I fell in love with the ocean and all the fun one could find there.

There was one more perk to spending time with Grandma: if we all did well and did everything she wanted, we could choose one big toy we wanted for Christmas, no matter the expense. She would have our selected toys at our home by Christmas Day; we could count on the toys being there. We always knew she would come through if Santa did not. Yes, I believed in Santa Claus, and I knew who he was and was not.

It was like a game of giving we all played, and it made us all happy to receive gifts and hugs and say thank you. We should have been doing all that anyway; however, Christmas made it all special, and Grandma was surely a Santa Claus to us. She always told us, "No matter what the gift is, it is the thought that counts." Truth be told, there was a Christmas or two when Grandma's gifts were the only ones under the tree. A Christmas like that made us all grateful and thankful.

When Santa Claus missed us in any given year, we hoped he would come back again—and when he did, we thanked God.

Our quality time with Grandma had a lasting impact on my brothers and sisters and me. We loved all our grandparents, but we especially adored Grandma Richardson for the many things she taught us about life and for the time she shared with each of us.

Most helpful to me as a young man was her insistence that I learn Rudyard Kipling's poem "If." I believe my grandmother knew what I was going through, and she not only helped me to memorize the poem but also aided me in closely studying every word. The words "If you can meet with triumph and disaster, and treat those two impostors just the same" helped me to cope with the dual lifestyles of my parents without going insane or retaliating against them physically. I read and recited the poem "If" over and over. I even gave a performance at one of my grandmother's church events. Later, the poem even inspired me to write poetry myself because I wanted deeply to know what a good man was so that I could one day become that.

I NEEDED PRAYER

My faith came from what I saw and experienced. I wanted to carry on with what I knew and believed. I believed that prayer worked and that God really answered prayers, and I was convinced that if God had answered my prayers in the past, I would trust God to answer my prayers again. I also knew my grandmother was praying for me, because I witnessed her on her knees by her bed many times, praying earnestly.

THINGS GOT CRAZY FOR ME...

Boy, did I need prayer a few times before we left our East Woodlawn Street home. My behavior became very defensive after my mom burned my hands. I felt I needed to protect myself from her and everyone else. I began to see people's aggression toward me in a different way. The gang members would taunt me, and I would now provoke them with my response. Going to school was all about avoiding fights and being ready to fight if I had to. I would arm myself with sharpened No. 2 pencils and wear a big-buckled belt. I would run my mouth with harsh cuss words and use the f-word in everything I said to give off the vibe that I didn't care and was poised to do anything crazy. However, I never cursed at home, as my mom would have killed me.

With that behavior in and out of school, I ended up in the principal's office. Even though I was a good student and did my work, I had an emotional problem that I did not know how to manage. I had an itch to get to someone before they even thought about getting to me. I wanted everything on my terms so I could control things myself. Much of what I was experiencing was simply paranoia and wasn't real, though some of it had legitimacy. All of it was in my mind, and I was prepared to engage with anyone first in order to be prepared to protect myself. I did not want to fight, but I also did not want anyone to hurt me. My behavior was due to my confusion, and my parents knew something had to be done with me.

Somehow, my parents thought I needed discipline and took me to an area Catholic school that was across the street from my elementary school. I was told not to be fighting or else. Their logic was that more structure would be a good thing for me. During my first and only day there, I was in a classroom with many kids I knew from the recreation center close to where we lived. It was a tough day for me, as I quickly learned what the physical consequences were for not sitting up straight with my hands properly placed on the desk while Sister was writing on the board.

It was a joke to think that Francis Clay Jr. could be settled or act perfectly in one day. At the Catholic school, my classmates hit me with spitballs while my teacher—a nun with thick black heels— was writing on the blackboard. Spitballs came from the first row in the front to the middle row, where I sat, and they all landed on me with precision. Those Catholic students were good at playing classroom games. As soon as I returned fire with the milk straw in my mouth, my Sister-teacher was heading my way with an eighteen-inch ruler. *Bam! Bam!* I got it across the knuckles on the hands my own mama had previously burned. That was a big mistake on her part. I grabbed the ruler. That was a big mistake on my part. She was one strong lady, maybe even stronger than my mother.

After convincing me of who was boss in her classroom, the teacher went back to the blackboard, and another volley of spitballs came toward me. The teacher must have known it was happening. As I returned fire again, just as stupid as I could be, the sister turned and approached me again. Her big shoes pounded audibly on the wooden floors. This time, Sister grabbed my ear, dragged me to the hot water pipe in the corner, and told me, "Don't move." Getting my ear pulled that way was a first, and it took me a while to realize that my ear was still connected to my head. However, it was impossible to stand next to that hot pipe. No one could have stood the heat from the steaming pipe. It was a setup, and the second I moved away, Sister "Big Shoes" was there with her eighteen-inch ruler, whipping me across my butt. I retaliated and ended up in the coatroom for being a distraction to the class.

In the coatroom, it was dark, and as I tried to find my way to the little light I saw reflecting from the floor, I hit something and knocked a bunch of stuff down onto the floor. I knew I was in for it, and sure enough, Sister "Big Shoes" opened the door, grabbed my other ear, and dragged me all the way down to the principal's office. There I stayed until my mother came, and I was escorted out of the school never to return. That was a rough day, but it straightened me out a lot because my mom used that experience to threaten me. She'd say she was going to send me back to Sister "Big Shoes" classroom, and I would plead with her not to send me back there again.

Worse, my mom said she would arrange for me to be put in jail— yes, jail! She told me if I did not change my ways, that was where I would end up. I played tough, as if I were all for it, because it seemed everyone knew someone who had ended up in jail, particularly those in gangs. It was almost as if I knew inside that something bad was going to happen. I would ponder when I would be the next one in the neighborhood to go to jail. However, my mom beat me to the punch and took me there before any police had the opportunity.

When the Officers put me in the cell after warning me I would go to jail if I kept getting into trouble, they said nothing more; they closed the cell door hard, locked it, and walked away. I said to myself, *Oh shit, what the fuck is this? I've got to get out of here!* I thought they were going to come back, but they did not for a good while. It felt like days to me as I sat on the hard bloodstained bench. The lighting was poor, and I could feel the temperature change where there was no sunlight. I must have examined every inch of that dirty, dark cell, and I positioned myself to be ready to come out as soon as I heard a voice or footstep. When the police came back with my mom, I said, "Mom, I'm sorry! I will do right! I am sorry, Mom. Please get me out of here." She did, and I never was arrested or put in jail. That place scared the hell out of me that day, and I wanted no part of it. Some of my friends' moms would say jokingly, "I brought you into this world, and I will take you out of it too." However, when my mom said it, she meant it literally. She would kill me if I did not do what she said and become the "better" young man she envisioned me to be. It puzzled me to know what my mom had exposed me to and what she expected of me. The same went for my dad, with all his drinking and smoking. Why were they so hard on me? Why the double standard wherein they would do wrong and expect me to do right? I reasoned that the end would have to justify the means if I became the man I was struggling to find.

GRATZ STREET

My dad was running around working three jobs to support five children and going to Temple University for his master's degree. He was given one of the first jobs associated with being an Equal Opportunity Officer within the government in the mid-1960s, when civil rights was emerging. The promotion meant more money and a move north from Woodlawn Street in the Germantown area to Gratz Street in the West Oak Lane area. It meant bigger and better for our family. We would move into a better neighborhood and in a larger row house on the corner, with larger alleys, and we were within walking distance of a better school. Getting me out and away from Woodlawn at that time was probably the best thing that could have happened to me. I would be forever appreciative of whatever it took for us to move. I believed it took everything we had. I say this because we had some days when there was no food in the icebox or pantry. We knew it was bad when we had to eat sugar sandwiches and the government block cheese given out at that time. The only time I saw my dad was when he was practicing piano in the basement before choir practice or a Sunday performance at church.

I attended a new school called Rowan Elementary School and got a new start at being a better person and a better student. I did just that. I tried hard to do what the teacher said, at the direction of my mom. My infatuation with my fourth-grade teacher helped me. She looked just like Annette Funicello from the movie *Beach Party*, and I made sure I was the first to do all the schoolwork requested just to get a kind hug from her for doing well. I knew the difference between a hostile and friendly classroom at that point. Rowan was a nurturing school that had the motto "Keep the light of learning burning." Yet outside the school walls lurked another type of gang life in the area.

It was not a major issue for me until the fifth and sixth grades. I had just come from the gang territory they called the Summerville area where the gangs threatened me, and now I found myself in Clang territory where the gangs wanted me to join them, or else. Adjacent to the area where we lived was an Italian gang called the Bricks. They were Catholic boys who loved their mamas—you did not do any stealing or fooling around in their neighborhoods, or they would get in their big cars with their shot guns out and drive through your neighborhood to make a statement.

There were many gangs in the Philadelphia area, and you did not go into another territory without knowing someone who could protect you. I don't think my mom and dad ever fully understood that. As we visited many churches where my dad played, I had to be careful. At that age, when the girls were approachable, it was even more of a concern to end up talking to a church girl who lived in another gang's territory. Back then, you needed to be careful in the City of Brotherly Love and with gangs in general.

Moving to Gratz Street required me to get an orientation of the gang life in the area quickly. On the playground behind Rowan Elementary, which had no grass and only a basketball court, I first became acquainted with the full-court game of basketball. I would come to develop skills on the court, and basketball would play an integral role in my getting through college one day. It started with daily play on the hard court next to the Northwood Cemetery.

I played ball with my neighbor Phillip, who lived one row house down from me, almost every day until sundown. We used a beat-up basketball that had a black hickey on it where the outer lining had worn away. To make matters worse, the sneakers I wore before my grandfather brought me my first pair of Converse sneakers had cardboard in the bottom sole area. The cardboard packaging that the Chinese cleaners east of Rowan Elementary used for my dad's folded starch shirts came in handy for that sort of thing. My father would say, "The Chinese cleaners is the best place to get your shirt starched." However, what I liked about the Chinese cleaners was that I could use the cardboard to protect my feet.

NEAR HOME

Opposite our house, one block away, was a diner that served my mom's favorite: liver and onions with mashed potatoes. I loved the desserts there, especially the pies and New York cheesecake. My mom would treat me to a piece of apple or lemon meringue pie if my grades were good—and for that reason, they stayed good. I learned an important lesson at the diner that has stuck with me all my life. During one of our visits, as we were walking toward the exit, my mom caught me going back to a nearby table where the customers had left behind some coins. I was about to take the coins, as I had done before, not knowing anything about the concept of tips. When she saw what I was about to do, she said, "Junior!" in a way that meant "Stop!" She asked, "What are you doing?"

I said, "I'm taking the coins left on the tables."

She sat me down to explain that people were leaving the change as a way of saying thank you, and it was called a tip. She said it was always good to leave money for people who provided services for you, such as a waitress. Then she added, "You also tip cab drivers like C. J. too." I got the initial message that others earned their living by providing services and that tipping was appropriate, but her random interjection of C. J. threw me off. Just the mention of his name brought back memories immediately, and it seemed I was being put in a compromising position again. I felt bad about all the coins I had taken in the past and always left a tip from that day forward.

Not long after I learned the lesson about tipping—which, again, I felt bad about because the waitresses were so nice there—my mother directed me to take a package to C. J. in front of Rowan Elementary. I took alleys to make sure no one would see me. I took the long way, running as fast as I could. I approached his car from the rear side next to the curb, and his window was down. I threw the package through the window and ran away, thinking, *I hope my dad doesn't see me!* I didn't see C. J.'s face again for years, until the day I attended the Penn Relays while in college.

GOOD THINGS WERE HAPPENING

Things were getting to be very good for me in my new community, but the world around me was changing fast. Some Caucasian men who were missionaries came into the community and took an interest in me and exposed me to the Cub Scouts. My first orientation was a hiking trip. I was asked to bring my lunch, so I went to the corner store down the street and bought an Italian hoagie, a Tastykake, and a Frank's orange soda in a bottle. During the hike, as we walked the trails around rocks as we climbed upward, the oil from my Italian hoagie dripped through the brown bag holding my lunch. As we hopped over one rock and onto the next up the hill, my brown bag broke, and my orange soda slipped out and broke. I held the hole closed and kept moving, as large flies began to follow me. The pack leader took notice and positioned me at the back of the troop because I was apparently drawing so many flies that it was causing a noticeable disruption among the other scouts. When we got to a place by a stream and all the Cub Scouts pulled out their lunch containers, canteens, pocketknives, and collapsible cups, I looked like an outcast. I only had my hoagie and Tastykake in an oily brown paper bag with a hole in the bottom of it.

A few of the Scouts had portable fishing rods, and they were casting their lines into the clear streambed. I had nothing like they had, but I could see fish hanging around close to the shore area, swimming around some rocks in ankle-deep water. I witnessed one of the Cubbies catch a fish, and I wanted so badly to say I'd caught a fish too. I watched the fish's movements while I ate my hoagie, and I took some bigger rocks and encircled the innocent fish lurking around in the cove. I threw some meat from my hoagie into the area near the fish to draw them into the trap and waited. As one of them approached the bait, I quickly stepped into the water, scooped it onto shore, grabbed it, and claimed I had caught a fish, to everyone's surprise. We threw it back into the water, and it swam away. The experience taught me the importance of coming to events like that well prepared with the essentials needed to enjoy what you are doing.

I was hiking, and they were scouting, but to be a Scout, you had to have what Scouts had. I was motivated to find a job and work at the local stores on Ogontz Avenue around my home, cleaning floors and putting out trash after school, to earn money for my uniform, canteen, books, and pocketknife. I loved the Cub Scouts, and I carried our den flag and stood in the front of the line. The Scout motto has resonated with me for the rest of my life: "To do my duty to God and my country and to obey the Scout law... To help other people at all times... To keep myself physically strong, mentally awake, and morally straight."

At school, I loved our music teacher, who had me sing the introduction of "Let There Be Peace on Earth" in the school's annual music program. Somehow, from the performance we put on, I got a chance to audition for the Philadelphia Boys Choir in 1965. It was an amazing honor to sing first soprano for that world-renowned choir. To get selected, I had to audition in front of the choir director, Dr. Carlton Jones Lake, who was choosing 250 boys to be in his choir. When in front of him, I had to sing the tonal scale (do-re-mi-fa-sol-la-ti-do) forward and backward multiple times, concentrating on breathing from the stomach as I went from one octave to the next. I thought I could sing because I thought I was Smokey Robinson with the Miracles. I could sing their hit "Ooo Baby Baby" like Smokey, and I had a sweet lead voice, or at least I thought I did. I loved singing with all the groups on the radio, and I loved learning from Dr. Lake, who took an interest in me. My only challenge was getting to practice on Saturdays at Benjamin Franklin High School, which was seven miles from my home. I had to take a trolley and subway, which required money that did not always come from my parents when I needed it. I could not stay in the choir if I did not come to practice, so I worked hard to earn money to be at practice. By 1968, Dr. Lake was conducting the Philadelphia Boys Choir under the purview of the board of education. The choir consisted of approximately 250 boys from schools all over the city who gathered at Benjamin Franklin High School at Broad and Spring Garden Streets. Dr. Lake had organized the choir in 1961.

I hustled in multiple ways: collecting empty milk and soda bottles to turn in for two and five cents, bagging groceries at the grocery store, and collecting old newspapers and selling them to the junkyard for five cents a pound. I would take my brother Darryl with me to make as much money as we could. The collected used newspapers we turned in to the junkyard led to my taking an interest in my first paper route with the *Philadelphia Bulletin*. I remembered the lesson my mom had taught me about tips and service. Now I wanted those tips for sure. So, this skinny little paper boy named Clay would be the best at folding papers and placing them wherever his customers wanted them: in the door, on the porch, on the run, or on the step. I wanted those tips, and I got plenty of them, and my route got better and better. It was a great gig and my first exposure to true entrepreneurship.

As I earned money to fund my way to choir practice, when my mom started to see the dollars coming in, I first had to give what I earned to her. Before I knew it, I somehow was supporting the family needs for food. I gave my mom the money, wanting to believe she was saving it, but I knew she spent it. There were times when the family needed my money to help out, and I was glad to do it. I knew my money was family money.

Unfortunately, a day came when the gangs showed up at the start of my paper route and surrounded me and my papers stacked high on my wagon. I tried to keep them from knocking over my newspapers, but there were too many of them to fight off, and I suffered a big loss as they took my papers and my wagon. I was still alive, but I didn't have enough money to pay for the stolen papers to take to my customers, especially since Mom had spent what I was supposed to have been saving. With great disappointment, I lost my route that quickly. I felt my dispatcher could have loaned me the money, but it didn't happen.

That same weekend, I had to jump the subway entrance and take my chances on getting caught just to make it to choir practice. I was incredibly close to not being able to participate in our grand performance. I could not miss a practice, as our performance was near. Wearing our choir blazers with emblems, we featured songs from *The Sound of Music* by Oscar Hammerstein. My favorite song was "There Is a Balm in Gilead," which I did not know at the time was an old African American spiritual. I love the following part of the song:

> Sometimes I feel discouraged
> and think my work's in vain,
> but then the Holy Spirit
> revives my soul again.

Those words gave me great comfort, and I pondered the Holy Spirit. Being in the Philadelphia Boys Choir was subconsciously a revival for my soul that I had yet to come to know.

My mom and dad came to our grand performance, and they took me to Friendly's on the way home. It was one of the few times I had both of my parents all to myself.

CHAPTER 2

Fighting Back

One day my mom, standing in the doorway of our corner row house on Gratz Street, witnessed a big fat boy in the neighborhood bullying me and hitting me. He was Jewish and the son of the corner store's owner. As he pushed me around in the alley by my house, my mom yelled, "Junior!" and I ran to her. As I approached the steps of our house, she asked, "Why are you letting that boy beat you up?"

I said, "Mom, you told me not to fight!"

My mom grabbed my collar, pushed me down the stairs, and said, "Go defend yourself! Don't let him push you around like that!"

Well, that was all I needed to hear. Many boys had bullied me in the past, calling me Sticks or saying, "You are nothing but a piece of clay!" With my mom's okay, I went off on the big fat boy that day. In fact, I became the bully and beat that boy's butt every day that week. Kids took it for granted that I would not fight under any circumstances because of my mom, and a few were not informed that she had recently endowed me with a hit-'em-back card that prompted me to set out to square some things away with those who had abused me in the past. Some things you never forget. Two blocks over lived a tall, dark-skinned boy who loved to hit me in the schoolyard to impress others. Before school one day, I went to the back of his house, knowing the way he walked to school, and as soon as I saw him, I decked him to the ground. I went on a rampage with him all day and ended up in the principal's office for fighting, which brought me back to myself.

Now word got out in the street that I was, in fact, a good fighter. I had a style similar to that of Cassius Clay, who had just beaten the great Sonny Liston twice. Their second fight was in May 1965 in Lewiston, Maine. Cassius won with a first-round knockout. I was excited over his win and watched how he fought and talked. Everyone thought I was related to Cassius Clay, who, later in my life, as Muhammad Ali, would say and write on his commercial photo that we were family. In addition, Joe Frazier's Gym, near Temple Hospital, was no more than five miles from my house and only blocks from where I had choir practice, so boxing and fighting were things we all talked about, and we anticipated listening to matches on the radio or on our black-and-white TV.

Soon the gangs confronted me to join them as I approached my teenage years. I said I could not because I knew my mom would not approve and would probably kill me. When you fight and win, it just means you have to keep fighting, and I did not want that. My new identity as a fighter required that I have someone to watch my back. I could think of no one better than my neighbor across the street, known to the gangs as Little Jeep. He was a small guy with thick glasses and the biggest heart. He had a brother named Big Jeep, who was a gang member before he joined the service as a Marine in Vietnam. Everyone loved him, and he loved his little brother, whom he never let anyone mess with. Little Jeep and I did way too much together, both good and bad. In fact, we became blood brothers by slashing our hands with a switchblade he had. We promised to keep each other's secrets; because we did so, I cannot say much more about our secret life growing up in the neighborhood. All I can say is this: it would not have been a good thing to mess with either one of us or our family members. That's all I have to say and will ever say.

By then, everyone knew of the gang wars that plagued the City of Brotherly Love during the mid-1960s. The conflict was about claiming territories block by block. I used to live in Summerville territory, and now I was in Clang territory. I saw friends of mine from Gratz Street fighting friends from my neighborhood on Woodlawn Street. The fights involved boys of all colors, mind you. Each gang thought I was snitching or tipping off the other side. It was a no-win situation, particularly when they were warring. On a weird kind of day, I was confronted in the schoolyard without my friend Little Jeep, but my neighbor Phillip came to my aid. The junior Clang gang members surrounded us in a circle, taunting us with profanities. Then they charged us and attacked, and it was on. I pulled off my belt that had a very big buckle and started swinging. Just when I was about to get my ass literally kicked, thank God the police came with the paddy wagon and their lights flashing everywhere as they came into the school yard. Phillip and I were exhausted from fighting, and I was glad to see the police, having just taken a hit to my lip before the gang members ran away up over the walls and through the cemetery to escape. Phillip and I were taken home in a police car, and Mom asked, "Did you fight back?" I assured her I had.

MY CHALLENGES—MY CHANGE

In 1966, the Civil Rights Act was defeated, and the mood of the country was not good at all. President John F. Kennedy had just been assassinated on November 22, 1963, and President Johnson was in office. They were calling for five hundred thousand more troops to Vietnam. There were riots from Mississippi to Chicago. It was the first time I heard the terms *black power* and *segregation* and the saying "Burn, baby, burn." We had witnessed firsthand the March on Washington on August 28, 1963; my dad had taken me to Washington, DC, to see the march as we drove through the crowds. Though we did not participate in it, we were there all the same. All this was going on while I was just trying to survive gangs in the streets of Philadelphia and feeling like I needed something to simplify my personal challenges and concerns. What was I to become—a choirboy, a Boy Scout, or a gang member fighting all the time?

The missionaries sent into the community from a small church across from Rowan William Elementary School approached me with an invitation to join them for Bible study on Wednesdays. Then I was drawn into the Sunday school sessions because they offered not only Bible lessons but also food: each child received a milk carton, an apple, and a cookie to take home. At that time, my family was eating government cheese and sugar sandwiches. I found it strange that no matter what, my dad always had his Ballantine beer and Camel cigarettes. In our house, we only got to buy food once or twice a month, so the food the missionary church offered on a weekly basis was a treat I did not want to miss.

Things got crazy with my dad and mom when somehow, he was at the scene where a woman dropped dead at a bar across from the church where he was the choir director and pianist. My dad did not go to jail, but the newspaper put his name in the article because he was with her after choir rehearsal. I saw his picture in the local paper and witnessed his arguments with my mom. Whatever happened, it for sure affected my dad in weird ways. It must have been embarrassing, and I never forgot its impact on me. Later in life, I was afraid to be in a bar with a woman, as I thought the same thing could happen to me. For my dad, from that time forward, getting his master's degree was very important for a few reasons. Foremost, all of my father's siblings had status and degrees except for him. One was a lieutenant colonel, another was a lawyer, one was a reverend, another was an accountant, the last brother was a professor of mathematics, and his only sister was a nurse. My dad was a musician and a government worker who smoked and drank, and my grandfather treated him differently. He was treated in a belittling manner and as a young man watching all of that, I didn't like it at all. The older I became, the harder it became to hold my peace about it. My dad was the government guy, the odd one out. Some said he was the black sheep in the family, but he was my dad. Because of that, I believe he felt pressure to finish his master's degree and thus drank more than usual in order to cope— so much so that his drinking got out of control, and he found himself out there running around and believed my mom was doing the same. It was a crazy thing. Yet knowing my dad as I did, I also realized he wanted to get out of Philadelphia, where the death of that woman had left a stain on his character that he would never overcome. My mom always had an issue with what had happened, and I wondered how he was still able to play for the church across the street, knowing what had happened.

One day Dad came home drunk with lipstick on his Chinese-laundered white shirt. My mom had fixed an elaborate dinner, which was set on the table, and we all were waiting to eat. Dad was late in getting home, and when he came through the door, my mom, who was very upset, immediately confronted him, and things got crazy physically. Mom went off and broke china, turned over the kitchen table that was all set up, and started beating the hell out of Dad. My dad then hit her and me as I got in the middle of the fight to break it up. Mom bit his finger badly, and blood was all over the place. Before I knew it, the police were at the house. They handcuffed my dad and took him away in the paddy wagon right before my eyes.

We went back inside, where there was broken glass everywhere on the ground, and attempted to eat our cold dinner off the kitchen floor while sorting out pieces of glass from our food. It was the worst day I witnessed between my mom and dad. I prayed I would never see anything like that again.

Another day around that same time, my mom asked me to get her some Wrigley's spearmint gum, which she loved, out of her purse. I had gone into her purse before, but that time, I saw Kodak pictures of the lady across the street licking her own breasts. I tried to understand what I was looking at exactly. I knew that someone else must have taken the picture. On top of that, why would it have been in my mom's pocketbook? I never told my mom what I'd witnessed with my own eyes, but I believed she knew because it took me more time than normal to get her gum and bring it to her.

From that time on, I was distant from our neighbor across the street and found it odd that she and my mom started going out together. Mrs.

Jefferson, Little Jeep's mom across the street, thought it odd as well. I overheard her cautioning my mom about the neighbor lady. Needless to say, at that point, growing up was challenging for me. Around that time, Little Jeep and I found some old *Playboy* magazines in his garage in the back of the house. We would sneak a peek at them and run away quickly, hoping we would not get caught. Seeing those nude pictures, I had an endless array of questions about women and their bodies, which presented all sorts of struggles to work through in my head. I had no male adult to really talk to at the time. I questioned many things. What was right, and what was wrong? What was love, and who really loved me? What was sex? What was a true marriage, why did parents fight, why had my mom and dad found themselves involved with other people, and why was beer more important than our having food? When would my dad really be with me, not to mention play with me? Why did we have to stay in the house all the time? Why couldn't people at church see that my dad drank? Yet still, everyone accepted and loved my mom and dad in their own way, and I did too—and life went on with all those unanswered questions.

While attending the little church by my elementary school, I started to believe in what I was singing: "Jesus loves me; this I know, for the Bible tells me so." I wanted to be loved and accepted. I loved the Bible and wanted one so badly that I actually took one from the church. Granted, if I had asked for it, they would have given it to me, but I was adamant about having one to take home with me to read overnight. In our Bible class, we would sing,

> The b-l-o-o-d that Jesus shed for me
> way back on Calvary,
> the blood that gives me strength
> from day to day,
> and I need that strength to keep it together.

The words in the song inspired me and stayed in my mind all week. I truly wanted to be the good boy my grandma talked about, the good Boy Scout my scout master encouraged me to be, the good student my teachers said I could be, and the "better" son I hoped my mom and dad wanted me to be. Why then did I feel as if I had to fight all the time? Why was I being exposed to things I didn't need to see?

Inside my Bible was the Twenty-Third Psalm, and when I read the verse "Yea, though I walk through the valley of the shadow of death, I will fear no evil for Thou art with me," I fell in love with those words. I concluded I needed a Savior to be with me to fight for me and protect me; then I would not feel as if I had to do it. I needed a Savior to help me find answers for all the questions I had and to put me in a place where I knew I was doing the right thing considering all the realities I knew about. When I had to run through the alleys in my neighborhood, I wanted a Savior. I wanted to stop fearing the gangs and my parents. I wanted to fear no evil, and I wanted Christ with me.

Through the ministry of that little church, I learned about the Ten Commandments, and it became clear in my mind and spirit what was right and what was wrong. I read the book of Proverbs, and it told me how to be a Christian man who made Christian decisions. After I heard the song "Come to Jesus, Come to Jesus Right Now," I wanted Jesus Christ to save me. I needed salvation and wanted to be saved. I accepted Jesus Christ into my heart, and he did just that—he saved me. I asked for forgiveness for the bad things I had done. Afterward, a remarkable thing happened to me. I changed inside. I rejected the nasty things about my life and sought goodness and forgiveness. I continued to read the books of Proverbs and Psalms daily, over and over, to learn how to be thankful, to praise God, and what it meant to be a godly man. Much around me was saying, "Get it," "Steal it," and "Take it." My Bible told me to ask for it, work for it, and pray for it (Colossians 3:23). I resisted falling into the trap of being an alcoholic like my dad. My saying no to drinking caused us to be distant on a personal level, as I would not have a beer with him. I knew that if I started drinking with him, I would end up like him. Beer and hard liquor prevented us from having many good times together. He drank all the time, every day of his life; I could not do that, no matter how much I loved and respected him. I saw what it was doing to him, my mom, and the family.

I would remember the Bible story about the woman by the well anytime I thought about my mom's and dad's improprieties. John 4:4–26 led me to reason that as they had not been the perfect parents, I had not been the perfect son, though I was trying. In her own way, I knew my mom was trying, though I never understood some of the things she did. However, Mom never left us, and she always made a way for us to have what we needed. I loved my mom and learned to forgive her without ever discussing any specifics of the wrongs she might have done that caused me multiple concerns and challenges. I could not change her or my dad, so I decided at an early age to change and control myself. I loved my dad and learned to forgive him too—especially for the over-the-top whippings he gave when he had too much to drink. I have a few scars for life to remind me of his abuse.

Once I had the love of Christ in my heart, I immediately stopped the fighting, stealing, cheating, and cussing I'd been doing. Francis Leander Clay Jr. was a born-again Christian—I was saved! I just wanted Jesus Christ to be with me and to guide me— and he would be, all the days of my youth.

CHAPTER 3

Moving Away for Better

A happy day for both my dad and my mom was the day my dad finally got his master's degree from Temple University. To his credit, despite working three or more jobs and being the father of five children, even with drinking, smoking, and all the other concerning acts of behavior, he did it! His achievement meant more opportunity for him to be promoted from his position as Employee Development Specialist within the Department of Defense to a higher-level job in the federal government. That meant more prosperity for our family and a better living environment for me to grow up in. My mom threw a big party for him with glitter and decorations. It was the first time we had a lot of important people over to the house from his job and from the school. Even my dad's brothers and sisters, who rarely ever visited us, all came over—some of them for the first time. With his grand achievement came a promotion and a move to Washington, DC, to be the assistant director of the Equal Opportunity Program. Thus, my family embarked on a new life in the Maryland area. It was obvious to me that a college degree meant more money. My dad's example created a vision of success for me. Though I did not see him much because he was working and studying, I did enjoy seeing the fruits of all that he had achieved.

It was a happy time, and God answered my unuttered prayers to get away from the gangs who wanted me. I was on their radar, and our move would take me out of the line of fire. Had we not moved from Philadelphia at that time, I truly believe my life would have taken a turn for the worse. Moving day could not have come soon enough. Soon a moving truck was in front of the house, and on to Takoma Park, Maryland, we went.

Our new home was a nice stand-alone old brick house near the corner of Boston Avenue, in a wooded area. It had a fireplace and a big lawn surrounded by large trees. It was close to the school I would attend, Takoma Park Junior High. I would walk there every day. Most noticeable to me was that there were no alleys in the neighborhood that I would to have to navigate. There were also no row houses, and the school had plenty of grassy areas to play on. I wondered why some people lived that way and others did not. I concluded that moving was a way to bring about change, and the Clays were on the move. It was a way out for me. God had answered my prayers.

It was fall of 1967, and we enjoyed playing in the thousands of leaves on the ground. It never even crossed my mind to rake them up, because they were so colorful and welcoming on the ground. We were now in Maryland, but there seemed to be some concern back in Philadelphia with our old house, which apparently had not sold.

THE CHESS GAME...

Our neighbors on the right side in the corner house were a Jewish family who had a son my age. He invited me over to his house for Hanukkah. Entering their house during a day when we had no school, I could see that my friend's dad was a photographer; photo equipment was everywhere. During my visit, I vividly observed a father spending quality time with his son, teaching him the game of chess. I knew checkers, and I had seen the pieces of a chess game, but I never had been taught the basics of the game. Though I was good at checkers and thought that was the game we were going to play, I found that I knew nothing about chess. As I'd learned by watching my grandfather Clay beat everyone at the family picnic in Fairmount Park in Pennsylvania,

I sat at my friend's house over a two-day period and watched my neighbor's father patiently teach him all the movements of the chess pieces and how to make opening moves. What I noticed more was that I had not had one-on-one time like that with my own dad. And I thought, I probably would never get it with all the sisters and brothers I had in my family. I observed youthfully that sharing, listening, and encouraging was very good things for a father and son to do.

On day two, my friend's father turned to his son and asked him to play me. I was alone on my side, and he had his dad behind him. I heard him say something that applied not only to the chess game but also to life: "Move to protect your king first." To me, that meant "Always protect what you have first," and I remembered that going forward when I found myself in the chess game of life. In fact, I created my own motto, "Use what you have," as the first step toward striving for better.

Chess was different from checkers, which was a faster game. Chess was a 360-degree game versus a north-and-south game. You had to be what his father called disciplined, thinking before you put your hand on a piece to make a move. I did just that in my first chess game with his son and beat him. We played again, and I beat my friend two times in a row. Then, to my surprise, I was asked to leave, escorted to the door, and I was never allowed to come back inside the house. It was a good two-day seminar on how to play chess and beat your neighbor. However, I never had an opportunity to play with my friend again. As I had realized before, nothing ever lasts. However, I went on to be a natural master of the game of chess, though I always was afraid of what it would cost me to beat my opponent. Chess players are like that. They want you around them if they can beat you. I would reason that losing at chess was an indirect way of admitting that the winner was smarter than you. Winning chess games became something I learned to enjoy and embrace. I got great satisfaction from beating anyone at chess, and if I lost, I felt like I was learning. Rarely did I ever lose two chess games in row, and if I beat someone badly, I never got a rematch. I could see the envy on their faces in a negative way. I would say to my opponents, "Don't play if you plan to stay. I probably will win, and that will be the end."

WE HAD PROBLEMS IN PHILLY

Something was going on with our move from Philadelphia. There was still some unfinished business there that took my dad away every weekend. Apparently, the house on Gratz Street had a buyer, but the closing was not accomplished. The house was not selling, so my dad and I had to make a Friday night trip back to Philly to address certain issues with the house.

My dad was drinking that night before we hit the road. In fact, he always had a few Ballantines stored away for me to retrieve from somewhere during the trip. When we left Takoma Park that night, it was late, and it was pitch dark as we drove to Baltimore and through the Harbor Tunnel on Interstate 95. I hated the Baltimore tunnel, with all the smoke from the exhaust pipes of the cars. If there was traffic, I got down on the floor. Somehow, the air was cooler down there, and I instinctively would prefer that air so I could breathe. My going to the floor was a clear sign that I had asthma issues back then, but no one paid attention.

My dad was driving our relatively new 1966 Dodge station wagon, which had a backseat facing the rear window. It was our first brand-new car and I loved the whole process of watching my dad test drive and ultimately seal the deal by purchasing it. It was like a boat floating down the road. The front seat was big enough for four people. On that trip to Philadelphia, I was sitting next to my dad, listening to the radio. I loved the AM/FM radio in the car, and I usually had my own battery-operated transistor radio by my side. Highway 95 was relatively new back in the mid-1960s, and it was well marked and wide open that night with very little traffic. We were flying down the road, when all of a sudden, the car went toward the median. I will never forget seeing the station wagon move across the dashed white lines on the road. I reflexively grabbed the steering wheel as we drifted to the left. I turned the large steering wheel to the right to avoid going off the road as I yelled, "Dad! Dad!" I glanced quickly to see his eyes in the back of his head through his glasses.

We soon were drifting too far to the right; we crossed multiple lanes within seconds as the road twisted and curved to the left. Before I knew it, I was the driver from the middle seat, and I was desperately trying to keep the station wagon in the center of the highway while yelling again, "Dad! Dad!" We entered the bridge going into Delaware with the bright toll lights in the distance.

With the guardrails of the bridge ahead, my dad woke up in the middle of the bridge as the car slowed down just in time for him to gain control. "I've got it," he said as he gathered himself to pay the toll ahead, as if nothing had happened. God was with me in those few seconds. I was not scared until it was all over and I thought back on how easily we could have fallen off the bridge. We made it to the next service island and slept in the car until daybreak. It was a close call, and from then on, I instinctively get frightening quivers whenever I found myself crossing over the Susquehanna River into Delaware from Maryland on 95 North. I did not know how close we were to falling into the river that night.

The challenge my dad and our family faced was that the house in Philadelphia was not selling because it needed work. We had no money, and if the house did not sell, we had to return to Philadelphia, plain and simple. My dad and I painted and redid the floors to make the place better. Man, did I hate painting back in the day, and I've never liked painting because of the bad experiences I had in rehabbing our old home. The oil-based paint affected my breathing, but no one would listen. My dad wanted to keep using the same brushes and rollers over and over again, and he would get mad when the wall would streak and run because of the cheap oil-based paint, which required two or three coats. Furthermore, I had to clean the old used brushes and rollers using paint thinner, which probably put my body at an even greater risk for having an asthma attack. I complained that I could not breathe, but my dad refused to take me seriously.

For reasons I would never know, we ended up leaving Takoma Park in a rental truck after a brief few months, returning to Gratz Street on a weekend, on a cold, dark night. We unpacked everything from the truck into a cold house with no electricity or water, which wouldn't be turned on until Monday morning. My dad got in the rental truck late at night and drove back to Maryland by himself, leaving my mom and all the children there alone that night. We huddled in front of our small gas-lit fireplace, with my mom in the center and all of us finding some part of her for warmth. My mom comforted us with tears in her eyes. She had so much to do in the morning all on her own. There was a long day coming, and none of us knew what was going on or what was next.

It was embarrassing to have to return to our home on Gratz Street after packing up and leaving only a few months before. We had been exposed to a life that seemed much better, and there we were, back at square one with no Dad and alone. My dad's job was still in Washington, DC, and yet we were now in Philadelphia, not knowing what to do. First, we needed the electricity turned on, some food, and some heat. My mom made it happen. How? I did not ask, but she did. We would be in that situation temporarily, according to my dad, so I kept things tight and just went to school and came back home. Everyone said, "What are you doing here? You left us, and now you are back?" I wanted to go back to Maryland, and I was pulling for my dad to come through—and he did finally.

TO MARYLAND FOR THE SECOND TIME

It wasn't long before we moved back to Maryland into Oxon Hill Apartments for a few months, and there I found my first real girlfriend. I was head over heels for her. Her name was Beverly, and she lived right across the hall. Our parents did everything to keep us apart, but we had signals, and I constantly looked through the peephole in the door for her. She was my *cherie amour*, and when Stevie Wonder came out with his song of the same name, I quickly thought of her in that way. Some would call how I felt a little puppy love, but oh, how exciting it was.

Our first Christmas in Maryland was a Christmas we all would remember. I received my ten-speed bike, and it was brand new, not used like most of our other bikes. I loved it. It had streamers and mirrors on the handles and red reflectors in the spokes of each wheel. It had a battery-operated horn too. Sadly, my new bike from my father got stolen within weeks of my receiving it. I told the police that the thief had taken my bike down Wheeler Street, which crossed into Washington, DC from where I was in a Oxen Hill shopping area. The police told me they could not pursue the thief because he'd crossed the state line. That was a hard loss for me, and I went back to the police station a couple of miles down the road every day, looking for my new bike to be returned. One day, after weeks of my checking in, the police finally asked me to pick a bike from the many they were holding in the lost-and-found cage. I picked a silver ten-speed and was pleased and grateful to the police for helping me in that way.

I reasoned that if you ever get something new, you have to guard and protect it before someone comes along and takes it away. I saw that play out over and over again. One minute, something is yours to have; the next minute, it's gone someone seeking to take what you have. Nothing lasts forever. Second Corinthians 4:18 was of great help to me in understanding that. To say my dad was disappointed that my new bike was stolen was an understatement. He finally had gotten me something new that I had always wanted, and I'd lost it. I felt bad for us and very bad for myself.

CHAPTER 4

Why Me? Why Not Me?

We were in and out of Oxon Hill, Maryland now after the house in Philadelphia sold. In less than a year, we moved again into a smaller duplex house in East Riverdale, Maryland. It was a very small house for the size of our family, and it sat on the side of a hill. I ended up going to an area junior high school near our home, where I had my first confrontation with real hard-core racism. In Philadelphia, people disliked others for no reason, but we all knew how to coexist and get along. It wasn't about black or white but more about what you believed and about protecting your neighborhood and working hard to get through school. Whether you were from a Catholic, Italian, Jewish, or Christian home or from a different gang, there was enough space for all of us to do our own thing. However, for people who knew nothing about someone to outright hate a person because of the color of his or her skin was pointless to me. I never had to give it much thought until we made this move. People in the neighborhood area near my school treated me as if I were a dog and it was not a friendly place for me to be. I had not encountered anything like that before back in Philly. I didn't know what racism against black people was all about, but I learned quickly.

In 1955, the year I was born, Dr. Martin Luther King Jr. led the Montgomery bus boycott near the city where my dad's parents were from: Selma, Alabama. In April 1968, Dr. King was assassinated by

James Earl Ray in Memphis, Tennessee, while he was planning the Poor People's Campaign to be held in Washington, DC. In that same year, as I was entering my new junior high school, as the only African American in my class and one of a handful of African American students in the whole school, George Wallace ran for president. My first day there, I found myself in a tough position, and the school found itself in a tough position also. "What should we do with this 'black boy' from Philadelphia who is not afraid of anyone?" was the unspoken question. I had not asked God to protect me from anything like that. In my mind, there was no reason to be afraid, but soon I had plenty to be concerned about.

From the first class to the last on the first day of school, the students there let it be known I was not wanted. I would go to a classroom to sit down, and a boy would come up and say, "This is my seat." Then I would move to keep peace, and another student would contest the next seat, saying it was his seat, until the teacher had to finally place me in a seat for everyone to accept; this was usually in the last row with me sitting by myself. At lunch, the other students threw food at me. It seemed no one wanted their glazed raisin buns that day, which were very good, as they hurled them at me from afar. I had to sit with a teacher to eat my lunch, and still a few buns came flying over my head. During gym, I was bullied, pushed, and shoved until I finally said that enough was enough. I zeroed in on the ringleader who I thought was behind all the unwarranted aggression. I waited in the bathroom and confronted the boy one on one. We had a few words as I held him against the wall. "Why are you fucking with me?" I asked. He had nothing to say.

As I let him go, he said, "We will get you, boy." And they did. I ended up fighting for the rest of the day, right into the principal's office. Those students were nothing like the fellow students I was used to. They hated me because of the color of my skin, and they wanted George Wallace to be their president. It was crazy. When school was let out, I was sitting in the principal's office, and I looked out his window and saw nearly the whole school waiting for me to come out as they blocked the only way

I knew to get home, which was to go through the woods northeast of the school entrance. I called my mom, who came to get me in a taxi, and home I went.

It got worse. Over the next few days, many of the students brought red and dark blue "Wallace for President" stickers to school and flashed them in my face all day. I didn't fully understand what the Wallace presidency represented; I just hated what was being done to me for just showing up to the school I had to go to.

I was constantly on guard at my junior high school because I knew a certain group was out to get me. I put up a pretty good fight when I felt threatened, able to take on two to three opponents at once, and they didn't like that one bit. I was not backing down at that point; going along to get along did not work. It was like in the streets of Philly, where I'd had to hold my ground by gaining the respect of those who wanted to take me out. However, at my new junior high school, I was all alone—that was, until one day when, while returning home, I heard a girl screaming, "Don't! Don't!" in the woods. I went to respond and saw some boys from school on top of my Caucasian neighbor's sister. Some would have called them "poor white trash," but being poor where we lived hardly amounted to the poverty in Philadelphia. My Caucasian neighbor was known as Sting. I ran to his house a short distance away, yelling, "Sting, Sting, they have your sister!" On instinct, we both ran back to rescue his sister, who was being raped by the guys. I had not known Sting could fight like he did, but we both took on about five or six of them. That day, Sting became not only my friend but also my protector. No one would mess with him, our families, or me.

One cold winter day when snow was on the ground, I was working on a shop project that caused me to leave the school late. I noticed it was quiet when I stepped outside. It felt as if the world had stopped, and I didn't see or feel the normal movement of people and cars. The walkway by the woods looked strange as I approached, finding my way to go home. Then, once I was on the pathway in the woods all of a sudden, I heard dogs barking. I could decipher a regular bark from a bark that was about to precede an attack having witnessed a Doberman Pincher kill our dog Snowball back in Philadelphia. What I heard now sounded like lots of dogs and I felt as if I were having a flashback of walking through the alleys in Philly. I felt as if I were in great danger and quickly set my stride toward the east as I ran toward my shadow in the snow, maneuvering around bushes and trees. I paused after running a good distance, and it sounded as if the dogs were still fresh on my trail. I ran faster and farther until it was apparent I had hit a body of water. I struggled, scared, as I kept running in icy knee-deep water. Stepping fearlessly, I knew I had to keep going, and I did. I ran and ran through the snowy and slushy ground. I sank deeper and deeper into the icy water and snow to get away from the dogs. I was so scared that I never got tired. I ran and ran until the hillside blocked the setting sun, and I was in gray darkness, all wet and cold. Luckily, I observed that the dogs had stopped barking, but I was totally lost. I was not only lost but also afraid. Now I wasn't afraid of the dogs; I was afraid of getting home late and getting a whipping from my parents.

I kept walking and walking until I heard some car sounds, and I ran toward the road. I had to make a decision: go right or go left. I prayed, *Lord, help me.* Left was downhill, and I just knew that way would take me home, so I followed my gut feeling and the Holy Spirit and went left. I soon saw the Riverdale shopping center close to my home and felt relieved, though I looked a mess. Things went well when I got home, because my mom could see something was drastically wrong. My new school was not the place for me, and Riverdale was certainly not like Takoma Park or Philadelphia. We had to move again soon, and I could not wait.

Later on in life, I came to realize that when I was running away from the dogs that day, I ended up running into a large pond area that now also includes a park with a pathway where people walk around the pond at their leisure. I realized it was that body of water that probably kept the dogs from getting me and saved my life. I never knew who organized that assault against me, but I quickly understood that while gangs might have been the main threat for me in Philly, in Maryland, the racial hatred of a few was something I needed to watch out for. Days like that one came again in different ways in my future.

THE THIRD MOVE IN MARYLAND

The following year, after the presidential election in early 1969, we again moved. We moved into our second single-home dwelling, on Magellan Avenue in Aspen Hill, Maryland. From the park up the street, we were about the seventh house down, just before a dead end near a basketball court at the top of the hill. The recreational spot had no signs of gangs or bullies I needed to be concerned about. People in the area were friendly towards me. In fact, many times, I practiced my basketball skills all alone. There I was free to play basketball without fear, and I did so almost every day.

When we first came to our new house, the first thing we all noticed was a little black-faced man with red lips on the lawn, holding a lantern. Back then, I did not know why it offended me so much. Without much thought, I immediately painted a white face with red lips. Later, we all questioned why I had done that, but it was something that had to be done to signal a change in ownership to an African American family. By that time, my knowledge of slavery had penetrated my mind deeply; I wanted to let it be known loud and clear that the Clays were not slaves living there. Later in life, I came to understand that the little black-faced man with red lips on the lawn was actually a significant symbol. In its purest intent, the statue was used to welcome someone and was a place where one could tie up his or her horse. Those icons were known as lawn boys or lawn jockeys. Historically, the Underground Railroad used them to indicate whether or not it was safe to travel. A green ribbon meant it was safe to travel, and a red ribbon meant otherwise.

We were blessed to have good neighbors on both sides of our house and lots of grass in the front yard and backyard. The living room had about a twelve-foot ceiling, which I would practice trying to touch. In fact, I was able to do so by my senior year in high school. I took an interest in taking care of the place. I repaired windows, did the lawn care, and even painted the house once or twice. We finally were stationary in Maryland, staying there well past my last year in high school. I would call it home, but my roots were still in Philadelphia, where I'd been made into a young man.

By and large, it was a peaceful period for my family. My dad had a good government job in Washington, DC, as an assistant director of Equal Employment Opportunity (EEO), and he played the piano and organ for all the local African American churches in the Rockville area nearby. I considered myself an African American and not black. People around me didn't like *black*. I was aware of the black movement that harshly affected those like me in the South, but I was not facing slavery or lynching, and there was no need for me to act like I was. At that point in my life, black and white references essentially pointed to the era's changing of the times. The multi-generational descendants of African slaves were on a quest to be duly acknowledged as Americans coming out of slavery and serious discrimination. I was no different. I was determined to live a life of equal opportunity regardless of the color of my skin. My dad was a fighter of equal opportunity and *for all we suffered I wanted my opportunity to have an opportunity*. I had my whole life to work through that though. Just trying to fit in would be my biggest challenge now.

I had another opportunity to get it right with those who did not look like me at another new high school, where, again, I was the only African American male student in my class of more than nine hundred students for three years. I first spent a short time finishing out my junior high school days at Parkland Junior High, and I quickly joined the Boy Scouts of America again—troop 731 after being recommended by Mr. Jennings, our scout master, on April 17, 1969. Getting with that group of guys allowed me to recondition my thinking that all Caucasian people were bad. I suppose I knew that anyway, but my previous junior high experience had taught me that some Caucasian people indeed were very bad—and also that I could be bad too if provoked. In the same way, some of the people in gangs were very bad too, but not all African American people were bad as well. Good and bad were issues of character, not color. *It would be my mode of operation to have the faith to find the good in all people, risky as that was.*

My goal in the Boy Scouts was to be first class. I went from tenderfoot to second class to first class fairly quickly, as I was getting good at camping out. I have always remembered the Boy Scout motto to "Be prepared," but I think that motto meant something different for me than the rest of the scouts. It meant being prepared to confront bad people. I also loved the Boy Scout slogan "Do a good turn daily." I also connected the motto and slogan to the Bible. Proverbs 21:31 says, "Do your best, prepare for the worst—then trust God to bring victory."

I got off to a relatively good year at my new school, Robert E. Peary High School, where the students were friendly and represented a variety of different cultural backgrounds. In the classroom, I performed above average, and I liked algebra and geometry more than any other subjects. I joined the JV basketball team and became part of the SGA (Student Government Association). After I learned how to drive, I also got a part-time job at the dry cleaner in Aspen Hill Shopping Center. I drove a 1965 Volkswagen Beetle stick shift, which I learned to drive due to an unforeseen emergency.

My parents bought the Beetle Bug mainly for my sister, who had challenges with shifting the gears. I knew because I was jerked around many times as my dad tried to teach her. One afternoon when just my mom and I were at the house, she had severe pains and had to get to the hospital. Unbeknownst to her then, she was pregnant, and not only that, but she was going into premature labor. I had never driven the Volkswagen before; I'd only watched my sister during her driving lessons with my dad and had just gotten my driver's permit. It clearly was an emergency that required me to drive, and my mom encouraged me to do so by saying, "Let's go. I know you can do it." I got in the car and imagined myself shifting gears the way my dad had taught my sister. I learned that my imagination was a good teacher for me in life. Later, I understood that to be the basis for the saying "Fake it until you make it." My timing for shifting gears was a little off in the beginning, as I would press my left foot on the gear petal before pressing the gas with my right. The letup of my left foot was a little slow, and man did I tear those gears up. However, once I was in gear, I had it. I got my mom to the emergency room, thank God, and by the time we got there, I knew how to drive a stick. My mom, sadly, had a miscarriage; however, my parents said little about it.

I got my driver's license with ease with the Volkswagen Bug. It was a great car to park because it was so small. Driving allowed me to get around, gain work, and participate in many extracurricular activities at Peary High School. All was good now, except I had one particular problem: speaking and comprehension. I still had a little Philly language in me that caused a few curse words to come out precariously when I was under pressure. There was a difference between English and language, which highlighted my limited vocabulary issues and my reading and comprehension shortcomings. *I remembered from Proverbs 4:5– 9 that it was important to get wisdom and understanding if you got anything at all.* I kept this verse in mind and applied it to my schooling.

I needed God's help to understand better and during my last few years at Peary, God answered my prayers again with good teachers, such as Ms. Sheehy, whom I loved deeply. She explained to me the importance of improving in those areas if I wanted to go to college. If there was any potential for me to get recruited for my basketball or soccer talents and achievements, I needed to make a big change in English and comprehension. I needed to get wise and get good grades. I had not thought about college in a serious way, and she made the observation that I was way behind in my skill level to make it to, let alone though, college. Ms. Sheehy offered to help me after school if I committed myself to doing the extra work to get caught up. I believed her and took on the challenge, not fully envisioning where all my effort would take me. I learned quickly that my after-school efforts were paying off, and before I knew it, I was being commended for my attitude, speaking, writing, and reading. Some creativity even started showing up as I began to write poetry. In fact, Mr. Gibbs, who was kind of different, suggested I enter a writing contest.

It was different relating to Mr. Gibbs, who posed for his drama club picture with a carnation in his mouth. He allowed me to have a role in the play *Billy Budd* and ranked my poems highly, showcasing them in our school's hallway display. I never got my typewriter-printed poems back, nor did I have copies. All ten of them were lost forever, and as a result, I was hesitant to give any of my poems to anyone for a long time. Nevertheless, I continued to write poems with passion. My progress with Ms. Sheehy also got me placed in a college-prep-course program, and college became an unintended reality for me.

The one person who made it crystal clear that college was a possibility was Mr. Hill, the only African American male teacher I had during my entire high school education. Mr. Hill was cool and calm, and he had a calming effect on me. He already knew my frustrations being an African American student before I could ever elaborate on them. His approach was to always get me to come back to his classroom, where he would give me one-on-one attention and fatherly instruction. I had algebra as well as geometry with him, and I remember him breaking down one aspect of geometry I was struggling with in particular. Mr. Hill stared at me and said firmly, "Francis, equal interior angles make a square. If you have a choice in answers, pick the one where the angles are the same. When it comes to parallel lines, all corresponding angles are congruent. Remember that!" As I became aware of my personal learning style, I discovered that it was always best when I could figure out what was important. I had a fleeting mind that tended to dwell on the unimportant. Mr. Hill helped me to focus on what was important so I could obtain the right answers. It worked. I proudly got an A in his class, not because he liked me or because we both were African Americans in an all-Caucasian school but because he helped me understand and be wise in math. Later, I would maintain strong grades in algebra in college.

I knew Mr. Hill loved me as a son. His influence was my first experience of having an African American professional male lead and guide me while knowing my strengths and weaknesses. When I was wrong and my behavior was not up to par at any time in or outside of school, Mr.

Hill would stare at me hard, and I just knew I was out of order. I found a true reality of life: there must be enough love and forgiveness for things to run smoothly. The less love that exists, the more forgiveness is needed. The more love that exists, the less forgiveness is required. I started to really love more—to love enough so things could go smoothly. Mr. Hill taught me how to endure in all my current circumstances by learning to love and forgive others and myself. I loved him deeply for that. He was one of my biggest fans on and off the basketball court at Peary High School and throughout my life.

Playing sports was my key to making it to college. By my sophomore year, everyone knew I was quick and could jump. All of my talents were playground grown; I had not played any organized sports worthy to speak of and certainly not at the level that was expected to be part of a top-rated high school athletic program, such as Peary's. Our football team was one of the best, and I was targeted to be added to the roster. The only problem was I had never played organized football before. The day I was invited and encouraged to go out onto the field was the first day the team got to wear their full pads and gear. I became a locker room story when I was given a jockstrap to wear and ended up putting it on backward, not knowing what it was or what it was used for. Everyone around me laughed as I tried to put it on. By the time I was outfitted, I felt like 8th Man, my childhood hero from when I watched black-and-white TV in Philadelphia. Most people now do not know anything about 8th Man, but he could do anything, and he was fast. The first drill the coaches ordered was a down-and-in designed to put pressure on the quarterback. It was a simple drill, really. Those who have played defensive end could probably do it in their sleep. Previously, I had not ever played organized football with a title or position—I'd just played. When Coach Williams told me to "get the quarterback," all I could think of was Dick Butkus crushing the quarterbacks on TV. As Deacon Jones would say, "Butkus was an animal on the football field," so I went animal. I thought that was what the coaches wanted to see.

"Come on! Get in there, son!" Mr. Williams said in his deep voice. In the back of my mind, his calling me son required me to give my best effort. The quarterback I was addressing was the all-metropolitan future NFL player drafted in 1977, and there came a skinny kid from Philly whom no one knew. In my first attempt to become a football legend, I used my 165-pound, six-foot-two frame to hit him full force and knock the hell out of his 220-pound, six-foot-four body—talk about a blunder. What in the hell did I do that for? I was just supposed to tap him at best, but I didn't know that. I busted him with a midair collision, and within seconds, he was flat on his butt. A black guy had clubbed the team's number-one quarterback—in practice, of all places. It was not a racial act on my part at all; it was pure ignorance—and I paid dearly for that act, which had many unintended consequences. It was the longest football practice of my life, and it was also my one and only high school football practice in full gear in my life. The coaches quickly moved me away from the team's quarterback. He wanted nothing more than to kick my ass, to say it bluntly. No more Dick Butkus acts for Francis Clay. I was pretty much done for the day and the season. I was now put on the line to be a defensive lineman, facing three-hundred-pound Bubble Boy, who enjoyed slapping the living daylights out of me in drill after drill as everyone watched. As soon as I got up, he bumped me down and rolled me in the muddy dirt again and again.

At the end of practice, the coaches lined the team up with half on one side and half on the other. Taking turns, everyone went down the middle and received a little rough bump and forearm touch from the other players—until my turn. I started up a tunnel of "Kick his ass into the ground." I could see it on everyone's face: "You hit our quarterback, and now we are going to hit you, fella. Welcome to the team!" I got a bump, stump, and dump until my face was in the mud. Some of that must have been a little racial, but there was never any name-calling. For sure, they beat the living crap out of me, but I made it through, though I was flat on my face with a crooked helmet at the end, and I could barely breathe. God, the football pads, and a helmet saved me.

CHAPTER 5

Choosing to Go Forward

Still on the ground, what I saw out in the distance looked like heaven at the time: students in shorts kicking a white-and-black-dotted ball while laughing and smiling. I said to myself, *That is a good sport, and that's for me.* I turned all my football equipment and jockstrap back in that same day; went to the football coach, Mr. Williams; and quit. He said, "Are you sure, son?" I quickly said yes and left. The next day, I went to play soccer for Coach Pine, who desperately needed a goalie.

I had never played soccer before, but it came naturally to me. All I had to do was stop the ball from getting into the goal. I just had to stand in front of the net and keep the ball from coming in. I knew I could do that well. The team needed a goalie, and I needed a team. More importantly, I needed a safe place to play organized fall sports, and soccer was it for me. There were players of other nationalities playing with me, and we all were kind of learning organized soccer together. We had Spanish players and Russian players—I was the "African" player. On our team we had the best soccer player ever: George Borowski. He was a superstar, a poetic soccer player in motion on the soccer field. Even his pictures showed his grace with the soccer ball. George lived on the other side of the park down the street from me. During practice, George's multiple shots at the goal while I was the goalie made me outstanding in that position. I figured if I could stop George, I could stop anyone. I should mention also that I loved George's mom, Mrs.

Borowski, and her Russian or Polish cooking, especially her pastries. So delicious! I would invite myself to their house as often as I could, and she always welcomed me like a son. All of that made George my best teammate and friend at Peary.

I had great success in being a goalie; I became one of the best in the county and state. I received many acknowledgments for my skills as a goalie, but I did not reach my full potential as a goalie until my coach arranged a one-on-one training session with Lincoln Phillips. In 1971, thanks to Mr. Phillips's coaching, Howard University became the first historically black college or university (HBCU) to win the NCAA Division I championship in soccer. When the great Pelé came to Baltimore, Lincoln Phillips was the goalie to defend against him. Mr. Phillips was well known among the best soccer players in the world, and there I was, training with him one on one.

Lincoln Phillips was the first African American coach to take interest in me to make me better. I think my soccer coach at Peary High School believed I needed, more than anything else, to be around a successful African American role model in sports, and he was right. I spent a whole day with Mr. Phillips, who emphasized closing out a player and knowing how to play all the angles of approach within the goalie box. Then he showed me how to lay out, catch, and block the soccer ball. Mr. Phillips was as quick as a cat, and I watched everything he did with good memory. Coach Phillips showed me that day what was important when playing the game properly. During the discussion, the possibility of my attending Howard University for soccer came up. As Howard was an HBCU, I considered his offer. I never forgot my quality time with Lincoln Phillips, and if I had played soccer in college, I probably would have played for Coach Phillips. However, my love for the game I grew up with was first on my mind. I wanted to play basketball in college.

I did not know how good I could be at playing basketball. I was fast; could jump high; and, being six foot two, was able to dunk a basketball. All those hours on the basketball court in Philly paid big dividends at Peary High School, where the team had just seen the greats of six-foot-nine Paul Coder, who had been recruited by North Carolina State in 1968, right before I came to Peary. Then there was Steve Nuce, who graduated in 1970, right behind him.

In 1971, my junior year, our team was not that good. My basketball coach, Mr. Bragonier, led us to a 4–16 rebuilding season. One incident in particular brought us together. Steve, the six-foot-four all-everything quarterback I'd decked on my first and only day of football, was now my teammate, along with many of the other football players. In one of our earliest practices, we were left alone in the gym to run a few plays. I was playing against Billy, Steve, and others, when Billy, our little guard, went to go around a pick, and I beat him to it. Billy firmly elbowed me, and to his surprise, I took him down. A team fight broke out. That, of course, was no problem for me, but like clockwork, the whole team came to Billy's defense and not mine. Before I knew it, I was fighting my own teammates. I decided that was not going to end up like my first and only day of football. I quickly ran toward the team's folding chairs and started throwing the chairs at anyone who came near me.

Right as I ran out of chairs to throw, Coach Williams, the football coach, came in and yelled, "What the hell is going on?" He asked me, "What are you doing, son?" When he said *son*, I practically melted in respect. In fact, we all respected Coach Williams and heeded his advice to work as a team. The whole team was given suicide drills until we were exhausted, and we were ready to go back to running plays as a team. That incident jelled us together because we had to make a commitment to care for one another as teammates—and we did.

I had a great time playing basketball in the summer basketball league and was successful against basketball greats, such as Adrian Dantley, who attended DeMatha High School nearby. He and I were the same size, and we both played in the summer league and both showed out down in Georgetown, where we played in the summer of 1971.

I wore number 33 my senior year, and I was featured three times in the Peary High School yearbook, *The Polaris*. I gained ultimate respect from the team when we were up by one point and our opponent went for a breakaway layup to win with seconds left on the clock—or so everyone thought. Like a flash of lightning, I caught the player with the ball going up for a layup. All of my attempts to touch the twelve-foot ceiling at home finally came in handy. With one of the highest leaps I had ever performed, I cleanly blocked the ball off the backboard for Peary to win. I was up so high that I almost landed on the stage that was behind the basketball goal. We won the game against Wheaton by three points, which put us in position to become Montgomery County champions. The joy we shared as a team was unexplainable.

We went all the way to the Montgomery County, Maryland, championship and beat our rivals by one point. That would have paved our way to go to Cole Field House, as my teammate predicted, except for one thing. The rule book stated that we only had one more game, and we were in a tie with Springbrook High School. Unfortunately, we'd played too many games to accommodate a required playoff. We had to win the playoff to go to state; at the same time, if we played in the playoff, we could not go to state because we had played too many games. We had no choice but to go down in history as the first team to win a county championship and qualify for state but not go to the state championship at Cole Field House. We played Springbrook with all our hearts and effort, winning by one point. It was a bittersweet victory. It was a great lesson in planning and scheduling for success! I was disappointed that my coach had not planned for that possibility.

Equally disappointing was the number of times my parents attended my games. They came to maybe two or three games the whole time I was at Peary, and when my dad showed up, he was lost, not knowing what to do or say or how to fit in. My dad never went to the basketball court up the street from our home either. He was clueless to all the talents I had displayed in high school. We had little to share when we were alone. He missed it all by working and doing other things that, frankly, were not that important. He and my mom finally understood how much of a role I had played at Peary when the team and coaches voted me Most Valuable Player (MVP) at our basketball awards ceremony. My dad was at a loss for words but gave me an empty hug and said he was proud of me. My mom did too. The county honored me as well, and my picture was in the newspaper when I made the all-county team. Somehow, that day, I felt I had to become the good boy that everyone wanted me to be. My grades were on point and my performances on the court were being talked about. I was in a prime position to be recruited by select colleges and universities.

Looking back on this reality, I probably didn't appreciate it accordingly, but I was thankful all the same.

There was one more sport I really wanted to try my hand at. It was a game I'd seen on TV, and it was what most of the basketball players did after basketball. They played golf, and I wanted to play it too for the first time in my senior year. Unfortunately, the reality of who I was in the face of civil rights and equal opportunity made it clear that my fellow students and teammates had privileges that I could not enjoy as an African American. I first witnessed that at a senior party at a house near a prominent country club near our school.

I was invited to a party for the basketball players, and things got out of hand. I might have been getting too close to one of the girls there, and for whatever reason, one of the guys then asked me to go fetch some beer from a car sitting across the street. Trying to fit in, I went to get the beer, and as soon as I did, a dog came running at me. I wanted to retreat back to the house, but when I saw everyone in the window laughing, I knew what the whole scene was about, and I ran home.

The next day at school, I was told that I could not play golf because the players' parents had to belong to the country club. I was not told that the country club did not allow black people to play on their course. The course was off Norbeck Road in Rockville, Maryland. The eighteen-hole regulation course at Manor Country (Men's) Club in Rockville was a private golf course organized by a group of men called the Syndicate. There had been a long history of discrimination at the country club against Jews and women as well. The wives of the husbands who were members there were not allowed to play. In fact, my friend, our class president, could not play there either because he was Jewish.

That kind of discrimination was being challenged all over the country, and I probably could have had my dad get involved, but I was too hurt about the whole thing. It brought me back to my previous junior high days in a different way. I thought, *Just because of the color of my skin, I cannot play on a golf course? Really?* If I'd been allowed to play golf at Peary, I might have devoted all my time to golf. Until I played, I often wondered why some kids had to play in the streets of Philadelphia while others could use up so much land to play eighteen holes for five hours while trying to individually put a little white ball into a little round hole. Many of my classmates did not know what had happened as far as my embarrassing golf incident was concerned, though they did need to know. One of my friends and basketball teammates knew, and he wrote the following in my senior yearbook:

> Francis Leander Clay
>
> This year has really been messed up.
> The rip off in Basketball topped it all off.
> I really enjoyed playing ball with a real champion
> like you. You were a great part of the team.
> You talked about pressure all year and I think you
> handled it very well. There's always pressure on
> the Negro in today's society. Well, before I close
> just remember that when you are feeling low
> Think about basketball and how sweet it is.
>
> Best of luck always
> Your friend

My family stayed on Magellan Avenue long enough for me to spend all my high school years at Robert E. Peary High School. During that time, I never had to be taken to the principal's office. I got along with everyone for the most part. Yes, circumstances challenged me at times, but I learned how to cope as the only highly successful African American male student in our class. I did not see myself as a black or Negro student while I was in high school. I was a Peary Husky, and I defined who I was for myself. I was a proud African American student who understood the realities of racial discrimination and the importance of personal perseverance and achievement—survival and seeking success. I had that success at Peary High School, and the teachers there took my skills to another level to prepare me for college. I will always be grateful to each one. They had an impact on me, and I know I had an impact on them as well. True, I was different, but so was everyone else.

The motto at Peary was "We will find a way or make one," which came from something Robert E. Peary said while on an expedition to the North Pole. It also provided an explanation of what I would have to do to make it in life, and I set the simple goal to always be better. When studying Rear Admiral Peary, I learned about Matthew Henson, an African American who was with Peary when he claimed the discovery of the North Pole. Henson's connection to that historic achievement was particularly important to me. It let me know that as an African American, black, or Negro— whatever label was placed on me—I, Francis Clay Jr., had a personal and significant destiny to fulfill.

Someday someone like me will be seeking his or her North Pole, and I hope my story will encourage him or her to press on toward something better. Henson published his memoir, *A Negro Explorer at the North Pole*, in 1912.

Basketball was a blessing to me. I had the grades to enter any college of my choosing thanks to all my teachers who'd supported me in my college-prep program. There were some teachers who did not like an athlete getting a scholarship for playing sports, when many students did not or could not but attended class. Why not give every student a scholarship versus having a privileged class of students who got money for entertaining other students with athletic abilities? Surely a good argument for the debate class I took.

I knew that if I did not get a scholarship, I would more than likely never attend college. Surprisingly, my dad had made no previsions for me to attend a college and be on campus. He suggested I join the military or apply for a job with the government. I did not understand why there was all this push for me to go to college growing up, only to now be of age and not be supported in going. As I'd worked so hard in all my college-prep courses, it was crushing to hear what my dad had to say. I could only reason that he was disconnected from my success and insecure, envious, and jealous regarding my achievements. In unspoken words, he was saying, "Go make it on your own like I did." It was crazy.

My parents witnessed the multiple offer letters I received from many colleges and universities, mainly ones on the East Coast. My highest-profile offer came from Boston University, which extended a full athletic offer. The letters *AO* were stamped on the application. All I needed to do was pay the processing fee of fifty dollars, which I did not have the money for. For reasons I will never understand, my dad repeatedly delayed giving me the money. When I confronted him about the time running out with the athletic offer in my hand, he told me again to join the service.

He had no clue what was being offered to me and was so busy doing his own thing that he never took time to find out. I lost it when I lost my opportunity to go to Boston University. I was so busy finishing classes to graduate that I did not have time to work for the fifty dollars, and I knew my dad had the money or at least could have come up with the money. I did not even call the BU coach. What was I to say—"My dad won't give me fifty dollars"? I was too embarrassed. I gave my dad the benefit of the doubt because right around that time, he had to pay for my sister's wedding, for which two busloads of family from Philadelphia and a few unexpected guests came. It was a major expense for us as a family, and I knew that money was tight. Still, my dad could have spared fifty dollars. There was more to his resistance than I was aware of.

After that, I learned I would have to take matters into my own hands. I started inviting coaches to the house as a way to let them speak for me and educate my parents. It seemed to work well. Charlie Fields from Towson State College was my dad's kind of guy. He was an insurance salesman when he was not coaching, and he knew how to get to my dad. He made two quick visits to close the deal with me. When I toured Towson, I felt better about college because all the buildings for my classes were centrally located on campus.

I had clear priorities when it came to college. I always felt I could go to Towson to play ball and graduate. I also made it clear to myself that I was going to go to college and graduate in four years on time. However, to do so and play basketball would not be easy. My biggest challenge now was my father, who wanted to keep me on as a dependent for tax purposes. He did not understand that doing so was in conflict with my getting the maximum financial-aid package with work-study for extra income—in addition to my scholarship money. My dad did not get it. He'd had to pay for his college education at Temple and did not understand that an athletic offer was free schooling for the most part if I applied and filled out the forms. And when we did fill the forms out, claiming me as a dependent meant he was paying for college, and he was not doing that. Everything being offered to me got delayed, and it was a big mess. I concluded that my dad was intentionally obstructing the process for me to go to college, which was crazy to me. My dad and I had it out. I challenged his professional existence as an equal-opportunity advocate. He supported opportunities for everyone else, yet he would not support his first son with the resources and money to take advantage of the opportunity to go to college and play ball. My dad went out of his way to make it difficult for me to get needed resources from programs I could qualify for.

Even without an athletic offer, with my dad's pay status, he made too much money for me to get any grants. That was an issue for me since he was still claiming me on his taxes. He wanted it both ways—to claim me and still get a tax write-off. It was a sad chapter in our relationship as father and son. I felt sad for him because he had been so distant from my athletic success that he could not embrace the rewards and benefits. My success benefitted not only me but also the financial interest of the family. It was money he did not have to pay. However, in his mind, he was not paying no matter what. All the scholarships I could qualify for had no value to him.

With time running out to enroll as a freshman at Towson, I had to complete my financial-aid packet and process my scholarship. I ended up going to my mom with the financial-aid enrollment papers and figures. I had completed the forms but needed a parent's signature. The information I'd filled out reflected the reality of my situation and what I had to do. My personal motto held up at that turning point in my life: "It's not what is right or wrong but what is the most appropriate thing to do at the time to make it right or make it work." Here I was doing something similarly underhanded to the actions I had looked down on my mother for doing, and in that moment, I realized why she'd done them. Her actions relative to my dad's position on important matters also made sense to me. I was doing what I had to do.

My mom, looking me dead in the eye, said simply, "I don't want to read it; just tell me where to sign," and she did. She knew I had her heart and wit to do what was necessary.

I was accepted into Towson and handled all financial matters without my dad's help. My dad ended up giving me a little money—and I do mean a little—yet he bragged to his friends that his son was going to college on a scholarship. "Wow" was all I could say to myself when I observed his hypocrisy and reflected on what I'd learned from Mr. Hill: "When less love is expressed, more forgiveness is needed to keep things going." In a special way, I wanted my dad to know I would make it somehow with or without him—but I never told him that. I just showed him and tried to have him enjoy the ride with me. I had an idea of why he was acting that way toward me, and I concluded that it had nothing to do with me. He'd had to make it on his own, and that was what he wanted for me. I saw things differently. We could somehow make it together, doing what we could to help one another.

CHAPTER 6

College Escapades

It seemed like it was no time before I had to enroll in classes at Towson State College in the fall of 1972. It was a big transition year for Towson, as it was the first year Towson allowed men and women on campus to be in the same dorm. Being on the basketball team once again had its privileges, as players were given priority to be housed in a dorm with a long waiting list. I first had to spend some time off campus because of my late enrollment due to my late financial-aid processing. Unfortunately, by the time everything was ironed out, there were few freshman classes left. In fact, there were so few classes left period, that I took my three-by-five-inch cards from station to station frantically trying to find any openings whatsoever and sign up for a class. I was nearly all alone during registration. Everyone else had been processed. It was the last day to find classes to be in. I was forced to take some tough courses in my major, with no elective or freshman courses like the ones my peers took. I had business management, accounting, and economic principles and politics all in my first semester. Frankly, I did not even know what freshman courses there were until the following semester, when I realized what having a major meant. I had no academic adviser to tell me I should have taken an elective class, which would have been easier in the beginning. The mistake was a self-inflicted penalty for signing up for courses in my major so late, but I had no choice. Those courses were quite a challenge for a first-year college student. Each required a lot of reading, and forced me to quickly learn the value of having a great amount of discipline for studying and exam preparation.

One of my evening classes, called Management Theory, was taught by Wayne Schelle, who was the Vice President of business and finance for Towson at the time. He wondered how I'd gotten into his evening class as a freshman. He even warned me on the first day of class that a lot of reading was required and told me that if I felt I needed to drop out of his class, it was okay. I assured him I would not drop his class. In fact, it was Mr. Schelle's class that forced me to hide in the library to get my reading done. That was the discipline I kept in order to properly study for all my classes.

The Albert Cook Library was my hiding place; I sat at a desk way in the back on the third floor and read without any distractions. Mr. Schelle's class was tough. All my classes were tough and challenging for me. Despite trying as hard as I could, I ended up with a cumulative 2.0 average for my freshman year after getting a 1.8 average in my first semester and being put on probation, risking my scholarship and position on the basketball team. Getting Ds represented death to my grade point average, which had to be much better for me to achieve my goals. However, when I was a sophomore, the worst was behind me. I knew what it would take to get through college, and I knew I could do it if I remained disciplined and involved with my studies. Instructors, such as Mr. Schelle, challenged me and got right in my face to communicate what was important. He pointed out very clearly that there were no freebies in his class. You got the grade you earned, and all you had to do was put in the work to study hard and show interest in the class.

I picked business administration as my major. Having been exposed to it hands-on by my uncle John, I wanted to know how the business game was played. At our house, we used to play Monopoly, and I always envisioned buying a block of houses, paying taxes, getting dividends, and collecting money for just going around the block. My dad showed me how to use credit cards to make it, and his approach was unique.

He had a spreadsheet and maybe thirty or more credit cards. He would pay the minimum and seek a large line of credit from the many offers he got weekly, paying off one card with another. To me, being in debt with compounding interest was not the way to live, and I committed my future and career in business to living debt free one day.

Getting a good education is invaluable. Knowing the basics of business prepared me adequately for a great future in business. At Towson, students got a sound fundamental business education from some great professors who taught the application of what we were learning. That was key in my college experience. I was learning, yes, but how could I apply what I had learned to make a difference? If I had to do college all over again, I would start an actual business my sophomore year. You have so much time to research the market and conduct market tests. Three years later, the respective business would be well established. Also influential to my business interests and savvy was my uncle John, who showed me invoices, showed me how to calculate profits, and demonstrated how to count inventory. The hands-on demonstration made the theory real, and when I got my degree, it meant a lot to me. At Towson I knew I had learned well regardless of my grades.

Each week, I went to the library and browsed through all the weekly magazines to get ideas for papers I needed to write about future trends in business. I was genuinely fascinated by businessmen and worked with the Baltimore Chamber of Commerce to help emerging businesses write business plans. The one thing I knew was that it took money to make money. How did one get money to start with? That basic question required an answer for me to achieve my dream, which was to own and operate my own corporation or business.

One person on campus in particular helped me stick with my major in business: my teammate Ray Tannahill. Having Ray close by in my dorm and watching what he did helped me to do the same. I took the classes he took in order to graduate. Ray also had an involved father who visited him often and brought him what he needed weekly, whether money, food, or liquor. Ray's dad never missed a basketball game, and he quickly became my college father figure. When he came to see Ray, he would come to see me too. I watched the two closely for four years. My father, on the other hand, did not come to visit me often. I can say for sure that he didn't even come four times during all of my four years.

Mr. Tannahill was the best father a son could have had, and he gave Ray all the things he needed to be successful at Towson. As fate would have it, Ray's dad eventually ended up in a nursing home out in Kansas, where I lived later in life. At that time, our roles changed. I visited Mr. Tannihill in the nursing home when Ray could not be with him, because Ray was living in Maryland at the time. The nursing home was five miles from my house in Overland Park, Kansas. I spent time talking with and praying for Mr. Tannihill. I was the one to summon Ray to come see his dad only days before he passed. It was funny how relationships at Towson played out in major ways like that during my entire life.

GETTING CLOSE TO THE FEMALES

Towson was a teaching college with many female students. In my freshmen year, all the guys had the opportunity to give their attention to many beautiful, smart, attractive young female students of all shapes, colors, and nationalities. We were attracted to them, and they were attracted to us. The real truth is that all the women were playing the men at Towson. There were on-campus and off-campus female students, and everyone seemed to be enjoying the college experience to the fullest, with the ratio of women to men being high. In addition to the general acquaintances, games, and parties, I also enjoyed the moments spent behind closed doors while in college. To put it bluntly and personally, I had way too many relationships with ladies at Towson. They all were good experiences that broke off in degrees of disappointment. Rarely were freshmen couples going to be together forever. In fact, it might have been good for some relationships to start during the junior or senior year so the possibility of being together forever had a chance.

I cared deeply about each female I was involved with at some point in time. For the record, I will never confirm or deny being sexual with any of them. I later wondered why I did not end up marrying at least one of them. The fact is that from 1972 to 1976, there were too many women on and off campus to have a good time with over a four-year period. Some said I had too many women or girlfriends. Even my mom said that, but it was a dynamic time in my life, when I did not have to look far to find someone to be with or love on. It was the 1970s, a time of love, peace, and everything else.

I held my first party on campus at Towson in my room on the first floor of Prettyman Hall. Most of the female African American freshman students were on the wing of the entrance to Prettyman. I could look down the hall from my room and see their heads peeking around the corner as all the guys waited for them to show up to our room. By now they all had been bombarded with their fair share of warnings from home or on campus about not hanging out in boys' rooms, let alone, becoming involved with one. My roommate and I had one bottle of Seagram's 7 whiskey and my portable turntable. It was not much, but we had enough to make the invitation to party. I waited until eleven o'clock that night for the girls to show up. "Let's wait until eleven, and if they don't come, let's invite the older girls on the upper floors." I said. When eleven o'clock came, that was what we did, and man, did they come down, with bottles of Matsu, Manischewitz, and cheap wine and cheese—stuff I'd never heard of. We partied to Sugarloaf, Jackson Five, the Temptations, Eric Burdon, and War—just a good old '70s party. If someone had a joint at a party, things really got grooving. I was introduced to marijuana in the fall of 1972, mainly by holding that party. However, the Vietnam Veterans who attended Towson on and off campus were the real bringers of pot once they caught on to how the campus party scene really was. They brought the drugs and influenced many of us to experiment with different kinds of marijuana, cocaine, and mescaline. Those were the three main drugs on campus. In light of my schedule and the few dollars I had, marijuana was thankfully my only drug of choice. I used marijuana mainly on Friday and Saturday nights when we were partying and there were no basketball practices or games.

The male freshmen on campus had to compete in many ways with grown men who had been in the military, had cars, and lived off campus. Everyone found hanging out at Towson, particularly at Prettyman Hall, a blast. We usually played the card game bid whist or whist, a game that I would later learn was played in the United States since the time of slavery and historically played by service members in the military. Many of us did not know that at the time. If you were African American, it was a card game you had to play without getting your feelings hurt. As time went on, card playing was a preparty activity that brought us all together before we figured out what we were going to do on Friday and Saturday nights.

Living on campus in the dorm had its advantages, you might say, when it came to the female students. They were right there 24-7, and anything could happen at any time—and it did. With all the freedom and plenty of time on our hands, we all got to know one another fairly well, and there was always a party going on, whether at Towson or at other colleges and universities nearby. Most home basketball games ended up having an after-party somewhere, which usually meant doing my thing with somebody somewhere. I knew I had to control myself to a certain degree because I needed to study and be ready to practice or play basketball.

Though I did not do as well as I could have grade-wise, I did develop good study habits to complete my class work and get passing grades. I would study hard on Friday afternoons until partying time. My goal was to complete all my work, say a prayer, and then party the whole weekend until Sunday, when I would usually attend church with my sinful self. I took studying and church seriously and would not miss church if I could help it. I readily asked for forgiveness, knowing full well what I had done during the two nights before church. I was doing the same things everyone else was doing and things I was glad my parents didn't know about it. Before some of the parties, I simply said, "Lord, allow me to survive!"

The partying we did over the years resulted in a few major evolutions. For example, my teammate Ray, who was not only a business student but also a businessman on campus, came up with a way to turn the dorm into a club. I was right there with him. We moved tables into the halls when I was a resident manager at Newall Hall and then got a half keg of beer and charged a party fee. We did pretty well, especially when more people came than expected, and made a profit to buy more beer and food. Ray and his close friends went on to buy and run the Charles Village Pub across the street from Johns Hopkins University, taking all the

Towson beer drinkers and partiers with him. I had a chance to get in on the deal but did not have any seed money to put up. Ray and the guys did well and put their learning to work. I learned the importance of having money to invest when an opportunity came up. That's something you are not taught in the classroom.

IOTA PHI THETA, INC.

The other evolution was that I was instrumental in chartering one of the first African American Greek fraternities on Towson's campus: Iota Phi Theta, Inc., Rho chapter. Truth be known, I actually was about to join a Caucasian fraternity on Towson's campus until I heard there was an interest group for Iota Phi Theta, Inc. circulating on campus who wanted me to come on board. We gathered an interest group of five led by Charles "Chuck" Meyers, who had a cousin in the fraternity. That connection drew me closer to the opportunity. Chuck and I were involved from the get-go, and my roommate Jerome brought Robert, his best friend from Richmond, Virginia in on what we were trying to do. We just needed one more to make a line of five, and we found Craig. We called ourselves the Five Star Originals because we were the founders of the Rho chapter at Towson. The name fit us because most of what we did was original at Towson, and it had a lot of class. Brothers came from Bowie State College, The University of Maryland, and from Morgan State College to make sure our chapter was put together right.

Being the first African American fraternity on campus was not easy. We had to do it right, providing full disclosure to the administration and dean of students. Everything we did as a fraternity in the beginning to create a meaningful social life for African Americans and all students had the blessing of our college president, Dr. Fisher, who looked and acted like John F. Kennedy in my opinion. I took the lead in the administration of getting our fraternity started on campus, working with President Fisher's administration, and providing the details and money to Iota Phi Theta, Inc.'s national office. This proved to be a taxing responsibility as the school administration was meticulous with becoming aware of the mission and purpose of Iota Phi Theta, Inc.

Everyone loved the Brown and Gold when the Iotas came to campus and sang in the perfect setting between Prettyman Hall and Scarborough Hall. It was a sight to see students looking out their windows at night to observe Chuck, Capp, and Sweetback with my Iota brothers, singing the hymn and other songs. We were creating a different culture for campus life at that time and we were definitely celebrating the importance of African American female students as we outwardly and intentionally treated them with love and respect. I loved the meaning of the five stars that represented Iota Phi Theta because they reminded me of the Boy Scouts and their focus on leadership, scholarship, citizenship, fidelity, and brotherhood. Personally, I had never had a big brother, so pledging allowed me the experience of having a big brother, and I had plenty of them. Pledging, in a way, helped me to confront my fears of in-your-face intimidation that had haunted me all my life. I always felt as if I had to deal with adversity in one way or another. From gang members in my face, both white and black, my father, and even teachers, I was frequently held hostage in a helpless mental state. Pledging allowed me to accept the aggression as a way to make myself better, and I realized how much better I was because I had survived the streets of Philadelphia. The big difference now was that I had a purpose. I was trying to become a brother of Iota Phi Theta, Inc.

We had the Iota Sweethearts, an auxiliary group for female students that got them involved with fraternal life on campus and made pledging fun. Ours were special, and we thanked them for making us pillows and keeping our big brothers occupied. We went over—or were initiated into—the fraternity on May 5, 1973, right after my freshman year. My grades had improved, and the timing was perfect, as the fraternity as a whole was celebrating its ten-year anniversary. Historically, Towson was only the seventeenth chapter in the Greek fraternity's ten-year history. Iota Phi Theta, Inc. had a short but rich history as the youngest African American Greek organization in the country, and it was on a roll.

We helped start twenty new chapters of Iota Phi Theta, Inc. across the country. I became Rho chapter Polaris and was elected to the fraternity's board of directors. In that capacity, I later wrote the fraternity's national strategic plan. Rho chapter paved the way for other traditional African American Greek organizations to come onto campus, such as the Deltas, Omegas, Alphas, and AKAs.

I attended Iota Phi Theta, Inc.'s tenth-anniversary conclave and had a ball. On campus the next year, we held our first bump dancing contest in the basement of Scarborough Hall, charging one dollar for couples, after the University of Baltimore County Maryland game on February 8, 1974. The place was packed, and we had some sore hips the next day. Twenty days later, we had a slave auction to raise money. We could be hired to clean someone's room, do laundry, or do whatever was requested. One girl literally handcuffed me—and the rest of the story I cannot confirm or deny. I was the dean of pledgees, or DP, for our first line. Our biggest event was our Coronation, during which we crowned a Sweetheart Queen; a woman who supported our organization overall and had a good rapport amongst our peers at large, as well as involvement in other Towson activities. We crowned our first queen, who was a good friend of mine and a member of Towson's cheerleading squad. Our most important act of good was raising money for a worker in the campus cafeteria who got sick. We collected the money from fellow students and took it to her home, and she used it to buy the medicine that she needed.

During that time, the ladies of the Delta Sigma Theta, Inc. sorority were also chartering a chapter on Towson's campus. A few of the ladies pledging Delta Sigma Theta, Inc. were close friends of mine. I was a student adviser to help get the Deltas chartered on campus. It was not easy to get established on campus. Apparently, I became an issue for the Deltas starting out. I was a significant distraction for those on the line—so much so that their adviser asked me to distance myself from them all until they had gone over. Having just pledged myself, I understood the request and obliged her wishes. All in all, I was glad to know that in some meaningful way, I was helpful in the Deltas becoming the first African American Greek-lettered sorority on Towson's campus. Together we created a positive social environment for African American students at Towson, and our legacies continue to this day. I was glad to have known so many Deltas, not knowing that one day my own daughter would be a Delta too.

When we graduated, President Fisher said, "A patriot is to be judged not by how loudly he proclaims his love of country but how well he lives up to the ideas of this country." It was not easy to start an African American fraternity at Towson, but we lived up to the ideas that, in the end, made our college experience more meaningful. With all students working together, we formed the United Front against Racism, which was a teach-in to explain what racism was about, and how it was affecting our country and the campus. Our administration supported the effort. We felt that students did not understand what racism was or the impact it was having on all of us. We were not passive, and it was refreshing to see all the students get engaged to create more awareness and understanding. I believe the teach-in prevented a major protest on campus because the lines of communication were open, and we were able to resolve some issues bubbling on campus.

Amid that struggle, while I was the Polaris, or President, of our chapter, a racist school newspaper editorial targeted our fraternity. I was the one to respond to the editorial, which was published in the school newspaper by "Name withheld upon request"—that was how it was printed in the newspaper, which showed a black person wearing a KKK uniform and holding a torch. Those types of acts were creating a bubbling of unrest on campus that simply would not be tolerated. The heading was "Would You Support White Studies or a White Student Union?" It went on to question, "How would you—yes, you—take the formation of an all-white fraternity on campus?" We as African American students got the message. Our concern was leveraging the KKK, which took matters to a whole other level. I personally had to respond because I knew that before Iota Phi Theta, Inc.'s Rho chapter was founded, there were already Caucasian fraternities on campus, because I'd been about to join one. The editorial was bad, with the picture equating Iota Phi Theta, Inc. to the hateful KKK. This was a mischaracterization of our fraternity indeed. It was not getting any easier to gain acceptance as an African American organization under those circumstances, and from many angles, it was an evolution for me to know when to stand up and when to sit down.

In writing the editorial response, I explained the rich history of African American fraternities' community service. By supporting the response with facts, we could educate and answer questions, calming any fears or concerns. As I said, it was not easy, and no one knew the challenges better than I did. However, by God's grace, I prevailed, and a year later, I felt that starting the Rho chapter was one of my greatest achievements in life. As I look at all the young men who have joined the Rho chapter since I left and now have an organization that affirms them as African American male students and as I see all the other African American fraternities and sororities that have come onto Towson's campus since the Rho chapter's beginning, it's a blessing to know I played an important part of paving the way for this historic change.

GUNPOINT

At the end of my junior year at Towson, I moved off campus into a fraternity brother's house on Riggs Avenue. Four of us would be staying there together: Chuck, Rick, Cos, and me. It was like our own inner-city frat house in many ways.

By that time, Chuck was in a relationship with a girlfriend who would later become his wife. His girlfriend had a roommate named Joy who would later become the wife of yours truly. It's kind of funny to look back on it now. Back then, we did not know how any of our lives would play out. In fact, our lives were almost cut short by a robbery at gunpoint that took place within the house on Riggs Avenue.

I was on the phone, talking to a close friend of mine, when all of a sudden, a guy broke into my room on the second floor, wearing an all-black mask and holding a woman close to him. He demanded to know where the drugs were as he pointed his gun directly at my left temple. I could see the inside of the barrel of the gun as he thrust it toward the left side of my face. I went into Philly mode with my attitude and showed no fear, responding as if I didn't care, saying, "I don't know what you are talking about. I have no drugs," which was true. The robber could have shot me as he poked the gun into my face, but I gestured with an attack response, standing up quickly. He then backed up from me, retreating to the hallway, where he had a girl hostage standing there embraced by his left arm. She happened to be visiting my fraternity brother downstairs.

The robber quickly grabbed the girl he was holding as a hostage, put his left arm around her neck, and pointed the gun at her head, which stopped me in my tracks. He said, "Downstairs!" and I followed his instructions, hoping he would not shoot her. Downstairs, he told us all to lie face down on the wooden floor, where there were two other robbers in masks with guns. They had gathered everyone in the house at that point. About eight of us were on the ground, and the robber I had confronted kept kicking me hard. I could see my veins pop up from my skin on my arms and legs. They were so noticeable that I was sure he saw them too. Compounding the fear of the whole ordeal, another girl who was visiting went into shock and began shaking. She was having a heart attack.

I sprang up in an angry panic. "If you are going to shoot, do it, but we need to call an ambulance right now!" I said to the robbers. All the brothers being held at gunpoint fearlessly came to the girl's aid, putting ourselves at risk of being killed at that moment. We were able to call 911. The robbers apparently did not want to kill us, which led us to believe they knew us or at least knew of us. Instead of drugs, they quickly took all the clothes and jewelry they could grab. Then they all ran out the front door before the police and an ambulance came.

Talk about God's grace and mercy! We certainly received it that day. I could have been shot dead two times during that ordeal, and I later felt guilty for acting so Philly bold, as if I didn't care for my life. My behavior scared the hell out of me in retrospect because internally, under pressure, I was unafraid of anything or anyone. Years later, however, the thought of what had happened that night haunted me. I thought about all the things I would have missed out on if the robber had pulled the trigger on me. Killing people, especially the young, simply cuts innocent lives from ever seeing the good that God has for the living. I thought of my friends from my youth in Philly who were jailed or killed. They missed out on many good experiences in life—all over nothing when you really think about it. Fighting, stabbing, and shooting at one another at such a young age—or any age, really—is pointless. The Ten Commandments highlight this. One commandment states clearly, "Thou shalt not kill." It's a tragedy to witness people dying so young. My motto is, "Stop the innocent killing! We have so much coming our way if we can just live long enough to see it."

BACK ON CAMPUS

Because I survived that day, I was alive to do many other things while I was still in college. During my time at Towson, I was active with the president's council, Student Government Association, the black student union, the marketing and business club, Iota Phi Theta, Inc., Towson basketball, and the United Front against Racism. I even ended up writing for Towson's school newspaper. However, I experienced my greatest moment in college during the last few seconds of our basketball team's triumph over Salisbury State during my last home game as a senior.

I'd played on the team since my freshman year, and many times I had vividly imagined making the last basket in a close game for Towson to win. Basketball at Towson meant so much to me. It was not about scoring the most points, because that would never happen. I played behind the great Larry Witherspoon, who should have been in the Hall of Fame for all of his accomplishments, but because he'd fallen short of a major requirement, his contributions to Towson basketball were missing from the Hall of Fame record. Bearing that in mind, one of my major objectives when I joined the team was to complete my degree on time in four years. Unlike most athletes, who majored in physical education during that time, my degree was in business. I loved sports, yes, but I knew full well that after my college career, I would want and need something more solid to fall back on.

Playing ball taught me about life and the roles one has to play to get in, fit in, and get along. It was about knowing how to bring value to a team, thriving on the team, and having the confidence to perform and produce when called upon. I was not my coaches' favorite, but Coach Angotti told me, "Pound for pound, you are the best I've ever seen play the game." Coach B. had taught me the fundamentals of the game when I was in high school at Peary. I knew the proper foot movements, passing lanes, and angles to the basket that made plays better than most. Fundamentals will complement or compensate for talent every time—particularly in a championship game. The truth was, Coach Angotti could have cut me anytime, and had good reason to do it, but I will always be grateful to him for keeping me on the team as I struggled at times to keep it all together, even though I felt I was his scapegoat for many of the losses we had. Playing a key role in winning the last game of the season was the best way I could show my appreciation to Coach Angotti for all he'd done for me during my four-year career with Towson basketball.

For me, our last home game made any sacrifices made by those around me worth it. In the stands were my dad, fraternity brothers, and sweethearts and even one of the senators of Maryland, Charles McCurdy "Mac" Mathias Jr., whom I took a picture with after the game. Close friends, such as Phil Jacobs, my frat brother Pat Britton, and Bobby Washington, were my teammates on that journey, and our connection became more meaningful to me over time. It was my happiest one shining moment while playing Division I NCAA ball. The game was not for a championship, but it was a goal achieved and a dream come true. We might not have been champions, but we were winners all the same having finally secured an overall winning season. On that day, my dad observed me as one of the three seniors who shared captain honors. I also was the first African American player to come into Towson as a freshman, stay on campus, and graduate on time in four years. The student who had earned a 1.8 GPA after his first semester now was asked to help our coach recruit new players by speaking to high school students about opportunities at Towson. They used me as an example of how young men could come to Towson, play ball, and graduate.

We played our last home game at Towson in Burdick Hall, which had bleachers only on one side and had a flat wall on the other side. No other school had a basketball court like ours. We played in an era when the basketball rims were not flexible, and dunking the ball was not allowed. In fact, the square transparent backboards had just been approved. We played our rival, Salisbury State, and it was an important game to end a successful basketball season. It was the best season for our coach in ten years, and we were shy of the conference title by only a few points.

The game was painstakingly tight, with leads exchanging back and forth. In the closing seconds, my defense on the wings was needed to stop their motion offense, which required our team to switch our man on any pick-and-roll. Salisbury was trying to run the clock out with a one-point lead. Coach wanted us to play tight defense and not foul. It was almost like a movie I had seen before. There I was, defending on the wing, and the ball was passed to my man, who quickly moved to the center of the court with seconds left on the clock. We were still down by one point.

I knew we needed the ball, and I could calculate with my eyes the rate of bounce my opponent would create with each dribble of his hand. I took stock of his every move and took a low defensive position, almost as if I were peeking under a table. Moving like a wildcat on the hunt, I saw my opportunity and swiftly swiped the basketball away with my left hand as the ball came off the ground from my opponent's dribble. The basketball was now loose and out of my opponent's hand. In a flash, with my left hand, I pushed the ball forward toward our goal. I was now in control of my dribble, crossing midcourt with my opponent trailing.

Nothing was in front of me, and within seconds, I jumped to put the ball in the hoop. As I passed the foul line in the air, preparing for a layup, I launched myself so high that I could see the inside of the hoop as my body floated forward. With my arm extended, I placed the ball to the back of the rim. Mind you, as I said, we could not dunk the ball in those days, so I had to lay the ball up right. The whole time, I could hear the crowd yelling and screaming loudly as the ball bounced back and forth as I descended gracefully to the floor to witness it falling through the net. It was a dream come true as the buzzer to end the game sounded. The last game of my college basketball career was over, and we ended it in the win column. How sweet was that? I'd made the last shot for Towson to win. That moment defined my four basketball years at Towson and taught me to always hang in there until the very end. I ended up being interviewed right there in the locker room alongside my coach and the governor for a featured article in the *Baltimore Sun* newspaper.

That play always kept me believing that just *one time*, if I could get an opportunity, I could win. I still get goose bumps when recalling that moment. It's the type of moment that few get to enjoy. The only thing missing from the locker room was champagne being sprayed all over the place. My dad was there to greet me and stood in the background, watching his son get all those acknowledgments, not realizing that his could have been the most important acknowledgment I ever heard.

LOOKING BACK

After my last game at Towson, when college basketball was over, I soon realized I had a tremendous amount of catching up to do to graduate on time. In fact, some professors changed their sense of understanding once the season was over and would not allow me to make up assignments I'd missed due to our basketball schedule. That was understandable yet unfortunate for me. Missing a class assignment that required a lab or working with a team could not be made up, and I would have to accept a C instead of a B in a required class, such as biology. I begged my computer-programming professor to give me a C when I turned in my last assignment at Towson. That coming Monday, my assignment to turn in a deck of punch cards was due. I had spent the whole weekend focusing on the assignment of organizing hundreds of punch cards. My classroom was in the basement of the historic Stephens Hall, with its eroded smooth, square marble steps. That was the class grade I needed to end up with a 3.0.

Monday morning, I walked from the dorm next door to Stephens Hall with my cardboard rack of cards early in the morning. I was going to be the first in line to have my punch card run. The only problem was that it was raining hard. I dashed toward Stephens Hall, running on tiptoe, and when I got to the marble step to open the heavy door, my foot slipped, and down I went with the cards all loose and falling out of order. I grabbed a large portion of the cards and brought them to my chest, but the project collectively was a mess and terribly out of order.

I had spent all weekend on the project, and I did not want to do it again. I was so stressed that I could have cried right there on the steps of Stephens Hall. Wet and dejected, I took my punch cards as was and faced my professor outright, pleading with him to give me a break and not require me to redo the assignment. Looking at me, he agreed that if the punch cards that stayed in order met the minimum requirements, he would give me a C. Some of my cards were too wet to process, but thank God enough of them were dry. I gladly accepted a C in the class, which dropped my average to a 2.85 GPA. From that incident,

I developed a phobia of trying new technology, always fearing that something unexpected would go wrong.

There is nothing like hearing the registrar tell you that all your grades have posted, you have enough credits, and your GPA is good enough for you to graduate and attend graduation ceremonies. With all the makeup work I'd had to do, my grades were the last to be posted. All the senior athletes faced that reality. Graduation day was the realization of another dream come true and a goal achieved. I was the first and only among my siblings to attend a four-year college, live on campus, and graduate on time. That achievement alone made my mom, who had not finished high school, proud. In fact, it motivated her to get her GED and attend college herself later on. At any rate, Mom was proud of me, and she showed it. I wanted to be an example for my other siblings, especially my little brother Sidney, who was taking notes.

I remembered what Mr. Hill had allowed me to learn in high school: "More love, less forgiveness." In other words, the more love you exhibit, the less forgiveness you have to extend. I did it. I graduated in four years with a degree in business administration. Everyone from my family was there to witness my graduation, and my mom and dad were proud and full of smiles. When I looked up at my mom from the floor where commencement took place, I realized that without her initial signature on those financial-aid and enrollment documents, my graduation from Towson might still have been just a dream and not a reality. I learned from my mom and dad that you do what you have to do to make it in life. Sometimes it is not all that pretty or right, but if your heart is in the right place, somehow, someway, it works out in the end.

When the diploma hit my hand as I crossed the stage, I thought about my friends in Philly who'd ended up dead or in jail and my blood brother, Little Jeep. Inside, I wondered, *Why only me?* How come all my friends from Philadelphia were not sharing that moment? The moment was better than I ever could have imagined. I was now, as the Boy Scouts said, prepared to take on my future, and I relished my high school motto and said to myself, "I will find a way or make one!" In the words of Malcolm X, whom I had gained an appreciation for, I found my way "by any means necessary."

The way forward is not always shown; sometimes you have to feel your way through until you can see clearly which way you need to go. It's all in the mind. What you can conceive, dream, and hope for you can believe and achieve. I was now a college graduate, and I was pleased with that accomplishment.

CHAPTER 7

I've Only Just Begun

As weird as it seems, I subconsciously thought a job would be waiting for me after I graduated from college. I was looking for all the attention I'd gotten when I graduated from high school, with multiple offers and folks calling me left and right. I did not think through the details of what I wanted to do post-graduation— or, more importantly, what I needed to do. At the time, I needed a job quickly and a place to live. It was that simple. I needed to make some decisions soon because I had no money and going home was out of the question.

In retrospect, I realize I didn't discipline myself to take advantage of the job information and recruiting activities my college's career center had to offer. I did not see the potential of networking amid the influential people I knew, particularly those in the Towson Alumni Association. Fortune 500 companies were looking for African Americans and other minorities. Affirmative Action was a catalyst for getting students like me their first jobs in an effort to meet quotas and invoke more minority participation. All of that was happening but not happening for me because I had not made getting a job a priority or a goal. I had no one to blame but myself, and I felt ashamed.

Thus, my first job out of college was cleaning offices at the John Deere building right outside of Towson, Maryland. I was on my own now and needed to pay the few bills I had as well as eat. I took the job because of the prominent name of the company and the fact that they were looking for an immediate hire. I was embarrassed to say at the time that I did not have a real career job. However, everyone had heard that I had landed a job with John Deere and congratulated me for graduating, though they never asked me what I was doing. I quickly would say, "I got hired by the John Deere Corporation," which I had, and then, to avoid another question, I would change the subject. The reality was that I was mopping floors and emptying trash at John Deere at night with a degree in business administration.

Being in that state of affairs quickly woke me up to what college was supposed to really be about in the end: finding a job and starting your career. With school and basketball out of the way, I seized the opportunity to redeem use of the career center and started speaking with alumni. After doing so, I eventually found my way to my first "real" job at a large Maryland-based insurance company as a staff control analyst. Within months of graduation, I got it together with a lot of prayer and grace. Sometimes you have to feel your way until you can see where you are going. I applied, interviewed, and was selected for a good position that would lead to a bright future in corporate America. I was on the right track, and I was grateful to God for seeing me through those ignorant and neglectful times of simply not knowing and being too embarrassed to ask for help in the right way.

Leading up to graduation, I had known I did not want to take the journey into real life alone and had proposed marriage to my girlfriend, Jackie, my southern sweetheart at the time, who was in a nursing program in Baltimore. We had met when I joined a few of my fraternity brothers in going to meet some nursing students at a party in Baltimore. I'd quickly zeroed in on that Georgia peach from Tuskegee, Alabama, which was where the Commodores had originated. In fact, she knew Lionel Richie and the whole group. At a concert in the Washington, DC, area, we met them all in a VIP setting because of her connections.

My relationship with my first fiancée took me deep into the South, where I gained a full understanding of the African American journey from slavery to civil rights by embracing some of the historic figures at her school, such as George Washington Carver and Booker T. Washington. While traveling to the historic Tuskegee Institute, which she attended and which was known for its outstanding nursing program, I saw my first Colored Only sign at a rest stop where my roommate, Jeff, and I were trying to get gas in a small town in southern Georgia, off Interstate 85, right before crossing into Alabama. When we stopped and I observed and connected with the sign's intended meeting, I told Jeff, who was driving, "I think we need to get out of here." I could sense we were in the wrong part of town at the wrong time of night. We left, taking the chance that our gas could run out along Interstate 85 before the next exit with a well-lit gas station. In that case, at least people could have seen if something went wrong. When you visit Tuskegee, you cannot overlook the contributions of Booker T. Washington and of George Washington Carver, who produced three hundred products from peanuts, including flour, paste, skin lotion, and medicines. Tuskegee was one of the first institutions of learning for the Negro in those times.

That trip south was to see my fiancée during her graduation and discuss our engagement. It was not one of our best times together. Because it was her graduation weekend, her family was there, and I could sense that things were not right between us based on how we were communicating. My fiancée and I, as well as her mother and a few close friends, all went through the motions on that visit, not really connecting to the truth about the way each of us was feeling. We were unsure about the future of our relationship going forward, and it appeared we had little time to understand one another and work things out.

I returned to Baltimore, where I had an apartment on Radecke Avenue, unsure about our relationship. Internally, I was feeling disillusioned about why things were not going right for us. To be honest, I never had a good handle on what really happened between us and felt like I could not go on with the engagement because I did not have all the answers to the questions I had. Therefore, emotionally, I called it off with mixed feelings right before I accepted my first career position. I rationalized to myself that I just was not the marrying type. I had been involved with many women at Towson and finally was willing to settle down with one woman, only to have the relationship not work out. I came to the following conclusion: "You can love anyone, but you cannot be committed to everyone." That became my mantra, and it was true. Even the Bible encourages us to love one another. I was in love, but from where I stood, I was not committed. My next objective as far as any long-term relationship with a woman was concerned would be to find the one person I could love and be fully committed to for life—and at the time, I knew that would be a big challenge.

MY FIRST PROFESSIONAL JOB

My new position as a staff control analyst, unbeknownst to me, encompassed the basics of all quality-control management, and it provided me with a sense of legitimacy after having just graduated. There was a solid career path communicated to me, and I would need to put in three or more years before I could become a manager. In retrospect, it probably was good for me to start my career while single versus married, so I could focus on my new position and the transition into my new life of working every day.

At the insurance company, I was responsible for performing work-measurement studies that created staffing standards based on production criteria, time, and the number of errors recorded. My participation in that discipline made a big difference for the company. It was my job to make substantiated recommendations to improve the processes that had a direct impact on staffing, performance, and production. The only challenge I soon faced was achieving above expectations too quickly. That caused me to stand out in management meetings among my peers, who were mostly Caucasian. I was good at justifying a position or eliminating a position based on the correlation of work produced in a certain period of time. That information was helpful to a field manager who was understaffed. He or she then had data to make a request for an additional staff person. With the company growing, it was a human resource tool to make sure we were supporting the growth in sales.

Being a young college-educated African American man in an all-Caucasian working environment gave rise to group dynamics worth noting. For one, some managers encouraged me while simultaneously using me as a rabbit in the event I was producing above average. That would embarrass the other team members and inadvertently influence their improved workmanship. Their predominant assumption was that African Americans did not work as hard or perform as well as their counterparts. On the other hand, some managers would use me and pay me less for producing twice the amount of work because it made them look good.

In either case, I was outperforming myself and working as if I had something to prove versus embracing the self-confidence I had in being competent in what I was doing. Such a disposition allowed my work to speak for itself. A better assessment of my situation at the company might have been made clearer if I had not had an unethical African American manager heading my department. He was having an affair with his secretary, whom I had to work with on a daily basis.

Unfortunately, I got caught up between the two. How did that happen? One day, while attending a client-sponsored boat ride in Baltimore, my manager asked me to pick him up, along with his secretary and the secretary's sister, whom she had invited. When I arrived, the secretary's sister opted to drive her own car, so she followed the three of us to our destination. We all headed to the boat ride on one of the early *Spirit of Baltimore* cruises, during which I had my official introduction to the secretary's sister once we were on the boat.

Everything was businesslike throughout the cruise, and I ended up entertaining the secretary's sister, who was a professional in the dental field. We'd had a few drinks, so my manager asked for my car keys, as if he were going to do some of the initial driving home.

Thinking he wanted to ensure my safety, I handed over the keys with no contest. As we returned to the dock, the secretary's sister and I were still on the upper level of the boat, while my manager and secretary were on the lower level. As everyone exited the boat, with the lower level leaving first, I lost track of them. When the sister and I reached the parking lot where my car was, they were gone, and my car was too. After we waited around aimlessly for a while, the secretary's sister finally suggested we go to her place, which was interesting. That was in no way part of my plan for the evening, but it was the start of a long night that went into the early morning.

At her place, which was laid out nicely, we talked more about our backgrounds. She had the notion somehow that I was related to the Clays who were big in the Baltimore area's construction scene, which I was not a part of. We waited and waited as I worked hard to be respectful, knowing that she was the sister of the secretary, whom I had to work with on a daily basis. It was almost three o'clock in the morning before my car showed up. I gave my farewell to everyone and headed home.

The next business day, when I returned to work, the atmosphere was tense. My manager and I had an unspoken man thing going on, wherein he knew I had to live with the truth about his affair with the secretary and what had happened after the boat ride. I felt played by the man I had to report to every day, and to make matters worse, he was an African American senior-level employee in the company. Everything was different for all three of us, and frankly, I did not know how to handle the situation and play the secrecy game. In my role as a staff control analyst, I minimized my contact with both my manager and the secretary, which probably was not the best thing to do, as it was blatantly noticeable. I tried to play their office game but did not communicate effectively, which showed up in an evaluation I was given. My work was good, but my interactions were too guarded.

In doing work-measurement studies on the sales administration side, I was able to ascertain that the insurance reps were making nice money, and they seemed to have a lot of fun doing it. I remembered that one of my fraternity brothers, Danny, ran a successful insurance business, and I approached him about becoming a life insurance agent under him. That was my subtle vision for exiting the awkward working environment I was being subjected to.

One of the things he told me in my initial meeting was to always be aware and read local newspapers, business books, and review magazines. He recommended books to read and magazines to look at routinely. That bit of advice helped me with my personal and professional development. I read the local newspaper daily to be on top of current events, particularly those in business. I derived a valuable principle in business from doing those development activities: you cannot have better customers until you better educate them about your products, programs, and services. I left my first job and became a licensed life insurance agent in June 1977.

My start under Mr. Danny Henson was outstanding; however, he was not my manager for long, and I ended up with a new manager. Right from the start, my new manager wanted to co-travel with me on deals I was about to close, although I really did not need his help. Then, when processing the applications, he always found something missing and volunteered to secure what was needed rather than allowing me to gather the information myself. I thought he was helping me, when in fact, he was acting in a way that would allow him to take partial commissions for the business I booked. He raised my quota for the number of applications I had to process and then delayed my compensation. That put me in a constant prove-yourself mode, which required a lot of cold-calling, which I became good at doing. Once again, I was facing an African American manager doing something unethical, and I did not want to make an issue.

The superior to my manager started to suspect something was not right. I learned that I could voice my concern and make a formal grievance, but I knew going about things the wrong way—by showing too much emotion versus laying out the facts or complaining madly—would be a waste of time, and time was running out. Once again, I simply did not know how to professionally handle the matter. My manager had me right where he wanted me. I wanted to leave because I felt that when you lost respect for the person you had to report to, you either continued to be mistreated or left. So, I left.

My first two jobs in corporate America in the insurance industry were indicative of the many recurring challenges I would have in working for middle-aged African American male managers who wanted to misuse my talents, skills, abilities, and accomplishments for their own gain. It was a sad thing to see. At the time I entered the workforce, racism and discrimination by Caucasians really was not my issue; they were giving me opportunities. For the rest of my professional life, my biggest challenge was dealing with people of my own skin tone, who were jealous or envious of my achievements and ambition or just wanted to take advantage of me for their own personal and professional gain. It was similar to the behavior my dad exhibited toward me. Later in life, I would discover the formal term for the behavioral pattern I encountered, particularly with the African American managers who engaged in unethical behavior with peers and subordinates: rankism. Rankism can be intentional or otherwise. Mixed with the psychology of envy, this is a reality that African American men should address and be prepared to confront properly.

In my case, I clearly understood it and knew it was intentional. The errors made by others in that regard clearly impacted my career early on. The worst part was that there was no one to tell at the time who could help me. My choice was basically to remain in the awkward subordinate role or leave. I chose to leave. Deep down, I knew I was prepared to move on. I said to myself, "I have so much to offer and could bring value to any business or organization. I will not be misused or restricted because of the selfish agendas of others." I was smart, humble, hungry, experienced, and attractive. I lacked only the wisdom that a good life of experiencing failure would teach me. I sometimes said, "No wonder black- and brown-skinned people do not get ahead. In part, it's because we are always misusing one another for the wrong versus properly valuing one another for our future good."

I engaged with too many African Americans who did not keep their word, have good ethics, or follow up in a timely manner. The quality of our relationships was unpredictable, and we argued over matters that were irrelevant in the long run. As a result, we were holding one another back or down within our communities and social settings. When you are on the wrong end of this behavior, everyone near you is disillusioned, hurt, and disappointed. What do you do? My goal in that regard was to make people better. If others were around me, I would try to lift them up in truth, believing that one day they would do the same to me or to someone else.

CHAPTER 8

Working Things Out

While dealing with coworker issues, I remembered what a Jewish mother in our neighborhood in Philadelphia had said to me one day. Her family owned a business that all her sons had a hand in. She shared the following in a conversation about discrimination: "I tell my boys not to ever, ever step on someone to get ahead; we don't do that. But I also tell them never to be afraid to step over or around someone to get ahead." I never forgot those empowering words, and it was clear to me that sometimes you have to be bold enough to step over or around people to reach your goals. There was no escaping the force in human nature to be the best among the rest, but there was a right way to do it out of respect. Putting people down or abusing others was not the right way, because you were putting down people you would need later to go to the next level. People are entitled to their preferences, and they have the right under the First Amendment to speak and assemble as they wish. To me, that meant if you couldn't beat them or join them, then you had to leave them respectfully and go another way.

I had gotten to the point where I asked myself, "Why work for someone else if I am going to have to put up with so much?" I said to myself, "Why not become a lawyer if you are going to have your values and work challenged so hard in life by someone else?"

My uncle John was a lawyer, and he'd become one by going into military service. Uncle John appeared to have the life I wanted back then. He always wore nice suits and drove nice cars with a big smile on his face. Following his example, I tested to qualify to be enrolled in the US Army and become a legal clerk.

I didn't realize that by making that commitment, I would miss my dream chance to try out for the Baltimore Bullets. While I was at Towson, the Baltimore Bullet players regularly practiced at our facility during the off-season. Mike Riordan, a notable player during that time, promised me an opportunity to try out if I could beat him in a one-on-one pickup game when he came to Towson's gym to practice. In fact, he gave me his red suede Pumas after I beat him in two out of three games to 21. It was not only a nice work out for him but also an opportunity for me to go to the next level in basketball. I think I would have made the team, because I was playing the best basketball of my life after I left Towson. I dreamed of playing in the NBA when I was playing in a local Baltimore semipro basketball league and averaging more than twenty points a game at the time I got my Baltimore Bullets invitation. Word had traveled about my success when I took MVP in our league. I unfortunately missed out on the opportunity because I had already enrolled in the military, and I was committed to going to basic in the spring.

Life happens like that sometimes, but I was grateful to Mike Riordan for keeping his word. In February 1978, I committed to go to basic training and was slotted to go into the US Army as a legal clerk with the intent of qualifying for JAG (Judge Advocate General Corps) School and becoming a lawyer. In that capacity, I could chart my own course in life, be respected, and achieve my goals.

At the time I made the decision to go into the service, I was involved with a beautiful young woman named Joy Holland, a hardworking graduating senior at Morgan State College. Joy and I had met years before at a party at a club near her campus. The first time I brought her over to my apartment, we quickly found ourselves in a serious talk about life, and I shared with her all my life challenges since graduating from Towson. I loved the conversation, her openness, and her willingness to listen and understand. We listened to music, had a bite to eat, and talked some more. Somehow, we got to the point of kissing, and after a while, I politely asked her to leave my apartment out of respect for the way we were mutually feeling. She was surprised, but I knew what I was up for. At that time, it was too soon for us to take the relationship further. I knew one thing for sure, though: I loved that woman and wanted to preserve the possibility of us living our lives together in the future. I did not know if I was ready to get involved in a deep relationship again, so I put us on pause.

Joy did not make it easy for me to resist spending time with her. In fact, I later ended up moving into her apartment in an unplanned sort of fashion. She had a bed in her apartment that we had to sit on when I visited. It had a valley in it so deep that I would inadvertently end up rolling into the middle of the bed and then on top of her because the slope was so drastic. I offered her my bed and then started staying with her right before the boat incident at my former job. As a result of that eventful night, Joy kicked me out of her apartment that morning when I returned late, saying, "If you can't come here at a decent hour, then you have to leave."

I ended up leaving the next day and moving into the place of the secretary's sister that day. She had jokingly offered to let me stay there the night before because neither of us had known when my ride was returning. It was a crazy twenty-four hours in my life. I called my fraternity brothers, gathered my stuff, and moved out of Joy's apartment.

Surprisingly, Joy ended up calling me at the place where I was staying. How she found out the number I have no idea. However, that conversation led me to come back to her place. It showed me a lot about Joy and her desire to be with and committed to me. She made her point and wanted me to be committed to her too. Joy was showing me what commitment was.

Furthermore, Joy's aunt Carolyn came to her apartment one day to meet me, and she made clear her expectations about how her niece had to be treated. It was established in my mind that Joy was not going to put up with me doing anything any old way. That was clear. But her fight to keep me brought out the best in me. It all sounded like a different kind of love to me.

In our talks about being serious and committed, I expressed to her the importance of finishing her degree and said I was willing to get out of the way so she could do that. Joy was surprised about my decision to go into the US Army, as were most of my friends. To be honest, I really did not think through the timing, and before I knew it, it was time go. I had a commitment to the US Army to keep, one I could not get out of. I left most of my things with Joy to pursue my goal of becoming a lawyer by way of the United States Army.

FIRST NEW CAR

A unique challenge I had before departing was figuring out what to do with the new 1977 Ford Granada I had just purchased. I had not had a genuine desire to buy the silver Granada at the time. In retrospect, I realize I was taken for a nice ride. I was looking for a new used car when I pulled up onto the dealership's lot that day, and I was invited to drive the new Granada. It was in the late evening, right before sundown. I drove it around to all my friends, and they loved it. I returned to the dealership to return the car because I really did not have any money to put down. Upon returning to the dealer, I was told my car had been sold, and everyone was gone. I was disillusioned. I was told to keep the car until the next day and come back, which I did.

When I returned, the salesman was waiting for me with a big smile and asked how I liked the car. I replied that I thought it was nice, but I wanted to know about my car. He said, "We sold your car when you did not return."

I was just as confused as I'd been the night before. I said, "I don't have a down payment for this car."

He immediately replied, "Don't worry. All you have to do is go to the financing office we recommend, and everything will be taken care of." In all honesty, I wasn't even mad. I didn't think I would get approved for the car in the first place. I drove there to find out what was what.

When I walked in, the financing office essentially said, "Sign here, sign there, and the car is yours." I signed and drove away feeling as if I had achieved a milestone as a car owner. All the while, I never looked at the details and the high amount of interest I would be paying on the debt.

With my commitment to go into the service, I originally thought I could take my car with me, but that was not the case, so I went back to the dealer and asked if I could return the car. They said, "Sure, just go to this garage on North Avenue in Baltimore, and they will take the car, and we will handle it from there." At the garage, they were waiting for me. They took the keys and wished me well. I left my new car there, as instructed, but that decision would later haunt me.

CHAPTER 9

Paying Uncle Sam His Due

Joy, my fraternity brothers Prince and Pat, and others gave me a joking farewell party where nobody took me seriously. I tried to firm up things with Joy, but I strongly suggested she focus on getting her college degree from Morgan State before we took our conversations and relationship to another level. I kind of left it like that, and we were free to do our own thing, but I knew I loved her and risked not seeing her again. She and I committed to staying in touch—and we did. My fraternity brothers just laughed and said I was crazy, giving me playful warnings, such as "You'd better come back!" with serious undertones. I would miss them all as life took a new turn for me. I was on my own, fostering a new vision for my life. I had taken full ownership thereof.

By then, it was apparent that my decision to further my career was also about my carrying on the family's military legacy. My grandfather was a Chaplain with the rank of LTC, and I had an uncle who was an LTC in logistics. I was subjected to the same fate as my father, uncles, and grandfather.

Going into military service provided a clear pathway to success, and my joining was no exception. My basic training took place at Fort Knox, Kentucky and it was the place where all the gold in the United States was stored. There were lots of tanks running around, particularly at night. Basic training was a unique situation for me. I was one of the few, in fact, to go through basic training two times—yes, two times! Not many in the military can make that claim.

That phase of my life was a challenge for me not because of what we had to do but because the drill sergeants were more about breaking us down in the beginning and then seeing us achieve with a firm respect for following orders. My first go-around at basic, I scored high on all the physical training (PT) tests, as I was in prime shape from my four years of college basketball.

I was in the top five of any individual physical test (push-ups, sit ups, pull ups, and two-mile runs in boots). I had few issues with individual competition, but winning with others on teams was a challenge. Some people didn't do their part, and failure to perform as a team could cost you sleep, details, and more work until you met the standards as a unit of one. Pushing others to be better and meet standards caused conflicts. Trainees with poor skills, attitudes, and abilities made working together difficult for high achievers like me. In the long run, the practice resulted in good teamwork that was rewarded by all of us working together and doing our best. I found myself a leader in that regard, always challenging those around me to be their best for the sake of the team. We all subscribed to the warrior ethos:

> I will always place the mission first.
> I will never accept defeat.
> I will never quit.
> I will never leave a fallen comrade.

It was funny that we subscribed to upholding those values but fought like cats and dogs with one another out of respect to achieve our unit objectives. The idea of what soldiers represent collectively, in reality, is greater than any soldier individually. The warrior ethos rooted within us great values for establishing a personal sense of priority and accountability, but working as a team, we could accomplish much more in less time. In that regard, I found my experiences with the Boy Scouts and even my fraternity helpful during basic training.

Basic Combat Training, or BCT, is designed to make individuals into soldiers over a ten-week period. You learn about military customs, such as saluting and following orders. Most importantly, you learn the Army's seven core values: loyalty, duty, respect, selfless service, honor, integrity, and personal courage. The first phase of basic is an indoctrination period wherein you learn to work as a team, get into top shape, and learn the importance of discipline. In the second phase, you get to show off your individual skills through marksmanship training, shooting the M16 rifle. In that training, I received the designation of sharpshooter. From there, we had a number of rappelling and land-navigation courses to tackle in order to develop skills and build confidence as soldiers. The last phase of basic training is live-fire weapons training with a .50-caliber machine gun, a grenade launcher, a ten- to fifteen-kilometer tactical foot march, and a night infiltration course.

The person I remember the most was a dark-skinned African American brother from the deep south we called Jo or JoJo. I felt a need to always help Jo and keep him near me because he struggled with reading, speaking, and administrative tasks. However, he was one of the nicest guys anyone would ever want to meet. He really wanted to be an Army soldier and had an inner desire that I had to respect him for. Jo was ready to die for his country and his fellow soldier, which showed me a flaw in my character. I was trying to become a lawyer, and being a soldier was merely a means to an end. I was a city boy, and he was sure enough country and incredibly strong. Jo could pick up logs by himself that required two people. He also could shoot. With a piece of dry grass in his mouth and a little chew, he could outperform anyone in our unit. He impressed everyone. He was on target at any range. I quickly made him my best friend, and he went on to protect me to no end for helping him out.

With all the values we had as recruits going through basic training together, we still had to watch out for haters. One time, a group of Caucasian guys and one Mexican had it out for me in the barracks because I was pretty hard on them about following the direction of our drill sergeant to keep our barracks clean. There was one guy who could not take receiving orders from an African American like me, and I know why. His preferences, or rather prejudices, were very apparent as he always provoked me and wanted to fight. As my name was Clay, he would play on the notion that I could and would fight. Both assumptions were correct.

One night, there apparently was a plan to jump me in my bunk, which was positioned in the corner of the barrack. My bed was on the lower level of the bunk. The group of them came six strong to tag me while I was lying on my back. Upon their jumping me, I started to fight back and yelled out, "Jo!" He came in a flash with only his white boxers on. The assault was on, and we kicked ass effortlessly that night, it seemed. Big Jo threw guys across the room, leaving us all in shock. I held my own, but Jo was a hell of a man in a fight. He was a force for keeping the peace, and thank God he loved me enough to protect me. Afterward, everyone in our unit knew how powerful Jo was, and he had the respect of us all. No one messed with me after Jo's display of force.

I demanded to have Jo put on our final land-navigation team when we got tested because I knew he had difficulty with orienting the map using the compass, and I could help him. At the same time, I had a hidden agenda. I knew Jo could walk a straight line given the direction in which to move. My man Jo could not only fight and shoot but also count steps and keep direction like an American hound dog—I knew that, though I'd never owned a hound. That brother would tear through bushes and eat fruit off vines and trees as if he were on a Sunday walk in the park.

We completed and ended up passing our navigation course. Jo was insistent that our final marked destination point was only steps away from where we were on the final portion of the navigation course, but we could not see it. Other team members were starting to question me as the team leader for putting so much trust in Jo. Jo looked up into the air, taking a good sniff, and then plowed into some bushes that had been placed in front of us as a deterrent. None of us would have walked through those vines except Jo. The setup was inviting for one to go right or left if he made it to that point, and many did—but not Jo. He pierced the entangled brush with his six-foot-three frame to see the posting we needed to reach in order to complete the course. Lo and behold, we were right there. The destination point was camouflaged, and we all learned another big lesson about trusting your information, staying the course, and believing in my man Jo.

I almost had completed my basic training, when I complained about my foot, having walked Misery, Agony, and Heartbreak Hills—some of the toughest hills to tackle with fifty-pound backpacks in the hot sun. Going up or down the hills required focus. If you fell while going down, you would roll down to the bottom of the hill. If you fell while going up, you could fall down and roll to the bottom if no one helped you up. If you helped someone, you were using a lot of your own energy needed to complete the five- and ten-mile marches. Quite a few could not complete that phase of basic and were let go. The walk was tough on my feet, and I made the worst decision I ever made in basic: with a week before graduation, I decided to have the pain in my foot checked out.

X-rays were done, and I was sent back to the barracks for rest. I thought I had made it through basic with one week to go. Instead, I was told I had to go to the hospital to have a cast put on my right foot because of a hairline fracture they had detected. Next, I was told it would take six weeks to heal, and I would not be graduating.

I refused to put on the cast and started to walk out of the hospital. The military police were called, as I was in a rage at that point. I was given a direct order to have the cast put on or end up in jail. I conceded and was given desk duty for six weeks. In addition, I would have to start basic training all over again. I was in shock and depressed because I could have gone to Advanced Training and recovered while sitting at a desk in class, but my request was denied. I would have to spend another sixteen weeks at Fort Knox. That was how my second tour of basic training came about.

During those six weeks of desk duty, I had plenty of time to sort out my personal priorities and my future. I attended church every Sunday and prayed, according to Proverbs 3:5–6, for God to show me the way, and he did.

Throughout my first go-around in basic training, I received letters upon letters from many women, including my mom, which, of course, I welcomed. My drill sergeant teased me about receiving so much mail. Sometimes I even had to share the contents of my many gift packages, especially my mom's baked goods. I would be called up to the front out of formation and made fun of: "Trainee Clay has a package from his mama again, and he wants to share it with all of us. Open it up soldier!" Sure enough, everyone would be invited to eat her cookies and other goodies.

Interestingly, most of the ladies writing to me were also propositioning me for marriage. A few were even willing to send me money or travel long distances just to have sex, and others wanted to get married or just have a baby. It was really getting to me. The way things were going, I did not know what was going to happen to me in the future. If something did happen to me, it might have been a good idea to have a child to leave behind. This type of inward thinking was toying with me.

The one person, however, who was really concerned about me in a consistent manner was Joy. She never asked anything of me other than what she had committed to do herself: stay in touch. Hearing from her gave me joy because she was different with her words. Her conversations on paper were refreshing. She would even accept my calls at the right time, which was whenever the drill sergeant allowed us to make and receive collect calls. Joy took each one and I was thankful for her willingness to do this.

While on break, when I knew I was going to graduate, I invited Joy to visit at Fort Knox. In addition to her willingness to come visit, it was her first time away from Maryland by plane. When she arrived, it was a very special time and her presence lifted my spirits. I was happy and grateful she came.

JOY COMES

During Joy's visit, I was granted leave to go off campus for the whole weekend in Louisville, Kentucky, which was kind of unusual for someone in basic training. However, my circumstances were different. I'd been there for almost twenty-four weeks by then. Joy came on post in a sexy yellow top and blue jeans, which was a good sign for me that it was going to be a good time for us. I had planned her visit, and we first stopped by the post exchange (PX) before going downtown.

I looked at her class ring, took it off her finger, and put it on my little finger to guess her size as I showed my admiration for her graduating from Morgan State College and getting her first new job. I asked her to sit outside while I ran inside. I had scoped out some matching gold wedding bands that not only fit us both in size but also fit my budget at the time. I purchased the two wedding bands. Neither had a diamond, as I'd wanted, but they were all I could afford. She had no idea I was contemplating actually getting married. We had discussed our expectations and ideals about marriage but had never taken the conversation to a serious place. Though it was not the most romantic proposal, I essentially said to her that I was not sure if I was ready to be married but would like to try it. I told her I would try my best and give us five years. Joy was understanding in her response, and then I proposed to her. "Will you marry me?" I asked. Her yes response set the tone for the weekend in downtown Louisville as we embraced. We were now engaged, and I knew that meant her visit would be something special for both of us.

We had a nice dinner at the Fig Tree restaurant to celebrate and stayed at the Stouffer's Hotel. I was so excited about our getting married, and we had so much fun while she was in town. It all seemed so natural, and it was tough to see Joy, my fiancée, go back to Maryland. Of course, I dreaded facing going back to basic training, but things were different. I kissed her goodbye, and I left her with high expectations that we would be married soon. I told her that as soon as I knew where I was going to be stationed, we would pull the string, but we would have to wait a few more months before that happened.

Finishing basic training brought on new challenges for me, as most of the drill sergeants knew I was familiar with what basic training was all about. I found myself constantly in leadership positions on many of the tasks given to our unit. Just like the first time I went through basic, I knew it would be about surviving multiple weeks of drills and exercises that were demanding both physically and mentally. I sought to match or better what I had done the first go-around and was mindful not to complain.

However, to stretch me, they assigned a new drill sergeant to be in my face and in my head all the time, and it got personal. He brought out the Philly in me, and I studied his methods of engagement toward me and found that my laughing at him frustrated him most. One time, I almost got into a fight with my new drill sergeant and somehow, he called me out, referencing Philadelphia, and we realized we came from rival gang territories. We knew instinctively that we did not want to bring the street game into the military. We both had run away from that life and our mutual aim was to make me the best soldier possible. From there, we had mutual respect for one another, having gained insight about each other's past. At the same time, we did not want to speak about it either. At this point, all the drill sergeants knew how to get to me and made sure I understood that their authority was no laughing matter. I learned to respect the title and the person behind it.

We got to the final phases of training, when I would get a chance to throw a live grenade again. The challenge this time for me was that I was put with a fellow trainee who was scared as hell. I knew this because I had watched him perform with the practice grenade. The kid had a phobia for doing the task. Throwing a live grenade was a required portion of training; we had to throw one live grenade to pass. There we were, in the same cube with the live grenade, which was to be thrown from his hand. He pulled the pin—and froze. Within two seconds, I grabbed the damn thing from him and threw it over the wall.

We could see the dust and hear the shrapnel clash against the concrete barrier wall on the range. It was the real deal, and it was a close call for me that might have killed my chances of getting out of basic training. I was commended for my quick reaction, but I did not need compliments for saving my life that day.

I also had to survive a low crawl under live fire during our final field training. I was led into a sand pit with barbed wire above my head. The last time I had done it, there had been sound effects of live .50-caliber machine guns and M16s firing bullets. This time, however, the first few shots were sprayed right by my helmet, and I could see the rounds fluff through the sand as I crawled in a panic. I did not think they would kill me, but they damn sure came close. My only defense was to get the hell out of there as quickly as I could, and I had plenty of motivation to do it. It was yet another close call before I finally graduated from basic training, although that time, there were no complaints—none at all.

Two tours of basic training taught me some great values and made me appreciate being able to endure hardships without complaining. Complaining only delays the eventual success ahead of you in most cases. My drill sergeants disclosed all their motives to me at the end of basic training and revealed the purposes behind their constant aggression toward me. They were fully committed to making a better soldier and leader of men the second time around, leaving nothing to chance. I, on the other hand, was focused on getting out of basic at all costs. All I had to do was follow orders and maintain the discipline required to do what I was told when I was told. Leaving basic training, I took nothing personally, did everything intentionally, and strived to do my best every day. I was a model soldier for those going through basic training for the first time; I felt I was in a good place mentally, and for once, I felt in control of my life and myself. I had a future with my fiancée, whom I loved and was committed to, and now it was time to move on and shape my life for the future.

After basic training, I received the designation of 27 delta, or 27D: an Army Paralegal Specialist. I felt like my journey toward becoming a lawyer was halfway complete. I was uniquely known as the one soldier who had completed basic training twice, which made me even more qualified to finish basic training without any celebration. I got my orders, and I was on to Fort Benjamin Harrison to become a legal clerk for my Advanced Training.

ADVANCED TRAINING

At Fort Benjamin Harrison, I excelled and was among the top three in my class. About a week before graduation, I was briefed about a special assignment to Key West, Florida, where there was no Judge Advocate General's Corps (JAG) Officer. The JAG Corps is the branch of the military concerned with military justice and military law. Officers serving in the JAG Corps are typically called judge advocates. They also serve as prosecutors for the military when conducting military courts-martial. My goal was to become a JAG Officer by doing my time as a 27D and taking on a dual role of defense and prosecutor while in Key West, Florida. In my new role, I would provide counsel to soldiers for their article 15 defense cases and also act to execute the prosecution responsibilities associated with conducting courts-martial. I would have a Huey helicopter (Bell UH-1 Iroquois) at my disposal to transport soldiers to Homestead AFB for their court-martial trials. Due to my dual role as defense and prosecuting authority, I was given unprecedented status and had off-campus housing as a Specialist (E-4) coming out of Advanced Training. After confirming the assignment, I suggested to my fiancée, Joy, that we get married now. She would enjoy the spousal benefits and join me in beautiful Key West, Florida, where I had secured a place for us to live.

WEDDING

To my surprise, Joy agreed to get married quickly and left her new job with a Fortune 500 insurance company, having just graduated from Morgan State College in December 1977. To me, that was commitment, because she was making way more money than I was. I knew that we would have a great time in Key West and that the relocation would give us a good start on our new journey of becoming one. When she left a good-paying job for me, I thought she was crazy, but I gave her my outlook on things, and she bought into the vision. Though it didn't make sense for her to leave a good job and delay the start of her corporate career, I made a good case for her to come to Key West for a few years by emphasizing the many things we could do together to give our marriage a good start.

Joy's mom and aunts insisted on a wedding. We had not talked about a wedding; I'd just said, "Let's get married." I was told we were going to be married in a proper wedding, and all I needed to do was show up. I agreed that having God's blessing for us was a good thing. Quickly, Joy's family put everything together for us to have a wedding at Joy's grandparents' house at the end of my Advanced Training. I asked Joy a key question: "What is most important to you in a marriage relationship?" I loved her response: she wanted to have me as her husband and have children, a job, and a home. I asked her again to be sure. I sensed that she wanted me never to leave her or her children and wanted to contribute to the household. I, in turn, wanted a few simple things too: I wanted her to cook, be the best mother to my children, believe in God, and believe in me. Outside of those requests, we would make a commitment to be what each other needed in the marriage. I was certainly willing to try to make it work.

The wedding was held on September 2, 1978, over the Labor Day weekend. Upon my arrival home in Maryland, there was a big full-page article placed in the Baltimore, Maryland, Afro-American newspaper to announce to the world and all the women I knew that Francis L. Clay Jr. was marrying Joy Arnette Holland. No doubt this was the handiwork of either her mother or aunts. The article blew me away because I had not had a chance to tell everyone who needed to know that I was going to be married, particularly all the women who had written to me during basic and advance training. I simply had not had enough time or money to call everyone while I was in training. It all happened so fast, but it happened the best way for me to move forward with my life.

I should have been happy about the announcement article, but the reality of getting married hit me hard. Joy's family made it too easy for me to participate in our wedding. All I did was show up; put on a tux; exchange rings; and say, "I do." I had Chuck, my fraternity brother, as my best man, and Joy had her roommate, Chuck's wife, as her matron of honor. My good friend Jeff was there, along with my family. I borrowed my father-in-law's Cutlass, and we headed to Ocean City for our honeymoon.

I wore my sunglasses at the wedding because my eyes were a little red at the time. It was an outdoor wedding, and I just knew someone was going to shoot me for getting married without telling her in advance. While I was overwhelmed by everything having to do with the wedding, when I saw Joy from afar coming down the aisle and then glanced at my mom, who gazed back at me with her smiling approval, I knew I had become the man that my mom and Joy wanted me to be. At that moment, Joy became the most important thing to me. I also knew that God had sent me a woman named Joy so I would finally know and appreciate what joy was. I could not believe I was finally getting married, and it felt amazing.

I had previously secured the wedding bands from the PX in Fort Knox. At the time, I had promised Joy I would get her diamonds as soon as I could afford them. The fact that she was so happy without the diamond again showed me how important being married was to her. It wasn't about my giving her bling-bling but more about my being who I was from the heart and bringing all of that to the marriage. Those rings, though minimal, had so much meaning because they signified our willingness to accept one another just as we were. For me, it was all about the love and commitment I had promised Joy I would give. That was my true intent when I said, "I do."

KEY WEST, OUR FIRST HOME

Key West was a special assignment for me as a legal clerk and was paradise for the newly married Clays. We lived on Stock Island, in

Lopez Apartments. Our apartment was a little three-room cement structure right around the corner from a junkyard and dog track. That was our first home, but I spent most of my time in the office, in the same building on base as the Commander of the Key West Air Naval Station. The first sergeant frequently assigned me to be the Commander's driver. One of my main responsibilities was to escort the Commander's wife on post and downtown, which could be a lively assignment if she had a few mai tais. I officially prepared Article 15s and courts-martial on a weekly basis, and my training at Fort Benjamin Harrison had prepared me for my new official responsibilities.

Due to the location of our base, our troops frequently had a problem in returning to base in a timely fashion in light of all the partying they were doing and the high rate of drug usage. Drugs in particular were a major concern, as I found out. One weekend, I took my Remington .22 rifle out to the channel between Stock Island and Boca Chica Channel, where the water moved swiftly at sundown from east to west and where many of us practiced shooting. I threw some empty bottles into the water for targets. As I did so, I noticed military trucks going down a dirt road by the water, which was strange to see on a weekend. I shot one of the bottles, when all of a sudden, people started popping up out of the water near the ocean side, out in the channel. Then I noticed floating markers near them, and I got the hell out of there. It later came to light that the drug dealers were using the military trucks to bring drugs into Florida. There were air drops of drugs that would float in the channel, and divers were in the channel to retrieve them, put them on military trucks, and drive them up to mainland Florida.

In one incident, one of the soldiers had to be transported to a unit for legal disciplinary action associated with illegal drug activity. The solider told us, "Just do your jobs; it's okay. I will be back shortly. You guys will see." The soldier was right; the legal papers were filed, and the charges were dropped. Instances like that taught me to have a keen awareness of the serious drug scene in Key West.

Most of the time, I prepared Article 15s for the misbehavior of lower-ranking soldiers who went out on the town, got drunk, and came in AWOL, which required a filing under Article 86, which states the following:

> Absence without leave: absent himself or remains absent from his unit, organization, or place of duty at which he is required to be at the time prescribed; shall be punished as a court-martial may direct; failure to go to appointed place of duty.

A good week in Key West always ended up with a Friday night visit to Captain Tony's, where all the fishermen went to tell their stories of being out on the water—with much elaboration due to all the vibrations flowing throughout the night. The saloon had a fireplace where empty bottles were thrown all night long, one after another. Back then, I made my contribution to the broken glass like everyone else, not to mention the bras and dollar bills that ended up being pinned and hung on the ceiling and walls before the place closed for the night. It was a great place for the young at heart with story-telling, good music, and dancing, where we had a lot of fun over the years.

Married life was good because we were always on the go together, discovering new places in the Keys each week, having a blast, and eating all the fresh seafood we could stand, almost daily. It was getting so good there that I came close to ending my military commitment and entertaining the idea of being a full-time fisherman. I had got a taste of good the life while doing some part-time work on a fishing boat that was more about hobby than provision. However, there was still some unfinished business I'd needed to address since our engagement: I needed to get Joy the diamond ring I'd promised. My promotion to Specialist 4, after Advanced Training, provided me with the funds to make that happen.

I waited until around Thanksgiving to present the rock I had purchased from a jewelry store on Main Street in Key West. My presentation caught her off guard when she opened the big box I had decorated for her. I will never forget her face as she glanced at the ring, which I thought I'd gotten a good deal on. With no embarrassment at all, she said, "This ain't no diamond; this is a zirconia."

"What?" I said.

She then made it plain for me: "This is a fake diamond."

Man, I was embarrassed, but Joy laughed it off, knowing I'd been trying to impress her with the size of the ring. It was then that I knew she had a good knowledge of diamonds, silver, and gold. I felt so disappointed and mad that I was at the doorstep of the jewelry store as soon as it opened the next business day to let them know. I told them, "I might not know diamonds, but my wife sure does." They quickly offered to exchange the zirconia for a high-quality diamond ring set that had the sparkle and glitter my wife was looking for. The next time around, I knew the particular cut and degree of clarity to look for in the diamond. The ring I picked out, though not the biggest rock in the display case, was the prettiest ring due to the setting, the quality, and the clarity of the center gemstone, which had a natural radiance and brilliance to it at a rating of 12. The ring weight was about one-third of a carat of high quality, with a grade of D in color—almost flawless. I knew all the details.

I made my presentation a second time when her mom, Annie Jones, was in town for the Christmas holiday. I had the ring by the Christmas tree, in a big box wrapped inside another box. When my wife finally opened it and saw it, she was a mess. She cried and cried along with her mom who was there visiting, and they both had nothing but praise for my selection. When we went by the jewelry store to thank them, they could see they had a satisfied customer.

CHAPTER 10

More than Just About Us

That spring, Joy told me she thought she was pregnant with our first child. She had missed a period, but to be sure, she went to the doctor at the Air Naval Station. After her exam, the doctor confirmed that her hunch was right, and I was going to be a daddy. Immediately, I said we needed more money, and it was the perfect time to further implement my plan to become a lawyer by going through Officer Candidate School, or OCS, in Fort Benning, Georgia. Becoming an Officer meant more pay, but it also meant the loss of our vacation-style life we had come to find in Key West, Florida.

I got all the letters of recommendation I needed, having just been promoted to sergeant (E-5) in a six-month period. Along with my college degree, the promotion qualified me for OCS. With my paperwork in and approved, I had only one more task to prepare for: I had to pass the physical fitness test (PFT), which meant a two-mile run. To prepare for the two miles of endurance, Joy followed me in our car each morning as I ran the roads around where we lived.

Well into my training, I noticed my foot injury from basic training starting to flare up again, and it hurt when I ran in boots. That was a concern, but I did not tell a soul because I had to get into the next OCS class. Running two miles in the heat—in boots no less—was going to be an unavoidable problem. I invested in the best military boots I could find, which helped some, but my foot still hurt after a mile. I kept having flashbacks to being held back from completing basic training the first time, and I was not going to be held back from OCS. I was not going to complain.

The day of the PFT to qualify for OSC was a hot day for a two-mile run. It was so hot that before we even got started, I could see the heat vacillating off the black gravel track we had to run on.

The gun went off, and I went to the front. I ran hard the whole time, and by the time I got to the last few laps, the pain was unbearable. I pushed myself, though. I ran with nothing but the thought that I needed to do this to provide more for my family and needed to get off my foot as soon as possible. When I crossed the finish line, I was sweating profusely, and drops of liquid were flowing from my face. The drops were not because of the sweat but because I was crying due to the agony. I limped away with much pain but also with much joy.

I came in second in the two-mile run, and I soon heard that I had been accepted to OCS. I had done it! I was going to be an Officer, thank God. Of equal importance, more money would be coming into the household, which gave me great comfort that we would have enough to bring our new child into the world. There was one more good feeling about the announcement: I would continue the legacy of Officers in the Clay family. I would represent the third generation as an Officer in the US Army carrying on the tradition of attending OCS and making a contribution of service to our country.

Sadly, the good news meant we would have to leave our first home as a married couple. We'd had nothing but good times in Key West, fishing all the time, having picnics on the beach, going to plays, having ice cream dates, going dancing, hitting up Mallory Square, visiting all the fine restaurants, and going to bars, such as Captain Tony's. I'd spent a lot of time at Ernest Hemingway's home, writing poems outside with all the roaming cats that found residence outside his house. We even had attended many of his plays at a theater known as the Club Chameleon.

We'd bought our first car in Key West and loved spending time on all the beaches, including the nude ones too—what a sight! I have nothing but fond memories of that time in our lives, and we would return there many times to celebrate our anniversaries throughout the years. Did we argue, as many new couples do? Of course we did, but we would work things out and pray our way through any challenges. It was all rewarding in the end. Joy was having our first child, and that was the priority now.

OCS

Following in the footsteps of my late uncle Lieutenant Colonel William Clay II, I was carrying on another important military legacy of the Clay family by being a representative for the second generation of Clays to attend and graduate from Officer Candidate School at Fort Benning, Georgia. I knew my double rounds of basic training had given me excellent preparation for the rigorous OCS training I was about to go through. At this point in my military career, I was not as emotional about the excessive aggression of the TAC Officers I was confronted by.

The technical, educational, and physical demands of OCS were not a problem for me; however, the mental and psychological demands on all of us attempting to complete OCS were an overwhelming challenge for even the best of the best. My injury to my foot somehow healed itself, and I wore an ankle brace, which helped out quite a bit. I was depressed by the number of African American Officer Candidates quickly and easily removed from the ranks within the first two weeks of OCS. It seemed the TAC Officers knew what to say to get on those experienced soldiers' nerves, as they dropped one by one, complaining that what they had to deal with had nothing to do with becoming an Officer.

In fact, in light of what we went through as African American Officers on active duty, OCS was the best learning experience we got to prepare us for the realities we would face. Our training reflected real-world scenarios we would confront. The verbal chastisement of an African American Officer was our unique reality after graduation. Even though we might have been called names we did not like, or may have been confronted by a soldier who rebelled against our command, we still had to complete the mission given us. When we were yelled at, disrespected in front of our peers, cussed out, discriminated against, and demeaned verbally, we still had to carry ourselves appropriately as Officer Candidates like everyone else. Early on during our orientation, language that was culturally insensitive or otherwise offensive was used to embarrass or belittle minority Officer Candidates of all colors. Unfortunately, that was used as a catalyst to get minority Officer Candidates to drop out of the program. On the other hand, for those of us who remained, that experience turned out to be good training, as minority Officers eventually ran into similar language after being officially Article. The TAC Officers would get in our faces, up close and loud, using forceful and threatening body language. For many, it was just too intimidating. However, I was from Philadelphia, had pledged Iota Phi Theta, Inc., and had gone through basic training twice. As I'd been through all of that, it would have taken much more than simple name-calling to get me to drop.

The behavior of the TAC Officers in charge was an old psychological strategy to divide and conquer by playing each candidate against the others in the beginning. Making us all pay for the weakness or failure of a few, they broke us down one by one. They gave it out hard the first two to three weeks.

Taking insults from TAC Officers was one thing, but taking crap from a fellow Officer candidate freaked out many of us under pressure. By the third week, we were so on top of it with the TAC Officers that their only play left in the book was to cause havoc and confusion among us. They leveraged race, sex, height, weight, and language to turn us against one another. Everyone was forced to polarize with his respective group to survive. Major tasks and learning about group dynamics were accomplished in short intervals of time. It was fast-paced and personal. The aim was to accomplish the mission given to you and obey orders.

DISSENSION IN THE RANKS

My father told me what his father had told my uncle: "No matter what, don't get in a fight with your peers and get kicked out." At first I did not understand the warning, but I would soon find out what the significance of the warning would mean to me. One morning, while in the weapons room, all of us were asked to check our weapons by taking them apart and then putting them back together before going into formation. It was another setup by the TAC Officers, creating a situation wherein we would have to act quickly under limited time constraints. Within seconds of breaking down our weapons, we were given minutes to be in formation with our weapons put back together. Then the TAC Officer would make an operational check.

A Puerto Rican candidate named Morrisco, who was in charge of the weapons room, began yelling at everyone to get moving. For some reason, he decided to come at me, pointing right at my left eye—the same eye at which the gun had been pointed when I was held at gunpoint in college. His aggression and actions were like the robbery, and I had a bit of a flashback having to confront his threatening gestures. Within a split second, I hit Officer Candidate Morrisco with my left hand from a sitting position and broke his nose. Blood was everywhere, and at that moment, I knew OCS was over for me. In the back of my mind I knew all I would ever hear from my dad was, "I told you not to get into a fight." I quickly told Officer Candidate Morrisco I was sorry, but he was afraid and in shock. "I am going to report you!" He said to me. He had to do this as he had blood all over his clothing.

That was not good for me, and I prayed, *Lord, help me.*

I immediately was called to my leadership's office with Officer Candidate Morrisco, who had blood all over his shirt and was holding a bloody towel to his nose. On the way there, I called my pregnant wife on the pay phone in the stairway, which we were not supposed to use at the time. I said, "Honey, I believe it's over.

I was in a fight, and I just wanted you to know what has happened. I love you." I hung up quickly. Upset at myself, I proceeded to my leadership's office as ordered. As I entered the room, I saluted and was put at parade rest with both hands behind my back and my legs spread apart. I was asked what had happened, and Officer Candidate Morrisco, standing in the same position I was, told an elaborate story that was far from the truth. He wanted it to sound as if we'd been arguing, and I'd started a fight, which had not been the case. After hearing his rant, I broke my military stance, exhibiting a lot of disagreement about what he'd said. My superior gave me the order to stand at attention. I was then given the opportunity to give my side of the story, which was short and sweet.

"I hit him, Sir, by accident," I said. "Sir, I apologize to Officer Candidate Morrisco. I did not mean to hit him. He just approached me in a way that caused me to react." Sensing Officer Candidate Morrisco's story was a little too much, the leadership immediately excused Officer Candidate Morrisco, who wanted justice for my breaking his nose. I went on to explain my college story about having a gun pointed at me.

Upon my completing what I had to say, one of the leaders got loud and in a nasty voice ordered me to take a front leaning rest position—the push up position. He then ordered me firmly, "Down, Soldier, and hold it." I did just that, and then he walked over to me and put his shiny boots in my face. I could see my own face, with my nose just above the tips of his boots. I stayed in that position until I was shaking. Then I heard the command "Up, Candidate!" I stood up with arms shaking, and one of the leaders said, "You're dismissed to your room."

I went back to my room, and my TAC Officer ordered me to stay there until further notice. I thought an escort would soon be coming to take me away. I prayed, asking God to spare me from that fate. To my surprise, I instead witnessed Officer Candidate Morrisco moving into my room, where he would reside with me for the rest of OCS. What was going on? We were ordered to room together and get along for the rest of OCS. If any incident between us happened, we both would be kicked out of OCS.

The scene felt biblical to me, as I recalled the scripture about the weeds and the wheat, as depicted in Matthew 13:24–30. I recalled verse 9, which was a response to whether one should pick the weeds out: "'No,' he answered, 'because while you are pulling the weeds, you may uproot the wheat with them.'" The leadership in charge of our class did not want to lose either of us, so they put us together.

To this day, I believe everyone in leadership knew that I was telling the truth and that I could be trusted to remain under control when put under extreme pressure. Having someone put his boots in your face truly tests your mental self-control. Our leaders were wise in their decision, and I learned an important leadership lesson from them. What do you do when two good men have their truths about a situation? The good will always surface over time.

Officer Candidate Morrisco and I became the best of friends from then on. That was the good in the end. I told him again that I was really sorry for hitting him, which I was. He was not the last person I instinctively hit in my life after being approached aggressively near my left temple. I self-diagnosed my condition as a case of PTSD that I would have to live with and continue to guard against for the rest of my life. I was now aware of what I was capable of and how I needed to manage my emotions in the future.

When we were well into OCS training, the *Soldier Magazine* staff wanted to do a special article on OCS and our class for their September 1979 issue. I was one of the Officer Candidates featured in the article as well as be honored to be on the front cover. I officially had joined the ranks of my wife, who, prior to my magazine debut, being a model, had had a debut of her own in the August 1974 issue of *Essence* magazine.

While it was an honor to be featured in the magazine, man, did the TAC Officers put me out on front street because of it—especially in the mess hall. I believe I had to kill every fly in the room, and I did enough push-ups that day to push America into the center of the earth. The day was filled with challenge after challenge. One of the challenges we faced was on the confidence course, where we had to leap from one bar to the next, going higher and higher, to the top level with no safety net below. If you missed, you ended up having a very bad day. I was one of a handful of Officer Candidates to conquer that task and the only one rewarded by being placed on the front cover of *Soldier Magazine* in 1979.

Toward the end of our OCS training, Officer Candidates led themselves, and we had our own commanding Officer and staff going into the last week of field training, which was known as Hell Week—a week of going through hell in the field under all kinds of conditions. The leadership made me the Battalion Commander for Hell Week. I was the one giving orders to our entire OCS class. What an honor and what a big responsibility. The unique thing about my command was that all my junior staff leaders (XO, ISG, platoon leaders, squad leaders, etc.) were African Americans and were in charge of leading the predominantly Caucasian class of OCS candidates.

One of the leaders gave me the following direct order before we pulled out: "Make sure you have formation and account for everyone before you leave the training area." He was the same leader who'd put his feet in my face after I hit Candidate Morrisco.

He now put his trust in me to lead our whole class through Hell Week.

HELL WEEK

We were in the field all week. It was a tough week, and we struggled as a leadership team to gain the respect of each other. Those who were under us were given the critical tasks we were asked to accomplish with the rain pouring down each day. When it did not rain, it was hot, and our mission went night and day. The Vietnam Veterans in our class seemed to always have different ideas on how to do things. Most times, they were correct from a practical point of view. Some candidates had skills that were superior to those of the leaders who reported to me, which had to be respected. On more than one occasion, I had to overrule the decision of my subordinates' direct reports and make them give the correct directive that would help accomplish the mission in an easier way. In one case, waiting for the rain to stop might have been more accommodating, but the decision to press on marching in the rain allowed us to be where we needed to be for a meal that day.

The last two days in the field, it rained hard, and we slept in muddy foxholes. Many asked why we had to do it. The answer simply was that we had been told to do it. The only thing on all of our minds was getting the hell out of there and back to the barracks.

When morning came, it was still raining as all five of the two-and-a-half-ton—or deuce-and-a-half—trucks rolled up. As soon as they got in position, everyone ran toward them to jump into the back and get in his seat. In amazement, I watched this happen quickly. What shocked me most was seeing that the staff persons who reported to me were among the mass of Officer Candidates who ran toward the waiting deuce-and-a-half trucks. In fact, one was the first to get onto one of the trucks. Keep in mind that everyone who reported to me then was African American and had gotten an earful from all our peers. Not one of them embraced his responsibilities for accountability to me or for his people as I stood in the rain alone for formation. I was the only one standing there in the rain, remembering what one of the leaders had said to me, so I gave a loud and forceful command: "Fall in!" I said it again and again.

From where I stood, I could hear all the swearing, profanities, and obscene words directed toward me. My leadership assured me that everyone was in the trucks, yet I commanded, not demanded, that we hold formation. The more they attempted to break me down by refusing to have formation, the more I insisted that we were not going anywhere until we had formation. They knew that by not having formation, they were disobeying a direct order, which carried serious consequences. I continued to call for formation and caught hell from the entire OCS class as they reluctantly dismounted the M35 series trucks.

It was a nasty scene as I took much verbal and physical abuse for just following orders. Some of my African American leadership even told me to my face, "Fuck you," and one of my female African American platoon leaders spat in my face, which almost caused me to slap the you-know-what out of her. However, I held my cool, remembering the poem "If" by Rudyard Kipling, which my grandmother had taught me.

> If you can keep your head when all about you
> Are losing theirs and blaming it on you,
> If you can trust yourself when all men doubt you,
> But make allowance for their doubting too;
> If you can wait and not be tired by waiting,
> Or being lied about, don't deal in lies,
> Or being hated, don't give way to hating,
> And yet don't look too good, nor talk too wise.

Upon calling everyone to attention, I gave the command "Report." Lo and behold, one of us was missing. If there ever was a person who demonstrated racist behavior, it was one particular Vietnam Veteran with many decorations and past military experience. He was the most proficient soldier I had ever met. If you did not love him, you certainly respected him because of all the invaluable insight he taught us during training. He was the one who was not in formation. Everyone in our class was more than willing to go out into the pouring rain to find him. I directed that we organize a search team with radios and strip maps. We conducted a time check, and everyone went his or her way with his or her assignment. At that point, we had a real mission: to find our lost comrade in the pouring rain.

By that time, we all were focused and on the same mission. No one was near the waiting trucks, because one of us was missing. Everyone was part of the search-and-find mission in real time. Within an hour of the search, we all heard on the radio, "We got him."

I called off the search and again called for and held formation, which the candidates did willingly, precisely, and quickly. With all of us accounted for, standing in the rain, which had now slowed down, I gave the command to move out. It all seemed like a movie ending on a good note. We all learned an important lesson about respecting the Commander regardless of who it was. We learned that being a good leader was all about following orders and holding people accountable. We learned that just because someone looked like you did not mean he or she was going to talk and react to issues the way you did. Anyone could turn on you under pressure. Respect for each other as future officers was a given. The color of your skin and your background or experience could never get in the way of following a direct order given to you. Those were all important lessons we learned in OCS, and we knew every one of us would one day be in my shoes, having to make difficult decisions germane to accomplishing the mission. Everyone gave me the highest respect and recognition for the rest of OCS. All of the leadership congratulated me and thanked me upon our return. I was given the status of Senior Officer Candidate and the honor of being the guidon bearer for our OCS class during graduation for my role in leading our class through Hell Week.

On August 10, 1979, at 1000 hours at Fort Benning, Georgia, my OCS graduation finally took place. In attendance for my senior status review were my expectant wife and my in-laws. My father-in-law—Pop Jones, as I call him—bought me the officer cap I requested, which permitted me to officially leave behind the issued garrison cap, or so-called cunt hat, worn by those who could not afford an officer cap.

I'd hoped my dad and grandfather would attend my graduation. After all, I was now carrying on the family's military legacy, but for whatever the reason, they were AWOL, or absent from their post, so to speak. It was a big disappointment that my dad was not there. He had always wanted me to join the Army. However, I was thankful to Pop, my father-in-law, who was there to say, "I am proud of you, son!" Those were words I did not hear often from my own dad, if I ever heard them at all. Inside, I was proud of myself, as no one would ever know what all I'd had to go through. I'd followed that path for my family and myself. OCS had made a better man out of me. I could now look at myself in the mirror and know for sure that I had accomplished my mission of finishing OCS.

At graduation we were given our formal commission as US Army Officers and assigned the rank of Second Lieutenant, the lowest of the official Officer ranks. Then we were given branch assignments. I was hoping to join the JAG Corps. When they called my name, they said, "Field Artillery." I was told that President Reagan had dropped the JAG program and I would be going into the field artillery. I was disappointed but equally happy to be an Officer making more money to support our new family. My monthly pay moved from approximately $460 a month to the ballpark of $780 a month, and that was good news for my family. I next headed to Fort Sill, Oklahoma, for more Advanced Training to fulfill my commitment to the US Army for another three years.

FORT SILL

My pregnant wife and I arrived in Fort Sill, Oklahoma, where real-life buffalo actually roamed the land. In our apartment, I used all the walls for bulletin-style postings of what I had to study for the daily quizzes and weekly tests in class. We rented an apartment that was furnished, and the only thing I had to do was put together a crib in preparation for our firstborn. My initial attempt was pretty good, except the sides were on backward, and I had to redo everything.

Lawton, Oklahoma, was our second home together after living in Key West, Florida. It was a big change for us, but bringing the little one into the world was our main focus as a couple. I was going to be a father for the first time, and my only example of a dad was my own dad, who had taken little time to school me on what to do. I pondered what was required of me in my new role, and I had few answers. My dad had always demonstrated the role of providing for the family, and I'd witnessed him work three jobs as I was growing up. With that example, I was prepared to work and do what I had to do for my own family. The nurturing part of fatherhood was where I would struggle. Some things you just know.

As we got closer to the time when our daughter was to be born, everyone realized how unprepared for being a dad I was. The first sign was when we started to accumulate items for the new baby, such as bottles and diapers. Joy planned our visit to the PX store to get the things on her long list. We talked about the list before going to the PX, but somehow, what we were about to get ourselves into really did not sink in for me. We entered the PX, got a cart, and started down the aisles, picking up boxes of diapers, bottles, wipes, and more.

When my wife added in the receiving blankets, bottle warmer, teasers, and formula, I started to reflect in my mind on the time when my youngest sister had been born. I had only ever seen the bottles, diaper bag, and diapers, which were delivered to us. I didn't understand why a baby needed all the stuff we were buying. I started to tense up, knowing how much everything was going to cost us. My wife pulled the shopping cart full of baby items up to the cashier, and as she was placing items on the checkout belt, I walked out of the store, leaving her standing there alone. That was a terrible moment for me because there was not much to say.

I felt bad about walking out, and I knew I had panicked. I just did not understand why we needed all those baby things. When we got back to the apartment, my wife got on the phone, upset, but I had studying to do, which was good in a sense, as it keep me preoccupied. We ended up sharing the store incident with our Lamaze instructor and doctor. Both suggested taking our time and buying one or two items a week, which helped our budget and me. When I was alone late at night studying, I would ask myself, *What kind of father will I be?* It was hard for me to recover from that embarrassment. It was as if I had failed as a father, and the baby had not even been born yet.

Word traveled about my little breakdown. My wife has three sisters, three aunts, college friends, and more. Packages full of baby goods started coming from all of them. The cadre of support gifted nearly everything that had been in the cart at the PX when I left her standing alone. I was embarrassed again on a different level. The showering of gifts said to me, "Mr. Clay, if you won't provide these things, all of us women will." Anyway, I got the message and felt intimidated whenever all of the women gathered in one place. The new baby would get what it needed and probably everything it wanted and more.

I found the Lamaze classes we signed up for to be a big help. Number one, the class took me away from my training, which was hard to do, and number two, I knew what a nurturing and encouraging role I could play to help bring our first child into the world. I learned the importance of breathing and encouraging breathing. I saw how I could help my wife be comfortable by supplying a pillow or having a cold cup of water nearby. I learned how to be firm in my support when the time came to push. I had not had a good understanding of any of those things before the classes. The Lamaze method gave me confidence, and I felt reassured when we got our certificate of completion.

The greatest amount of pressure placed on me while at Fort Sill came from my urgency to graduate from the field artillery school's basic course. Designed for newly appointed lieutenants like me, the training provided a complete understanding of the field artillery systems, with an in-depth knowledge of observed fire, fire direction, and skill development while becoming fire support team chief. It also included how to be an Executive Officer and Maintenance Officer. All of the work was challenging for me because I kept thinking to myself, *I did not sign up to do this.* I'd wanted to be a JAG Officer in the legal field. I also knew if I did not pass that course, nothing good was going to happen to me, and I would end up in the infantry. Given that I had a college degree and experience in working with the field artillery in Key West, I was given the opportunity to be one of the few African American Officers selected for the advanced course.

After successfully completing the basic course in field artillery, I was prepared for responsibilities as a Battery Commander, fire support Officer, and more. I then learned about target acquisition, surveying, and communications and electronics. I also was one of the few to attend the nuclear and chemical target analysis course, which required a top-secret clearance.

We had a lot of bookwork to do and tests every day. In a way, it was much tougher than college because they not only tested what you knew but also tested your ability to apply what you knew to specific situations. What helped our class tremendously was the opportunity to learn and train with Israeli Officers who had a lot of practical experience in real warfare. They were our age but much more mature military-wise, particularly when it came to their understanding and application in wartime environments. When someone gave them a task, they were quick to execute it, and they worked well together to accomplish any mission. I befriended those Officers, which was to my advantage.

Often, they would explain why they were learning particular information and how they would apply the military knowledge to real combat situations they had experienced. Those stories helped me to retain the abundance of information being poured out. To the Israeli Officers, a sense of urgency could mean life or death for their families and their nation. I took being an Officer more seriously because of the time I spent with them.

While I was in basic field artillery training, I was selected to Advanced Training to become a Target AquisitionOfficer. Our class was introduced to the first instruction on computerized targeting. We were the first to be trained using that technology. The old method we'd been trained on was called "sound and flash." Our mission was to locate enemy artillery, adjust the friendly artillery units, conduct surveys, and provide data. We worked closely with radar and flash observers. The goal was to detect a flash or sound from a minimum of six locations and plot the findings on a plotting board designed to establish an intersection of all incoming signals to create a target.

That was the old way; the new way was much faster and required a top-secret clearance to perform the special assignments given to us using computers. The training was intense and involved a lot of precision in calculating and working with the big guns and learning how to call in missions from land, air, and sea support. In my new assignment working with the newly formed Twenty-Four Mechanized Infantry Division, which was reorganized to support NATO the year I stepped foot on post, that skill came in handy for all the mobile missions we trained for. I was assigned to a mechanized 155-millimeter self-propelled battery that supported units with the best in class M1 Abrams tanks and M2 Bradley fighting vehicles. All of that was part of the newly formed rapid deployment force.

On December 7, 1979, my first child, my first daughter, was born at Reynolds Army Hospital on the Fort Sill Army post. I had to prepay only five dollars for the whole ordeal. I was in the operating room with my camera, excited to see what God was going to bring me. It was an intense process that resulted in a perfect little girl born into this world. We named her Brianne Lakesha Clay. I was happy that Joy was okay and even more committed to passing my advanced class requirements. The timing could not have been better. I recalled learning in church that the number seven had significance in the Bible, from the number of days in creation to honoring the Sabbath and so on. I thought it no coincidence that just seven days after Brianne was born, graduation day came, and I passed the field artillery Officer basic course, class 1-80, on December 14, 1979. I also finished the Field Artillery Target Acquisition and Survey Officer Course, Class 2-80, by March 11, 1980.

CHAPTER 11

Here We Go

In preparation to leave Lawton, Oklahoma, I got a U-Haul and then drove to Hinesville, Georgia, where I'd been told there would be housing waiting for me. What was in fact waiting for me was a waiting list for government housing on Fort Stewart post. With the Twenty-Fourth Infantry Division just reorganizing, that year, housing was a premium, and I was at the bottom of the list.

After spending all day in Hinesville, Georgia, looking for a place, we were referred to Savannah, Georgia, to secure an apartment. We got there late the night before Saint Patrick's Day, 1980. I remember it well because I saw the river turn green, and everyone was drinking green beer. My wife let me go out for a drink while she nursed the baby. I didn't stay out long because I wanted to be with them. All the training was done now—almost two full years of being in some type of military training course. It was time to get to work now. And not only as far as my career was concerned, but it was time for Joy and I to work on our family as well. We would certainly give it our best shot.

Traveling from Savannah every day was a big challenge due to having to get up so early to make it to formation before dawn. The return home was so late that Joy and my baby girl were just about ready for bed. The gas associated with traveling back and forth fifty miles for fifty minutes every day was costly, and even with my increase in pay, we struggled to pay the rent. Joy had to find work and put her smiling, happy little girl in day care after six months. We did not want to do that but had no choice. The cost of day care barely made the decision workable, but we tried, knowing that if it did not work, Joy would have to go home until I found proper housing for my family.

Well, it did not work, and it all came to a head when Joy started working and I had to come home to pick up Brianne from the day-care center, where she had only been a few times. My baby girl, Brianne, usually was smiling and moving around when she was at the apartment with her mama; however, when I came to the day care one day, popped in, and asked to see my child, apparently, they were not ready for me, and she was lying there alone, stinking because they had not changed her. The staff cleaned her up and fed her, and off we went to meet Joy, who was coming home from one of her first few days of work. It was a strain for me to get back to Savannah after a full day of work and an hour drive and then have to pick up my daughter. We made it to the bus stop just in time to pick up Joy. Before she came, however, I smelled a number two and proceeded to change the diaper. I laid my baby on the backseat of the car and noticed stinking yellow stuff everywhere. I had no wipes or receiving blanket—and I now fully understood why those items were needed.

I tried to clean up all the yellow-colored doo-doo, but it was everywhere—in her clothes, in her socks, up her back—and it ended up on my hands. I quickly wiped my hands in the grass under the car, which was parked on the side of the road, only to return and find that my baby had rolled down the incline of the backseat. Doo-doo was everywhere, it seemed, and it smelled bad. I finally got my baby girl as clean as I could using another diaper and a bottled water in the car and wiped my hands on the grass again. When she was decent looking, Joy's bus arrived, and I motioned for her to come quickly because the baby was crying. As I put little baby girl Brianne in her hands, Joy sensed that it had been a long day for me. I told her right then and there on the side of the road that the current arrangement was not going to work; she would have to quit her job after going to work only a few times. There was no other option. That decision led to Joy going back to Maryland for a while to stay with her grandparents. She made arrangements to stay there with Brianne. We will be forever grateful to Grandfather and Grandmother Crutchfield for their love, support, and generosity during that difficult time of adjusting to Army life on post. I will always remember what Mr. Crutchfield told me… " a rolling rock gathers no moss." At first, I said to myself, I am not in the business of gathering dirt. However, I ask myself the question, with all the moving around I was doing, what had I establish… what had I built… what did I have to show for all I was doing? I got the point. Having a little moss under my feet might be a good idea.

I was assigned to the 333rd Mechanized Field Artillery. Lieutenant Forward Observer (FO) was my first position assigned the Second and Ninth Cavalry, where I applied my computerized training skills. While processing through the headquarters, I met another new lieutenant who had the same housing issue and was looking to live off post. Sam McDonald and I quickly became friends, as we were among the mere handful of African American Officers at Fort Stewart. To avoid living on post, we put our money together and bought a brand-new three-bedroom home at 624 Second Street in Hinesville, Georgia. He allowed me to have the larger room, knowing I had a family who might be coming to join me. We would hold on to the house while one of us was stationed there and then sell it and split the profits. With that understanding, I moved from Savannah to Hinesville at a great savings. It was one of the most profitable business deals I ever got involved with in partnering with another African American male and friend.

One of the duties usually given to a lieutenant around the Christmas holiday was watching the punch bowl during the Officers' Christmas party at the Officers' club. It was a huge, beautiful punch bowl made out of pure sterling silver. It held red punch, liquor (probably grain alcohol), and ice floating on the top.

In the reflection, I could see the lights of the two Christmas candles burning brightly on each side of the punch table. The assignment came with a warning about a long history of Second Lieutenants who had been previously warned about sipping on the punch at the beginning of the party. Like any other Second Lieutenant given that duty, I was duly and properly warned.

As the evening started and I was standing fresh in my dress blues, I thought to myself that the assignment did not seem to be an impossible task. As it got hot in the ballroom, I took a sip of the refreshing punch next to me and felt fine, saying to myself, *What is there to be afraid of here?* The gala got more exciting as the Commander and his wife were presented to the attendees with music serenading them. As I stood there, I took another sip or two. Everything was pomp and circumstance, as they say, and then, when the music stopped and the invocation started, we were asked to bow our heads. I did, and in doing so, I quickly saw the print on the old rug of the Officers' club right in my face. Down I went onto the floor in the inevitable tradition of Second Lieutenants before me who had fallen prey to that responsibility. Sometimes it pays to pay attention to the past. I was carted away as if I were part of the program: "The Second Lieutenant has fallen, so let's party!"

Falling on the floor was not my only spectacle involving drinking at the Officers' club, which was the watering hole for all Officers, particularly after being in the field for days and days. Our training was hard and as real as it could get. An Officer was mainly the focal point for communicating between various command structures and the troops. When training was done, we needed to unwind quickly because at any time, we could be called back into our roles as Officers and become responsible for some special duty or called to go to war.

A normal trip to the Officers' club bar usually resulted in a round of toasts with a few shots of tequila. The bottle with the worm always had my number, and that could mean there was an amazing performance by yours truly for the entertainment of others. My last time performing before my peers, I faced the hard reality that I could not hold my liquor like I thought. By that time, my wife had returned to Hinesville with our child, and I returned home to her waiting arms. That trip home,

I did not remember how I'd gotten home, but in fact, I'd driven, just desperately wanting to get there. I clearly had had too much to drink, but I was in a happy mood. I was so happy, in fact, that I decided to take a shower with my clothes on.

My wife, thinking it would be a fun time, started tickling me. Laughing, I eventually said, "Stop!" as she kept on. Finally, I yelled, "Stop!" laughingly. She attempted to grab me by my face, taking the wrong angle, and all I remember next is pulling my hand back, which I had punched through the hallway wall. The act was unintentional, spawned from another college flashback, and the last thing I would ever have wanted to do. I had made a fist-sized hole eye level to my wife's face. She was in shock, and so was I. I sobered up quickly, trying to apologize, thanking God that I had not hit her, and knowing that if I had, it could have been serious and perhaps the end of our marriage.

Two things occurred to me that night. One, I knew Joy would leave me if it happened again. Had we not been joking and having fun, maybe everything would have been okay, but on the other hand, maybe it would have been a lot worse. I had the PTSD issue again, and being drunk, I did not even know when or why I reacted that way. Two, I admitted I had a drinking problem that needed to be brought under control. The hole in the wall served as a constant reminder of that, even though I later patched it up.

I immediately stopped going to the Officers' club after they allowed me to stumble out in such an intoxicated state. Though it was still my responsibility, the bartenders were pouring the drinks and they played a role in all of it. Who knows what might have been put in my drink or how many I had? I finally realized I was being provoked to drink crazily and was doing so to fit in. Doing shots of white liquor put me in a bad place, and it quickly needed to stop. I also knew that as the only African American Officer, seeking everyone's acceptance by drinking was not the way for me. I realized it was a road to nowhere. I never stepped foot in the Officers' club again while on active duty at Fort Stewart, Georgia.

There was no more drinking and driving for me.

My performance in the field was noteworthy, and I soon was given additional responsibility and promoted to first lieutenant. It was the first time my mom and dad came together to see me get a military recognition or citation of some kind. My youngest brother, Buddy, also came down to Fort Stewart, and they saw my unit, stood on my armored personnel carrier, and took a family picture with me in front of the tank that stood at the entrance of the post. My dad was so proud of my achievements that day. He had been in the service as an enlisted man, but his older brother had been an Officer. Just like my dad, he had a son who was an Officer too. My dad never talked about his military background, as my being an Officer now seemed to make it immaterial. I do not think he ever understood that I was enlisted before I became an Officer. Still, I was glad for him. Mom, of course, was just Mom and had love for me regardless of my status in the Army. She was all smiles and lent her support for all I was doing. I am glad she came and saw what I had achieved. She really enjoyed her time with me and I thanked her for all of the cards, letters, and packages that had lifted my spirits over the years.

With my promotion, I was a Battery Executive Officer (XO) and ran a Fire Direction Center (FDC). I had a new unit leader who made no bones about the fact that he did not want me as his XO, even though he did like the way I commanded the troops. He knew I could get my troops to do what needed to be done because they respected me as an African American Officer in the Field Artillery. Stemming from jealousy I believe, he constantly gave my platoons challenging tasks just to see how well we performed. It soon became obvious that we were doing much more than the other platoons. It seemed to make matters worse that he had not gotten commissioned by going to ROTC or OCS; he'd been commissioned by the United States Military Academy at West Point. There was a discriminatory factor in play that established West Point Officers as the cream of the crop of all Officers, and all other Commissioned Officers from OCS and ROTC were not as good.

West Point Officers made it a point to gain the respect of everyone by being vocal and tough. My unit leader made unreasonable demands with unreasonable timelines, but he never showed up himself to do his job. We had one-on-one talks about it, and his ultimate reply would be "Do your job, Lieutenant!"

One day, out of the blue, he called me into his office, asked me to sit down, and told me a matter had come to his attention that required my immediate attention, or I could lose my commission as an Officer. I wondered what was going on.

He said, "Officers cannot be in debt," as he produced a letter from a credit collection agency that showed I owed the value plus interest of the car I had bought in Baltimore right before I went to basic training. It was a scam from the start, and I was caught up in it. My unit leader was going to leverage this matter to end my military career because he could, and I believed he would. Why would a fellow Officer do that? He did not offer any counseling or any sort of time to straighten things out. He said only, "Handle it quickly," and in the same breath, he cited an Article 134 reference that could be filed under the Uniform Code of Military Justice.

I learned there were people who would catch you in the wrong or with a mistake, whether the wrong was intentional or unintentional, and use that wrong to destroy you, but I knew my relationship with God would prevail. I knew somehow it would all work out. As a trained legal clerk—and a good one at that—I had read Article 134 and knew that it carried a higher standard of conduct for Officers under (5)(a) and paragraph 59c for offenses committed by Commissioned Officers, cadets, and midshipmen. A charge under Article 134 for dishonorably failing to pay a debt was basically characterized as fraud or deceit. I prayed about my situation, and I was convinced not to settle for leaving the situation in the hands of my unit leader. There was no time or room for chance when it came to losing my commission because of that situation. I needed a quick remedy to put my unit leader in check because I did not trust him or the credit collectors who had apparently been trying to track me down since basic training to get a piece of my wages, which my family needed. Now not only were my wages at risk, but so was my commission as an Officer. I had to protect that at all costs.

I quickly called my lawyer from college, a young Jewish man I'd become friends with while at Towson. He advised me I was not the only one caught up in a scam in which dealers took cars back from recruits entering the service and then attempted to recapture the value of the car plus interest through credit collectors. He admitted he had never counseled an Officer in that situation and advised me not to file bankruptcy and to take a different path to negotiate a solution. I did not think I had time for that. I needed to silence the issue, and the only way to do that was to file under Chapter 11 using that strategy. Sometimes you cannot leave a decision to chance. You have to accept the reality of the situation and own the consequences. I knew that once the filing was done, my leader would not be able to mess with me or threaten my commission. I thought that was my best strategy at the time.

The bankruptcy was an effective resolution. Unfortunately, my leader's threat had gone too far, and I was advised to meet with a JAG Officer on post. When I did, I supplied my bankruptcy filings. All actions against me were stopped at that moment. It was the right move at the right time. My leader was reassigned after the matter was reviewed, and I was given a special assignment to work with the National Guard and Reserve units that had just been activated within the Twenty-Fourth Infantry Division. In filing the bankruptcy, all my debts were paid in cash except the car that was involved in the scam. With my lawyer's help, my record was cleared and I would not have to mention having filed due to the fraudulent circumstances surrounding my filing.

In my new assignment, I was working with the National Guard, which was showing up for live training much more than before. My unit was calling in fire for the National Guard and Army Reserve 105th Field Artillery units, which, in the beginning, were dangerously bad. We were on our observation post (OP) within Fort Stewart. The Vietnam Veterans on our team heard the sound of a 105-millimeter round coming near our position and yelled, "Take cover!" They yelled like they meant it, and we all instinctively hit the ground and hid behind anything that was protective. As we hit the ground, my NCO said, "Sir, we need to dig in if we are going to stay here." The land where we were that day was a national protected area where disrupting the landscape was not permitted. Fully aware of the challenges in the fire direction center, when my NCO brought me fragments of shrapnel, I felt we were in danger and ordered everyone to dig in, putting safety as my highest priority.

My team was on the OP for the weekend, taking shrapnel, as if we were was too close for comfort. I called for a cease-fire after the next volley of rounds landed even closer to our position. My unit leader came on the line and called for everyone to stand down. By then, the finger-pointing had started, and I had to verify that the coordinates I was sending down to the National Guard artillery units were correct and that all checks were in play. My unit leader arrived on the OP and chewed me out loudly about messing with the terrain, which was against our standard operating procedure for our position. That was his style to call a wrong a wrong. Then, in the same conversation, considering the threat to life posed by initial inaccurate firing of the National Guard and Reserve units, he commended my troops and me for taking corrective action. The firing got much better, but by then, we had dug in for good, and it was an amazing thing to see.

The foxholes on the OP were the most elaborate pieces of construction I had ever seen made out of wood pieces, rocks, and dirt. The Vietnam Veterans in our group showed us a thing or two—how to dig in quickly, how to listen for incoming rounds, the importance of sighting where rounds landed, and if you were advanced, how to determine the direction in which to create openings for your foxhole. They even created a man-made trap to kill a wild pig that was roaming around our area. Using leaves, string, and sharp sticks under wet leaves, they set the trap. They caught the wild pig and smoked it for Sunday breakfast with the C rations: old green cans of ham and eggs. That one big wild hog was enough for my whole unit to eat off of. I was given the honor of splitting the cooked pig open with one motion of the knife. Talk about some good eating! My team's performance during the first campaign of the corps operation readiness exercise gained us great recognition for setting high standards of performance. I received a certificate of achievement for exceptional fire support and readiness.

Hinesville is in the South, and I faced a few discriminating acts from law enforcement, though I probably got off safely merely because I was an Officer in the US Army. On the way back from visiting my wife and daughter, who had gone to stay with Joy's grandparents in Annapolis, Maryland, I pulled off Interstate 95 at the Fort Bragg exit. After I pulled off, the police pulled me over as I parked in a fast food parking lot. The Officer's approach was quick and assuming, and he stated he was pulling me over for speeding. I knew I had not been speeding, and pulling me over when I was parking did not make sense. Back at the highway exit, I knew I was being eyed, but for what I did not know. I accepted his charge and voiced my thoughts that I did not think I had been speeding. Then, before I knew it, police cars and motorcycles surrounded me. I was asked to get out of the car, and as I did, I overheard on the speaker of the motorcycle the timeliest words of relief I've ever heard: "You have the wrong suspect." Was this racial profiling or a case of mistaken identity? I would never know.

As I began to relax, I quickly became pissed off at the policeman standing there in front of me holding my license. Trying to intimidate me, he then said, "You know, your Commander would not like to hear that you were speeding, so slow it down," and he handed me my license back as if he were doing me a favor. The police never apologized for pulling me over incorrectly. The whole scene got to me. The policeman knew he had pulled me over for no reason, but what could I say? Looking back, it was for my benefit that I didn't say anything at all. I was in a helpless situation but remained humble. It could have been worse. Thank God for his mercy and grace.

I got back on Interstate 95, frustrated, and took my Cutlass up to ninety miles an hour, thinking, *This is what speeding is!* Then I caught myself and humbled myself. I slowed the car down. God was watching over me again. I was thankful I hadn't gotten locked up for no reason.

Another incident emerged with my unit when I was XO. I was responsible for the Battery's Annual Christmas party, which we held at the Hinesville armory outside the post. We brought food and our own liquor. Some local ladies I knew who worked on post fixed the foot. We squeezed the party in on Christmas Eve due to scheduling challenges. The party ended around ten o'clock at night, just in time for us to get back home to our families. The troops left the armory, and I was left there with the ladies, the leftover food, and all the alcohol. After cleaning up, I had to drop the ladies off at their houses before returning home myself.

The armory entrance was on the turnoff of Highway 84 heading southwest. Upon my leaving the armory, as I approached the turn, I immediately saw orange traffic cones in the middle of the two lanes. As I went around the cones slowly, a policeman pulled me over for no reason. Fortunately, I had not drunk hardly anything that night; still, it was not a good scene to be pulled over on Christmas Eve with two women, food, and open bottles of liquor. The police apparently knew who I was and had been waiting to take me to the police station in Hinesville. They had no interest in the ladies, who got out of the car and found another ride home, taking everything with them. The police wanted me as the executive Officer of my unit.

I was taken to the police station, where basically my whole unit were standing behind bars with their hands sticking out and yelling. It looked as if every last one of them was crammed into the cells. Some of them who'd been driving while drunk should have been locked up. However, that did not apply to the entire unit. I was surprised to see them there. The police never locked me up or put me in cuffs. They told me I needed to provide seventy-five dollars per soldier, and they would let my men go. They sat me down at a table with a phone, and I called each person's family or friends as they yelled their phone numbers while locked up behind bars. I would tell whoever answered the phone to bring the money.

By close to midnight, I had everyone home for Christmas. I'd had to bail out one or two myself. I then was given a ticket and told to go to a specific location to pay a fine to the judge in cash after Christmas. It was a weird location; when I walked into the old building's hallway, it was dark, with only a naked lightbulb above my head and an obscure table underneath. I thought I was going to the courthouse. This was the hallway of an old office building. From the shadows towards the end of the hall came a voice that told me to leave the money on the table, tear up the ticket, and go. I did just that and left. I never saw the person's face.

It was another intimidating situation that left me feeling out of control and suspicious of law enforcement in the South. Not all law enforcement was bad, but there were enough bad ones, of all races, to be concerned about. They mainly reared their heads at night, it seemed. I always wanted to proceed with caution, and I drew upon the knowledge that God was aware those situations occurred. He makes clear the following in Ecclesiastes 9:11– 12 (KJV):

> I returned, and saw under the sun, that the race is not to the swift, nor the battle to the strong, neither yet bread to the wise, nor yet riches to men of understanding, nor yet favour to men of skill; but time and chance happeneth to them all.
>
> For man also knoweth not his time: as the fishes that are taken in an evil net, and as the birds that are caught in the snare; so are the sons of men snared in an evil time, when it falleth suddenly upon them.

I would read and pray over and over again reflecting on this particular scripture, "So are the sons of men snared in an evil time, when it falleth suddenly upon them." Stuff happens, and it can happen to anyone at any time. There is evil in this world, and to think otherwise is a mistake. We always need to be on guard and have what the Army calls "situational awareness." This element helps our personal conduct to be influenced by staying alive but also, more notably, enjoying life while doing so. In the Boy Scouts, we were taught to be prepared, and what I learned years ago certainly helped me to stay away from and out of trouble to the best of my ability. Even in college, I was not one to be around a lot of drama, name-calling, and fights. The mere insinuation of such violent acts like fighting, had me locating the nearest exit. Too many times in Philadelphia, the small guy wanted to fight the tall guy. I was the tall guy and tried my best to avoid a fight on any day. I wanted to live. Avoiding conflicts and evil people was a good thing—particularly while I was as an Officer in the U.S. Army.

CHAPTER 12

A Fork in the Road

That Christmas, my wife Joy decided to go home after opening up the toys with our daughter Brianne. At the time she was leaving, I had a career decision to make. I could extend and qualify for the rank of Captain with 20 more years until retirement, or, I could leave the service in one year with only one year left to finish my current commitment. Choosing to stay active in the Army would mean my next duty station would be South Korea for a year alone without my family, or I could finish my commitment in twelve months at Fort Stewart and come out if Joy could find a job.

Both options looked attractive. I was ready and prepared for my tour in South Korea. Whether or not my wife found a job would be the determining factor. Since she had left her job to be with me when we first got married, I was certainly willing to give up a career in the military in exchange for a career in corporate America. My wife went home with the intent of doing just that. On a Friday between Christmas and New Year's, we all flew home. The next day, Joy ran into a contact from her former employer in Annapolis, Maryland, at the local mall. The two happened to discuss employment opportunities, and the next thing we knew, Joy had accepted a role that would start the following Monday. Our decision was made!

I returned to Fort Stewart by myself to finish out my commitment there. I was getting out and going home! I told my Unit Leader, whom I respected greatly, that I was going to leave the service. Keeping a minority Officer, like myself, would have helped his diversity goals, and he did not want me to go. He first tried to reason with me, and I replied that I had made my decision. Then he went into interrogation mode, saying, "Lieutenant Clay, you need the field artillery. You love being an Officer here."

I replied, "I understand, sir, but I've made my decision."

He then went on to belittle me by saying, "You will never be anything without the Army. You're Dismissed."

Those were his parting words, which I never will forget. They killed any thought of reconsidering the decision I had made. I've always wondered if he really meant the words he said. It hurt to hear them then, not to mention having to remember them for a long time thereafter. However, people will put you down if they cannot keep you down under their control and get their way. Some things you just know.

Still, I could not believe he'd said that, and I wanted to retaliate with a few comments of my own, but I had to let it go—and quickly. I had learned my lessons about keeping my composure during moments of plain injustice. The truth was, before I left, there were times when I thought my Unit Leader was right, because he usually was. In analyzing my military accomplishments, I had done well and was promoted frequently. Yes, I had a few issues along the way, but by and large, I was one of the best officers in our unit. Sometimes people will say anything to get you to stay in their corner. Even for all of the right reasons. To make good use of my time before my ETS (expiration of term of service) on September 9, 1982, I enrolled in the on-post master's program with Central Michigan University's Institute for Personal and Career Development in their Management and Business Administration Program. I spent much more time in the field and on special assignments between classes. Many times, I studied by candlelight in my Armored

Personnel Carrier (APC) to get all my readings done, starting in the summer of 1981. It seemed I worked even harder my last few months in the service.

In March 1982, I realized getting out of the regular Army might be a good thing for my family and me. From everything I was seeing, some type of war was about to happen again. I could just feel it. Any time there was a live-fire exercise, I knew things were serious. In my last major field exercise, I played a dual role in the Gallant Eagle 82 Operation, Fort Irwin, California, which involved three thousand paratroopers of the Eighty-Second Airborne Division and ninety air force cargo planes.

What I remember most about that operation is the strategic targeting we did. Much pre-planning went into establishing targets for the assault. The wind conditions that day made the exercise challenging. Helicopters were flying sideways, and on the training battlefield, when the Ranger paratroopers dropped, all of them flew right past our APC positions with their parachutes stuck in the wild, windy conditions. Soldiers hit rock and equipment. It was a crazy scene. From an operational standpoint, we were sitting ducks in the sand with our jolly green giant colored vehicles, and it was so noticeable that when we returned to Fort Stewart, all units were called in to paint the vehicles the sandy brown colors soon seen in the wars in Kuwait and Iraq. Sure enough, I missed going to those wars by deciding to leave active duty.

BEING ON THE OUT...

I know that some of the training and missions I was involved in went a long way toward making the US Army a lot better, particularly for combat in the Middle East. This was real life training that had me ready to fight and die if called upon. In many of those situations, I was not viewed as a black or African American Officer; I was just an Officer doing my job, and I often got recognized for my outstanding performance during these secret training missions. However, I did not receive total acceptance from my Officer counterparts and peers, as I was not invited to the private ceremonies and was excluded from certain Officer gatherings I should have been invited to. Most of those events involved a lot of drinking and mischief, but they undoubtedly bonded the Officer core together on a personal level, and I was left out intentionally, maybe for my own good. Having been included in these "offline team building activities" you might say would have made me complete as an Officer in so many ways. This was not new. The African American Tuskegee Airmen of the 447th Bombardment Group were arrested on April 3, 1945, when they tried to enter the Officers' club set up by their unit Commander. Those Officers were jailed for just entering the Officer Club to send a message that this was a place for just them, but there was a change... charges were later dropped. My experiences were never that bad, yet at that time, there was a preference-preferred category that Officers could classify under. I was neither a preference nor preferred. It was a sad thing to work as hard as my peers and not be included in the group 100%. Many African Americans of higher ranks experienced that isolation and disrespect. It was not my peers driving this. They were just following orders that did not include me. Because our rank garnered respect in and of itself; I just went along with watching the "hidden parties" from the outside looking in and found our own thing to do to cope with this reality.

A somewhat funny example of what I am saying occurred when I was a part of the Second Squadron's Third Armored Cavalry Regiment training operation Border Star 81. I was controller—a coordinator of activities and an evaluator of the unit's performance in those activities. We were in the field for days. In fact, the training was extended because certain units failed badly and had to go through the operation again. I had to stay to evaluate.

Well, while the Officers of the unit gathered in a vehicle and headed to the Officers' Club, I was left in the field with no transportation. I was an outcast; no one wanted me around, nor did they like my making evaluations of their unit's performance, which I received an honorable handwritten note of appreciation for.

I decided to go into town in my dirty uniform. I flagged down a man in a pickup truck who said he would take me to a club that was open on Thursday nights if I bought him a bottle at the liquor store. It was a deal. I decided to just go in for a drink at the club and then head back.

When I got to the club, I was told that Thursday night was ladies' night and that I could stay only if I participated in the all-male review. I had no clue what that was, but wanting to get some relief after being in the field for ten-plus days, I agreed. I was given a table, and before I knew it, ten women were buying this soldier boy drinks—and plenty of them. I was in heaven for the moment, getting more attention than I needed or could handle.

Then a staff member called me to the back to pick out a song. I asked, "For what?"

The reply was "You are going to dance."

I said okay and picked James Brown's "I Got the Feelin'." Boy, was I feeling it. Before I knew it, it was my turn. They played part of the song, and I danced, went back to my table, and took something off. After each song, you took one more piece of clothing off. Quite interesting!

Before I knew it, I was in the finals, with Mr. Muscle Man in blue tights and me in dirty white Fruit of the Loom underwear. Half the crowd were for him, and half were for me. I had not paid for one drink but surely had had too many. It was a blast, and the emcee called a tie. One final dance would be the tie-breaker, and I went at it, thinking I could win. The place went wild with my best move, and then Mr. Muscle Man in the blue tights sprang a Slinky from the front of his pants, and the whole place went wild. I got second place.

As I was being awarded $50 and some nice prizes when I saw the front door of the club open, and I staggered toward it, drawn to the shadow of the light from outside. In fact, I ran to the light, as I needed fresh air. As I did, a cab drove up to let some ladies off at the club. As they were exiting, I fell motionless into the cab. That is all I remember from that night.

I ended up on the floor under a bench at a holding station for troops, in uniform. It was not one of my proudest moments, but I was thankful to be alive, and I always will be thankful to that cab driver, whom I never saw or knew. God was with me. There you have it: a well-intended night that ended up amiss. From that experience, I developed the following motto: "Don't let your fun, fantasy, folly, or foolishness be your failure."

Looking back, I realize I did not get what I really joined the Army for: to become a JAG Officer and practice law. I decided it was time for me to go, knowing I had made a significant contribution to the US Army. I cannot speak about some of my missions and work, as they were top secret. With my clearance, I saw some important things accomplished. Being an Officer with so much responsibility made me a man at an early age. The difference maker was my wife, who also was seeking to make a career and a life for herself as well as our family. We were committed and survived a flighty time in our marriage. I cannot confirm or deny any wrongdoing during the time she was away. There are certainly things that I wish had not happened or that I should not have done, either knowingly or unknowingly. However, in the military, you live two lives as an African American Officer. One life is full of honor because you accomplished a mission and respected your family, friends, and fellow service members. The other life can be personal and masquerading as you work through frustration, disappointments, challenges, and failures—particularly when you are viewed as one who cannot fail. Reactions to military life can release themselves in unpredictable and unintended ways. One might say secretly, "What happens in the Army stays in the Army." At the end of the day, there are three things you give honor to: *(1) you obeyed all the orders given to you, (2) you accomplished the missions given to you to the best of your ability under the circumstances, and (3) you recognize and give honor to the fact that it is only by God's grace and mercy that you are alive and in your right mind.* This is important when you think about training and preparing to kill others if ordered to while still possessing the desire to live a normal life in peace. Every veteran is impacted by this reality in some way.

This happens to many of us in the military in one form or another. You tend to escape the reality of being a soldier for some other reality that is more ideal—whether good or bad. It is a sacrifice for you to be a soldier and to face death in both training and combat in order to be the best. You are constantly pushing yourself beyond caution, and *the raw truth is that you know you will not get affirmation for all you do.* You witness the higher-ups get the citations and awards. You witness being assigned to other duties when conflicts or acts of war are contemplated. Though those who play together fight together, too often, we don't get to play as other soldiers do.

It was a privilege to serve my country and the state of Maryland as an enlisted, Noncommissioned Officer, and Officer in the United States Army. It was an honor to well and faithfully discharge all of the duties given me while I, Captain Francis L. Clay Jr., was in command of the 2-110 FA MDARNG from December 1982 to December 1987. From the time I was a guidon bearer as Senior Candidate Clay for our Officer Candidate School (OCS) senior status review at Fort Benning, Georgia, on August 10, 1979, I accomplished each mission given to me as an Officer. At the same time, I followed every order given to me as an enlisted before I went to OCS to become an Officer. It was a privilege to receive two honorable discharges, on June 20, 1979, to go into OCS and on May 24, 1989, to eventually leave the US Army and National Guard. I was honored to receive two certificates of achievement.

My active-duty days were over. I'd discharged all of my duties to the best of my ability and observed and obeyed all orders given to me. I remembered all the oaths I took, and it was a good feeling to be released to a new calling in life while being blessed to still have my life to live.

CHAPTER 13

Taking Charge after My Discharge

There was no other way to say it: I was done with my commitment to the Army. I was now back in civilian life with my wife and back to finding a good job, just as I'd been doing before I went into the Army. The only difference was that now I was a whole lot wiser.

Due to my serving in the military on active duty for five years, we were entitled to some good benefits coming to us. I had been away from my family due to the decision my wife and I made together. She would find a good corporate job with a Fortune 500 Company, and now it was my time to follow her and her career. During the year we were apart, as I said, I would use my time alone to attend graduate school during the evenings and weekends as a student of Central Michigan University. I was just six credits short of finishing my master's degree in business when I returned to civilian life in the Maryland, DC area.

Coming home, I felt immediate pressure to find a job when I was really looking for a career. If an Army recruit doesn't do twenty years, he or she leaves military life with no severance and no money coming his or her way. Though I needed income, I did not want just any job. I wanted a management career in business or corporate America since I was going to have two degrees in business. Academically, I was well prepared, and now I had first-hand managerial experience in being an Officer in the US Army. Adjusting back to the corporate world was not much of a challenge, but I underestimated the adjustment significantly. By then, I was used to giving orders, having soldiers salute me every day, having a driver whenever I needed one, and having approximately two hundred men and women report to me each morning in some form or fashion. What I now faced on a daily basis was a big change for me personally and no one understood what I was going through. Some days would go by, and I would talk to no one at all. On the inside, I felt alone even when I was not.

I felt very isolated, particularly in the mornings. I was alone and felt as if nobody really cared about who I was, where I was, and what I had to say. The only one I had to report to now my wife and that was difficult for me. It was a fine line that had to be respected between us and rightfully so. I was used to giving the orders, which I'd done just weeks and days before, and now everything was different.

Finishing my degree, however, gave me the immediate sense of purpose I needed to properly adjust to civilian life and secure a good career. I attended my final courses in the classrooms around the Georgetown area in Washington, DC. My last two classes were intense, particularly the course on managerial economics in the fall of 1982.

One day my wife and I got into a heated discussion over nothing. I cannot even recall what the issue was. She was aware that I'd broken one of her nice glasses unintentionally during the day. It had fallen out of my hand while I was walking, and even I was concerned about why it had happened. My wife asked me over and over again what had happened, and my answer did not change: "It just fell out of my hand." My classes were giving me all kinds of anxiety, which caused me to be short with my wife. She pressed for me to do things around the house since she was working, but all my attention was on studying. She was persistent, and I told her, "If you don't leave me alone, I am leaving." I gathered my luggage to head to a hotel to study for my course, as I was serious about finding some uninterrupted time to get my act together. I just had to pass that course. I had to put finding a job and everything dealing with the family on hold for just a second.

However, I forgot I was never to say, "I am leaving," to my wife, Joy. In light of her past, those words meant something different in her mind. She had not known her father as a child, and my saying I was leaving probably sounded as if I were abandoning the relationship. That was not the case; I was simply trying to make the point that I needed to be alone to study. I wasn't really leaving; I would always be there for her. It would have hurt too much to really leave her and my daughter at that time.

In response to those words, my wife called everyone in both of our families, and within hours, her mom and dad and my mom and dad were there to stop me from leaving. Now I had five adults on my case, and I was not getting any work done. It just goes to show how words miscommunicated can cause various issues.

In my quest to get relief and some time alone to study, I had made matters even worse, because they all wanted to speak with me immediately—especially when they took notice of my luggage by the door. After explaining to everyone that I just needed some dedicated study time, everyone agreed to take my wife and daughter away for a few days. I agreed to stay at our apartment to study. Thank God I had the time to focus on that class, as I ended up passing my finals and completing my master's degree in business administration (MBA). That achievement made me more marketable, particularly because I had a 3.5 GPA, and on paper, it looked as if I were fresh out of graduate school. Everyone was happy about this achievement.

Soon after finishing my course work, my best opportunity for transitioning from military life was with a major publishing house in Westminster, Maryland. I was looking for an entry-level management position and interviewed well. They liked my background, and I connected with everyone. They gave me an initial offer, but it was in the order-processing area, in a non-management position. It was a good offer with benefits, which my wife found attractive when I showed her the offer letter. It would have meant I had a check coming into the house, and for a quick moment, I was happy, and my wife was happy, but I was not satisfied.

When the human resources lady called to follow up on the offer, I told her I was excited about the offer but then said, "I can't take the offer. But I am interested in any entry-level management position at the company. I went to school for business management, and that is what I'm looking for." I said it just like that over the phone, and I could tell by my wife's expression that she was deflated and amazed I had turned down the offer. I was somewhat surprised and depressed myself by what I had done, not realizing why I'd responded that way to their initial offer. I'd had a job offer and turned it down, and I had not even prayed about it. It was a crazy feeling, and I can't say I was proud of myself for taking such a stand, but for sure I started praying. I started to question my own judgment because my family needed me to have job, and I had just turned one down.

Twenty-four hours went by, and an amazing thing happened: I got a call back from human resources, and the woman said, "Mr. Clay, everyone was so impressed with you that we wanted to revise our offer. We have created a position for you wherein you will spend six weeks in each department as a management trainee, and then we will assign you to an area as a supervisor once your training is up." The pay was more than the first offer, and I gladly accepted.

I was more than happy to look my wife in the eye and say, "I am going to be in management!" I had held out, believing God would make a way, and he had. I learned an important lesson about holding firm and trusting myself for what is best for my future versus settling for what is convenient at present, even if my family had to suffer some in the short term to receive a greater blessing in the long term.

My academic and military training, particularly as a Supply Officer, came in handy in my management trainee position. I excelled in all areas of my orientation. I was given a special assignment to help manage the opening of a new 350,000-square-foot warehouse, scheduling the movement of books, and writing the safety manual for the new facility. I coordinated the opening ceremonies and managed all the tours with the public. It was great exposure for me to sit at the table with all of management seated around me. I had finally set foot in corporate America.

I was quickly made the small-order pick supervisor on the night shift and was recognized for my detailed reporting and my ability to plan for achieving any task. My approach was to get clarity on the objective at hand and answer the five Ws: *who, what, when, where,* and *why.* I also added one more W: *with.* With what resources or with what unit or team? The question lends itself to determining how the objective will be met with certain budgets or with allocated human and material resources. Given the right resources commensurate to the objective, a team can be very productive once everything is in the right place.

I made one observation that cannot be overlooked: a manager must have awareness of corporate and office politics, particularly when faced with unions and collective bargaining. Positioning and posturing to influence others is a strategy all members of management need great awareness of.

There was an attractive lady on my Small Order Pick staff who got my attention and the attention of others due to her ability to do great work quickly. I was delighted to challenge her to reach her full potential of becoming a team leader, and she did. Stationing her at the correct position on the picking line allowed her to multitask and pick up the pace of filling orders to avoid backups, which was critical to our success. She could handle three to five orders at a time.

We had a positive working relationship until the union push came upon the team and created havoc for the company. It was to my benefit that I'd studied collective bargaining while in graduate school and was attuned to the wide range of methods and strategies a union deployed to get into a company. My personal assessment was that employees were better off without a labor union, considering the benefits they enjoyed at the time with the company.

I scheduled evaluations of employees and conducted a one-on-one meeting with each employee in my office located on the floor. I thought my team leader's evaluation would be an easy review, but her demeanor was suspicious. My military experience caused me to act on my situational awareness. When we got to discussing areas of improvement, her voice got loud and accusatory for no real reason, and to my surprise, she got up and walked out. As she walked out, she threw her evaluation in the trash in a deliberate act of defiance. I must say I was disappointed in her. I knew that the way she was expressing herself at the time would have an impact on people's opinions of me as a new supervisor. It appeared like she had been mistreated in some way and it felt that way to me too. You always have to manage the perceptions of others when you are in corporate management. Negative perceptions can be divisive and even dangerous.

Proceeding with caution, I pulled out a Polaroid camera, which all supervisors kept on their floors for documenting accidents, and took a picture of her evaluation in the trash. I wrote a detailed and timely report of what had happened and then called my manager.

In the next few days, there was to be an election to vote for the labor union. During a rally in my area, which management observed during the lunch hour, my team leader got up and talked about how management treated the employees and specifically claimed I had thrown her evaluation in the trash inappropriately. A meeting with senior management of the company and the labor union was called. My team leader, as beautiful of a person as she was, told the story of how she had been evaluated and how her evaluation had ended up in the trash. The truth of the matter is, I was being used, and she was being used as well, as both sides allowed the matter to escalate to make a point that everyone was taking sides. No one in management believed her account of the story nor did they believe I would do anything like that. I won out because of my thorough documentation of what had happened, and she was embarrassed when my pictures and report were provided to both the union and management at a joint meeting. I told her I knew we both were being used. She told me she was sorry, and I accepted her apology. We went back to work after the labor union vote failed, and my creditability as a supervisor and manager was strengthened as a result of my handling the matter correctly.

While on the night shift, I took some day time a visit my alma mater Towson and used the career center to look for any opportunities that fit my background. Spencer and Spencer Medical was recruiting. I applied to Spencer and Spencer Medical for the second time only to get turned down. Then Mr. Wayne Schelle, the Vice President of finance at Towson, heard of my inquiry and ended up calling me directly about an opportunity with cellular phones he was considering. Mr. Schelle remembered me from my freshman first semester, when I'd taken all those tough courses, including the one in which he was my instructor. He had seen my work ethic in his class, along with my achievements on the basketball court. Mr. Schelle suggested I take an offer in sales and join him in a new start-up. I thought that for him to leave Towson, it had to be a legitimate opportunity.

The company he joined was a Baltimore-based American Radio and Television service that could have been described as a run-of-the-mill family-owned business if not for one feature: it held a license from the FCC to set up an experimental cellular network in Washington, DC. By the time Mr. Schelle arrived, the license had laid dormant for three years. The family had sought out Mr. Schelle to breathe life into the cellular project. Mr. Schelle later learned the only other experimental cellular license in the United States was held by American Telephone and Telegraph Company in Chicago.

Because I was working night shifts at the publishing house, I had time to explore the start-up cellular phone company. At that time, they had only two cellular towers in the Baltimore and Washington, DC, area. I was given an opportunity to cover the Annapolis area, but it had no coverage there. That was a great challenge for me when it was first proposed. Mr. Schelle was offered a salary or stocks with options to run the cellular phone company as the CEO and CFO. He said he was taking stock options, which revealed his belief in the company.

I needed money, so my offer of a minimal salary with a chance for 10 percent commission on all sales sold was important. Each Motorola cellular phone was selling for approximately $4,500 then. That meant $450 for each phone sold. However, I never fully understood the opportunity Mr. Schelle had given me until American TeleServices was later bought by Cellular One. Only then did I recognize the difference between settling for the pennies versus seeking the dollars when considering a new business venture. However, at this point in my life I was thinking money and security. I kept my eye on the dollars in business going forward. Still, what Mr. Schelle offered sounded good. I'd wanted to work for Spencer and Spencer Medical all my life, but not having direct sales experience was a hindrance for me. Now I could get the sales experience I needed, so I jumped at the opportunity and left the publishing house distribution center to sell cellular telephones and get sales experience.

I had an immediate impact on sales by doing my own marketing study. While doing my territory planning, I asked the question "Who in Annapolis, Maryland, travels frequently between Baltimore and Washington, DC?" I came up with the answer "Bankers of large loans." I was correct.

Troubling to me was that the inventor loved demoing the new cellular phone in his Baltimore office. I suggested doing a demo in a rental car, mainly because I did not have a decent car that was nice enough to merit demoing a $4,500 cellular phone but also because seeing the new cellular phone perform between the towers would be the best experience for the customer, particularly if we could stage a call-in while driving.

My first in-car demo proved me right. I asked, "If you could place or receive a call on a cell phone to close a deal on a multimillion-dollar loan that you otherwise would not have gotten without a cellular phone, the money made on that deal would pay for the phone, wouldn't it?" In the initial demo, we made a call to my prospective customer's DC office. Like clockwork, he received a call from that same office on the way back to Baltimore to close a deal. He bought three phones that day using a special offer three for $12,000 and he also gave me five creditable hot leads who also bought. I was on to something very successful marketing-wise.

I next sought out surgeons who got business by being on call. If hospitals could reach them directly, they could get the business. Cellular phones were a game changer in business because they provided immediate access for important decision-making. My success in selling cellular phones continued with one sale after another. It was amazing to see the new phenomenon play out in a short period of time.

One day, when I was at a business show at the Baltimore Convention Center, I was told to cover the company's booth while CEO, Wayne Schelle and the sales management team, went to get something to eat. I was the only African American in the sales group, but I had no problem doing what I was asked as the newest sales representative. In fact, I was pretty good at generating leads at shows throughout my career. As soon as everyone was out of sight, a short man came up to me and said plainly, "I want to buy a phone." He had a serious facial expression as if to communicate, "I want the phone now!"

I said, "They are $4,500, sir."

He replied, "I have that in cash."

"You have $4,500 in cash?" I asked, as if to say, "Show me."

"Yes," he replied.

"I have a phone in the car," I said.

"Let's go," he said.

I left the booth empty as we casually went to my company car in the parking lot. We got to the car, and I opened the trunk as he counted off forty-five one-hundred-dollar bills. I gave him a new cellular phone and a receipt in note form, and he left. Upon returning to the booth, I had a big smile on my face.

My manager was waiting to give it to me for leaving the booth, with top management standing all around me. After I let him say what he had to say, I politely replied, "Why are we here? To sell cellular phones, right? Well, how many phones have you sold today?" I heard no reply from the staring faces stunned by my question. Looking at my manager, I energetically said, "Well, guess what? I just sold a cellular phone, and it was paid for in cash." I then whipped out the forty-five hundred-dollar bills and flashed the spread of bills so everyone could see. Mr. Schelle congratulated me, smiling. My sales management team then scrambled to figure out what to do with the money and how to deposit it so late in the evening. Collecting that kind of money at a show had never been done before. I became the talk of the sales group that evening. More importantly to me, I made $450 in commissions which was equal to a month's pay when I started out in the Army.

That was not the last cash deal I made. In a short period of time, I got more requests from unique places. Customers who called me for cash deals were one of a kind. It was clear I was selling to a network of customers that were referring me to one another. One of my last calls was kind of weird: I was called to a house with black Cadillacs all around outside. The house I entered had another house inside of it. The owner told me that the homeowners' association did not like the way his house was built, and he did not want to change it, so he'd framed in the house with an outside that complied with code—so I was actually inside a house that was inside a house. You had to be there!

Apparently, there had been a big party the night before my visit, as I observed people passed out everywhere. I then was surprised by a robotic table that approached me and asked if I wanted something to drink as I sat in the kitchen-like area across from a bedroom. The bedroom door opened, and my name was called. Through the opening, I could see a bed with pool-like tub to the right of it. My customer said, "Francis, you probably are wondering what the fuck is going on.

Well, we are celebrating my going to jail for robbing a million dollars from a bank." I was stunned by what he said. He then challenged me by saying, "Francis, you have a degree and went to college for four years, and look at you now. You're out here trying to make money. Where I come from, we rob a bank, go to jail for a year, and come out rich. We are just celebrating before I have to go in."

He then went to the back wall. There were shoeboxes on the wall, and he started throwing me wads of twenties. I caught all $9,000 worth of them. "Francis, that should be enough for the two phones," he said. I was too shaken to count the money, and I gave him the cellular phones, wished him the best, and left as quickly as possible.

I called my wife on my cellular phone in the car on the way home and told her, "If I don't make it home, just remember I loved you." I was serious. I came close to seeing how another world with a different set of values operated in this country. All the referrals for cash deals came from the first one I'd had at the company's booth. They were all my trusted customers. I trusted them, and they trusted me to sell them the cellphones and say nothing more. Some things you just know.

Ironically, it was not until later in my business career that I appreciated the full impact that cash deals of that magnitude could make for the bottom line of a start-up business. Cash is king, and no one ever complained about my cash sales. Having cash coming in the way it was certainly impacted the start-up cellular phone company's ability to get more credit and draw additional investment dollars. Showing cash improves a balance sheet versus having increasing accounts payable and enlarging debt. My last commission check was so impressive to me that I told my wife on a Friday to just be ready with the baby because we were heading to our honeymoon spot in Ocean City and would buy everything and anything we needed while we were there. I cashed my check and took cash with us. When we entered the hotel room, I made it rain dollars all over our king-size bed, and we had a great time with all the money in my pockets.

A DREAM COME TRUE WITH SPENCER AND SPENCER MEDICAL

When we got home that Monday after contemplating how great things were going to be with the cellular phone company and how well I was doing with selling, the phone rang as I walked through our apartment door. I took the call in the kitchen, on our yellow wall-mounted phone. A recruiter from Spencer and Spencer Medical was on the line. She wanted to set up an interview with me the next day because the hiring manager was in town.

My roommate from Towson State College, Jeff Woodard, had just won the Luxury Trip Award for 1983 with Spencer and Spencer Medical. He was one of three sales representatives I knew personally to get the award. His recommendation to interview me carried some influence. I had nearly forgotten he'd told me to expect a call and hadn't expected it to happen at that time. I turned to Joy while standing in the kitchen and mouthed silently that Spencer and Spencer Medical was on the phone. The discussion was brief. They wanted to do a face-to-face interview with such short notice. It would be my fourth attempt at landing a job with the big Spencer and Spencer Medical, but now I knew I had the successful sales experience they were looking for. Thinking of my family, I knew the opportunity would create a secure and stable job environment, and I just had to see one more time if Spencer and Spencer Medical would turn me down once again. This time would hopefully be different, however, as I now had outstanding sales experience under my belt.

This time, my dear friend and former roommate gave me one more bit of advice. Jeff was smart, quick-minded, well studied, and articulate. He told me, "Francis, if you want to get hired, you need to wear these." He pointed to his expensive black Johnston and Murphy shoes. I believed him, and I wore mine on the next day for my initial interview in late February 1984.

It would be unique to join a company where many of my oldest and dearest college friends worked as well. Already there upon my arrival was my Towson basketball teammate and roommate Phil Jacobs. Interviewing at the same time as me was another basketball teammate, Bobby Washington. Knowing I would be among all those Towson graduates was special. Four African American Towson graduates would be working for the same Fortune 100 company. Three of them had been basketball players and played on the same team. All of them were top sales representatives, including me. Jeff had attended my wedding, and I ended up attending his as well. Rooming with Jeff at Towson was one of the best decisions I made to impact my career. With all the serious partying we had done, I'd never thought he would end up so big-time in corporate America that he could recommend me for the job I'd always wanted. Timing is everything. You cannot control it; you just have to be prepared for it. You never know when your paths will cross again; when you meet again, let it be a good thing.

To make my dream come true, I had to interview well. The interview was at the Holiday Inn near Baltimore's Security Square Mall. The day of my first interview, I was only minutes from the exit I needed to take, when traffic came to a halt. Rule number-one for interviewing is "Never be late," and I was about to break that rule. Rule number two is "If you are going to be late, give notice." There I was, on the day of my interview, stuck on Interstate 695 in slow traffic. When our movement had come to a stop, I picked up my phone in my car from the cellular phone company and called the Holiday Inn. I asked the receptionist there to speak to Mr. McCarter, who would be waiting for me in the lobby. I got Mr. McCarter on the phone and explained to him that I was in my car in traffic but only minutes away. I told him my car was at a standstill, and he quickly responded, "Right. If you are going to be late, you might as well not come."

I continued by saying, "I believe I will get there right on schedule, but I wanted to call you just in case."

He asked, "You are calling from your car?"

"Yes, I have a cellular phone," I said.

He said, "You must be kidding me! In your car?"

I could tell by his tone that he was skeptical, but we kept talking. As we did so, the traffic started moving, and I kept Mr. McCarter on the phone, as I was only a few minutes away. I continued speaking about my background. "Yes, I sell cellular phones, and I have one right now in my car."

As we continued to talk, I saw the hotel, and I asked him to come out to the curb. In seconds, I sped up to impress him. When I got there, I invited Mr. McCarter to get into my car, which I kept very clean. I then showed him the cellular phone and gave him my normal sales pitch. He said, "I have seen and heard enough. Anyone who can sell this phone can sell our products."

I got my second interview around March 2, 1984. It was one of the quickest and most interesting interviews I had ever had. My second interview with the trainer, Karen, was equally special. She previously had found herself at a happy hour, talking to some men from American TeleServices I worked for, who'd ended up sharing about cellular phones and trying to recruit her, describing me and my amazing sales success as one of the cellular phone company's top salespersons in a territory that had no coverage. As I began to tell her about myself during my second interview, within a few minutes, she interrupted, saying, "I know all about you." I was concerned about why and how she knew so much about me, but she explained what had happened during happy hour. You never know who knows whom in business. If you hang around bars at happy hour, you'll find out just how small the world is. For this reason, keep your reputation and your life clean.

Karen's key concluding question hit right to the heart: "Why would you leave such a good situation?" It was a grounding question for me because I needed to give an honest answer to her and to myself. I told her from the heart that I always had wanted to work for Spencer and Spencer Medical from the time I was a little boy traveling up Route 1 with my parents. Further, my goal at American TeleServices had been to successfully sell cellular phones to get sales experience.

After my heartfelt reply, she said, "I wanted to be sure before telling you that we think we want to make you an offer." A big smile came over my face, either because I successfully had gotten an offer or because I had avoided failing another Spencer and Spencer Medical interview for the fourth time. Either way, it was a good feeling and a personal dream come true.

The Bible is right: if you are faithful in asking, seeking, and knocking at a door, the door will open if it is meant to be. I came to realize that in life, it was important to never give up on your goals, hopes, and dreams. Anything worth asking for is worth waiting for. Once again, I was proud to cleave to my grandmother's priceless impartation of Rudyard Kipling's "If."

> If you can dream—and not make dreams your master;
> If you can think—and not make thoughts your aim;
> If you can meet with triumph and disaster
> And treat those two impostors just the same.

I could treat success and failure the same. I now knew the true meaning of achieving one of my life's ambitions. The little boy from Philadelphia who'd pointed and said to his dad, "I am going to work there one day" was doing just that.

I agreed to go anywhere after my training, but training presented a big challenge for me because I could not pronounce a lot of the medical products, specifically the name of one of the ingredients of one of Spencer and Spencer's most profitable products. The product was 2.4 percent alkaline glutaraldehyde solution, and the word *glutaraldehyde* was a grueling tongue twister for me. I had quite a time pronouncing it.

It all came to a head during the final examination with Mr. McCarter. I was nervous as hell after six weeks of product-knowledge training. I stumbled as if I had a stuttering problem and had a panic attack over that one word. Mr. McCarter finally told me, "Just say it really fast, and tell me why you like the product," which I did. He said, "You passed. Now let's go celebrate." We immediately went out to eat, and after a few libations, we laughed because I finally had passed all the training requirements. Ironically, I suddenly was able to say the word *glutaraldehyde* all night long without a problem after struggling with it for six weeks.

With the celebration, I was nervous about telling Mr. McCarter something I had held a secret. I had bought a house locally in Pasadena, Maryland, which looked bad because I had agreed to go anywhere after my training. Prior to interviewing with Mr. McCarter, I'd met a Realtor selling houses at the end of a new development where I'd been casually looking at new houses. Buying new was my preference because I did not want to buy into old problems and be surprised and upset about spending more dollars to keep a used thing going. The Realtor wanted to sell, and I wanted to buy. She knew how to get it done, and I was willing to do my part to make it happen. In light of her connection to a bank that was approving veteran loans, my bankruptcy filing and past credit history were not a problem after I wrote a letter explaining what had happened. She indicated they had seen other veterans with similar stories and her bank was there to help.

My lawyer told me that my bankruptcy case would be completely wiped off the books because I could prove I had paid all my creditors, except for the unfortunate new car debt associated with the well-documented scam that service members were exposed to. At the time, my wife and I did not know if we would ever be able to buy a house in Maryland, but when the opportunity came, we jumped on it. During my Spencer and Spencer Medical final exam, I told my wife to handle it while I was away in training, and she did. Getting a new home was also important to her because our second child was on the way.

We decided I would keep my commitment to Spencer and Spencer Medical and go by myself wherever I was required to. Joy and the children would stay at the new house until I could transfer back to the area somehow.

I laid it all out for Mr. McCarter, who was not happy with the decision but understood. Joy and I closed on the house a few days before my final training requirements. I thought that even if I did not pass, we would at least have a new home. Unbeknownst to my wife and me, after much prayer, a sales territory nearby in the Washington, DC; Virginia; and West Virginia area opened up. The sales rep assigned to that area pulled out a sharp instrument known as a trocar in front of a surgeon and pointed it at him maliciously during a sales call. The action was accompanied by an exchange of words which were not good. Her actions created an immediate opportunity for me, as she was removed from the territory. What a break for me and my family!

I joined my peers from Towson and was assigned the Washington, DC; Virginia; and West Virginia territory, which was one of the worst of all the territories in the division and the region. My first few weeks in my territory, I realized that it was the worst territory because of the many complaints about the representation and products. I began to question what I had gotten myself into. It was so bad that I recommended my Division Manager travel with me to witness the negativity toward Spencer and Spencer Medical, which was uncharacteristic to hear. It was a great company, and the folks in my territory expected and wanted more quality and service. With my reputation on the line, I deployed a strategy of TLC—tender loving care—to get things together, which included fixing all the product complaints and being a better sales representative than the ones my customers had previously worked with. My challenge was the following: Would they let an African American be the representative they wanted?

Well, they had no choice, and neither did I. I resolved to have the following personal philosophy about self-acceptance: "To avoid being a hypocrite and living in self-doubt, who you are and who you want to be have to ultimately be the same person." I wanted to be in the top 10 percent of all the sales representatives and be given the Sales

Achievement Award and make Ring Club. Being recognized as one of the best sales reps in the company was important to me as a person who had two degrees in business. My roommate Jeff had had success, and I knew I could too. I was now in a position where going up the corporate ladder was the only option. Nothing could stop me as long as I had faith. I would be faithful to my wife's favorite scripture, Philippians 4:13: "I can do all things through Christ who strengthens me."

BEING A PROFESSIONAL SALES REP

As part of operation TLC strategy, I brought Dunkin' Donuts or cookies with me on all morning calls. I worked hard to find out something my clients and I had in common that we could have a personal conversation about, whether it was their kids, the food they ate, their favorite sports team, or whatever. Building rapport was simply about finding something we had in common or could agree on. Taking the time to build rapport showed that you were a sales representative that cared, and caring for my customers was my immediate goal.

On a business note, I offered quality product alternatives to the current products my customers were complaining about. Sometimes the cheapest product is not the best product to resolve a complaint. I would let the customers decide on the quality and how much they were willing to pay to have their problems stopped or eliminated. For example, one surgeon complained about the white surgical drain they had been using because it tended to break upon removal, which was painful to the patient. I offered a higher-quality alternative drain called the Grove drain. It cost more, but it did not break, and the patients preferred it in the case of a removal.

It became one of the products that provided breakthrough sales. For weeks afterward, I started my day with an empty detail bag and returned home with it full of failed products with issues. I made time for daily follow-up trips back and forth to West Virginia, getting at home late after fighting through traffic every day. One of the perks of being a Spencer and Spencer Medical sales representative was that I had a company car in excellent condition.

As the summer of 1985 approached, I had earned the right to sell new products in the majority of my accounts, and all I had to do was present products that were much better than the ones the hospitals were using. Even with my best efforts, with a few key accounts, I lost sales after evaluations, mainly because the pricing in the market was significantly low. That was mainly due to a Regional independent contractual agreement that had no relation to any of the national contracts that Spencer and Spencer Medical had in play. Customers had to honor those contracts, which favored low-cost and low-quality products. It was strange to see professionals being forced to use inferior products because of contractual agreements. In my mind, something had to change for me to have success in my territory.

My graduate studies at Central Michigan had taught me to conduct a market study within my territory to find the underlying reasons for the trends and perceptions about my territory. That informal study or review of contracts and agreements led me to observe my competitors' sales representatives, their contracts, and what they were doing that was different from what I was doing. I found that a particular competitive female sales representative commanded the majority of the business using a low-cost Washington, DC– area independent contract that impacted 60 percent of my territory. That was good competitive information within my company, as most of the marketing managers who knew the area understood the tremendous upside within my territory. On my own I would write a sales & marketing plan to gain significant market share in my territory. The key to my strategy was to negatively impact my competition's sales commissions by securing contracts she historically enjoyed. Girlfriend was bringing in the money and it showed! She looked to be high maintenance, and I knew it. How? Because I observed my competition. I could not help but notice the new Mercedes-Benz she drove, which was not too common for medical sales reps. She always went on her calls with hand-wrapped gifts. That was common among sales representatives back then; it was the way that many customers expected to be treated. However, I was not authorized, nor could I afford, to employ her methods with the expense allowance I had. As it was summertime, she would pick her hospital customers up for an early lunch around eleven o'clock and then drive them to Annapolis, Maryland, for an early afternoon boat ride. She was first class with her sales approach. I had to admit that she had it going on with all her accounts. They loved her.

To counter what she was doing, I asked the marketing department for the lowest prices in the company for a period of six to nine months. With that pricing, I believed my major competitor would lose the business of customers who wanted to buy quality Spencer and Spencer Medical products at an affordable price.

I targeted the contract renewals and won them over with the aggressive pricing given to me by marketing. When that happened, I knew she had big numbers to go against going into the new year in order to keep those commission dollars flowing. Without those contracts in her control, she left the company before seeing her total compensation drop. I had been right on with my prediction. We dropped pricing, and before I knew it, she was with another company, selling operating room devices, leaving the door wide open for me to secure new business and hit my Sales Achievement Award objectives for 1985.

That December, my second daughter, Karrah, was born, and I was able to bring her home to our new house. Excited about the new addition to the family, I had a great year in 1986 and was ranked among the top 10 percent of all sales representatives.

The big break I needed came in Virginia with the start of managed care. Historically, we would call on one hospital that did its own purchasing. There was a new hospital administrator in town, representing three hospitals collectively known as FairFax Hospital System. His goal was to reduce the supply budget by 20 percent. Spencer and Spencer Medical had just announced a regular cotton gauze substitute that absorbed twice as much liquid, had less lint, and cost 20 percent less than cotton gauze.

The new hospital administrator gave me the opportunity to convert this new product. I did the absorption and lint product demo to all the key staff in all three hospitals, and they loved it. I brought the new administrator a spreadsheet showing the savings of converting based upon the usage. There was concern about converting three hospitals, so a deadline to convert was proposed and accepted. With the new product due on the shipping dock by Friday, I had a deadline to convert all three hospitals by the following Monday.

When the new product was not at the shipping dock on Friday by the close of business (COB), I was concerned and had to make some last-minute inquires. Somehow, the product was sitting on a Spencer and Spencer Medical dock right outside Philadelphia. I alerted the hospital to the situation, and I was told if the product was not there on Monday morning, the conversion would be stopped. I alerted my management and marketing to the situation shortly after COB Friday and decided to rent a truck and go pick up the product myself on Saturday to deliver it on Sunday. When I finally got there, the dock was closed. Somehow, I found someone to open the dock for me to unload late that Sunday. The most important thing was to be ready Monday morning with product in place. I used my Spencer and Spencer Medical company car to go to the local Dunkin' Donuts shop near the hospital. I bought all the doughnuts in the store that morning, saying to the manager, "I am going to need all these doughnuts," and stuffed them into my car. The customers stood there amazed when I bought every last one. I had multiple boxes of dozens in the front seat and backseat of my car for the staff of each of the hospital locations. After driving up to the front of the hospitals, I used all the volunteer carts on wheels to take the doughnuts and coffee from one floor to the next. Tired, yet relieved that everything was going well, I soon realized I had completed a major achievement in corporate America that had put me in the top ranking of all the Spencer and Spencer Medical sales reps in the country. That milestone gave me the relevant sales experience to take on bigger initiatives and bring on new business opportunities. The experience of making something happen was a big deal because it signaled my ability to leverage the organization to generate sales.

Interestingly, all four Towson graduates now ranked in the top 10 percent of sales representatives. Phil Jacobs joined me on a luxury trip to Hong Kong and China. However, despite all our success, none of us as African Americans had obtained the coveted Division Sales Manager job coming through the ranks. I was interested in taking that step, but the company wasn't sharing anything about when my opportunity would come around even though I was more than qualified to be a Division Manager. So, when my patience ran out, I decided to take matters into my own hands to make a point.

Each year, before the awards ceremony, the divisional and Regional Managers would assemble in tuxedos at the president's reception. The year I was expecting to be promoted, I bought my own full tux and brought it with me to the national sales meeting. I hoped I would get an invitation to the president's reception since we had a new president coming in. Everyone expected my promotion before our national meeting. It was getting late, however, and there was no sign of such information coming forth. I decided to wear my own tux and make a surprise visit looking like a Division Sales Manager, in hopes of actually becoming one.

My timing was such that the new president and I showed up to his reception at the same time. It was almost as if we had planned to walk into the event together. I paraded down the steps in full view, and I could see everyone below me. I felt as if I were walking in a fashion show, with all heads turning as I walked by everyone directly toward the new president. My Regional Manager introduced me and gave a quick overview of my recent achievements. The new president spent a good amount of time with me, giving others the impression that we knew each other and also that he was an advocate for diversity, which he was.

The evening went on, and no one made an attempt to reprimand me or shoo me from the new president's presence as everyone thought I knew him. He sure made me feel welcome in his presence. I was promoted to Division Sales Manager a few months after that entrance.

Sometimes you not only have to speak your future into existence but also have to walk your future into existence. Some say, "Fake it until you make it." I say, "You have to be it until you achieve it." I never liked the idea of faking it, because when the time came to be real, many failed. I was fully prepared to be a Division Sales Manager. I had studied management during both my undergraduate and my master's programs and as an Officer and leader in the US Army, and I was a seasoned senior sales representative and trainer. I had become one of the first African American Division Sales Managers promoted from field sales.

On April 18, 1987, I was recognized as Division Manager of the Year and had the Division of the Year stats before being quickly promoted into sales planning, while Phil Jacobs, my roommate in college, was promoted into sales training. Now two Towson basketball players were in the management ranks.

Our achievements as a group of African American Towson graduates were impressive. We generated millions in sales for Spencer and Spencer, and it was a blessing to interact with them on a professional basis. I always thought we could have done more collectively to help our college and hometown communities if we'd been better informed and solicited properly on a professional basis. For example, I donated thousands of dollars to the newly constructed St. Joseph Hospital in Kansas City, Missouri, as part of the Heritage Society when I had the ability and funds to do so as a Regional Sales Manager. They solicited me, and I responded.

Towson never had expected us to achieve as we did. I say this because there was no solicitation or coverage of our success. While on the basketball team, none of us ever had thought our paths would cross professionally in that manner. We never had contemplated pooling our money to buy a business together, leveraging our relationships, talents, and resources. At Towson were some of the smartest, handsomest, and most charismatic African American men and women one could ever have met. Many of us got into deep relationships and were involved in interpersonal experiences that stopped us from being connected to our friendships. We did that to ourselves, not realizing we could have gained much more by remaining cordial, kind, and supportive of one another in life.

NEW BRUNSWICK

For selfish reasons, I wanted to go to Spencer Hall in New Brunswick, New Jersey, where the rich tradition of Spencer and Spencer's medical products was headquartered. I knew I would miss out on the commission dollars associated with being in sales if I took a fixed-salary staff position in senior management. I would have done well as a Division Sales Manager having just received Division of the Year honors, but I was told that when asked to come to headquarters, you did not want to say no.

In Spencer Hall were some of the brightest and talented businesspeople I had ever met. They were empowered to think strategically, with a primary focus on improving health care for all patients, regardless of who they were or where they came from. As I traveled on Route 1, I passed by a big red Spencer and Spencer Medical sign on the lawn of one of the manufacturing plants, which reminded me that dreams do come true.

The housing costs in the central New Jersey area were three times what they were in Pasadena, Maryland. We moved from our new $72,000 four-bedroom, 1,400-square-foot duplex with a big yard to a new $220,000 three-bedroom, 1,800-square-foot town house with a little yard. We took a financial hit by using both our 401(k) savings to make the down payment and incurring all the penalties and taxes. Then, to make matters worse, we had to put our firstborn into private school because on the first day of public school, I witnessed drug dealers lingering near the school property and declared the area unsafe for my baby girl. Private school meant the comfort of knowing she was safely learning, but it was a major tax on our budget and cash flow. I was in Spencer Hall, doing my corporate thing, but we were broke and unable to save a dime. My wife had to travel one hour north to get to work, and I was working long hours, going back to work after picking up the kids, and not seeing my wife return home from work until late. I was living my dream, but life was a challenge.

Taking these realities into account, I asked to go back out to the field in sales and gave the president a deadline for when I wanted to do so. He had me on a few special assignments, including doing a study to find out where our next moves would be. My research indicated my family needed to go to North Carolina, Georgia, or Kansas. Those places would have affordable housing, growing economies, and we could work our way out from the super high mortgage. By then, it was the late 1980s, and I was tasked with developing a plan to split our sales force to better cover hospitals, with an emphasis on coverage of surgery centers, nursing homes and home health, and multiple hospital systems.

However, before we addressed the changing of our sales force, we were challenged with a decision to recall potentially defective and possibly deadly products, and our sales force was called on to do it. One would think everyone would volunteer to participate in such a humanitarian gesture. Unfortunately, in corporate America, heart and treasure do not come from the same place. In a boardroom of business professionals fighting for awards, promotions, bonuses, stock options, and commissions for that year, all that humanitarian stuff seemed to go right out the window as top leadership of every discipline fought to protect their own interests. From 1986 to 1988, the problem Spencer and Spencer Medical faced was bigger than any of us could have imagined.

When anyone talks about customer confidence in a company and what it is worth, he or she simply has to study how Spencer and Spencer Medical handled that crisis. Our chairman issued a directive to deploy more than two thousand sales representatives to take millions of pain-reliever capsules off the shelf. As part of the national sales planning team, our job was to manage that process within the hospitals and associated medical facilities. We performed the task quickly and precisely, with 100 percent accountability.

Spencer and Spencer's shareholders were hurt only briefly. In 1982, the stock, which had been trading near a fifty-two-week high just before the tragedy, seesawed. In a panic, people sold, but it recovered to its highs only two months later. Investors have had little to complain about since then. If you had invested $1,000 in Spencer and Spencer shares on September 28, 1982, just before the infamous pain-reliever episode, you would have twenty times as much today after multiple stock splits.

On the day of the final decision to recall after a number of episodes, there was a closed-door meeting wherein matters got a little heated and ultimately physical as senior managers and executives struggled with their tempers, desperately trying to find the appropriate response. Sales time and sales were lost. However, what finally got everyone on board was the Spencer and Spencer Medical mission.

When the first sentence of the mission was read, the discussion essentially was over. We were going to put people first over our own concerns and professional agendas. By doing so, we would set Spencer and Spencer Medical apart from all corporations and make history. To this day, many business schools will reference the pain-reliever case study as a way to handle a corporate crisis and provide superior customer service under adverse conditions from a management point of view. What really stands out is the importance of having guiding values and principles as a compass to guide an organization through difficult and prosperous times. I was never prouder of our leadership team, particularly my boss, Mr. McCarter, the man who'd interviewed me on a cell phone years before. He fought for us to do the right thing, and we did.

Our department led the recall, which was professionally executed. Each of us in that boardroom walked away knowing that we had continued a living legacy and that Spencer and Spencer Medical's decision would be the standard on safety for many years to come. Today all medications have antitampering devices for everyone's safety as a result of our finding a long-term solution to that crisis. I was there when it all went down, and I am proud to have played a part in the execution of it all.

A CHANGE IS COMING

Soon the time came to respond to the emerging concept called managed care, and the old Spencer and Spencer Medical representative I initially had been trained to be was no more. The good times, when fortunes were made by reps calling on one hospital at a time when the hospital owned and controlled the buying customers and users, were over. The issue at hand was reducing costs within the hospital, and consumables were prime targets by the MBAs who'd authored the industry-wide change.

The company would have to be broken up, and the more experienced reps would go into Spencer and Spencer Medical Hospital Services to represent multiple Spencer and Spencer Medical companies among the 150-plus companies that were in existence back then. My new boss in national sales planning handled the strategic plans for the newly formed company secretly. Others merged with the southern based Medinet, a pack and gown company, which now would be called Spencer and Spencer Client Care. Still, many employees from Spencer and Spencer Medical would be laid off after many committed years of service. This is sometimes the cost of strategic growth.

CHAPTER 14

Real Challenges to Overcome

I will never forget the day the merger was announced, because my mother called around three o'clock in the morning, when my wife and I were deep asleep. That was strange because she never had called me that early before. Joy answered the phone and quickly handed it over to me. I said, "Mom, what's going on?"

My mom said, "Junior, I just called to tell you everything will be all right!" Those words were the last clear words I ever recall hearing from my mom. She had a stroke shortly after that call. It was almost as if she knew what kind of day it would be.

When I got to work, the President of the company himself personally came into my office and said, "Frank, you got your wish, but you can't tell anyone today. You will be going back out to the field as a Division Manager in Kansas." Then he said with emphasis. "Congratulations! Make sure you are there in Kansas by January 1, 1990 and remember—do not tell anybody but your wife."

I was so excited that I raised my hands up and down while turning in circles. I thought, *I have a job still, I can pay off this huge mortgage, and I am back in field sales as a Division Manager,* which actually was a Regional Manager. While heeding his instruction not to tell anyone and reflecting on what my mom had said, I immediately asked myself, "Where is Kansas?"

Though it was a great day for me, it certainly was not pretty for many, and I heard the crying and shouting outside my office. It was sad to see Spencer and Spencer Medical eliminated. It was a great company with talented people. The whole experience was a blessing for me. My immediate concern became finding out where in the hell Kansas was. I had never been there; I'd only heard Dorothy talk about it from *The Wizard of Oz*. I went into Mr. Walker's office, as he had a big map of the United States on his back wall. I asked him casually, "Where is Kansas?" He pointed to the center of the huge map, where there was a big black dot that looked like the point where the map in the opening credits of one of my favorite TV shows, *Bonanza*, started to burn. Even though *Bonanza* actually took place a little farther west, I got the idea that I was moving a long way from my birth place in Philadelphia, Pennsylvania.

It seemed as if everyone in the corporate office disappeared as we approached the Christmas holiday after the layoff. I had been told to be in Kansas by January 1, but no one was saying anything more. I waited and waited for someone to tell me what to do, and then, after Christmas, I took the initiative to plan and organize my move myself. I had the authority and ability, so I got my relocation package approved and processed. The movers soon came after the company agreed to buy my home to get us out from that mortgage.

By that time, my mom was in the hospital, with tubes everywhere, showing a serious decline in her health. My brothers and sisters always said, "Come see Mom," as she always perked up when I showed up. The day I came to tell her I was leaving, I could tell our visit would be different—a sense of finality hung in the air. I started to tell my mom I was moving, looking directly into her eyes with a deep focus, but before I could explain anything more, she quickly looked away to the left side of her pillow, as if to say, "Go."

I replied, "Okay, Mom." There was nothing more I could do there, and I had to go. As tough as it was, I kissed my mom goodbye. As I exited, my sisters and mom started to sing "Blessed Assurance, Jesus Is Mine," a song that would forever bring me to tears in memory of her. My mom could not sing the words clearly, so she loudly hummed the tune to let me know that she had accepted her fate and, more importantly, that she had accepted Jesus Christ as her Savior. She knew I often wondered but could never bring myself to ask her flat out, knowing so much of what we both knew. I never asked, but it was good to know she was trusting in Jesus at a time when I could do little to change things for her.

Leaving my mom to go to Kansas was difficult for me, but I remembered a home video we had made that was relatively recent. In it, while I was taping, my mom spoke her directives to me saying, "Junior, be sure to take care of my granddaughters, and make sure they get a good education." I never forgot those words. My quest to move to Kansas now had a purpose: I had to make sure my girls went to college. My mom would not be disappointed in me in this regard, as both of my daughters would have the best education and go to college and graduate.

It felt as if we had to rush to make sure we were in Kansas by January 1, 1990, but I had already started executing my moving and relocation plan. At the same time, in the back of my mind, I thought, *Where are we really going? Where am I taking my family, and what have I gotten them into? We are going to Kansas. Wow!* It was hard to imagine going to the Midwest. I had researched possible places to live in Kansas and decided on Overland Park, its new and growing city. It was also affordable, and we could get more house for our money. I subscribed to the local newspaper, the *Kansas City Star*, particularly for their Sunday edition, and I looked in the new homes section, which mapped out all the new developments. From the number of new housing developments depicted on a map in the real estate section, I could see that Overland Park was the place to be. I specifically had my eye on anything close to the newly constructed Johnson County Community College (JCCC), which was ranked among the top ten junior colleges in the country.

A key criterion of mine for finding a new home was that it had to be at the top of a hill, and there were not many hills to choose from. There was no real reason for my request other than that when I turned into my subdivision, I wanted to see my house from a distance. At that time, there were single-lane highways all around the JCCC area, and there was a public park positioned south of the junior college. As we'd exhausted all our savings while living in New Jersey, I thought that if we could just live close to JCCC, my kids could live at home, walk to their classes, and at least get a good junior college education if push came to shove. That thought was predominantly motivated by my mom's directive to make sure her grandchildren went to college.

Bedford Downs caught my attention because it had a new elementary school within the development that was walking distance from all the new homes. I prayed for God to show me the way, and while still living in New Jersey, from the *Kansas City Star*'s new-housing-development section, I picked out the location of our new home in Overland Park, Kansas, and made it happen.

We arrived in Kansas two days before the New Year. I had no contact with the new management of Spencer and Spencer Client Care in Dallas, Texas. With no communication, I did not know whom I was reporting to, and I did not know what my new compensation would be in the new company. On January 1, 1990, my family and I were on pause in a Residence Inn in Overland Park, Kansas, waiting for a call. When the call finally came, my new management jokingly said, "Where the hell are you? We have been looking for you to be here in Dallas." No one knew the president of Spencer and Spencer Medical had told me to be in Kansas on the first of the year. In Kansas I was, as directed. From the phone conversation, I gathered I was supposed to be in Texas by January 1 according to their understanding. I believe that had I not followed what the president told me, I would have been in Dallas, still in the same position as the national planning manager for the new company. That would have been a big disappointment.

The new management wanted me to conduct the first sales planning meeting on the transition plans, which were detailed. I understood the need for my assistance but had no plans to go to Dallas. Yet they requested that I come to Texas, as if that were the only priority I had at the time. During the call I firmly said, "I am not doing anything until I can settle my family, and to settle my family, I need to know my new salary and bonus package offer to look for and buy a home." I was unafraid of the negotiation to establish my position, salary, and bonus package. I learned this lesson during my time working in home office, you have to stand your ground to gain the respect of those around you. My new position was as a Division Sales Manager, which really was a Regional Sales Manager position, considering the nine states I had to cover under the new organization: Kansas, Missouri, Nebraska, Iowa, Illinois, Indiana, Kentucky, Arkansas, and Tennessee. In my new position I would travel five to six days a week and have eight to ten representatives under me in the new corporate configuration.

The initial offer my new company made was an insult, as it included a drop in salary, plus a commission. It was a nice try, but I knew better than to take a drop in salary to make the move. No one takes a drop in pay for a lateral move into sales management. No one takes the first offer in a negotiation either. I knew I was in an negotiation at this point. This was to be more of a promotion for me, not a demotion, and I was to be responsible for nine states. From there on, it got funky for a second because my welcome to the new organization was questionable, and I could feel it. I ended up with some of the worst territories in the new organization.

When you are a professional African American in corporate America, you sometimes wonder why you are treated certain ways. For me, it was apparent that when I dined out, I always seemed to be seated in the back of restaurants or near the kitchen, away from others conducting business, who were wearing suits and ties just like I was. I would be seated next to moms with rambunctious and noisy kids and always had to be reseated. Other times, when I was checking into a hotel with a preferred award status, the front desk person more often than not gave me a room at the end of the hall, farthest from the lobby. The rooms at the end of the hall were usually damaged and had worn-out beds with evidence of excessive smoking or mattresses that were not the best. Furthermore, almost every time I flew, I was seated next to families with sick and crying children despite other open seating—and I flew more than fifty times a year. The constant occurrence of flying near children caused me to buy Bose noise-blocking headphones to block out the crying, and I also carried medical masks to avoid getting sick from coughing kids that always seemed to be found behind me. Traveling as much as I was, I often had to challenge those inconveniences and ask to be moved; other times, I just prepared to make the best of the situation. In the same way, in Kansas, I had to make the best of my situation and work things out with my new company.

After a few days of back and forth, we finally got my salary right, and I actually got an increase, plus other incentives and commissions worthy of the position of Division Sales Manager and all the traveling I would be doing. When it comes to salary, I learned that you should negotiate hard up at first. Do your research, know what you are worth, and ask for what is appropriate. Hoping your salary would change down the road, or if you worked really hard that your salary would increase, were not strategies for success. I reasoned to myself, *you are going to work hard, so ask for the increase up front.* I had to have the right salary to be able to close on a new home in Bedford Downs, where there were only three houses standing. So, we finally got my compensation right and now I was ready to move on with the new company.

My wife would be blessed with a transfer to her new office in Corporate Woods in Overland Park, only five minutes from our house. Our kids could walk to school and to Stoll Park, which was only a block from our house, and there was also a hidden satellite police station around the corner. Those factors gave me much comfort while I traveled 90 percent of the time. Our house was 3,200 square feet, almost double the size of our New Jersey home, for two-thirds of the price. Not a bad move for her and the family!

While all of that was going on, I shared with my wife that my mom's situation was still on my mind and heart. It was tough to leave her in Maryland and be far away in Kansas. It hurt, but I couldn't let it get to me. I resolved to put all my trust in God for her condition to improve—only it did not. One year and nine months after I arrived in Kansas, she was not with us anymore. Her last words to me before the merger always stayed with me: "Junior, everything will be all right."

SPENCER AND SPENCER CLIENT CARE

I was invited down to the Texas home office for the new Spencer and Spencer Client Care complex, and my first task was to meet the new president, Mr. Don Archer. I was brought into a room with a nice outside view overlooking a pool of water with a fountain pouring out of the center. I was in a room by myself with many empty chairs. The big class room where I was waiting, dramatically influenced my first impression. I didn't care for the welcome, but I was all about business. To be honest, it reminded me of an interrogation setting back in OCS. I was told to wait in a chair specifically positioned by a window whose curtains were spread only slightly. It seemed kind of odd to be sitting there alone in a room full of empty chairs that was lit only slightly by the rays of sun coming in from the windows. Nevertheless, I did what I was told and waited. Then, all of a sudden, a man in a suit, with his hand behind his back, walked past the gap in the curtains, and the sun cast his shadow on my face. As he paraded slowly by, I noticed his lit cigar, which seemed to indicate, "I am the general in charge here." After a delay, he came back again in the opposite direction. That went on for about ten minutes and again reminded me of an interrogation tactic. The whole setup was similar, and I went into survival mode and let none of it impact me mentally. It was merely a game, in my mind. Then, like clockwork, a gentleman came into the room and said, "Did you see him? Do you know who that is? That's Don Archer!" as if I had just seen Superman or something.

At that point, I knew all of this was an intimidation technique intended specifically for me. It had little effect on me, however, as Officer Candidate School was the last time I had been intimidated by something like that. I simply replied, "Oh." I never got to meet Mr. Don Archer that day or anytime soon thereafter. Maybe I should have said, "That is Don Archer? Can I meet him?" Maybe I would have gotten my chance. I will say this, however: from what was being said to me, everyone knew, loved, and respected Mr. Don Archer. I left the room to go to my next scheduled meeting.

In the meeting, I made my presentation on the strategic sales plan from the old medical products company. Halfway into the presentation, I was asked to stop. I assumed management did not want everyone in the room to hear about the details I was sharing, particularly the financial folks. I was about to discuss the financial numbers that backed up the transition planning, but my presentation was put on hold. You always wanted to have a proper handle on forecasts and profits before you entered a meeting like that, and I understood the sensitivity. The second half of my presentation would need to be approved by senior sales management before sharing the details with marketing and finance. In Spencer Hall in New Jersey, I'd learned the importance of establishing good numbers during the planning process. Establishing the right forecast was critical to establishing budgets and compensation. If you put numbers out there, you must do two things: make sure they are accurate, and be able to back them up. Securing a grassroots forecast was the best way to get the numbers right and hold field sales managers accountable for the numbers they forwarded so that course corrections could be properly made. I had shared enough for the management team there in Texas to know that I knew what I was talking about. They wanted to establish their own numbers for the new company, and I could not fault them for that. In fact, I knew it was always a good thing to take ownership of your own numbers and I encouraged senior sales management to do that which was appreciated.

It was a tough day for me in Texas, and that was not the way I'd wanted to be initially introduced to a new management team, but things were the way they were. I was the only one who could help me at that time, and that was tough.

Before I left Dallas, I met with my new boss, who was a nice guy but was a company man of many years. He had his marching orders for me and he was clearly up to the task. We reviewed my territories and briefly went over the sales team I would inherit. Of the eight people I inherited, two were veteran senior sales representatives with previous home-office executive positions who were now being sent back out to the field to be with me. I thought one of them would be a mole and report my every move back to management. Anyway, I questioned why they were being sent back to the field. I got no answer. Three were African American, and all were classified as underperformers, though no specific reasons were cited as to why. My boss told me to fire all of them and hire new ones. I thought that had to be a joke, but it was not. I was being asked to terminate employees who I did not know and had no verifiable grounds to do so. I did not agree with it; it was unethical, not right, and not becoming of a first-time Division Sales Manager to take those actions right at the outset of taking on a new position in a newly formed company. Furthermore, for me as the first African American Division Sales Manager, I felt it would be disastrous to fire a large portion of the few African American sales reps—one of which was a senior person with twenty to thirty years of experience with the company. I was asked to do this without any regard for EEOC and the protections for older workers.

At first, I said to myself, *I am being tested once again.* Then my gut said to me, *It would be outright suicide for you to fire all these people and face age-discrimination charges.* I had to send a statement to my new management about who I was, what I stood for, and what I was there to do.

I abruptly closed the office door to get my new manager's attention. I approached his desk with respectful intensity, determined to be clear and upfront with him concerning what I was about to say. In a few words, I quickly said that in all my years of leadership, I had always been about developing people, not firing people. In fact, I had never fired anyone in my career. Most people got better, or they found out that the jobs they were in were not for them under my management. My mode of operation had always been to work things out so I could be in a position to help those under and around me to reach their goals in exchange for their helping me to reach mine. I said to my manager, "If these people are that bad, they should have been fired before I got here and before the merger; but since they were not, before I fire any one of them, I deserve the right to work with each of them over the next six to nine months. If I cannot turn things around, I will do as you have requested—I will fire them." Then, frustrated with the way things were going, I walked out of the office and headed back to Kansas understanding that I had to succeed for my team and for myself.

It was quite an introduction to the new management team at Spencer and Spencer Client Care as the only African American Division Sales Manager in the company. I had, however, learned from the best at Spencer and Spencer Medical, and I understood all aspects of corporate business, having worked with the publishing house, American TeleServices, and two insurance companies, all in the field and in the home office. Intimidating Mr. Clay was not a good plan of action, as I had been well trained since my OCS days to handle all situations and accomplish my mission.

ON A MISSION

One of the first tasks for me in Kansas was to find office space and hire an administrative assistant. I picked out a place with office services inside the Commerce Bank building in Lenexa, Kansas. I would leave the task of finishing off the inside to the person I hired. My final choices came down to a lady with great office-management experience and another lady named Linea, who could type more than one hundred words per minute. Linea had boys who all had attended college, and she played the piano and organ for her church. During the interview, I asked Linea to type something for me on a typewriter we had in the office. She blasted through the request in an impressive manner, showing off her skills, though she was nervous. The fact that she listened to me was a big positive; the other candidate, for all her experience, seemed a little bossy in her responses. She always talked about what she would do and never asked what I wanted her to do. I decided to hire Linea, as she seemed loyal—and I was right about that, as she was always loyal to me, my team, and the company.

I brought the whole team into the division office in Lenexa, and Linea went above and beyond with her baking talents and cooking ability. I never asked for and she never charged us for those special homemade delights, but she created a warm environment for my Division Office meeting, especially when I had to draw a line in the sand with the whole team. Before any slide presentation or sharing about the division's goals, I said simply, "Folks, I am the new Division Manager on the block, and this is a new division. Either we stick together and work together to achieve our individual goals, or within twelve months, I or some of you will not be here. I have been asked to let some of you go because of past sales performance, but I have never terminated anyone in my career, and I do not plan to do that here. You have to decide if this is the place for you. The only way to know that now is to do your best under my new leadership. This is what I am asking all of you for: your best effort." I shared that the territory I'd been given had the worst sales in the country and that the pricing in the division and region was awfully high. It also appeared that in the past, commissions had been paid to managers based on the profit profile of the division by account. I had no problem with that, but if one only had a few accounts, in order to make a good living, those accounts needed to be at their highest profit levels. I knew how to make that assessment.

The other side of the coin was to have more profit dollars and more accounts or customers to grow the business in multiple ways. That was my preference, and we used brown gloves as our key focus because the marketing folks were paying 20 percent commissions—yes, 20 percent commissions on a reusable product that the industry had to use. For a major corporation to pay that kind of percentage on a potentially viable product was unprecedented. In sales, to maximize your compensation, you have to have a high-dollar-value product or service or a large user base. To sell in a major city is the ideal scenario. At that time, in the operating room, everyone was using one-size-fits-all gloves. My division was going to promote the use of a hypoallergenic glove that fit the user's respective hand size. We would approach the business like selling shoes, allowing the customer to try different sizes. Since no one knew his or her hand size, we employed a simple sizing-party marketing strategy to make selling fun and informative.

We came up with the 20-20-20-20 sales plan and sales strategy: twenty people in twenty hospitals using a brown glove twenty times a week for twenty weeks. Do the math! In approximately six months, that would be 160,000 brown gloves and a lot of commissions.

I hired a bartender named Albert Dock, whose dad was a prominent doctor. As a sales representative, I asked him how much he wanted to make. During our first visit together, he said $100,000 in a partly joking, yet partly serious, manner. I shared the math of the 20-20-20-20 plan with him and the need for hard work. I guaranteed he would make $100,000 and more if he could hit his numbers.

I asked the entire division to focus on the highly profitable brown gloves also because I knew the math behind the 20-20-20-20 plan would take my division to the top and turn things around—and it did. Our division was ranked number one for the majority of the year. There I was, the odd man out, at the top of the newly formed Spencer and Spencer Client Care. I knew I would not be chosen for Division of the Year. I was an old Spencer and Spencer Medical guy from the merger, and the only African American sales manager in the company. I had made big producers out of people who were on the block to be fired; I had made my mark. Surely Frank Clay would not be given that honor. One reason, I knew, was that many found me intimidating. I came off that way because many expected my performance to be only average, and I turned out to be above average. I led the most profitable division to success against all the odds. My success alone was intimidating. For me, there was no choice. I had been a champion since high school, and winning was part of my nature as far as competition went. This competition among other divisions in the new company would be no different.

I said to my wife, "Don't get your hopes up too high for a company trip. This management team will not choose me because they don't prefer me to be the face of the new company." She saw the standings of my division, which was in first place month after month. However, regarding Division of the Year in 1992, I knew I would never be given that award. They liked me, but that was it. Some things you just know.

I was cool with it all and told my wife to still plan for a trip because with the money I was making that year, we could afford to go on our own trip. I was on guard because I knew all too well from my time as a national sales planning manager all the games that were played with sales numbers to gain the upper hand on someone else. Sales reports are sometimes like statistics: you can make them say whatever you want them to say from one moment to the next. No matter what sales reports came to be, my sales team would be at the top. In my first year, my division ranked third in sales, an increase from sixth in 1991. In 1992, we recorded $18 million in sales, a 7 percent increase. We were ranked first for eleven months straight. In 1993 and 1994, my division ranked in the top ten, with $634,000-dollar increase in 1994. In 1995, my division ended up with a million-dollar increase in new business, and I had ten sales representatives reporting to me before a reorganization in 1996 to focus on continuing care.

OVERCOMING THE BS

My success as Division Manager always was challenged by others in some way. One way was by discrediting me. Some things you just know are going to happen when you are on top. You stay alert and anticipate the worst but hope for the best.

I had to put up with a lot of BS that other Division Managers didn't necessarily have to deal with—and I knew it was coming. Being a Division Manager was so enjoyable as you worked with your reps and engaged customers and the corporate office staff. However, to be recognized by your management and peers… something was odd. One year, we had a Division Managers' meeting in Dallas, right by the airport, at a place called the Fan. The meeting coordinator asked me to go to the bar area before the meeting started. I knew senior managers usually met before the main meeting to do all the final planning, which was what I'd done as national sales planning manager at Spencer and Spencer Medical. Since I was new, I thought it would be an opportunity to get to know my peers better before the meeting. It was like an early happy-hour invitation, and I arrived at the bar area with the music jumping and lights flickering. I saw the bartender and two cheerful women with balloons. I felt I did not deserve all the fanfare as they approached me with a big welcome and words of flattery.

I ordered my favorite drink at the time: a whiskey sour. I realized I was the only one who had responded to the invitation, as I was the only one there. As I approached the bartender to order another drink, he gave me a tip that I was being set up. I nodded, gave him twenty dollars, and said, "Every time I order, use the same type of glass, but fill it just with water, and bring it to me." I then started to play it up with the ladies there, pretending to have a joyous time with them, drinking, laughing, and making small talk.

Before I knew it, as I had anticipated, select members of senior management walked in, and they had front-row seats at a table behind me to observe me doing my thing. They did not join me, and I wondered if they ever were going to. Some things you just know.

As soon as they sat down, I paid each of the women twenty dollars and said, "It's your turn now to have some fun."

"Sure," they said as they took the money, and they proceeded in the direction of the senior management. I immediately got up with a sober look, walked past their table, and walked out. No one in attendance said anything to me during the rest of the meeting. I considered it a honey trap gone bad, and it was back to business.

There were other such acts to isolate me, discredit me, or embarrass me. I'd learned in the military to be constantly aware of the situation and my surroundings and never let my guard down when in a battle. Merging into the new company was like moving into enemy territory. What I saw out in the open was professional and somewhat normal. What I did not see was some type of negative force at work to distract, disrupt, and discredit me at all times—particularly in light of the business successes I was achieving. I could not call it out because to do so would distract, disrupt, and discredit all the good that was going to be happening to me. But I knew the threat to my reputation and success was there.

Another example of what I was experiencing occurred when the company participated in the AORN (Association Of Registered Nurses) convention in Atlanta. At the hotel we were staying at, I was rooming with someone who was clearly envious of me, and he was in sales development. My guess was that I posed somewhat of a threat to his promotion chances in the management rankings because we were peers in a sense. He was someone I kept an eye on. I was surprised we were assigned to room together, and I said to myself, *What did he do to have a room assignment with me?*

By then, I'd made it a practice to always get to meetings early—I mean really early. That applied to my check-in habits at the airport when traveling as well. I never knew when security would do an unwarranted search. "Random" searches seemed to be routine with me because of all the traveling I did out of the Midwest. Not many African American men traveled like I did, so I had my fair share of searches at the airport.

When I got to the front desk at the hotel, the front desk clerk told me that someone had recently canceled my room and there were no rooms left. "Really?" I said. "My room was just canceled and there are no other rooms available? I am early!"

I had been to that hotel before and knew the management from my national sales planning days with the old company, when I was responsible for coordinating national sales meetings and I reserved rooms for hundreds of sales representatives and managers. With a little prayer, I hoped they would hear me out because they could see that someone was trying to lock me out from being where all the action was at this hotel. My roommate had been reassigned to another room, but I had not. Who had canceled my room? I would never know. Who'd reassigned my roommate but not given me a new assignment? I would never know. In an instance like that, I was glad to have arrived early. My prayer was answered. The hotel staff reinstated my reservation, and I ended up with a room by myself. In the back of my mind, I thought, *What happened to my roommate?* I saw him in the foyer area, and neither of us said anything. He looked surprised to see me standing around the hotel, knowing we were supposed to be rooming together. Neither one of us questioned what had happened, but he knew, and I knew. I made it a habit never to expose the challenges I was facing, particularly by outwardly expressing my emotions. There was a time for that but this was not the time to me, it was about having a job and taking care of my family first and foremost. Keeping my job was about doing what I needed to do versus finding out who was trying to take me out. It was better to wait and see others' reactions to my nonreaction, which in some circles is known as passive resistance. In my thinking, it was not a good thing to expose the enemy to your thoughts and feelings. it was better to survive than to stand out and be put out.

Another incident further gave evidence that my feelings of caution were not misplaced. All managers at AORN in Atlanta were to wear rental tuxedos contracted by the company for the opening champagne reception held for most of the powerful head nurses of all the major hospitals in the country. I had ordered my tux like everyone else through the rental company. There I was physically waiting in line to pick it up in the early afternoon the day before the event took place. When the attendant gave me my black tux with my name on the plastic cover, I quickly noticed my pants were embarrassingly short. I was told I had to wait until all the tuxedos were issued to see if someone had my pants to make a switch, or I could place a request for changes. One thing was for sure: without a tux, I could not attend the Champagne Reception, as it was a formal event with a mandatory requirement to wear a black tux. I think there were others knew about my tuxedo woes, because it felt as if I were being watched. Some things you just know.

I went along with waiting to see who would help me get my tux right, but no one in the company showed any concern or sense of urgency. After all the tuxedos were issued, we checked to see if my pants were among the tuxedos left there hanging. My pant size was a 35 long enough for someone six foot three, and none were found. The company then sent forward an emergency request for my pants and told me to come back at five o'clock. The event required us to be there at six o'clock. Wanting to be at the Champagne Reception to meet my customers, I waited and picked up the pants that were left for me. and then quickly headed to my room to change. By then, everyone else was heading to the event in his tux, and there I was, out of uniform, so to speak, rushing like a chicken with my head cut off. Into the shower I went, and I was soon ready to put on my rented tux pants. I put them on and quickly noticed, with much disappointment, that one leg was longer than the other. I said a few curse words prompted from my Philadelphia days in response of what was happening to me. I concluded my rant with a big "Damn!"

I was not just angry at the fact that I did not have a company tux or that the hotel had canceled my room; it was unbelievable that someone was deliberately trying to disenfranchise me at that event. What they did not know was that something had told me to bring my own black tux—the same one that had gotten me promoted within the old company. I'd had it the whole time. Within minutes, I made a grand entrance to the reception, to a lot of people's surprise.

By the looks in their eyes, I felt that some people were thinking to themselves, *How did he get a tux to be here? Why is he here?* Considering all that had happened to me, there I was in my own tux, which fit me to a "T." I made the most of my grand entrance by immediately hitting the dance floor—which I could do much better than most. It was a wonderful night, and I opted to make no mention about what had happened to me during that first day trying to get my room, nor what happened when I went to pick up my tux. Actually, the convention opened up many more new business opportunities for my division and brought us closer to the Division of the Year award. During the whole AORN convention, I had the respect of all my nurse customers, and I showed them all a great time. I even had two nurses driven to their nearby hotel in a horse-and-buggy ride. In return, they invited my reps and me to come visit them and provide more information on how we could mutually do business in the future.

My 20-20-20-20 plan worked, and my new hire, Mr. Dock, became one of the best decisions I ever made as a Division Sales Manager. That year, Mr. Dock was named Rookie of the Year and Sales Rep of the Year, winning a luxury trip and a promotion to senior sales rep. He was honored on the awards stage, but I was not. Again, some things you just know will happen. All of my reps performed beyond expectations except for one. They did so well that a few created opportunities for themselves to leave the company and to be promoted.

Unfortunately, one rep needed more of my attention than others. At our national sales meeting, I had to make a tough decision regarding one of the senior representatives, named Adam. This senior sales rep was one of the nice older guys who'd been sent back to the field, and he was doing okay but had a serious issue about carrying the bag and doing things the right way, particularly when I accompanied him during a co-travel. Every good sales rep knows that when the boss travels with you, that is the time to do things by the book. Adam had a big problem in adhering to that unspoken rule, especially when he and I traveled in Tennessee, because it appeared to be socially correct to have the African American manager carry the bag into a meeting, but that was not going to happen with me being the Division Manager. Basically, at his age, in places like Memphis and Arkansas, Adam felt embarrassed to be seen carrying a detail bag while walking alongside a young African American sales manager who was clearly his boss. No doubt he was struggling with that image.

I understood his internal concerns, as I'd experienced that reaction many times as a young African American lieutenant giving orders to older senior sergeants and Warrant Officers. However, I was the one in charge, and I had to demand the respect of my position because without it, I would have the larger problem of not being able to be the leader I needed to be in order to be successful. Respect will always connect you properly to the person you have to have a relationship with. All too often, I would ask him, "Adam, where is your detail bag?" Without it, we could not detail, demo, or leave samples with our customers, and taking two or three trips back to the car was a waste of precious sales time and, more importantly, a missed opportunity to share and make our point. That could result in a lost sale or a costly return visit that could have been prevented with a properly stocked detail bag during the initial sales call. "For God's sake," I would say, "at least carry the detail bag when I am traveling with you." He did not do it and was not going to do it, so I had to address the issue, and the sales meeting was the best time.

Before the sales meeting, I pulled Adam aside on a balcony where no one was around and said firmly, "Adam, I have your termination letter in my left pocket, and I do not want to give it to you, but I will if you don't agree to change your behavior and improve your performance." I was not even able to finish the sentence before Adam broke down with overwhelming emotion. His face turned red, and he apologized and said he knew what he had to do. Adam told me to expect a change in his behavior and said he respected me. He thanked me for giving him another chance. I pulled the letter out of my pocket, showed it to him as if I were going to give it to him, and then tore it in half and gave it to him, expressing my thanks. We then walked away together, both knowing that Adam had just missed a close call. I was not calling a bluff—I was making a point.

The power of the moment indeed brought out what I needed from Adam. He needed to do his job knowing I had his back and trusted him. Tearing up the letter was a sign that we both trusted each other and that I was concerned about Adam's success. That was one of the greatest and shortest counseling sessions in my career. Adam closed the year strongly and set up a great year for the division with his turnaround in attitude, performance, and sales. Adam and I also became good friends after that.

CHAPTER 15

You Can Only Go So Far

With all my success, my disposition with the new company was suspect, as I was definitely aware I could only go so far within that management structure, no matter how good I was. Too many times in my corporate career, I heard, "You are only going to go so far." In fact, it was a true statement, and the saying was true for a lot of African American employees—men and women alike. Only a few get to earn their way to the top with promotions. Some do not have to earn their way to be promoted; they are chosen, and you just have to watch them rise and pass you by even though you might be more qualified. They don't teach you that in college, because if they did, there would be a lot more entrepreneurs coming out of college. However, when you are told those few words—"You are only going to go so far"—you come to realize their meaning for yourself, pay attention, and do the best you can until you can go somewhere else.

At our managers' meeting, I was isolated and singled out and felt alone. Usually, someone leading in sales as I was would have all his or her peers seeking a few mentorship tidbits for success. That was not the case for me, and I wondered who was noticing my sales success.

During one of the breaks by the hotel pool, I was alone, with my elbows resting on the pool bar in the privacy of the shade. After months of being aware of Don Archer, the president of the newly formed Spencer and Spencer Client Care, I had never had any up-close and personal time with him. A Division Sales Manager with my success normally would have had a lot of interaction with senior management about what was going on and what was not.

As I was chilling out there in the pool bar area watching the television that was on, a body quickly came up right beside me, and a disturbing cloud of smoke surrounded my face from the cigar he was puffing. A voice said distinctively and quickly, "Frank, we like what you are doing. Keep it up." With that, he blew smoke directly in my face and walked away.

That was my one and only meeting with Don Archer. Now, what does one do with a corporate gangster move of gratitude like that? To someone else, it might have seemed cold-blooded, but to me, it was another rite of passage I had to endure in order to be accepted. Every organization seems to have an in-person testing of the will, especially if you are African American. I had no one with whom to share what had happened in that brief moment. An adverse response to tests like these, have the potential to distort the image of the true professional you are trying to be. I recalled my OCS days, when my leader put his shiny shoes in my face after I punched Morrisco in the nose. It was just another test, and I guess I passed once again.

Many African Americans I know would have made a scene and said a few words, as they would have deemed the act insulting and disrespectful. However, scenes like that were usually setups, with others around to witness my emotional response. The overall objective was to design an act or scenario provoking in nature. If I fell for it with a hotheaded, emotional, or ghetto response, then I'd fail and lose. It was designed to catch me in the wrong and unable to explain myself. A personal saying of mine truly applied to that situation: "See the trap, avoid the trap, and don't fall into the trap." Let those types of situations skip by you because they have no relevance unless you make them relevant or significant by a negative reaction. However, always remember them just in case. Some things you just know.

Time went by, and I was given more responsibility within Spencer and Spencer Client Care. Within my territory were three well-known hospitals under the Barnes-Jewish Christian Hospital System, which had a new president who was dynamic and wanted to leverage all three hospitals for better pricing and one contract. Reflecting on my work at FairFax Hospital System, I knew that was becoming a leading-edge way of thinking among hospital administrators involved with managed care. The serious formation of contract-buying groups, or consolidations, usually cut out the middleman and reduced profits due to per capita health-care increases in medical technology and spending.

I warned my new leadership at Spencer and Spencer Client Care that this was coming, but they played me off. I now faced a major loss of business—three hospitals—if we did not respond. In fact, I was told I would lose all the business at Barnes-Jewish Christian if I did not produce a contract by the deadline given to me. Barnes-Jewish had been created by the 1996 merger of Barnes Hospital and the Jewish Hospital of St. Louis. Facing that situation, I called on the people I knew from my previous days at Spencer and Spencer Medical who had gone over to Spencer and Spencer Health Inc. (SSHI). SSHI represented many of the 150-plus Spencer and Spencer companies in deals like that. The president of SSHI flew into St. Louis and established the first managed-care contract for Barnes-Jewish Christian Hospital System to the surprise of all those above me at my company.

In the end, I saved my business at Barnes Jewish Christian, but the new leadership at Spencer and Spencer Client Care felt I had gone around them—which I had. I had been successful but at a cost to my reputation and status. Either way, I would have been impacted; however, if I had not made a move to save the business at Barnes-Jewish Christian, that would have been more costly to my pocketbook and status. Corporate politics probably was not my strong suit, but for me, surviving and excelling in corporate America was oftentimes a "Damned if you do, or damned if you don't" game with an hourglass constantly being flipped. Some explain it like this: "If you are not at the table, you are on the menu."

AN UNINTENDED FALL

What probably forced me out of a career with Spencer and Spencer and caused me to give up the constant fight to be at my best and recognized for my achievements was an ignorant mistake on my part. It taught me a revealing lesson about the evils of businesspeople who spend their time manipulating the perceptions of facts and their relationships with others like pieces in a chess game. I learned the value of paying attention to details and being truthful to yourself and others at all costs. However, sometimes we miss our mark; sometimes we are unavoidably caught like fish in nets thrown by others, as Ecclesiastes 9:11–12 (KJV) tells us:

> I returned, and saw under the sun, that the race is not to the swift, nor the battle to the strong, neither yet bread to the wise, nor yet riches to men of understanding, nor yet favour to men of skill; but time and chance happeneth to them all. For man also knoweth not his time: as the fishes that are taken in an evil net, and as the birds that are caught in the snare; so are the sons of men snared in an evil time, when it falleth suddenly upon them.

As I was one of the only African American corporate managers in the Midwest, multiple sources sought my help in finding and recommending minority candidates for Fortune 500 companies wanting to make placements in the Midwest. If a candidate got placed, I was paid a finder's fee, which was generally an okay practice as long as one was not paid for candidates being placed within his or her own company.

There was a time when compensation was paid for referring a candidate who got hired within any of the Spencer and Spencer companies. The company paid an employee for making a successful referral, but it was not paid to an employee by a recruiter. By then, I had a recruiter whose clients paid him, and he would get paid by the company as well if we hired his referrals. In essence, the recruiter was getting paid twice for the same placement. He would charge his clients for the preparation process he put them through. He made each candidate stand out in the eyes of potential employers, but he was aggressive with his approach in getting them to appreciate what needed to be said as well as what shouldn't be said in order to be hired. He was also classy and generous with his thank-you's, which led me to be careful with him. Often, he gave me a nice pen or something for my desk.

Early in my management career, I'd viewed gifts and awards as signs of accomplishment and acceptance. However, as time passed and I gained more influence and power because of my position and responsibilities, I noticed that many people wanted to have access to me in order to influence my decisions and solicit my commitment to their economic agendas. Though their gifts were in good taste, they ultimately sought control over my authority and decision-making abilities. In Philadelphia, on the streets, we called it pimping, and no one ever wants to be pimped or enslaved.

In 1997, I was given the responsibility of being the acting Vice President of sales for a new nursing and home health-care division we had started within Spencer and Spencer Client Care. Hearing of my new status, my recruiter approached me with a proposal: he wanted me to give him a multiyear contract as the sole recruiter for the new division. I found it strange that he knew a lot of details about the new division. In fact, I had the pen authority to sign off on such a contract with my temporary status as VP, but I would not ever sign off on any agreement without the support of our senior leadership team.

To my surprise, in my recruiter's quest to make the multiyear contract happen, he—the same person who gave me gifts in good taste—got loud, obnoxious, intimidating, and forceful in my office. He coarsely said, "If you don't get this done, I will expose you for personally taking a cashier's check for the hiring of one of your current employees." When he said that, it hit me: I had asked my wife to cash a cashier's check for the referral of a minority candidate at another company, but something about the check had seemed strange. It had not been made out to anyone when it was presented to me until the last minute. The fact of the matter was that the recruiter had his clients pay him with blank general cashier's checks, but he never put his name on them. Spencer and Spencer could trace the cashier's check to the Spencer and Spencer Client Care employee who had been his client. The employee who had originally drafted the check was now one of my employed sales representatives. By my cashing the check, it appeared the rep had paid me hire him, when in fact, that cashier's check had been redirected to me for a legitimate referral for another company placement, but also to pay for legitimate recruiting service fees. I'd had no idea the check originated from the bank of the employee.

At that moment, I knew I was being tempted, scammed, blackmailed, and coerced into making the biggest blunder of my life. I was being pimped, and I was about to be enslaved if I fell for the okie doke. My recruiter said, "If you don't get this done, your career is over. Done! I will put your name on the state's blacklist, and you will be done." He smiled while saying it and then walked out of my office. He smiled as if he had me. He smiled as if I were his for the taking.

I felt an *Oh no* inside, and I wasn't sure if it was the Holy Spirit or the Philly rising up in me. For sure it was a tough situation. There I was, at the vice-president level after finally having been given that temporary assignment just a few days before, and now my ethics had been challenged. I knew that what was happening to me was wrong, and a lot of things that happened to me in totality were wrong, but that was a different wrong. I would have to explain the situation to my wife in full out honesty. I did not do anything wrong though it appeared that I had. I had to do the right thing, no matter how embarrassing it was or how low it took me. If my career ended because of all this mess, it would be because I chose to do the right thing.

I knew the leadership at the company wanted me out, and the check debacle was all they needed. I knew it was a scam, and I thought the company would stand by me if I did the right thing. After all, that was what our credo was all about. In retrospect, I realize Spencer and Spencer Client Care did the right thing legally by me.

I went to the Vice President of the company and laid everything out in the open. The move surprised my recruiter, who'd thought I was his good business friend whom he could control in light of all the great hires he'd helped me put in place. I owed him his due for bringing me good people, but his last move of greed had been out of left field. The situation was turned over to human resources and security, and Spencer and Spencer Client Care corporate conducted an investigation. The investigator told me on the side that he saw my innocence, but the cashier's check presented a major problem. He said the recruiter was compromising the employee associated with the cashier's check, preventing him from telling the truth. It was messy, and there were many other details I was never privy to that had a negative impact on the company. In fact, my recruiter friend was also planning another trap for another rising superstar in the company. I was advised that the matter was ultimately settled to protect the company, my family, and me. Even the lawyer I had hired apparently was satisfied. I elected to accept a nice severance from the company, realizing there was no one in my corner to fight for me to stay, nor did I want to fight to stay at that point. I had witnessed worse conduct from other corporate managers over the years, and they had kept their jobs and still had their careers. At the core of my decision was the fact I would never go to Texas to work and live after the way I had been treated from the first day I got to Kansas. One thing is for sure: I did the right thing and exposed the scam by telling the truth. It was time for me to move on, and I did so knowing I had done the honorable thing. So, it was true that I would only go so far. Some things you just know.

My personal saying came back to my mind: "See the trap, avoid the trap, and don't fall in the trap." As you move to avoid the trap and stay clean, the effort of some to eventually trap you continues.

One inappropriate or unintentional step by you can knock you out.

Through my faith in God, I was always provided a way out when tempted by things that were not good to me or good for me. I thank God for bringing me through the unintended fall. My Spencer and

Spencer Client Care days ended on somewhat of a bad note and not one of my choosing. A senior leader within Spencer and Spencer Client Care once had told me, "You are only going to go so far," and he'd been right. Yet I had gone far enough to experience some incredible things in corporate business. I'd had a wonderful ride of sales success for thirteen years, maintaining a consistent status in the top 10 percent in sales and receiving some of the company's highest awards. Most importantly, I had taken care of my family and made a way for other African Americans to chart their course in the company, demonstrating that African Americans could be successful in sales management against all odds, particularly if they were allowed to do so. On my last day, the Vice President I had been filling in for returned and came to Kansas to pick up the company car. It was a humbling experience when he took away the keys to the car. He offered me a ride home, which I refused. I said, "No, I will walk." It was a good thing for me to say because I had to literally walk on my own now.

I prayed and thanked God while walking down College Boulevard in Overland Park, Kansas. It was midday, and the sun was hot on my back. Then, all of a sudden, a car pulled up beside me, and a pretty lady asked me if I wanted a ride. I said, "Sure!" It was my lovely wife, who somehow knew to be nearby, and took me home. I was happy to see Joy at that moment. I knew that even though I had to walk on my own in business from then on and move on from Spencer and Spencer Client Care, I knew I would not be by myself because my wife would always be there.

THE LEANDER GROUP

I immediately became a self-employed proprietor and did business as the Leander Group, a name that reflected my middle name. I had started a consulting business on the side to do recruiting years ago, and now that I was a full-time entrepreneur, I made that my focus.

Almost immediately, word got out that I had left Spencer and Spencer after thirteen years of being in sales in all capacities, from a sales rep to Vice President. I had seen and done it all at every level. I loved training and developing young salespeople and managers; however, sales would always be in my blood, going back to my days of selling for the *Philadelphia Bulletin* newspaper in Philadelphia. I'd loved those tips for doing a good job, and now that I was older, stock options, rewards, a commission, and bonuses were nice carrots one could dangle in front of me at any time.

As finances from my severance were drawing to an end, I looked at multiple opportunities in the Kansas City area to do business and even invested in a start-up. I joined a local chapter of Toastmasters, breezed through the required courses, and became a certified Toastmaster. I always recommend Toastmasters to anyone wanting to work in corporate America, start a career in sales, or improve his or her self-esteem. I believe Toastmasters is the quickest way to sharpen your speaking skills and get honest, unbiased, affirming, and immediate feedback, which many of us need from time to time.

Around that time, during the beginning of 1999, my father's health took a turn for the worse. I never knew or wanted to know the details of what actually was causing his problems. In fact, he never told me anything about his health, but I remember the way it all ended. Before his death, I joined a major Fortune 100 insurance corporation to market life insurance for businesspeople traveling and living overseas. The opportunity came about through my participation in a Toastmasters course, wherein I was contracted by a regional VP.

I was working on a project with my friend Warrick Graves, who was with Prudential in an investment capacity. Warrick was well known and the coauthor of *Stop Probate Now: The Only Living Trust Book You'll Ever Need to Read*, published by Trust Publishing Company in 1991. He was also a family friend. We came across a big opportunity in Africa that required a large amount of insurance, and the company I represented was one of the companies that could provide the insurance for a public-private initiative where the opportunity was. I had a valid insurance license and the authority to sell that type of insurance for international businesspeople.

I took the new business opportunity to my local regional Vice President, who did not take me seriously due to the magnitude of the opportunity but allowed me to pursue it anyway, which I did. I needed to get to the highest level of management within the company, so I reviewed the annual report and got the name of the president who headed the international division. I was required to send him an introductory email to arrange a meeting. Surprisingly, I got a quick response: he asked me to come to New York for a meeting and bring Warrick and the client. I arranged it all and told my boss.

When word got out in my office that I had officially arranged a meeting in New York on my own, my management team got nervous and distant. They told me that the meeting could take place but that I did not need to go. That was strange, and I told my boss that I had to go because my client wanted me there in person, which they did. My boss tried to find every way to talk me out of going and even said that if I had to go, I had to do so at my own expense. When I heard that, I said to myself, *Here we go again.*

Some things you just know.

I went to New York on the same plane as Warrick at my own expense, and we met my business client at the Waldorf Astoria, where he was well known. In fact, he had the title of prince in certain circles, which explained why the president of the company knew much more about the business opportunity than I. The initial meeting took place as scheduled. I introduced everyone in order to make claim on the commission for bringing the deal to the table. The commission on a deal of this magnitude would be significant if everything went through as planned.

As the meeting got legs, I was asked to go to the waiting area. Warrick and my business client remained in the meeting, which ended early and looked promising. After we left the company building on 70th Pine Street, which was near Wall Street, we all had lunch at a famous restaurant nearby. We tried to change our flights to leave sooner but could not. Warrick asked, "What shall we do until our flight?"

I thought for a moment and then said, "I know; we could run down and go see my dad, who is in intensive care in Philadelphia."

Warrick looked at me and questioned abruptly why I had not told him about my dad. I said, "I knew how important this meeting was, considering all I had to go through, so I did not tell anyone. But now that we are here, let's go."

We rented a car and were in Philadelphia in no time. On the way down to see my dad, Warrick revealed that he believed the situation was meant to be: we had come that far for him to pray for my dad. Warrick told me he was preparing his sermon to be an ordained minister, and that coming Sunday, he had to preach his final trial sermon. I asked, "Why didn't you tell me?" It was funny; we both knew God was in control and had used this trip to accomplish His purpose.

I will never forget that day. The medical staff had my dad strapped down, with his arms secured. He could not speak but had some communicative movement with his hands. When I went to introduce Warrick, his eyes popped wide open as if he were in shock because he thought he was seeing his brother, Nathaniel. He kept saying, "Nathaniel. Nathaniel." I had to admit Warrick favored my uncle Nathaniel a lot.

My dad could write, so we exchanged words that way. The nurses motioned that they were about to move him, and Warrick declared that he needed to pray for my dad before we departed. He did just that, and he gave a powerful prayer. I leaned down close to my dad to say goodbye, trying to make out what he was saying as we were about to leave, and he pushed himself up, lifted his head, and kissed me on my left cheek, near my lips. I was shocked, but I realized what the gesture meant, and I said, "I love you too, Dad." He never had shown that much physical love toward me ever as an adult, but I would remember that kiss forever. Warrick and I then departed.

Warrick and I returned home, and I attended church to hear him preach that Sunday as he gave witness to how God had moved in our lives that Friday on our business trip to New York. That was the good news. However, the bad news came on Monday: as soon as I walked into the office, I was reassigned to just marketing insurance and not selling. Out of nowhere I was put in a room with a copier and told to print, fold, address, and stamp thousands of mailers all day. A rental truck rolled up, and as I looked out my window, I saw that it was filled with boxes of plain copy paper. All the paper came to my room, and I was insulted and embarrassed. My task as a marketing representative was to copy and fold thousands of marketing sheets each day, stuff them inside envelopes, stamp them, and mail them. I did that all day, every day. My management had put me in my place where I could not go anywhere if I wanted to get paid. My boss was doing exactly what the higher-ups required of him: restricting the travel and movement of Frank Clay. Some things you just know.

What was being done to me was a personal issue because I was blocked from conducting the follow-up to our New York meeting.

Sometimes in business, things get personal, and those above you usually have the upper hand and the last word. With so much commission on the line, I started to ask questions, but I got no answers. At that point, I knew it was all about who was going to get commissions off the deal. I'd experienced the same type of treatment before I'd left the two previous insurance companies I'd worked with and when I'd been in the running for Division of the Year at Spencer and Spencer Client Care. In all those situations, the truth as I saw it was that they did not want an African American like me to be that successful and receive the kind of dollars and recognition that went along with the success. I now understood that I would need to be prepared to fight hard for what I deserved. In a good fight like that, someone wins and someone loses out in many ways.

There was a difference with this insurance company that brought caution to my resisting what was going on: my wife had a good job and career with them at the time, with many years in. In no way did I want the situation to impact her. At one point, I brought my girls into the office to witness what I was doing to keep a check coming into the house. I said, "Sometimes you have to do things to keep getting paid until something better comes along. This is what I have to do."

The company was paying me well to make copies to support our mail campaigns, but they knew I was not happy, and I got the message they were sending in no uncertain terms. Honestly, the Philly in me wanted to fight back, but sometimes it's better to lose a battle and win the war. Winning the war was allowing my wife to keep her career going, so I contacted human resources in New York, who were aware of the situation. Using my Spencer and Spencer corporate experience, I was direct and said, "I know you are aware of what is happening, and these are clearly grounds for claiming workplace discrimination and unfair treatment of a broker agent. However, my concern is my wife. I do not want her to be impacted by this situation. I don't want her involved, and I do not want her consulted or contacted. I am making the decision independent of her. I am proposing that you give me a severance and let me walk away."

It was that simple. The human resources lady agreed that my wife had a spotless ten-year career with the company, and we mutually agreed that my proposal was the best way to go. They gave me a nice severance package for the short period of time I was there, and I left the company. I never heard anything more from the insurance company, and they allowed my wife to continue her career until she retired. The lost battle for me again was exposing the truth and walking away from a commission opportunity sitting on the table. That was the hardest thing to do. Some things you just know are best. Once more, I referred back to my grandmother's sharing of the poem "If" by Rudyard Kipling, particularly the following part:

> If you can make a heap of all your winnings
> And risk it on one turn of pitch-and-toss,
> And lose, and start again at your beginnings
> And never breathe a word about your loss.

LGC

A natural transition at the time was for me to get more serious about recruiting and coaching minority clients with major Fortune 500 companies. I had learned many lessons about being successful in corporate America, and I felt I could share those lessons with others. I knew how to move up the corporate ladder. What I had to offer from an African American perspective would help my clients go further in corporate America and avoid the mistakes I'd made; as well as prepare them to overcoming obstacles that were sure to come with their success. I would at least help them to cope with the realities of corporate America, wherein the success of an African American was restricted more often than not.

In the capacity of an executive coach, I was able to leverage what I was offering on a consultant basis, and I went back to Spencer and Spencer companies in the Northeast to consult with their human resources department. My aim was to help their sales managers identify, recruit, coach, and train highly talented minority and female candidates. Some viewed that as racial and sexual profiling but in a positive sense.

I conducted profile assessments to determine character strengths and tendencies to help properly position clients for future opportunities. Doing the assessments helped my credibility to contract with Spencer and Spencer corporate because it allowed me to offer an objective voice to help assess a candidate's potential for hire.

By networking in Kansas City with various groups, such as the National Association of Market Developers (NAMD), of which I became president of my chapter, I was able to source potential candidates for hire by leveraging NAMD's past connections in corporate America. As part of NAMD, I briefed Kansas City on the annual Urban Consumer Market Report, which was issued to media and marketing people and reflected innovations, strategies, and trends within the urban community. I personally headed the marketing committee that generated the first African American consumer survey for Kansas City, which was planned for release at Black Expo USA in 1995. We called the survey *Snapshot*, and it was published in May 1996. I was able to connect with strong professionals, including the founder of a consulting company called LGC and Associates. She was also active in NAMD. She had recently come from Hallmark. Many corporate people with twenty-plus years of experience were leaving corporate jobs to do great things business-wise on their own while making good money. She was my mentor in learning how to do consulting properly.

It was evident that everyone in corporate America needed an exit strategy to position all his or her knowledge, experience, connections, and resources back into his or her local community. Many times I advised corporate professionals confidentially on how to plan their last two years with their companies to maximize leverage with contacts and achievements properly. No corporate job, no matter how great it looks and feels, will last forever. Those who stay in corporate America too long trade off what they could do on their own, including making more money and being free to pursue their own visions, for the sake of towing the corporate agenda. Staying in corporate America is not always a bad thing; however, you need to know what is best for you, and you need to know for sure where you sit within your company's succession plans. You should analyze both scenarios with an open and objective business mind because timing is everything, and preparation makes a thing work when the time is right—this is true whether you are African American or not. When your opportunity comes, you have to be prepared and ready to go.

For two main reasons, I explored a partnership with LGC and Associates: first, the founder wanted to get into a process called executive search with all the top companies in the area, such as Helzberg Diamonds, Sprint, and St. Luke's Hospital. Second, I thought it would enhance my business presence and image to be with LGC and Associates on an independent contract basis. I was given an office in the downtown business district, in Country Club Plaza. Location is an important key to success when it comes to marketing yourself locally. I always say, "To be successful in business, be where the action is, or be where the money is." County Club Plaza, with all of its water fountains, was the place to be. Many people did not know that Kansas City was said to have the most working fountains in the world. That was a great talking point for conversation that I used in networking with clients and partners traveling to Kansas City.

At the time, LGC and Associates was big on diversity, and the founder, a previous executive of Hallmark, did not have a staffed executive-search offering. I developed that aspect of her business, with a focus on professional sales reps, engineers, and high-level executives, which paid well. The firm was sought after all over the country and the world. It was nurturing for me to be in her office, and I was able to coach many corporate clients on how to find better recruits and hire and retain minorities so that productivity and advancement could benefit all concerned.

One of the most rewarding accomplishments of my work at LGC and Associates was finding jobs for the children of prominent people in the community, including top executives, celebrities, presidents and Vice Presidents, doctors, and sports figures. Often, their children wanted to find their own path in life versus capitalizing on the legacy of their parents. Those candidates for employment had to be properly positioned and oriented into a hiring company to be successful; their placement could not be too high and or too low. Placing high-profile candidates was good for me because it greatly helped my referrals. I successfully placed African Americans in roles that pioneered some of the first African American management positions for local companies with national presence. Helzberg Diamonds was among those companies, along with other emerging businesses who were intentional in bringing highly qualified African Americans onto their management teams. Ironically, I continued to make quality referrals to Spencer and Spencer. Why not? It was one of the best companies anyone could work for, and I certainly knew what they were looking for.

By then, I had established myself as a true headhunter. In corporate America, being sought after and placed is much different from being let go and having to go solicit a job. A good headhunter involved in executive search will know where you are in your career and will help you find your next position. In fact, every corporation should have a headhunter to call upon and take guidance from. With all the dot-com companies doing well and the emphasis on Affirmative Action high, movement among companies in the early 2000s was the norm, and the best companies wanted the best people. I was good at finding high-profile African Americans in corporate America, so now I was sought after for my strong headhunter reputation.

Personally, the money was flowing, and I thought I was doing well, but something happened in the market. Though it was an exciting time with all the dot-com companies starting up left and right, I was carrying a little too much debt, to be frank. My investments were healthy, and I was on my way to becoming a millionaire on paper. However, in life, major things can happen that change everything. The real deal is that you don't want to see the market change on the downside and find yourself personally stuck in debt. The dot-com companies at that time soon were in trouble in a fundamental way. Many of those companies, which were regarded as the future of our growing economy, had revenue, growing numbers of customers, and unbelievable financing, but not many were turning a profit. That being the reality, the market tolerated them over and over again. I too tolerated them, and I told myself those companies were going to fail because they simply were not turning a profit. How could the market be so high on businesses that it went against what I'd been taught in business school? Meanwhile, I was sitting too heavily on those investments, knowing I needed to pay off the large debt I had.

The reality is, you can get caught up in the financial circus of being on the upside of achieving wealth without recognizing the downside of taking care of your everyday business. In my portfolio were two main stocks I was in deep with. One large investment was with Enron, which was trading at ninety dollars a share leading up to the year 2000, the century leap year, when the world was supposedly about to come to an end. Well, the world did not come to an end, but Enron did in a serious scandal. I lost a great deal of my investments before I was strong enough mentally to make a change. Enron stock was not my only problem. My hometown's Sprint stock dropped to crazy levels, and the reliable AT&T stock evaporated in value over the next few years. My investments were in trouble.

Right before it all slipped away, I put my ego in check and cashed out enough money to pay off the compounding interest on my credit card bills I was not paying attention to. Those pieces of plastic were more than a means of making a purchase; they were addicting and reflected my desire to be the "I can buy anything" man. I gave the Holy Spirit inside me credit for alerting me of the market crash to come behind the scandals, such as Enron's. While in prayer my inner being was troubled over my prideful stance of holding stocks while hoarding credit card debt. Finally, I got out of the market without consideration of the tax impact, but I got out with enough money in hand to pay off all the debt I had. To me, it was a matter of running to safety, which left me with little in my portfolio. Yes, I admit I did well with my savings, but I did a disgustingly poor job of managing my credit card debt, which never seemed to go away, especially with all the perks.

I concluded that I would rather be debt free than a millionaire who was deep in credit card debt, as my dad, a master of credit card debt, was. He'd taught me how he transferred balances to get a new card, and he had a stack of them. I was tempted to do as he had done. In fact, I realized that I was like him. The only difference was I had money invested and saved. Credit cards and home equity loans allowed anyone to have what he or she wanted in a way that appeared to be okay. Credit card companies say, "Buy what you want, and don't worry about tomorrow," when all the while, your interest accumulates on a compounded basis.

The reality was that I was not going to be a millionaire with all the debt. I had to say that to myself over and over again. My financial planner did all the great projections but never asked me about my credit card debt and assumed I had enough personal cash flow to pay off any debt. That or he simply did not care. My planner also did not stress the importance of paying off the home equity loan and the debt that was about to kill us in upcoming balloon payments of compound interest. No, that was not the recommendation, because that would have meant I did not have the money to keep my portfolio going, from which my financial planner made his commission as well as annual awards. He said, "Just keep putting your monthly amount in your account, and you will reach your goal." With my wife beside me, it all sounded great.

Things were going well with LGC and Associates, and I was starting to source and place executives into small businesses. An assessment would be conducted, and I was put in motion to find candidates to fit the job descriptions and hold confidential interviews until a match was made. I did this successfully until I ran into one particular client and asked, "Which of these prospects would you like to interview?"

He replied simply, "You. You are what I am looking for."

Yes, my client recruited me when I was supposed to be doing the recruiting for him. I sensed that he needed my help and his business model reminded me of the days when I used to sell cellular phones. It seemed like an exciting new opportunity and so I went for it!

Interestingly was some readings about an African American business man who had it all and did it all, who was called the "Potato King of the World." Reading about Junius Groves certainly was an eye opener about what was possible if you took to heart some basic business principles that could be applied to starting any new business venture. What was a revelation to me was how successful Mr. Groves, an Exoduster, was as a "entrepreneur farmer" from 1879-1925. His amazing success was only minutes from where I lived in Kansas. I knew something big could happen in there with an African American business because it had happen before in a big way. Maybe this was my opportunity now. Junius Groves should be a must read for anyone starting out in business with very little wanting to find good, better and the best that a business can offer. I was ready and inspired after my readings about the "Potato King."

CHAPTER 16

To the Motherland

Alfred Gonzales Jr. took me from what I was doing at LGC and Associates to be an employee with his thriving telecommunications company. I'd been doing an executive search for him to find a director of new business development using my custom process called Select Search, which was all about understanding the company well enough to find the right person. As I selectively produced a few candidates and knew a lot about the company, Mr. Gonzales made me an offer I could not refuse: he gave me the title of Vice President, with the potential to become president and part owner of the company in the future if a venture in Africa were to materialize. To me, the proposal sounded great, and it led me into conducting international business in Guinea, Africa, in the motherland. This would be one of the places that my DNA testing revealed my ancestors had emerged from. Nearly everyone who is African American wants to know something about where his or her ancestors came from. To do business in Africa was appealing, but to go experience it in person was overall a blessing. Though Guinea is just a small portion of Africa like a state is in the U.S.A., it would be a return to the motherland for me would answer many questions that I had always wondered about.

Guinea literally had very little no telecommunications worth speak of, and Gonzales Communications had a solution that would make long distance calls to the U.S.A. affordable. Though I knew the telecommunication market was suspect, in a way, Gonzales Communications Inc. (GCI) was an opportunity for me to get back to that millionaire status that I had missed out on at American TeleServices. I was all in. My immediate task was to look at the financials and bring the cost of operation under control. As the Vice President, I focused on the numbers and looked closely at the financials, and in doing so, I was able to see many possibilities to improve on controlling costs and increasing profits. In any small or medium-size company, you have to have checks and balances to make sure you are delivering the best bottom line to maximize profits.

Generally speaking, you have to inspect what you expect and anticipate what you can't contemplate. In growing a small company, such as GCI, which was doing business with the Regional Bell operating centers (RBOCs), AT&T, Verizon, CenturyLink, and Qwest, we had to account for labor hours and materials used in order to cost our projects and bill properly. We made great strides in managing the engineering, furnishing, and installation. The work was strategically plentiful, and we had teams in Kansas, Missouri, Denver, Arkansas, Texas, and other states on a special assignment basis. The workload was such that we traveled on the company's private jet, a Cessna Citation, flying out of the old airport in Kansas City and from the local executive airport. There I was, flying on a private jet to various executive airports, leaving early in the morning for another state, and getting back home shortly thereafter before sundown. Mr. Gonzales and I would conduct business on the company's private jet, meet with our customers and installation teams upon landing, and be back in the air in practically no time.

Flying on a private jet was a little different, as our pilot would work around weather and get us to our destination quickly and safely. One time, we had a close call while going west to a meeting and had to call for an emergency landing. In those situations, it pays to have an experienced pilot, as we had. I will never forget when our pilot announced that we had to divert to the closest airport because we were losing fuel drastically, and he did not know if we were going to make it if we kept traveling towards our destination. "Prepare to brace yourselves," he said.

I began to pray. "Lord, help" was my plea. With the airport in sight, our pilot maneuvered the plane to glide us down to a safe landing. After we landed and got out, we saw fuel gushing out, and it was plain to see we had been in big trouble up there in the air. On the ground we were now safe but had barely made it. Had we not landed the plane when we had, it might have been all over for us.

That was the only flight I was ever concerned about. Flying on a private jet was one of the highlights of being with Gonzales Communication.

Al Gonzales Jr. was the president, and his hometown was Atlanta. One year, we had to attend a conference in Atlanta to solicit new business and meet with our customers and potential customers. Normally, we got to take customers to a dinner near our hotel, but that time, we wanted our key customers to have a southern experience. We came up with the idea of using a local African American business to give everyone an unforgettable evening. Mr. Gonzales had a friend who sold soul food from an old gas station in the hood called Po Freddie's, on the corner of Campellton Road and Dodson Drive. I had done something like that before, and Al was all in. We planned to pick up our customers from a hotel in downtown Atlanta in a party bus at six o'clock in the evening, bring them to Po Freddie's, and rotate the buses, which sat fifteen to twenty people, every hour, thinking the event would last three hours.

We gave Po Freddie about half of what we would have spent downtown to prepare for our guests. He bought steaks, lobster, fish, chicken, burgers, corn on the cob, gumbo, sweet potatoes, potato salad, and fruit—the works and plenty of it. He had enough money to paint his seating area, put in new lights and new gravel, and even have a mural painted with a big pink elephant and the words "We're back." It was amazing how he transformed his soul-food restaurant for the event. He also had two gorgeous hostesses who took orders and mixed drinks that were off the chart.

When our guests arrived, they could smell the food in the air, and it was on. With music at a party pitch, the parade of soul food hit everyone's palate, and mouths were smacking and knocking everything down. People were having a great time, and we all knew it. Locals passing by tried to look over the fence to see what was going on. Mind you, the majority of the guests were Caucasian, and no one left. Po Freddie was a master entertainer, and part of his act featured various varieties and degrees of hot sauce. The regular red bottle was on every table, but we were challenged to go to the next level, which came in a different presentation. The rotation went from the red bottle to a soda bottle, a teacup, a test tube, a baby bottle, and a dip. Next was having the hot sauce brushed on our food, and finally, the last one was a killer: a medicine bottle with a syringe. Po Freddie played it up, asking, "Do you really want to try this one?" Still, no one left.

It was getting late, and we had to pay our driver overtime to make sure everyone got to his or her individual hotel. Many people stayed around and left huge tips. One guy who had a wedding planned enjoyed himself so much that he recruited Po Freddie and his team to handle all the food for the wedding. The point is this: by our taking our show to "the hood," the locals ended up having a better place to come to after we left. Po Freddie profited greatly from our business, which in turn made a big difference for his business. More importantly, the next day at the convention, Gonzalez Communication and Po Freddie were the talk of the town. Our customers had a great experience, which strengthened our relationships, and we saved a lot of money on entertaining.

Everything we were doing strategically was leading up to setting up and promoting our cellular services in Africa. Around that time, something I never had thought would happen happened, changing the world and drastically impacting our company. Gonzales Communication was positioned to make operational satellite communication from Guinea, Africa, to Kansas, United States. I had tickets to travel to Africa to set up a sales team to promote calling cards. I was in my bedroom, watching TV, when the news broke that the Twin Towers had been hit by two commercial planes. It was a stunning scene.

Forever known as 9/11, that tragedy spread across the lives and hearts of the world, and it was a heartbreaker for Gonzales Communication as well. As a result of the incident, the needed financing we were close to receiving immediately stopped, and so did the New York Stock Exchange. After a period of sixteen days, it finally opened to a 7 percent drop, setting a record for one day. By the end of the day, the Dow Jones Industrial Average (DJIA) was down 14 percent for a loss of $1.4 trillion. I had to make a big decision: whether or not I was going to keep my trip to Africa. My family was concerned about my safety, but my company did not know if the deal would be stopped because of 9/11. For the sake of the company, I had to go to show good faith. After much prayer, I decided to go for it. I was committed to the opportunity to help set up satellite communications business for Gonzales Communications in Guinea and still viewed it as a once-in-a-lifetime experience. It turned out to be that and more.

I flew to Guinea alone for two weeks, and when I landed, it was almost dark. In Guinea, nighttime comes fast, is very dark, and the moon and bright stars in the sky provided just enough light that I could walk and see the shadows of others near me. As I was a guest of the president, a government official picked me up, and our first stop was a convenience store, where he grabbed a handful of condoms and put them in a bag. He gave them to me when we returned to the car. I was shocked at the introduction, and off we went to my private quarters in the dark, where I had my own armed driver and cook, who would kill one of the chickens running around for dinner or bake one of the fresh fish that came from the waters nearby. My meals were healthy, either fresh fish or a freshly killed chicken with a potato and a salad.

After getting me settled my first night, the government official left and then returned shortly, bringing to my place five women who did not speak English. They were all gorgeous. He had been drinking and motioned for me to pick one or two. I had not even fully unpacked, and there I was, in a precarious position on day one. Not knowing what to do and compelled to appear as if I was going along with my escort's plans, I picked one of the women to take back to my room just to get away from him and lock the door to buy some time to figure out what I was going to do. I was halfway around the world, and the next flight home was in two weeks. I was concerned. If I did not cooperate with the government official's proposition, what would be next? I said a "Lord, help" prayer and dealt cleverly with the situation. Clearly, the woman was mainly there to have sex with me, but that was not going to happen. I began to entertain her, even though we could not speak each other's language.

To keep her interested and occupied, I showed her different things in my luggage. My CD player caught her attention. They say music is a common language we all speak, and that thought came to my mind. I gave her my headphones and put on Earth, Wind, and Fire. I played songs from the *Open Our Eyes* album, starting with "Drum Song." She listened to the whole song in amazement. I kept sharing my music, and before I knew it, a knock on the door came. It was time for her to go. Before she left, I gave her one of the purses my wife had sent over to give away. I let her pick one out. As I heard the call "Time to go!" we hugged, and she went to the car with the other women and drove away, staring at me out the window. Though she had not had sex with me, I'd known she wanted to the whole time. God was with me that night, and what his Word says was true: "And God is faithful; he will not let you be tempted beyond what you can bear." After that temptation, I was on my guard from that point on.

The next day, my driver took me to the school where the Gonzales satellites were being put together for final inspection. I needed to pick up some antimalarial medicine I'd been advised to take, and after going to multiple places, I ended up at a hospital, where I saw all the Spencer and Spencer products I knew well. I ended up meeting a nursing professional who spoke English, and she was interested in my knowledge about the products. We hit it off, and I invited her to the place where I was staying. I needed someone there to help me figure out what was going on and whom I was dealing with. She was the right person; I could speak English to her, and I needed her help.

She came by the compound, which had an armed guard at the front gate, and I asked her everything I needed to know about how people in Guinea were using and paying for their communications. She shared that many were still using coin-operated pay phones, using phones at an internet café, and buying phone cards. To call out of the country, there were long-distance phone centers, but there were also bootleg places in houses where people intercepted the phone lines and were able to get calls out but charged the users a high fee for access. I tried to sample these makeshift phone locations by making a call to the States. It worked sparingly and I got to speak to my wife for about five minutes.

My newly found nurse friend's initial visit was very cordial. Before she left, the government official came again with three or four new women, as he had the night before. In English, I asked my nurse friend to stay with me. Her presence made the other women nervous, and because we could communicate in English, they all just got up to leave. As the government's women and my nurse friend stared each other down, my nurse friend put on a protective expression, so the government official and the women abruptly left—never to return. I kept my nurse friend close to me and paid for her to take me to places that were not on the official government agenda. I asked to see where she lived and met her family. That was a good thing but also a not-so-good thing because I did not know I was inadvertently setting big expectations by making this gesture.

Within a few days, I found a bilingual brother who was with the school and made him my sales manager during our initial sales training. I told him my vision for starting a sales team and asked him to recruit four people. I wanted to prove to him how the business model would work when we started selling phone cards for Gonzales Communications after everything was up and running.

I had brought a suitcase of Irish Spring soap and Lipton tea bags for my sales team to sell. I had heard the locals loved soap and tea. I got a great deal from Sam's Club so we were able to distribute in Guinea for pennies on the dollar. I opened a bank account with American Express checks, which I had brought with me. That was all the money I had.

My sales manager was my translator when I spoke to the other four team members. I asked them to sell each bar of soap for $10,000 GNF (Guinean Franc) or 1 US dollar, and bring the money to the sales manager, who would give them back $5,000 GNF, or 50 cents. They could keep $5,000 GNF and receive another bar of soap. We had a similar arrangement to sell tea bags. The manager would then have to deposit $20,000 GNF, $5,000 from each sales person, and show me the deposit slip to get more soap for him and his team. They had to sell all the soap or tea given to them in order to get more to sell. The sales manager was on each of his team members to sell everything they had because he would make an extra $5,000 GNF if they sold everything. In other words, he made $1.00 while the others made 50 cents if everything was sold.

They sold their allotment of soap and tea in a few hours, and my sales manager was diligent in making his deposits, as he could see how he and his team benefited if the team did their part. We sold all the soap and tea in a few days, and I achieved my training goal. We had a workable sales model for selling phone cards. When we had had everything in place, we would use the same selling strategy, putting our trust in the people selling for us.

Meanwhile, my nurse friend had arranged to take me into the country to visit her village. I was amazed at how everyone worked together. I even spent the night in my friend's family village. I stayed by myself in a guest home with one bed that was very nice and clean. What struck me most was how the men were protecting their communities. On the way to a village, many men engaged us, asking us questions: "Where are you going? Why are you here? Who sent you?"

All the questioning took place until sundown, when I was positioned in front of the village leader. I sat facing the sun in a room, and the village leader was opposite of me and my escort was strategically positioned in the shadows where I could not see his face but hear him talk. An image of the village leader was embedded in the sunrays in my eyes as I sat facing the setting sun. When I turned around, all the people who had questioned me were standing behind me to validate my conversations. I could see each of their faces clearly and recalled each one from our previous encounters on the road that led to the village. My meeting with the village leader went well and I was welcomed with opened arms as my answers were all collaborated.

At night, the men guarded their village. They knew who came in and knew who was allowed to stay. They dragged big tree logs in the street to prevent someone from driving through the village without being checked out. I witnessed a community tribunal and saw a woman crying. Apparently, she had an issue with a man who was positioned in the center of a circle that all the men in the village had formed. All the other men grabbed the man and then allowed the woman to confront the man. She slapped the living daylights out of him again and again. Then the men took him to the edge of the village by the main road and threw him onto the ground. It was something to see, and I couldn't help but wonder if it was also a warning to me.

Throughout Guinea, I saw trees so big that a road ran through the trunk of one of them. It must have been hundreds of years old. I witnessed a butcher killing a cow off the side of the road and cutting it up as people from the various villages came to get their portions of meat, whether a leg, a side, or whatever else. The children coming home from school blew me away, as they ran and played, picking fruit like candy from the trees and vines that were everywhere. There were no stores anywhere; everything they needed was right there. It was something to see. This was the motherland, and all it had to offer took care of its people. It had to have been the closest thing to the Garden of Eden. It seemed as if everything I wanted or needed for survival was right there growing all around me.

During the second week, when I'd completed most of my work, the government official apparently was disturbed that I had done many things on my own and had not cooperated with his personal agenda for me. By then, I had visited the president's wife's foundation for children, and I had even played soccer with the locals near me, scoring two goals through goal posts signified by large rocks, as we played on the dirt.

Everything was good until I got news that the government official had set me up to face a real tribunal with one of the country's ministers, accusing me of bribery and wrongdoing. With only two or three days of the trip left, I could not believe it, but I knew he was out to get me. This was some serious stuff, and it all came out of left field. There I was, being escorted by an armed guard into a meeting with armed guards and people speaking a language I did not fully understand, yelling back and forth. I was concerned that Mr. Gonzales would not understand what was happening, because I sure did not. I heard the charges against me as the interpreter explained them. I had to think quickly on my feet and find a way to get out of that assault on my character.

What saved me was the fact that by then, my selling experiment was over, and I had been a guest of the president's wife's foundation for children on a tour early that week. After leaving the tour, I'd gone to the bank and cashed out, closing the account. Fortunately, I'd instructed the bank to make out a cashier's check in the name of the president wife's foundation. In fact, the foundation had given me, in writing, acknowledgment of my donation. When the minister articulated the charges against me in more detail in English, I was floored and then made my case that I did not have any money to bribe anyone. First, I showed I did not have any intent to take advantage of anyone. I had come to give and not take anything from anyone. I reminded everyone there that my wife had given me twenty women's pocketbooks and purses to give away, and I had taken them to a women's shelter near where I was staying. I showed everyone the stubs and amounts of the American Express checks to compare to the money I had deposited and withdrawn from the bank to donate to the foundation. I was able to show that all my money was accounted for. Immediately, all charges were dropped, and the government official who'd brought the charges against me was immediately reprimanded.

I lost my driver and cook all of a sudden. I called my nurse friend to help me get to the five-star hotel where I was advised to go to if I was in trouble. I did not know if I was in trouble, but it sure felt like I was due to the sudden abandonment of services that were being rendered to me. On my way out of the house, I saw the upset government official and gave him back all the condoms in the same bag in which he had given them to me. Every condom was accounted for, with not one missing. He was not a happy camper and left me on my own with no protection right at the entrance of the president's compound.

Apparently knowing more than I did, my nurse friend showed up and informed me that I was indeed in trouble. She felt it was best that she stay with me until I got on the plane the next day.

Unselfishly, she stood by me even at the airport.

As my plane circled around, I never had been so happy to get back on a plane. I just hoped they wouldn't shoot the plane down. I never got a chance to express my sincere thanks to my nurse friend, the gentleman representing the president's wife's foundation who'd helped me to validate my donation, or the minister for looking at the evidence and protecting me.

Within months of my returning to the United States, the telecom industry completely went to the tubes. As Vice President of the company, I told Mr. Gonzales we needed to make drastic layoffs immediately due to cash flow. That included laying me off. With the satellite finally working, it was hard to get the capital to close the deal to keep me on. After 9/11, everything was different, but I would be ever grateful for the opportunity of a lifetime to go to Guinea and see the motherland. I was wiser for it, and I had no regrets about going. I learned a big lesson while working for Gonzales Communications: never get too close to your clients; you might get sucked into what they are doing and forget what you are supposed to be doing.

CHAPTER 17

New Ways to Share

When I stepped down from my position as Vice President of Gonzales Communication, I realized I had a complete understanding of how a small business needed to run in order to be successful. I had seen firsthand how people with limited views could stifle the growth of a growing company. I'd seen how individuals sought to control decisions to get their way. I was familiar with the multiple ways costs could get out of control if there was no process of checks and balances. I'd shared both the excitements and the disappointments of an owner on many levels. One disappointment stood out as hurting the most: having family and friends renege on their commitments. In a small business, you tend to want to give your friends and family an opportunity to participate even when they fail to communicate, show up, or just do what is asked. Situations like these require strong leadership to resolve impending problems. If that meant I had to recommend that my own position be eliminated for the sake of the company's survival, then so be it.

Having been exposed to so much at Gonzales Communications, I decided to go on a speaker's tour across the country to share my business knowledge and relevant experience. Realizing SkillPath International was headquartered in the Kansas City area, I approached them for an opportunity to speak. The interview to qualify to be an independently contracted speaker with SkillPath was pretty easy for me. I thoroughly knew the subject matter that was to be covered in any seminar inside and out. In fact, I had my own original material registered with the Library of Congress to speak from if needed.

As an independent contractor under the Leander Group name, I was designated as an authorized SkillPath seminar trainer from September 2002 to July 2004, presenting two different programs: "The Managers and Supervisors Conference" and "Coaching and Teambuilding for Managers and Supervisors." I presented those seminars more than 120 times for SkillPath. One responsibility presenters had in addition to presenting the subject matter for each program was to market and sell books to reinforce participant learning. I fell in love with a book called *The Leadership Challenge* by Kouzes and Posner. I believed strongly in the five practices of leadership therein. The book reflected studies and research on leadership and provided excellent data for new and emerging leaders to assess their leadership style. The book's focus was on becoming more confident and competent.

I conducted seminars at conference halls and hotels all across the nation, which helped me travel to all fifty states—something that was on my bucket list of items to do. I thoroughly enjoyed engaging the business community by conducting SkillPath seminars. I helped many businesses with specifics on how to deal with their issues, which made me feel like a consultant as well as a speaker. Nothing gave me more joy than seeing a person leave one of my sessions with an action step that made the seminar worth his or her while.

By networking with consultants and coaches in the Kansas City area, I ran into Ramon Corrales, PhD, who was a true professional as a coach and was a breath of fresh air to talk one on one with. He knew so much about human and group behavior from a personal and business point of view. I came to the conclusion that, "you can never make a better professional or employee until you make a better person." You actually make a better person by helping someone to think correctly. Ramon Corrales had much to say on that topic, and I was willing to listen.

CORPORATE MASTERY

I got more interested in business coaching and sought to become certified as a coach with Corporate Mastery when I was not speaking in SkillPath seminars. With Corporate Mastery USA, I became skilled at performing executive coaching using assessment tools and the teachings of Ramon Corrales, PhD. I perfected the four great dimensions of a relationship: rapport, initiative, structure, and commitment.

On my own, I found another assessment tool with Profiles International. Their assessment looked at thinking style, behavior traits, and interests to come at a total person assessment. I loved their assessment so much I made the investment to be trained and designated as a Profiles International distributor in Kansas in 2004. All of that fell under the Leander Group, and I was well positioned to do coaching, consulting, speaking, and executive search locally or nationally. With the number of my corporate and personal clients growing, I was excited about the future and how I could help others be placed in roles of greater authority and responsibility.

MR. TOMBS

In late 2004, I was invited to a Republican holiday party for a business-networking event. It was held at a house, and the place was packed. I made my way to the food. They had my favorites: wings, cheese dip, potato salad, baked beans, and punch. Not really knowing anyone, I hung around the food until a short dark-skinned man of distinction appeared under my elbow with his black-framed glasses and inviting smile. We began chatting. Chatting with Mr. Tombs, whose vocabulary was very complimentary, made me feel important—more important than I was. He got my attention that's for sure, when he mentioned that he had been an adviser to President Ronald Reagan on small business, and personally knew Senator Bob Dole, who was then a presidential candidate, well. He also said he had been a member of the National Advisory Council on Economic Opportunity under President Carter. When he mentioned that he had been a chief petty Officer twenty years before I was a Commander, I had the utmost respect in the world for him. However, I always wondered how this man had so much influence and reached into both political parties.

Mr. Tombs was an African American with twenty-three years in the US Navy, and to have achieved that rank in those times was remarkable. I was talking to an American legend from World War II. We had one thing in common: we both were veterans and had paved the ways for others. I had done so as an Officer, and Mr. Tombs had done so as a Noncommissioned Officer. Our achievements paved the way for other African Americans to be their best in the military and to come of the service with honor and dignity. Oddly, the whole time I spent talking to this man, it appeared Mr. Tombs knew way more about me than I knew about him. Our conversation was the only one I had that night. He said, "Son, you see all of this? It means nothing unless Kansas has more African American businesses. Kansas will never be all it can be until that happens. It needs a functioning black chamber of commerce. Think about that." With that, he walked away. With so much running through my mind, I left the event. Our discussion had been informative and compelling.

Later, I researched Mr. Leroy Tombs and found out all the things he had accomplished in business but never mentioned during our conversation. He owned a car dealership, was in the janitorial and food business, and had been the US Small Businessman of the Year in 1974. Then, by circumstance, my curiosity took me to Mr. Tombs's hometown, Bonner Springs, which was fifteen minutes from where I lived. In fact, many people I knew lived in that area, and I did not know a street recently had been named after him in 1999. I wondered what had happened to make him so prosperous.

From the time I met Mr. Tombs, I was richly enlightened about our country's business history, particularly in Kansas and Oklahoma. I learned that in the Treaty of Guadalupe Hidalgo in 1848, after the Mexican-American War, Mexicans lost most of the land that is now California, Nevada, Utah, Arizona, and Colorado. Furthermore, many American Indians lost all their land as this country negotiated its existence. This boy born in Philadelphia, with all my academic and business achievement, was humbled by the greatness of the historically rich place I now lived in. In no way was I inventing the wheel. I knew a comprehensive understanding off all the history I was discovering would be meaningful to me as I took on the next phase of my life in business.

Months later, Mr. Tombs called and made arrangements for a formal introduction to Mr. Tyrone Simms, president of Commercial Express. He was hammering nails into a wall when I was introduced to him and greeted by him. The wall was for the board room inside a mostly vacant historic Kansas City mall where Mr. Simms was spearheading the creation of a business incubator for veterans like myself.

One had to wonder what had happened to the thriving mall, which sat in a prime location where two major interstates intersected right in the heart of the African American community of Kansas City, Kansas. I drove by that site every week when going to the airport, and my first visit there, after hearing so much about it, what I saw was depressing. Nevertheless, Mr. Simms had a different vision for its future, and our meeting featured charts of new developments in the area, which called for new business and new commerce.

Nationally, there was a lot of movement to build the economy by increasing the number of small businesses nationwide, particularly within minority communities. In all the consulting I was doing, I was witnessing a major move of African Americans leaving corporate America to start their own businesses and leveraging their knowledge and contacts. I thought it was a noble strategy, but most prospective entrepreneurs had not completely thought out their business plans for success. Everyone had a business plan, but not everyone had a business plan with the necessary details that would provide great success and future profits.

For example, I observed many African Americans using their lifelong savings to start businesses, and their attachment to those dollars handicapped the new entrepreneurs in making sound business decisions. They literally approached getting into business with the mindset that they could buy their way in. With a little coaching, I advocated leveraging those dollars with a bank to get an interest-only loan to position their business for greater cashflow. I then advocated a focus on generating customers which required hard work. The kind of work that you can't cut corners with. At many banks, customers needed a relationship with the banker at their VIP levels in order to secure those lines of credit. An interest-only loan required only a percentage of the annual interest to be paid monthly, which created great cash flow for a new small business and, more importantly, allowed for the proper decision-making required to gain customers and grow the business. In short, that practice would allow an entrepreneur to capitalize the business properly with a keen eye on cash flow. However, a good work ethic would certainly create a positive environment for strong business growth.

My awareness of President George W. Bush's advocacy for more small businesses at the time had me in a very good place to understand what Mr. Simms was trying to do with his vision for the business incubator for veterans. When President Bush put out executive order 13360 in October 2004, providing new opportunities for service-disabled veteran businesses to increase their federal contracting and subcontracting, the prospect for more veteran small businesses was huge. It was an opportunity many wanted to take advantage of.

An incubator to bring veterans up to speed on how to take advantage of that executive order made a lot of sense. However, I had concluded that one would need more than a government program to start and be successful in a business. Regardless of the individual business endeavor, entrepreneurs had to respect the fundamental principles of business in order to be successful. An entrepreneur or business owner needed to know the basics of accounting, the fundamental steps of the sale, marketing and pricing products, business management, etc. Most business owners who started out were unaware of these basics. I saw a great need to coach new business owners who had no idea what they were getting into or that the potential for success was just a contract or two away.

During my official but informal visit with Mr. Tombs and Mr. Simms, they double-teamed me to encourage me to start thinking about putting together a black chamber of commerce. They challenged me to start a 501C3. I had done a lot of things in business, yet I never started or ran a nonprofit organization. I certainly had never started one from scratch with no money or required resources. This would be a first. I prayed, "Lord, help on this one."

Using the 2002 census, I did my due diligence of researching the data on small businesses. Just a quick review of the information pointed out a couple of key things. One, there were few African American businesses that employed people in Kansas. Most of the businesses for African Americans were working as a sole proprietor. The numbers for the minority business community in general, including women, were low. I realized there were more African American sole proprietors or entrepreneurs out there than anything else. Two, in many parts of the country, the numbers were getting better or increasing. African American businesses were growing in number, but they were nowhere near what they could have been, considering the number of African Americans in the country.

The 2002 survey showed that the number of black-owned firms had increased 45 percent from 1997 to 2002. Black households had $631 billion in earned income in 2002, which was a 4.8 percent increase from the previous year. As an MBA graduate student, I would be all over these numbers, which said simply, "If you sold to this community, they would buy." In my mind, it was like a gold rush for those who understood and controlled the marketing message to the African American community. African Americans bought and consumed everything but did not hardly own any of the businesses they bought from.

I found the intentional labeling of African Americans in the US census interesting. By its nature, it caused a perception of *we* and *they*, or blacks and African Americans. I saw that and said, "I have to choose between being black or being African American?" I then saw that *black* was not capitalized, but *African American* was in the reports. To the average American, that would not have been a real issue, but for people in business like me, it was. According to the census, someone like myself had three choices: to be an American, African American, or black. My choice to just be an American businessman was not an option for me. Believe me—it makes a difference when it comes to marketing. A fundamental basic of business is letting the customer know who you are. Why let others limit how your business is perceived by accepting a label of color that might be linked to politics or shortsighted stereotypical association?

Black, minority, and *African American* were catch-all terms, designed in my opinion, to confuse the buying community and to isolate the marketing potential of the business. Labels tend to define marketing programs designed for those business segments, i.e. black products being marketed to black people. However, to reach greater market potential and the buying community, one had to think green, as I used to say. To think green meant to label neutrally to any market segment, knowing exactly what your business is about, while also knowing that your business identity reflects what the business is and what it does. I thought African American business would succeed greatly if their positioning was correct and their marketing approach was on target. If you were an accountant, it was not necessary to be a "black accountant" when you could be officed where the "best accountants" were and be known as one of the "best accountants" in the area.

As I continued looking closely at the numbers in various market segments in the state of Kansas, I found my research of the number of African American businesses in Kansas City alone alarming. From the data I saw in the census, I understood why Mr. Tombs was thinking the way he was. There was much potential in the state of Kansas that was not reflected in the growth occurring nationwide. Just looking at the numbers alone, politics aside, I realized much could be done to make things better. But there were politics to consider, and I appreciated the role that politics played in local and state governments. However, I had no idea at the time how everything would play out.

Only a few African American businesses with employees were doing any major revenue. Commercial Express was one of them. Among the minority-owned businesses, Mr. Simm's company was at the top in revenue. I was never a top-line admirer of a business's revenues. I was not impressed with revenue alone.

Ranking the businesses according to their revenue and profitability would have been a better indicator of success for me. However, there was surely room for more multimillion-dollar businesses in the African American communities across the state.

Quickly, I realized that starting a African American chamber would make a difference and be a good way for me to give back to the African American community through the extensive business knowledge I had obtained over the years. I assumed many needed some assistance, even though I personally did not live in the African American community per se. I knew up front that it would not be a moneymaking venture for me personally, but I thought I would be rewarded greatly in other ways for helping African American businesses succeed. That assessment was true.

The odds of any small business staying in business were low and were even grimmer for an African American business. I wanted to know why. And how did one beat the odds? Why would there have been a difference in outcome just because a business owner was an African American? Those questions had been on my mind since I started my own proprietorship, the Leander Group, after my departure from Spencer and Spencer. Considering starting a chamber of commerce would require more prayer, time, and research. This I knew: business success was possible and very rewarding if the entrepreneur or business owner could conceive and believe the impossible.

Beginning in 2003, I made a point to copyright the materials I had been using over the last few years in coaching small businesses. All my intellectual material would be my own from my own experiences in business. I could officially say I had my own entrepreneurs' and business managers' seminar—"How to Drive Your Business: Getting into Business and Staying in Business"— produced by my company, the Leander Group, doing business as Right to the Point Seminars, which is registered with the United States Copyright Office. My material was right to the point and designed to help entrepreneurs make it past their first three to five years in business. It was a day seminar held on a private basis and included a lot of practical fundamental business information designed to ensure a business had longevity. I loved private seminars because more information could be shared for real solutions and strategies. At public seminars business owners ran the risk of sharing proprietary information with others in attendance.

RIGHT TO THE POINT SEMINARS

Year after year, industry reports say that only about two-thirds of businesses with employees survive at least two years, and only about half survive at least five years. There is no mention of color or ethnic background. As one would expect, after the first few years in business, survival rates flatten out. For a business to have longevity, it would take ten years, in my opinion. Though the critical years still would be years one through three, the main focus had to zero in on developing and maintaining new profitable business. If a business did that, longevity was assured. That was my solution to beating the odds.

Another explanation for the low success rate, in my opinion, was that many entrepreneurs, particularly African Americans, did not understand a known phenomenon called the change curve, which simply suggested that entrepreneurs tended to give up too soon and did not have the right type of support to meet the challenges of a new business. According to the change curve, things start out okay, increase slightly, and then take a deep dive until things get really bad. Then they make a correction and get better than ever. In coaching businesspeople on change, I have witnessed an increase in their capacity to be more determined when things get a little rough. If they just stay committed to making the business successful and continue putting in hard work with long hours, they become confident that all things are working for their good. That is what it takes to see successful change many times.

My past corporate success had brought me a long way from the living conditions I'd grown up in—conditions I had no desire to return to. Many of the leaders in the metropolitan Kansas City area were advocating a return-home message for young African Americans. Yet, I did not see any of those leaders living in the same neighborhoods where their schools and churches were in.

Like those who lived near me, I preferred nice, cleaner living outside the city, where it was more peaceful. I heard few sirens from police cars or fire trucks. My thinking was in conflict with the desire of local community leaders who advocated for more successful African Americans returning to their communities and bringing their dollars and investments with them. However, many successful African American leaders I saw were choosing to live outside the African American communities they represented and loved. They were not going back, though a few noble leaders did. There was no possibility of having one's cake and eating it too in that regard because there was no stated plan to draw successful African Americans back to the communities they'd come from. Much change would be required, and many safeguards would have to be put in place.

A functioning African American–run chamber of commerce could not bring past residents back into the community, but it could allow for their dollars to come back into the community in various ways. The primary deterrents were crime, drugs, and unattractive housing, which all had to be addressed for real and lasting change. I had this thought: *You only have community or a family when you come together.* The African American community would be forever split among the haves and the have-nots—that is, between those who could live with the drugs, crime, and theft and those who ran away from it all. Collectively, though, African Americans had everything they needed to proposer like any other ethnic group. The key was to communicate that possibility by having an active African American chamber of commerce that was attractive and accommodating enough for everyone to interact with the African American community at large. Change was a process, not just a simple act or show.

I began to see a chamber of commerce as a bridge or an interstate road, figuratively speaking, taking people from one community to another based not on color but based on what business they were in and what they had to offer. That would allow for the proper interaction and inclusion of others to exchange their dollars for products, goods, and services. The vision for a chamber I would run was not just a circle of black businesses that were only for people of color to deal with one another. That was not the American way, and that would not be a successful business plan in this day and time, particularly in Kansas. In fact, I was confident that African Americans as consumers had proven to support any African American business that promoted its products, program, or services in a way that attracted money. Also, America was about supporting culturally oriented businesses. We had China Town, Little Italy, etc. So clearly, there was nothing wrong with African American people supporting African American products, programs, stocks, and services. The issue was this: you don't know what you don't know. Too many African American businesses could not brand themselves in a way where buyers knew who they were or that their business was. Effective marketing was needed, and these businesses had to learn to properly budget this expense in their business plan.

I soon agreed with Mr. Tombs and Mr. Simms to start an African American chamber of commerce in the state of Kansas if we could contract a space on a low-rent basis. The chamber of mostly African American businesses also would work with the veteran businesses in support of Mr. Simm's vision for an incubator for service-disabled veteran-owned small businesses. My first challenge in putting the organization together was finding a name, because surprisingly, there was already a Black Chamber of Commerce registered in Kansas City, Kansas. That was strange because no one had said a word about it. In fact, the Greater Kansas City Black Chamber of Commerce represented

African American businesses in Missouri. In doing my due diligence, I found there seemed to be some image problems at the time with the black chamber. The organization in Kansas City had a questionable reputation with key corporations in the area.

I was also concerned that the title Black Chamber sent a message that limited the scope of its potential to lead the masses. I did not want anyone to conclude that we only had room for African American members doing business with African American customers. That perception would limit the affiliated businesses from reaching their potential. We wanted to communicate that our businesses serviced any customer who wanted to buy products, programs, or services. It was not good brand marketing to be profiled as a "black business" if you were trying to reach all your potential markets. With business names, business owners mainly wanted the buying public to know who they were and what they did.

After thinking through all of that and a few other key factors, I personally registered the organization as a new statewide minority chamber of commerce (SMCC). I handled all the filings, including the registration with the state, and obtained a bank account, and I was the official founder of SMCC, Inc. which was registered as a 501C6. We were located in a mall, in a back-room area next to Commercial Express and their developing incubator area.

I wondered many times why the Chinese could hire their own people and have the majority of the community patronize their businesses regularly. Jewish people had their own community centers and schools, kosher hot dogs, and food stores catering to the Jewish community. Italian restaurants had their Italian wines and pastas, which were fully accepted, just as all the Mexican restaurants served in English and spoke in Spanish. The only place well known to the African American community that hired African Americans and had an excellent brand in the Kansas City area was Gates Barbeque. Gates was an inspiration to me as I began the journey of establishing the minority chamber.

In getting the SMCC going, I first needed a person to create a business presence and do the administration. With a 501C6 with no funding, I donated my own funds to get started. However, more than anything, I needed someone to handle the phones. I happened to be at an office one day, doing business, and asked the receptionist there, "Do you know of anyone who needs a job doing what you do?"

She quickly said, "Yes, my friend Tamra Beatty."

I told her to call me, and within days, we set up Tamra's first and only interview. I soon interviewed a beautiful young woman who was very smart and had been taking college courses. However, something was not right. She seemed to be struggling with her confidence and was even shaking during the interview. I explained that this was a start-up opportunity, and she did not seem to mind. She just wanted to start right away. She actually seemed a little too excited to work, as I recall.

Her work experience and education indicated she had a lot of talent, but there was something going on personally, and I decided to address it right away. She was concerned for her children and told me her story in tears. The interview quickly turned into my helping her to cope with her personal situation more than she could help me with my business one. My skills in coaching were just what she needed. Our conversation ended with me saying, "Look, I am willing to help you. I can coach you through your current situation if you are willing to follow my guidance and help me start the minority chamber."

She eagerly said, "Yes! I will do what you say."

I took a disciplined and professional approach to Tamra's coaching. She took a profile assessment, which helped me validate her potential to do the job and strengthen some of her weaknesses. The profile assessment also provided unbiased suggestions for her to be more proficient. Tamra absorbed my every word and was willing to get objective feedback.

Many businesses have successfully benefited from the use of a profile assessment. Knowing more about Tamra helped me to gauge how much responsibility she could handle. Our main task was to control her emotions and build her self-confidence. She was a quick study, and I put her through a basic selling course using my coaching and previous sales management experience. Two things motivated Tamra at the time: she did not want to disappoint me, and she seriously needed the money she would generate from securing memberships for the SMCC. That was where her compensation would come from. We negotiated a minimal salary on a part-time basis, based on projected revenue from memberships and sponsorships. Tamra would also get a percentage of each membership. I then had her sign a coaching agreement with a zero for the services I was going to provide on a formal basis.

In short order, I knew this young woman did not fear anything but herself. She did not mind making cold calls, greeting people, or setting up meetings. Tamra was in a good space because the minority chamber was a safe zone for her to turn her life around. Within a month of heavy soliciting, we had enough members to start talking about corporate memberships, which she got a percentage of also. Now I was coaching her on how to be an event planner and how to promote the SMCC activities.

During that time, personally, I suffered a bit financially. After I paid Tamra and was reimbursed for expenses, there was little left in the SMCSS's checking account—but the organization was growing rapidly in reputation, numbers, and content. We were fully empowered by our members to address the challenging landscape for emerging and existing black businesses labeled by the US census. I preferred to refer to our members as African American businesses, but that did not complement the SMCC's name. We were mainly African American business owners but we were very clear about what our members did or could do. That gave us a lot of traction because we were not perceived as just a black organization. We were an emerging group of businesses ready to do commerce. That was the message. We started to brand the SMCC, and most people did not know who we were until we explained the meaning: Statewide Minority Chamber of Commerce.

We branded a different vision for African American business. As the founder, president, and executive director, I believed the most important attribute we had was a clear mission to bring African American entrepreneurs and businesses together for the purpose of doing more profitable business with any potential customer. Yes, we knew we were African American, but we also knew we had great businesses to offer to the community. We had unique ways of presenting ourselves to the public in order to draw customers all over the state. That was it—getting business for the members. All the other stuff was not my focus. I used my marketing and sales background to help each member with his or her business development by personally conducting what I called private strategy sessions.

More often than not, I found African American entrepreneurs focusing on the top line and not the bottom line. I would ask, "Are you making a profit?" and most could not answer that simple question, or they did not want to answer it thought it was key information. The strategy sessions mainly amounted to me sitting down one on one with someone and looking at the business and the business owner. A session was never about having a classroom full of people sharing intimate details about their businesses to people who did not need to know their business. Confidentiality was key, and I was able to provide appropriate consultation in real time.

In general, most of our members benefitted from hearing details about topics like finding low-cost vendors to increase profits, increasing marketing, wooing clients, dressing to attract clientele, having proper legal counsel in place, and much more. I was honest and to the point in each private strategy session. I would say, "I can either wait to see if what I am thinking right now is correct, or we can save some time if you give me permission to speak from experience about what I'm thinking. Now, I could be wrong, but I think I am probably right." Everyone gave me permission and that allowed me to give immediate feedback. What entrepreneur wants to wait?

After giving some honest feedback and setting goals for improvement, I would ask for just one thing: "Support the SMCC annual luncheon, and help me sell a table." It was no secret that as a chamber, we held our annual luncheons with a lot of class and professionalism. This was one way of demonstrating who we were and what we were about. It was how we marketed the SMCC, Inc. Our board was one-third corporations, one-third small businesses, and one-third community leaders. The way we were running the SMCC, the business-minded board members saw the vision and knew their ability to help raise money for the SMCC would ensure its longevity. The board would be a blessing in the beginning, but time would reveal the hidden agendas of some of the board members.

CHAPTER 18

Politically Correct

I learned a lot about our board members' agendas and politics as we pulled off our first chamber luncheon. I used my own credit card to float the funds needed to support the event's budget because no one really believed we would make it happen as we did. I had a good idea that things would go well because I had received personal commitments from every chamber member. However, somehow politics came into play as our sponsors raised questions about whether or not the event would draw a crowd worthy of the dollars we were asking for. When planning an event, all I can say is that the upfront planning and communication of the details are keys to the event's success. I was leading everyone to believe that the event we were putting together was certainly something they did not want to miss out on if you were a proprietor, entrepreneur, or planning to become one.

I knew the event had to be a success for the SMCC's creditability with our corporate sponsors, who had been promised features in our program and signage at the event for maximum media exposure for their products, programs, and services. I knew who had promised sponsorship dollars but had not paid. Many in attendance held their checks of support to wait and see who came. I found the posture of the notable Republican and Democratic businessmen interesting. Both quietly wanted to support what we were doing. When one side held a public-relations stunt during the SMCC's first annual luncheon—which was inappropriate because we were a nonprofit 501C6 and did not endorse either party—I had to take a bold stand for the creditability of all the SMCC members by making it clear publicly that we did not endorse any political party. With this declaration we ended up getting more dollars than expected at the end of the event, as no one wanted to be left out of the high level of participation.

The abandoned mall had not seen that many folks walk its floors in years. The parking lot was full, and the message was out. I had to conduct quite a few sidebar discussions to clarify that the SMCC was not and would not endorse any particular party or candidate. We were there to serve and build the African American business community and the corporate community at large by promoting all SMCC members and helping them to be more profitable.

However, there was a force in the community that was not comfortable with our instant success and momentum. In any community, the status quo is hard to change when they are benefits from the way things are. So, there was dissension in the air. Some things you just know. I received threatening calls when I was alone in the office, which brought back feelings of confronting gang threats and words of intimidation in Philadelphia. On some calls, I was cussed out. This kind of chastisement made it difficult not to feel bitter at times, however, my OCS training would once again prove beneficial for handling such instances. It reminded me to always keep my composure under pressure and stay focused on the mission.

There were times when my office manager Tamra was not around, and a well-dressed lady would want to meet with me alone in my office. It was the perfect honey-trap setup to get me caught up in some mess. I would address all meetings with females by requesting that our meeting be scheduled with Tamra until I knew them well enough. One lady would never show up again after I made this request of her. Fortunately, I had seen it all before. Some things you just know.

Someone even broke into my home and our office and took a few things that clearly indicated someone was trying to find out more about me and the inner workings of the SMCC; but I never said a word to anyone about any of the negativity because I knew it all was being done to discredit and disrupt what we were doing and the success we were having. Too often, when you are trying to do something new, some will execute block-and-tackle tactics to bring your efforts to failure. It is to be expected, and you must rise above the distractions and distractors. There is a strategy for dealing with these things, and I quietly employed it and dealt with it successfully using myself as an example. Because of how the SMCC handled its challenges, at every level of the organization, we still were having success and that was all that was important at the time.

By then, Tamra was full-time due to the number of memberships we had, and members were benefitting instantly from the strategy sessions centered on helping them get more profitable business. To keep tabs on our progress, I monitored and worked closely with ten chamber member businesses that I thought could scale up and handle more business. In fact, I helped some with their new business-development strategies and prepared them for key customer meetings. It was a huge success, and the group started getting multiyear agreements or contracts. It was then that I knew we were on to something significant. Securing multiple year agreements was a significant turning point. It was a clear way we could say that the SMCC was bringing value to its members and sponsors.

From then on, at our future annual luncheons, we could not only share details about our growth as a chamber but also talk about the growth of our members and how they were impacting Kansas's goals for economic development. The SMCC's vision was clear— continuous commerce in our community—and its strategic goal was to provide leadership for the economic development of its members, partner corporations, and the community at large.

The second full year of the SMCC was full of firsts. We had our first official ribbon cutting, which was covered by the press. I will never forget the photograph featuring the SMCC, Keith Slider, and I cutting the ribbon to welcome Slider Funeral Home into the community a few days before my birthday. It was an image of growth. Though his particular line of work as a mortician wasn't my cup of tea, they offered needed services to the community and I was very proud to see a young African American entrepreneur pursue his vision.

At the same time, we joined a prominent citywide Kansas City networking organization and were one of the first chambers to do so, providing resources for our members. The board of directors were very active and engaging making this journey a "we thing" as we continued to grow as an organization. They went above and beyond the call of duty to make things happen. Expanding our membership statewide brought in additional revenue for the SMCC, which kept our bank balance in the four to five digit range for the first time. Mr. Tombs was our chairman at the time, and I remember his words at our year-end board meeting:

> Days for covering up are over. People need to know who you [our chamber] are and where you are coming from. They have to see you and know you. Black America is in good hands. America will need you [the black chamber]. Your behavior is in your hands ... This is your fight. 2006 will be a make-or-break year. Establish what we need to know to win. Carry the word back and forth. America needs you [SMCC]. Do it now.

When the 2002 Survey of Business Owners (SBO) came out, it showed definitively that black-owned firms in America had grown 45 percent from 1997 to 2002, but Kansas was not seeing that type of growth. I issued a chamber press release when President Bush attended the Black Expo during that time and gave a speech in which he said the following:

We got some interesting ideas on how to build on this progress. We're working on a new initiative to help more African Americans and other minorities become business owners. My administration is joined with the Urban League, the Business Roundtable, the Ewing Marion Kauffman Foundation, and others to create what we call the Urban Entrepreneur Partnership.

What better timing for the SMCC to have the President of the United States of America advocating the same thing we were? He was even referring to people like me as African American versus black or negro, which were names associated with previous political movements. The SMCC was doing what the president was talking about: building on the progress taking place in America. Locally, the Ewing Marion Kauffman Foundation, which was headquartered in Kansas City, was part of that mandate to have more small businesses in the African American community. In fact, I was so in tune with what the Ewing Marion Kauffman Foundation was doing that I invited the president of the Urban Entrepreneurial Partnership (UEP) program to speak at our annual luncheon, which was an excellent draw for all the right reasons.

Our programming in 2006 was outstanding. Tamra, now our official office manager, created a 2006 virtual directory of our members, and we had key sponsorship from companies, including the newly constructed Kansas Speedway, which was bringing NASCAR racing to the state. Our host member, Commercial Express, provided great exposure to the local government. J. E. Dunn, Aquila, PepsiCo, Security Savings Bank, and Lowe's all stepped up big with significant sponsorship dollars. Most notable was Best Harvest Bakeries, which was minority (African American) owned by the Beavers family and Ed Honesty and serviced all the area McDonald's and the US military. Best Harvest Bakeries was a model company showing how one could leverage one's corporate experience to start a business of his or her own. There were a number of businesses that leveraged their contacts and experiences in corporate America to establish a reliable base of business starting out. This reduced the amount of risk and solidified the business relationship long-term. To be in this group of African American businesses was special and there was no desire to be labeled as a "black business." However, owners of these businesses knew that most African Americans would never have these business opportunities.

There were multiple success stories of African American businesses throughout Kansas, including in Wichita, Topeka, and other cities, that needed to be told the right way. Most of the businesses would not declare themselves black businesses and were reluctant to even say they were minority-owned businesses. However, they were excited to say they were successful businesses, and partnering with the SMCC was not a threat to their brand. This positioning helped with new business or was a source for suppliers or employees in the state of Kansas. I knew how to bring opportunities to members who were not 100% qualified to receive them. I gave partnering strategies to engage new business opportunities which made all of the difference. I was sensitive to ensure there would be a return on investment for the SMCC's sponsorship which surely made a difference to their bottom lines.

As the bigger money started to come in, we made it a priority to have the proper accounting of all funds. It's important to have the oversight that brings integrity to what you are doing and how you handle the money. Before receiving compensation for myself according to my agreement that I had with the SMCC, I solicited the services of one of our newer members: Five Star Tax and Business Solutions. Mrs. Marquita Miller was on point in the proper accounting of all our funds, reporting independently to the board of directors, providing reconciliations, and filing 990s in a timely manner. Most important, her honesty in keeping me straight about what financial practices were proper or improper would be something I always would value about her. In a strategy session with her, I gave her one key piece of advice to help her business grow based upon what I'd seen during multiple visits to her office. Kansas City was the headquarters for H & R Block and I knew this had significance. "Move your office location to where the major accounting firms are." I would advise. I went into the details of why knowing that co-locating with other businesses in your industry has tremendous benefits and some risks. But as they say, "If you can't beat them, join them." Mrs. Miller instinctively understood, and when she was ready, did just that in time for her next tax season. Her business took off in many directions. It was probably one of my greatest joys to see members' businesses and corporate sponsors benefit from their investment in the SMCC.

Working with a local design company, we created a new logo and website, which enhanced our brand marketing of the SMCC. Their creative work was the best I had ever seen. We upgraded our website to demonstrate to the members how important it was to invest in their own brand marketing. I could clearly see the impact of what we were doing when we partnered with UniverSoul Circus to sell tickets. We sold a lot of tickets and had a lot of fun with our families. Our branding was strong everywhere, and it helped us to drive ticket sales.

The rest of the year, we held strategy sessions and greet-and-eats in Geary, Sedgwick, Shawnee, Johnson, and Wyandotte counties across the state, sharing the SMCC's message and inviting potential members to our third annual luncheon. We even participated in Chamber Day at the Kansas Speedway and won an award for best attendance and participation. That was a surprise, but it certainly gave notice to the full potential of drawing African American entrepreneurs into NASCAR racing. In fact, that year, all who attended rallied behind Bill Lester, the only African American driver racing at the Kansas Speedway at the time. It was Mr. Lester who actually took time to help us understand what the sport was all about. He was so appreciative of the support we bestowed upon him and were thankful for his time with us.

Those were some of the little things the SMCC could do to make life better for everyone in all markets. With all that was going on, I quickly saw the emergence of competitive initiatives being headed up by prominent African American businessmen within the community. There was awareness about the great potential in the African American business community within the Kansas City metropolitan area. The SMCC had tapped into that potential without the sustaining budget that other 501C6 chamber organizations had.

The Greater Kansas City Chamber of Commerce and the Minority Business Alliance Inc. were promoting their POWER program. The Urban League of Greater Kansas City had a Business Development Platform and Urban Entrepreneur Partnership initiative going. These were significant and useful programs that I fully supported. However, of most importance to me were the findings that came out of the November 2006 Kansas City Consortium Disparity Study. Entitlements for minority business were the issue, considering the projected growth in that part of the state. The local government had a supply diversity coordinator put in place to manage the outcomes of that study for the mayor.

I knew the numbers concerning the disparity in business just by looking at the U.S. census data. However, correcting the situation by building and cultivating African American business was necessary to take on the emerging business opportunities. That was where the politics came into play. I knew the SMCC could help ensure that African American participation in those local and state-wide opportunities was adequate and proper. Establishing partnerships and training were key, as we needed more funding to make it all happen. Essentially, the capacity and capabilities of African American businesses were not adequate to support the emerging demand for minority participation in the economic growth of the state. This was a fundamental reality of supply and demand. In my view, it would take three to five years to develop the capacity and capabilities required of the corporate partners who had a vested interest in the economic development of Kansas statewide.

During that time, I worked closely with the Department of Development in all the major counties in Kansas and attempted to get up to speed on their strategic zoning and land-development plans. You often hear the phrase "Follow the money." I learned quickly to follow the zoning approvals, both known and unknown. To strategically build a business, one has to follow the politics of the local government in that regard. When you consider financing a major project, considerations of tax incremental financing, tax exemptions, tax credits, revolving loans, and more all are part of the calculus. That was nothing to be afraid of;

they were all pieces in the economic-development chess game, which I understood. However, none of that meant anything if you didn't have relationships with the right people, particularly in Kansas. Slowly but surely, the SMCC placed me in front of the right people, and I started building relationships that could make things happen. Still, something was happening behind the scenes that was hindering the success we were having. Some things you just know.

I think many people were surprised the chamber accomplished so much in such a short period of time. We did so because we were flexible and had the ability to manage resources that could best benefit the members. I did not need, nor did I seek, any particular acknowledgment for what I was doing. The best acknowledgment would have been to find a way to compensate me for the time I had given to the SMCC in accordance to my agreement; however, we had not yet reached those funding levels, and the SMCC board had not taken ownership of funding the SMCC's vision.

At the same time, I was not trying to be a hero of any sort and would not continue doing what I had been doing if the business community at large would not properly fund the SMCC long-term. I did not want the future leaders to have to sacrifice like I was doing. We had demonstrated its capacity and capability, and now our board of directors, business leaders, and the government needed to recognize our success by establishing some real funding. To that end, I asked for the revamping of the board of directors to make sure we had people who could help get funding for the SMCC long term. Thinking through a financially supported succession plan was critical to the chamber's future. Not enough people realized the importance of this. Why build a car, only to later lack the means to fuel it? Eventually, the former effort would count for nothing and no future progress would be made.

It was 2006, and the man who had put the vision in my mind died at the age of eighty-five in the month of May. Mr. Tombs was the SMCC's first chairman, and he must have known his time was drawing near, as he expressed a clear sense of purpose for the SMCC going into the New

Year. Things certainly changed after Mr. Leroy Tombs was gone. Mr. Alfred, the chairman of the National Black Chamber of Commerce, later wrote comments that made it appear that Mr. Tombs and Mr. Simms of Commercial Express had started the SMCC. He was right; in many ways, they had—by getting me to come to the table and make it happen. However, I clarified the facts when I needed to. I'd written and paid for the original paperwork for the SMCC. The record showed that I'd started the SMCC with my own money and I was fully vested in its long-term success.

Before he died, Mr. Tombs pointed me toward my next mentor— a good mentor in fact—in his stead: Bill Zirger, who had helped us get resources for all of our luncheons and had a lot of experience with boards. He had been close to Mr. Tombs and was a childhood friend of our Senator Pat Roberts who was from Holton, Kansas where Bill championed the Banner Creek Science Center for students. He was also a close associate of 1996 presidential candidate Bob Dole. His friendship and guidance were amazing in Mr. Tombs's absence. I could always tell when I was barking up the wrong tree, as Mr. Zirger would gently but firmly suggest I reconsider my plans.

Almost like clockwork, after Mr. Tombs's passing, I overheard a conversation between an owner of a major sponsor of the SMCC and their diversity officer. The owner said, "Look at what the SMCC is doing. Why am I paying you to create diversity programs if they are doing the same thing?" In my opinion, that type of thinking, by default, created a big divide between our chamber and all of the minority and diversity officers in the area. It would be equivalent to the proverbial strategy of divide and conquer and would be a good question that would motivate some minority/diversity officers to do more for the chamber, without being at the chamber's expense. Some things you just know.

Soon, the key minority and diversity officers involved with the SMCC began to distance themselves with their comments, presence, and money. I was surprised at first, but I understood their plight. They got together and held their own programs that mirrored what the SMCC was doing. Another block-and-tackle was plainly in play. Ironically, African Americans were the ones taking that action.

In 2006, I not only lost Mr. Tombs but also lost my dedicated office manager, Tamra, who went to work full-time with Mr. Simms at Commercial Express, which was a surprise. There she could have benefits and make a good hourly wage. She would still work with the SMCC but not as she had before. One thing I have never done was to prevent someone from pursuing a better career opportunity. Given the courtesy of advance notice, I would support their decision to move on as well as endorse it with a letter of recommendation. I fully believed in the adage, "What goes around, comes around." Therefore, it was always a good idea to do unto others as you would want them to do unto you. I believed strongly in the golden rule and in doing what was right.

A lot was changing, but new opportunities were emerging. Fortunately, a new SMCC business, Things to Do, proved true to their business name, as they were a tremendous help with the many things we had to do for the Annual Luncheon without Tamra to count on. Their business was mostly about being a virtual administrative assistant, and the owner helped me by being an in-person administrative assistant on a limited basis.

After Tamra went to Commercial Express, I formed my own business to take advantage of the opportunities for service-disabled veterans. At the time, all one had to do was produce his or her DD 214 and self-certify. In November 2006, I started The ClayGroup LLC while I was consulting with the owner of Commercial Express to help him establish what was essentially a building and building-materials business targeting affordable housing. He also had had a key role in the SMCC's development and held a board position.

With a following of about six hundred members, mostly African American entrepreneurs and sole proprietors, coming from all parts of Kansas to attend our annual luncheon and other programs, we went into 2007 with a more focused agenda than ever. By that time, we had joined the National Black Chamber of Commerce (NBCC), whose leader was a fraternity brother of mine, Harry Alfred. Alfred was nationally recognized as one of the most notable businessmen of Iota Phi Theta, Inc. and had started taking notice of our accomplishments.

At our Third Annual Urban Entrepreneurial Luncheon, he spoke about Mr. Tombs's legacy, and Mr. Robert M. Beavers gave a speech titled "Upscaling Your Business!" The event was a huge success because we had sponsors that included Cessna, Global Aviation Technologies, Cereal Foods, H&R Block, Helzberg Diamonds, and more representing more than just Kansas City, Kansas.

Also, to put a Kansas City, Kansas touch on the event, I asked F. L. Schlagle High School to bring their jazz band and high school seniors to meet and interact with the leading African American businesses in Kansas. I was also working with my contacts to have the staff at Schlitterbahn Water Park hire high school students from the Schlagle music program to provide entertainment at the park—sort of like what Disney World does their parade. To me, this would strengthen the bond with the community and also integrate the Kansas City culture into their entertainment business model. I believed by creating memories with the youth in the community, companies like Schlitterbahn had so much to gain from young people embracing their brand at such a developmental age. It made good business sense for their longevity and growth.

Without a doubt, our chamber was well positioned to do great things for the African American business community, contributing significantly to the Kansas economy. We were putting out beneficial business-related information using a newsletter we produced and authored, the *Observation Post*. It was important to have a source of communication worthy of a chamber member's attention. When you are growing a youthful membership, sharing fundamental business information is essential. Short and precise statements to trigger one's interest were key to bringing significant value to the SMCC membership and pointing the membership to professionals and potential customers who could help grow their business. It was all about giving back to the community for me and not necessarily about getting any recognition for the things that were going well. In fact, at the time, most members could not afford to compensate anyone for the kind of advice and support they were receiving. In return, most members were only able to render a heartfelt, "Thank you,"; that along with their membership was enough at the time.

African American businesses across the state were seeing and understanding the fundamental reality that a chamber could provide a safe, fair, and validated marketplace for commerce with the general public. It was a source of referrals and a place to recognize new and emerging African American businesses within the state of Kansas. The SMCC was accessible to the business community at large, and when we recommended members, I made sure they were capable and competent. That brought credibility to what we were doing. No other chamber of commerce could match our statewide recruiting, awareness training, and networking at the time. The truth was simple: we only had a powerful chamber of commerce when we came together as a community to support the SMCC. Creating those opportunities to come together was critical to the SMCC's success. When we did come together, we did so on time.

One of the interesting projects the SMCC took on was establishing a sister-city relationship with China. I traveled to China, where I received an official welcome and conducted discussions about the possibility of bringing NASCAR to China and having a contingency of people come from China to attend a NASCAR event. For me, this proposal was big and political because the SMCC was spearheading the initiative.

As we sought to finalize plans, all of a sudden, an organization from Kansas City, Missouri, popped up and took over what we had started. They indicated that there was already a Kansas City sister-city initiative in progress that no one in our community knew about. We yielded to the initiative, which included the Kansas City metro area, and followed the wishes of NASCAR, which had entertained our initial discussions.

Personally, I did not think it had to be an either-or situation; the SMCC could have been included in the discussions, and we could have looked at which cities each organization was engaging. China is a nation of many cities, and surely there was room for multiple business relationships with China. You might say the SMCC was international at the time.

The ultimate low of my tenure in running the SMCC was watching one of our members fall out of grace with the business community, chamber members, friends, family, and church members. Led by an aspiring young entrepreneur who drove a high-profile car and lived lavishly, the organization lost it all in what I came to call a Bernie Madoff scheme. In fact, he was a prominent financial adviser and active member of a local church. Helping young African Americans to manage their success is critical. An important fact to be aware of was that they were often targets for those who would want to mislead and misuse their success to create a public symbol of failure. The traps to see this happen are many and African American businesses with successful profiles have to be cautious and intentional about gaining success and protecting that success by listening and following prudent advice on how to properly handle the fundamental responsibilities of doing business in a fair and ethical manner.

All of that happened only months after Mr. Tombs's passing. Never had I been more convinced of the importance of having proper checks and balances in all business dealings. Reconciliation was a fundamental of balancing all bank statements and testing the movement of money to ensure access to any investment dollars was essential. With nothing to hide, I always welcomed an inquiry to make sure my business fundamentals were straight. However, I reflected on when my house was broken into and my personal computer was taken, I knew someone had information on the SMCC and me. I also knew there were people who questioned me because they questioned other SMCC members too.

When certain people wanted to volunteer and shadow me concerning the SMCC, it felt strange because they wanted to know only details about me and how we spent chamber dollars. Surely, every member of the chamber was entitled to know these details, but to observe me was somewhat insulting. Fortunately, I never compromised my beliefs and fell for the multiple honey traps or crazy political party offers extended to me during my time at the SMCC. I now knew that what someone wanted to do to me was serious, and maintaining the highest standards in business was essential. Some things you just know.

One evening, I joined a board member in doing business, and when it came time to sign his American Express, he gestured that he needed to go to the bathroom and told me to sign, extending his pen. I waited until he came back and let him know in clear terms that I did not sign my signature for other people. I began to see how someone could use entrapment in that regard to bribe people to do what he or she wanted. The old, "you sign for me trap!" These things happen in business and you have to be on guard the best that you can. Some things you just know.

You have to be on guard 24-7 in business, especially when you are a nonprofit organization. If you are successful in business as an African American, you can count on being tested and tempted to do things that could end up leading to your demise. My saying is valid: "Don't let your fun, folly, foolishness, or fantasies be your failure." At the same time, you can't let the many failures of others intimidate you into feeling that you're next. When African American businesses fail in the face of fraudulent schemes, you can start to believe you are going to be the next one to get trapped. However, I did not get trapped, and I avoided many of the devilish schemes that sought to take advantage of me both professionally and personally.

Soon two of our key board members who were diversity Officers and corporate supporters of the SMCC resigned. They said that due to my leadership style, which had never been questioned for three years, I needed to go. I was surprised to hear that. Almost instantly, the two board members duplicated what the SMCC was successful at doing, which essentially stalled the SMCC's progress and stopped the funding from certain places, including the Kauffman Foundation.

However, I knew they were not capable of doing programs like we were doing. We were empowering businesses to represent their own interests, and we dealt with business issues that were personal in nature and required confidential networking to resolve. I was making it happen through private, one-on-one strategy sessions, which I loved to do. In my opinion, emerging and existing small business owners often put too much personal information in public settings—in the chamber's case, settings that were organized by my ex–board members and others. Truth be known, I had no problem with other programs emerging—the more the better. However, what the SMCC was doing was working—and the numbers were proof. Everyone knew it!

When it came to helping entrepreneurs and small businesses, I suggested a nondisclosure agreement (NDA) for one-on-one discussions involving sensitive business details. I also recommended that letters of intent or term sheets be drafted before a formal contract was commissioned with a lawyer. Too many good business ideas were stolen or blocked by public disclosure in owners' quests to tell the world how they wanted to do business. It was important to teach entrepreneurs the importance of privacy and proper disclosure. My days as a legal clerk in the US Army served me well in that regard. I could read contracts with great attention to detail, and I recommended entrepreneurs do the same.

Restructuring of the SMCC after Mr. Tombs's death moved me to the position of founder-chairman, and we had a new president. Soon after, the new president asked me to move aside without cause so that more funding could come to the SMCC. That was the explanation given to me. It was a hurtful thing to hear that after I had founded and guided the SMCC to so many milestones. The bank balance of the SMCC was solidly six digits for the first time, with the majority of funding going to administrative expenses and our accountant, who could see how the money was flowing. When I was about to make a withdrawal to compensate myself according to my contract, members of the SMCC board started to wonder how I had survived two years with no salary and wanted me to expose more of my personal finances, along with the SMCC's financials, which I did. Surely, I was okay financially with my wife's support, or I would not have embarked upon the journey from the beginning. However, to be questioned the way I was fueled a sense of distrust which was unfounded.

I gave my personal time and my Social Security report, which had literally recorded a zero for two years. That was a clear indication of the personal sacrifice I was making at the time. I had no clue what was going on. The SMCC had money in the bank, and chamber members were reporting record sales. I had received no formal complaints.

One evening, I got a call from a close friend, who I am forever grateful to, indicating there were plans to discredit me in the press the next day. In no way was I going to spend my personal money to defend myself against some act of defamation. In no way would I put my family through anything like that. Whether this was a threat or not, being approached with that type of concern was the straw that broke the camel's back.

I immediately called an emergency meeting with the SMCC's president and resigned as chairman without a challenge or explanation. I asked my good friend Bill Zirger, who was on the board, to take my place and accept my resignation, and he did. As soon as he accepted, he boldly told everyone on the board to hold his or her hands up and then said, "No one here has holes in their hands, so none of you are perfect. What you were trying to do to this man and my friend was not right." He then graciously resigned, and we both left the emergency board meeting.

That was how the SMCC ended for me. Sadly, the SMCC board accepted my resignation as well as the resignation of my good friend Bill Zirger. We'd been forced out by a few African Americans on the board that I'd served faithfully alongside, who all had personal agendas of their own instead of the best interest of SMCC members or the community they had businesses in. I asked God why he allowed such a thing to happen, but I thanked him just the same for not allowing me to be consumed by those who sought to have the Founder and sitting Chairman of the SMCC removed from the board of directors.

I did not have one regret about my involvement with the SMCC. I knew I had provided something special and meaningful to the African American business community for those brief few years. The ten businesses I personally had coached continued to have longevity and benefit from the coaching I'd provided. I missed helping them with the challenges of doing business. The goal was to have fifty businesses in that group prove that with proper coaching and advisement, expectations for success were greater.

I think people failed to realize that God had appointed me to lead the SMCC. I had come with the sole purpose of giving what I knew many did not have: the knowledge and experience to overcome the normal pitfalls of starting and running a successful business. My spirit echoed peacefully the scripture Isaiah 54:17 (NKJV):

> "No weapon formed against you shall prosper, And every tongue which rises against you in judgment
>
> You shall condemn.
>
> This is the heritage of the servants of the LORD, And their righteousness is from Me," Says the LORD.

I did not want to be where I was not welcome, and I'd always believed I could succeed anywhere I chose to be.

Everyone speculated about what had happened to the SMCC for years and asked me what had happened. My answer was short: "I resigned." I did not give up or give in—I just stepped aside so that the inevitable could be. In life, you don't just waste your time where you are not wanted. I understood this priceless principle better than anyone else. In some ways, nothing is new. I studied Black Wall Street and saw how many had lost much at one time. I also realized how politics could stifle business growth and be a distraction while important business was negotiated without African American businesses at the table. In fact, we should not be at the table if we don't know how or have the wherewithal to stay at the table when the going gets a little tough. Just like in poker, no one walks away from a good hand. The truth of the matter is that African Americans, with their buying power, can sit at any table with the hand they have. We just have to learn to stay there and play all of our cards to win the game.

Another scripture settled the SMCC matter for me once and for all:

> And if the house be worthy, let your peace come upon it; but if it be not worthy, let your peace return to you.
>
> And whosoever shall not receive you, nor hear your words, when ye depart out of that house or city, shake off the dust of your feet. (Matthew 10:13–14 KJ21)

Years later, Bishop Steve Houpe and Harvest Church International Outreach in Kansas City, Missouri, recognized me for my contributions to the community. It was a surprise, and I was honored by the recognition, particularly with a tribute from my daughter Brianne whose voice brought me to tears. It was a sign that God was aware of what had gone down with the SMCC and my heart's longing for an overdue thank-you for fighting the good fight during this period of my professional career. The unselfish recognition from Harvest Church, which I had supported over the years, but am not a member of, was clearly a move of God. Sometimes in life, your blessing might come at another time and place. If you believe, some things you just know.

> And God is able to bless you abundantly, so that in all things at all times, having all that you need, you will abound in every good work. (2 Corinthians 9:8 NIV)

CHAPTER 19

The ClayGroup

Service-Disabled Veteran Owned Small Businesses (SDVOSB)

I'd had multiple opportunities to look at the daily operations of Commercial Express, which had been established in 1996 and had great longevity as an 8a company in the Kansas City, Kansas, area. At the time, one of the major concerns of its owner, Mr. Tyrone Simms, was that it had only until August 2006 to transition its 8a status, or he would lose his 8a business, which was in the millions. Riding out his last year of eligibility, Mr. Simms hoped his son would take over and allow the business to transition. I was aware of that in late 2006 when I was consulting with his company.

I was also investing in a new restaurant called Pelican BBQ, which would be located on Shawnee Mission Parkway in Shawnee, Kansas. I had always wanted to be part of a restaurant enterprise, and this was my chance. We had the right location, the best equipment, the best cook, an outstanding layout, and good partners. Our trial runs were impressive, and the initial reviews were noteworthy. I was a minor silent owner in the deal, and as such, I should have used my critical eye to assess what was going on with the numbers. While I still had my hand in the SMCC, along with this investment, I was also consulting with the First Step FastTrac program, doing general business training as part of the Urban Entrepreneur Partnership. However, I was particularly excited about the restaurant deal. Because we would be creating jobs in the community where I lived.

In this business endeavor I would learn an unbelievable lesson about business: you have to plan to protect your investment 24-7 at all costs because haters, competitors, or "the evil one that comes to destroy" (John 10:10)—whatever negative term you see fit— will surely come to hinder your success. You have to beware of the "Judas factor" anytime you try to do right and be successful. There was likely to be at least one person with a hidden agenda to sell you out. I'd experienced and witnessed it many times at the SMCC. It was hard to see such occurrences with a casual eye. An anticipating, critical eye was needed to make the proper threat assessment. Having a guarded presence was essential for seeing who was in your corner and who was not.

At the Pelican, although I was just an investor from the outside, I witnessed the takedown of the business from the inside. The opening was noteworthy. It was successful and went according to plan. The management expected a rush, and the rush happened. However, they did not expect the rush to keep going and going. The Pelican was so successful in a short period that lines of people would wait outside for thirty minutes. The food was that good. However, that sudden success brought the evildoers near.

The first lesson we learned was the importance of having cash for needed resources to run successful business. In our case, resources, such as food, were in high demand. Though having a line of credit was important, that did not help on the weekends, when the banks were closed, we needed more food, and everyone was paying by credit card. The Pelican ran out of food based on excessive demand. It was something they'd dreamed about but failed to properly plan for, which was a very costly mistake.

The next issue that surfaced was an internal problem with the newly hired staff. As we got into the second and third weeks, management received major complaints about the service, which customers once had rated as excellent. All of a sudden, reviews that had once been excellent, quickly turned bad. Management was so busy cooking that they lost their control of the service levels performed by their new hires. In their quest to hire employees to meet the immediate and growing demand, they brought in people who had intentions of ruining the Pelican's reputation. I called it out for what it was: sabotage.

To detect what was going on, I pretended to be a customer and witnessed the poor service firsthand. Food was late to the table, the presentation was poor, and servers displayed disrespect to customers. The restaurant quickly established a bad reputation, and the lines existed no more. As a result, the Pelican was overstaffed, had too little food for its high demand, and faced major cash-flow issues. It failed in short order, and I lost all my investment dollars in this venture. I should have pulled a Frank Clay and gotten more involved. All in all, we learned a lesson about not stepping back to regroup when things were going good. We were not prepared for success, and we lost a great opportunity by not selling within our means. We grew the business too soon too fast.

With the Department of Veteran Affairs taking a lead in helping Service Disabled Veteran Owned Small Businesses (SDVOSB) by promoting teaming agreements with major corporations to help them scale quickly, a new opportunity to do big business arose and it had my attention. Realizing the momentum of the movement, I started to focus on the ClayGroup and positioned myself to find partners to team with. In fact, there were corporations looking to team up with veteran businesses like mine to meet the president's mandate, which was backed by an executive order.

On December 22, 2006, President Bush signed Public Law 109-461, the Veterans Health Care, Benefits, and Information Technology Act of 2006, which told the Secretary of Veterans Affairs to "give priority to small business concerns owned and controlled by veterans." Also, Congress put emphasis on the Veterans First Contracting Program, which gave preference to service-disabled veterans. I had learned to follow legislation and the opportunities it afforded. I thought the act was big and could be bigger than 8a. What I also knew was the mission for the business had to be as big as the opportunity.

The day before my birthday, February 22, I was watching my favorite TV shows, *60 Minutes* and C-SPAN, and I saw a tour of the living quarters of the outpatient facilities at Walter Reed Hospital in Washington, DC. What I saw on TV reminded me of the military barracks I'd had to stay in while in basic training and on active duty. The bathrooms were deplorable, and I wondered why they had to be that way. As a Commander, I had put emphasis on cleaning the bathrooms, but we simply had not had the right chemicals and supplies to do as well as we could have. I knew the VA hospital bathrooms were not any better, with toilet paper on the floors and rusty old towel dispensers. I knew things could be better, because commercial hospitals did not have that problem. It was then that I uncovered the mission to use The ClayGroup, LLC to provide products that would help to make the VAs cleaner and safer.

Working closely with Tyrone Simms and Commercial Express, I developed a strategy to team up to market a clean-restroom solution using Commercial Express's main manufacturers. Commercial Express had a GSA contract, and in September 2007, after The ClayGroup had registered its CCR trading partner profile and secured a D-U-N-S number, we were awarded participating dealer status, which allowed The ClayGroup to sell janitorial and other products listed on Commercial Express's GSA schedule. With a cooperating contract officer who understood our mission, we were able to establish multiple team relationships in a short time to distribute products as an SDVOSB.

The ClayGroup soon became a master distributor, as Commercial Express was. Our teaming arrangement was not a partnership, and it posed some concern to Mr. Simms. On one hand, The ClayGroup, as a SDVOSB, surely was a threat to his previous business because we were being positioned as a participating dealer using Commercial Express's GSA schedule. This of course gave us access to his pricing and his strategy. Mr. Simms and I had to make a major decision that no owner wants to make. Giving up a controlling ownership position and losing control of the business's final decision making is a difficult thing to do; however, to take advantage of the SDVOSB directives inside the Veterans Administration, smart minds needed to prevail because it had to be that way. I needed to be the majority owner and 100% in control to take advantage of the SDVOSB programs being offered.

There was also another threat to the Commercial Express business as a result of the Federal Acquisition Regulation (FAR) being emphasized. Products that Commercial Express was selling in their generic form were classified as essentially the same, or ETS. That meant those products were on the AbilityOne list, which carried a mandatory compliance requirement and could not be sold by businesses like ours. However, the new public law required the VA to consider veteran businesses first, which was controversial among certain contracting officers. Yet that was the opportunity that everyone was speculating about.

Having a legal-clerk background helped me to read and understand the regulations as I broke each sentence down to strategize on how to approach contracting authorities. I had to know the Federal Acquisition Regulations (FAR), the legislation, the executive orders, and the public laws to be competent in approaching contract officers. I quickly learned that there were two buyers in the federal government: the user and the contracting or buying authority. It was good to be educated regarding both. The way to do that was to establish an effective capability statement using the format that contracting authorities liked to see. I was very good at putting that document together.

Many people in Kansas did not know at the time that while working at Spencer and Spencer Medical as the National Sales Planning Manager, I had been responsible for government sales, and I knew a lot about doing business with VA medical centers and selling off a GSA schedule. I leveraged this experience and got busy selling, and as a participating dealer, in just a few months, The ClayGroup was averaging $30,000 a month in sales by simply sending out a SDVOSB capability statement. It was a clear sign that the SDVOSB opportunity was real and could blow up.

Mr. Simms had a previous relationship with the current Office of Small Disadvantage Business Utilization (OSDBU) Director, whom was over the Center for Veteran Enterprises, or CVE. The CVE had been formed to certify SDVOSB and promote teaming agreements with major corporations to hit minimum participation goals. They actually had matchmaking sessions in Washington, DC. We found it appropriate to fly to Washington, D.C. before their annual OSDBU convention and hear firsthand what was coming down. The opportunity was real, and I purposely did not go to the OSDBU convention because I had heard enough from the director that I knew just what to do: get certified and registered with CVE. That was the message. I heard it loud and clear.

Like a waterfall, multiple unsolicited SDVOSB opportunities came into The ClayGroup once word got out that we were in business. I credited the passing around of capability statements to all the VAs in the country—so much so that I knew I had to now apply for a disability rating concerning my injury with the VA. However, I did not want to fill out the long application at the Kansas City VA Medical Center. I just could not get myself to do it. I did not want to re-live what had happened and I did not want the anger to rear its head again. Way too many people fail to realize the mental trauma that can stem from events during active duty. In my case, I think it came down to the fact that I was injured while following orders. Had I had full control of my life, I would have done something different and not put myself in harm's way. However, I was a soldier and I followed orders and got hurt. It was just hard to reconcile. Who does this? Well, our active duty soldiers do this every day. They put it on the line and they follow orders. When placed in the context of serving the country with honor, however, more often than not, veterans find a way to accept their sacrifice with honor, no matter how great or small it was.

Fortunately, I ran into an old Army first sergeant who made it his personal mission of hanging around the Kansas City VA Medical Center lobby, where manual applications for care were filled out at the time. He knew that far too often, veterans, especially African American veterans, had a tendency to be easily frustrated and did not have good interactions with the VA staff.

The challenge with the VA application process is that it forces you to relive what happened in the past, but it does not get into who, why, and what else was going on at the time. By the time I got to the section that called for explaining what caused the injury, I went into a pause mode of reflecting before writing anything down. I was prompted to start my writing by saying, "Signing up caused my injury!" But, I knew that wasn't the answer they were looking for. You don't really want to recall the details of situations, including facing who or what caused the injury, you just want to get up and leave. I was not immune to that mental state of denial. I started to leave with the government pen in my hand and tears in my eyes. At that moment, I just wanted to say, "Forget this!" and throw the ugly black government pen onto the floor. That was what I attempted to do; however, the first sergeant was right there and gently put his hand on my right shoulder and said, "Sir, hang in there—you can do it." I took a deep breath with watery eyes, trying to remember what I needed to do in order to answer the questions but not wanting to remember any of it.

Sweat ran down my face as if I were having a heart attack. I did my best to remember exactly where the incident had occurred, but I could not, because I did not know. The VA wanted me to know something I did not know. I wished I could remember; I would have gone back there and conquered the anxiety I was feeling. I never knew where I was exactly when it happened. It all had happened so quickly, during a special training mission in which we were transported by helicopter to a mountainous area where we had to use a rope in a dangerous monkey-crawl position. I could not finish the application without getting up and walking around to make sure I was okay. I prayed and gave thanks. *Only God saved me that day.* That was my final thought as I finished the application to enroll in the VA's system.

The VA evaluated me that day and took x-rays verifying my injury. However, on my way out, a VA staff member told me, "We see your injury, but we cannot verify that it is service-related." I almost lost it, and I left the VA mad and very frustrated. I did not want anything to do with the VA or the SDVOSB certification process anymore. I did not want to deal with the people at the VA period.

However, several days later, out of nowhere, while I was cleaning out the attic, my wife brought me an old love letter that she had just found in the guest bedroom of our house, not knowing the situation I'd confronted at the VA a few days earlier. To my overwhelming surprise, inside the envelope containing the love letter was my original copy of my sick slip on which I had complained in detail about my injury the same way I had written about my injury on the VA's application.

In the love letter to my wife, I complained about my injury in detail. I took that factual evidence to the VA as proof that my injury had occurred while on active duty. Within days, I had a valid disability rating, making me officially service-disabled veteran.

I immediately registered with the newly formed CVE and became one of the first SDVOSBs to be verified under the new program. Though being CVE certified was a business move, I never forgot the sergeant who'd helped me with the VA application so I could get my disability rating. I went on to coach multiple veterans through the same application process. Two veterans come to mind in particular. One was a Sergeant in the Army who was an electrician by trade. He was a subcontractor on a job at the VA, and he looked like one hell of a man with his tight-end frame and deep voice. I saw him cussing up a storm in the parking lot after having just left the VA: "That bitch! I could have killed her! Who does she think she is, telling me about the pain I feel?" He then ripped his long sleeve off his shirt and said, "See this?"

I almost fainted as I looked at where the skin had been so damaged from combat; I could see his burned veins. That veteran indeed knew pain. I had wondered why he always wore long-sleeved shirts in the heat of the summer. At that moment, I realized why. As if I were back on active duty as a Commander counseling a returning Vietnam Veteran,

I calmed the Sergeant down and heard him out. When veterans get like that, you just have to be there with them. Once the Sergeant had finished venting, we talked about next steps and how the VA benefits could really help him. I walked him through the VA application process and said, "Soldier, hang in there. You can do it."

Another veteran, Mike, was a golfing buddy of mine who worked on the railroad with a very good job. It turned out that over the years, he'd had heart issues associated with Agent Orange. I knew the VA had special programs and compensation for any veteran who'd done active duty in areas where Agent Orange had been deployed. All those years, he'd been paying high dollar for his medicine, when he could have received all his expensive medicine for free from the VA—but he wouldn't go there. I stayed on him every time we got together once I knew he was not getting his VA benefits. Nothing bothers me more than being in the presence of a Vietnam Veteran without his or her official VA health-care card. We finally made an appointment and went to the VA together.

Anyone exposed to Agent Orange had no problem being processed by the VA. Getting his rating and medical was no problem because while we were in line, Mike ran into a guy who had served in Vietnam in the same area of combat. The other veteran yelled, "Where the hell have you been, Soldier? You'd better come get these benefits—you deserve them." And my friend Mike certainly did deserve them. He got his high rating and back payments for his service and sacrifice. I was honored to help him in that way.

To this day, if I know you are a veteran, I will strongly advocate that you take advantage of the benefits the VA offers. The Commander in me will always look after the troops. There is some consolation when you have the benefits you are entitled to have. I want that for every veteran.

TEAMING: CVE ONLY

With my service-disabled status with the VA, I quickly developed a ClayGroup SDVOSB business plan based on what I knew. It was clear to me that Commercial Express would lose all its business if I did not step up quickly and put my foot into making the SDVOB opportunity work.

I didn't convince myself to jump all in until I had done my due diligence and would strongly advocate to others to do the same before starting a business. Having access to the client base of Commercial Express as an SDVOSB the basics of doing business with the VA and other government agencies looked very promising, The numbers just had to work out long term. I wanted to have a SDVOSB business for at least ten years—beating the odds of failure—and then have an option to retire. The owner's character is always found in the numbers, the financials, and if they are not right, the owner probably is not right. If the numbers are good, the owner is probably okay too. If the owner is busy and not reconciling the numbers to bank statements and vouchers, the character of the financials will reflect that. Knowing the numbers in your business is a good way to know a lot about yourself. I knew me. I wanted to know the financials inside and out going into the business venture, and I took the time to be confident in all my calculations to the best of my abilities.

The good thing about my primary market, the VA medical centers, was that it was based on a fixed number of locations. That made it easy if I knew a few predictable details about the primary customer and other medical facilities included in the customer count. The VA hospital locations were easily accessible by going online. Plus, being a veteran and taking notice of the full parking lot of every VA medical center I had ever attended, I knew that stays at the VA were short, which meant a lot of consumable products were used at the VA hospital at a higher rate than at regular commercial hospitals. The other notable was that most of the patients were men.

With my background in selling to commercial hospitals during my thirteen years with Spencer and Spencer, I was confident the new venture could bring in some major profits if managed correctly. The only requirement was that I needed to be in 100 percent control as a majority partner with Mr. Tyrone Simms to have The ClayGroup acquire the client assets of Commercial Express. The arrangement would have to be done quickly and with a high degree of trust between us. It was a challenge for Mr. Simms to give up his brand, which was well known as Commercial Express. That was a concern up front.

The major consideration of risk for me was in finding the right valuation of Commercial Express to make the deal legal, prudent, and acceptable. It was a huge risk for me as well. However, I knew taking calculated risks was necessary to be in business. I needed to be willing to accept those risks with a plan to minimize any unnecessary debt over time. Having myself as the 51 percent owner and being 100 percent in control would essentially put all the risk in my hands to a greater extent. I was now feeling the pressure of being in business on a personal level because failure would be at the hand of my pen and pencil, which made me more adamant that the business had to be run my way. I wanted to share control of the company, but I knew from flying on planes so much that only one person could fly the plane at the time, and someone had to be in control.

The structure of the SDVOSB program created that disposition and dilemma for the service-disabled veterans and their partners. It was a psychological illusion of the mind. You had a partner, but you really did not have one. Who would ever partner with another person and give up all control in a company when he previously had had all the control himself? No one. The government forced us into this predicament in their attempt to have veterans running the show. However, basic business principles would lean toward a partner sharing in the decision making and control of the company. Mr. Simms would simply have to trust me, and he had to make that decision soon, as his 8a status was running out. Under the new CVE program for SDVOSBs, you could not be a participating dealer; you had to be certified and have your own schedule. That forced me to make a definitive decision soon. The vision I had now for The ClayGroup was to have more diversification, which would require adding products to our GSA schedules quickly. More importantly, with audits soon forthcoming in the transition, I knew that having professionals managing that aspect of the business would help our creditability with our major manufacturers by making sure our GSA schedule was in good standing.

The essence of a good agreement was to craft language in the agreement that allowed for growth and proper remuneration and protections for both parties, considered the tax implications of the deal, and ensured Mr. Simms could be back in control if I decided to back out. Too many times in business, or in any close relationship, two people have a difference of opinion and attempt to challenge one another on the issue and exert their will just to make a point but usually don't make progress. I always focus on making progress and generating profits. I could care less about a discussion about whose point is better, because profits always win. In business, cash and profits are the bloodline of the business. You have to have them. I always say, "Get the profits, and then make your point." However, being ethical and out of respect, I always listen with a guarded mind toward protecting profits and cash. If you are going to take the time to listen, then take a notebook out, and soak up the informational wealth to aid in the decision making. You can gain much wisdom by listening. In other words, take time to listen for understanding and comprehension. More importantly, I had read in the Bible that two heads were better than one:

> Two are better than one because they have a good return for their labor: if either of them falls down, one can help the other up. But pity anyone who falls and has no one to help them up. (Ecclesiastes 4: 9-10) NIV.

After my partner and I cleared the air on our personal, business, and legal concerns, it was time to, as my lawyer's uncle would say, "Fish on!" Sales were coming in at a fast rate, and they were there for the getting. Everyone wanted to do business with an SDVOSB at that time. The 8a status of Commercial Express ran out, and when it did, The ClayGroup was ready and sales went from $30,000 a month to $300,000 a month rapidly. Our prepositioning of The ClayGroup's capability statement was strategic to our initial success. It felt as if we had done everything right to launch the company's SDVOSB initiative. Because we were one of the first SDVOSBs to get certified by the CVE, we caught the competition off guard as they struggled to get certified due to the backlog of applications that had to be processed. I knew if we got in line first, we would have the "first to market" competitive advantage coming out. Some things you just know.

With the VA medical center as our key customer, it was important to know a few basic things. First, it was important to know that most of the Environmental Management Staff (EMS) were veterans, and most veterans learned by repetition, so patience was essential for success. Everything had to presented and articulated over and over in most cases for maximum comprehension and execution. I knew that from my experience in working with soldiers as a military Commander. Second, I knew veterans loved to be hands-on to be at their best. They needed to be given direction. They needed to see something done and be able to do it themselves. Therefore, a proper demonstration with training was another pertinent factor for success. Third, we were dealing with soldiers who had sacrificed in some way for their country, and they deserved respect. That meant they were entitled to have a bad day. When they did, having understanding and just visiting with them versus selling to them paid great dividends. Giving respect to their ranks was also a big plus, because dealing with a previous first sergeant and treating him like a private, for example, was not good at all. The point is, it was a challenge for a veteran to transition to being a civilian and take on a government job. Knowing that helped when it came to communicating with anyone in the VA, which is truly a remarkable place, considering the tasks they are given.

Once we finally became certified as an SDVOSB and implemented a systematic selling approach to the business, our sales ended up being above projections quickly, and I had to slow down selling the products we had, because our line of credit was not big enough to handle the growth. I remembered the start-up and failure of Pelican BBQ and quickly worked to resolve all our line-of-credit issues. In light of the financial institutions, the dot-com losses, and reality post-9/11, it was a different story at the time to get approvals. Every effort to go to a bank ended in rejection, mainly due to the tight restriction on borrowing. One bank even thought I was pushing drugs because they could not follow our business model not having a physical location. A manager asked, "How do you go from $30,000 a month to $300,000 with no brick and mortar?" That was the bank where I had banked the most, and their senior management trumped the branch manager's recommendation for approval, to my disappointed surprise. I closed my account when that happened and learned a lesson about applications: you do not fill out an application unless you have a verbal agreement that your application will be approved. Yes, get that pre-approval first and then fill out the application to protect your credit rating. These institutions know you can't afford to have a rejection documented, which will have a negative impact on your credit record while the institution gets credit for their quota of minority submissions. That feeds into the narrative that African American businesses do not have what it takes to secure a business loan. Trust me, the banks can loan money to whomever they wish, so you just have to find the right bank or credit union who believes in your business model and in you. Share the information, but don't sign the bottom line until you have been verbally preapproved in some way.

I ended up going to the source of financing for the SMCC and made a commitment to Mazuma Credit Union that The ClayGroup would stay with them if they could extend a line of credit and find a way for me to have an interest-only loan. By our depositing the dollars we were projecting, other small companies could have a better chance of getting start-up and business loans in the community. We negotiated a healthy line of credit with a lockbox that would satisfy our partners who needed more security from The ClayGroup in order to increase its buying power. We used our accounts receivable as collateral to back up our line of credit, which was somewhat limited since we were paying our partners in twenty days. However, the quick movement of cash was attractive to every stakeholder supporting The ClayGroup's business. The average payment terms for a business like ours was forty-five days. We cut our payment term in half, which provided for an excellent cash-flow in our business model.

There was one other aspect of the business that needed a good eye on it: the credit card processing fees, which could represent a lot of profit dollars and could actually impact pricing if one was managing the business from the bottom line up, as I was. The ClayGroup was blessed to have me forge a relationship with a young entrepreneur named Brad Oddo. His business was locally known as Marathon Processing or, later, BASYS Processing, which was tracking to become one of the largest merchant credit card processing companies in the United States.

His company afforded us great creditability and provided us with a Peripheral Component Interconnet (PCI) compliance certification, which we marketed heavily to contracting Officers. We not only were the best SDVOSB but also wanted to be the safest SDVOSB for the government to deal with. Brad's business was in a growth phase, and he was quick to see the vision I had for The ClayGroup. As about 90 percent of our orders were credit card orders, partnering with a merchant credit card processing firm only a few miles away made sense. If we could save a point or two on our fees for processing more than seven figures a month, how much savings was that? Do the math! Some things you just know. The ClayGroup never had an issue with BASYS Processing or any other creditor during our eleven-year run.

CHAPTER 20

Defining What It Will Take

With an adequate line of credit in place and with one of the best credit card processing rates a small business could get, we had to implement a few basic actions to make The ClayGroup a success. One, we needed to manage the company's accounts receivable and make sure we collected what was due us on a routinely and timely basis. The task was more of an art than simply carrying out a fundamental business requirement. I would solicit Tamra to join The ClayGroup as my office manager as she knew how to collect money, having been trained to collect membership dues during our chamber days together. We billed intentionally on Mondays, Tuesdays, and Wednesdays to make sure we had maximum deposits or money in the bank on Fridays to pay our bills. That was huge in managing our cash flow. This strategy and area of focus increased the rate of collections that enhanced our cash flow tremendously. Next, we strongly marketed a SDVOSB hands-free dispenser program that carried with it no-charge installations and no-charge dispensers. The plan included my traveling seven days a week with the goal of visiting every VA medical center over a two-year period. I was a firm believer in the seven touches for achieving marketing success. My Spencer and Spencer experience and the spirit of their credo resonated in a motto I established for The ClayGroup: "Make the hospital environment better for the veterans first and their caregivers." I needed to see that all of The ClayGroup's partners and staff were doing that by offering products and services that supported our VA facilities. We wanted everyone in the VA to know that The ClayGroup was there to find solutions that made things better for our nation's veterans, their family, and friends.

Part of the formula for our success was knowing the buying cycle of the federal government and realizing that marketing continuously and routinely would pay dividends over time. You might be the best salesperson ever, but if the buying authority doesn't have any money or if there was not a budget for what you are selling, you have to wait for things to change. That reality was a neutralizing factor for all of us doing business with the federal government. We had to know how to play the waiting game until federal budgets were approved. We had to know how to get our product, program, or service on what many called the "wish list."

September ends the fourth quarter of the government's fiscal year, and there is a "Use it or lose it" phenomenon at that time, which I fully understood as a previous Headquarter Battery Commander. Basically, if you were given a budget and did not use it all by the end of the quarter or the fiscal year, you couldn't ask for more money the next time, because you'd failed to use what you'd been given the first time. With that awareness, buying authorities always spent heavily at the end of a quarter to use up their budget dollars. I always told my vendor partners to prepare for big orders at the end of a fiscal quarter. Many times, when spending was authorized, contract officers would approve those products on the wish list.

Again, the timing of getting an order was just as important as securing the order itself. One year, The ClayGroup got hit with an unexpected advance payment right at the end of the calendar year—right after Christmas, which is the end of the first quarter for the government. The advance payment had a great impact on profits, which caused us to pay more taxes that year. We learned that with better tax planning, we could have reduced the negative impact of our success.

We learned to have bills waiting to be paid if such an occurrence happened again in the last few days of the fiscal quarter. Having a good line of credit to tap into to pay bills in advance was also an important requirement for closing out the year when working with lawyers and accountants to minimize taxes. That was key for partners of an LLC trying to make a distribution during the first quarter of the new calendar year. It was also important to take advantage of discounts that could be incurred if we made payments early. A key to that strategy was to negotiate early payment incentives in our agreements. When you are processing a million dollars a month, a two percent incentive became important marketing dollars.

As with any other SDVOSB, the veteran owner was the figurehead for the business. People wanted to know who the owner was and what he or she was about. In other words, did the owner know what he or she was doing and talking about? I was more than qualified with my thirteen years of selling to hospitals and handling government sales as the national sales planning manager with Spencer and Spencer. More importantly, I was a veteran, and I used those facilities. However, I still had so much to learn when it came to working with the various contracting officers and other buyer authority locations. Reading Federal Acquisition Regulations (FAR) was my favorite pastime activity, and boy, did it pay off for the benefit of The ClayGroup and the nation's veterans.

KANSAS

In government contracting, if you are not pushing your agenda, you are being pulled away by another competitor's agenda. In contracting, there are people with power and preferences. It is not always about fairness unfortunately. Too many times, it's about precedent, preference, power, or politics. As a vendor, we had a right to fight for fairness, because if we did not, unfairness could reign in the end. On a side note, the contracting officer I started out with in Kansas rose in the contracting authority ranks and did the same thing nationally that he had formerly done in Kansas. I had to survive his procurement policies of exclusive standardization for eleven years. The first five years a decision made by this contracting officer locked The Claygroup out of doing business in our own state. That goes to show that one monkey can actually stop a show. However, when you are doing business nationally, you know there is more than one show and you learn to go where the "getting is good."

During the next eleven years, The ClayGroup recorded millions in sales, positioning itself as one of the leading SDVOSB companies that supplied janitorial products to the VA Medical System. We were on pace to install one hundred thousand hands-free dispensers in more than two-thirds of the VA medical centers within the United States. I told everyone, "The ClayGroup and our corporate partners collectively are responsible for changing the image of the restrooms in the VA by installing hands-free technology that promotes good hygiene and routine hand washing." As a veteran myself, I will always be proud of that achievement in my lifetime.

In the beginning, I competed heavily with another competitor SDVOSB stationed in Arkansas. At one point, we competed for new business at a VA medical center in Massachusetts, of all places in the United States. By then, it felt like the word on the street was to stop the momentum The ClayGroup was enjoying at any cost. Some things you just know.

I had a planned and scheduled meeting at the VA with the EMS chief in Massachusetts. Once I arrived at my customer's office, I was greeted and asked to have a seat at the boardroom table that was inside their office. When we were all at the table, all of a sudden, the sales manager from the competing SDVOSB in Arkansas busted through the door to the boardroom where we were meeting and threw his company's brochure and business card onto the table toward me in an aggressive and intimidating manner. He yelled in a deep voice, "Consider this!" I started to rise from my seat to throw his butt out of the meeting, but the EMS chief quickly held me back and told me he would handle it. He escorted the rude intruder out of his office. I had never seen anything like this in all of my years in sales. That was in-your-face, personal provocation, but I was never one to be intimidated. That was beyond the pale, as they say. It was a prime example of what people would do to throw you off your game when you are on your path of success.

GOVERNMENT

Not only did you have to face the competition, you had to accept the realities of some contract officer's indiscretions. There are clauses that give contracting officers a great deal of latitude when a decision is said to be made in the "best interest of the government." By and large, the government's procurement system works and reflects the politics of those in charge. To say individuals in the government process can prefer or not prefer one vendor to another at critical times, such as when awarding a contract, would be a statement of great accuracy. Considering the big task of contracting, most decisions are made with the best interest of the government in mind, but there are times when that decision-making has to be challenged because it supports the personal agenda of the buying authority.

To say certain individuals manipulate the staff and the system to achieve their own agendas of favoritism is sadly the truth when you look at some of the career staffers in contracting within the VA and other federal agencies. These individuals can and will intimidate, embarrass, isolate, and even infuriate you if you let them. At the same time, some behave this way to see if you have thick skin and will hang in there when an unfavorable decision has to be made. It happens. It's the government.

It was par for the course for me to challenge negative communications that were a concern for The ClayGroup. I had to prepare a proper response to address the inappropriateness of any action that put The ClayGroup at a disadvantage. I had to challenge because not challenging was silent consent. Sometimes, there would be memos that would be sent from staff persons within VA logistics giving directives to our customers that would imply their preferences for procurement. The thing about these communications is you never know how they are affecting your business until you start losing orders or opportunities. Part of doing business within the federal government is to make sure you know what is happening with your government customers. It literally is a full-time job. Making sure your company was in good standing was crucial.

The ClayGroup, under my leadership, had an impeccable record of passing all audits and inspections and being certified in a timely manner. Furthermore, our rating with Dun and Bradstreet was always acceptable, and our payments to creditors were beyond reproach. We were listed with the Better Business Bureau (BBB), and we never were upside down with any vendor. In other words, we tried to do the right thing at all times. We did not want to do anything to hurt our cause and provide evidence of being incompetent in any area that would disqualify our business for any new business opportunity.

I knew the importance of protecting the market share we had. We deployed every regulatory, legal, and political strategy possible within our means to keep our name clean and business dealings intact. Hundreds of veteran businesses lost business by not having the wherewithal to defend or protect the business they had earned, because they did not have their house in order.

I never understood why some contracting authorities said The ClayGroup, an SDVOSB, had too much business but were willing to give all the business to some other company. It did not make sense, but some people just didn't want you to have the business in the first place from day one. That was evident to me, and it was an ongoing fight to have The ClayGroup continued the success it had knowing that some people awaited our demise because we were doing so well. Some things you just know.

One of our biggest challenges came in an area called VISN 33, wherein The ClayGroup was enjoying the restroom paper towel business. We were experiencing abnormal competitive challenges. I realized the challenges were adverse to how we conducted business when we had a scheduled vendor show that The ClayGroup had paid for to promote our newest products. Inappropriately, the VISN asked me not to attend the show by sending the message through our vendor show coordinator, with whom we had a great relationship.

In instances like this one, I inquired about who was behind the decision and why I was being asked not to attend. You can never be afraid to ask? If everything is on the up and up, you will get a legitimate answer in return. If everything is not right, expect an answer birthed from diversion or no response at all. In this situation I was told, "Because you know all the staff, and you have the business." It was a tough discussion to have with the show's coordinator, whom I admired and respected for many years. She told me all that she could, but she could not give me the names of those behind the directive. Everyone was emotional and embarrassed to have this discussion because we knew what VISN 33 contracting was doing to me and The ClayGroup was not right. Though I knew I was in good standing to challenge the directive, I stood down to see how events would play out. Though I was not allowed to be at the show, my SDVOSB competition was, which was unfortunate and revealing.

Needless to say, I was disappointed. The request seemed designed to ensure that no favoritism was extended to The ClayGroup. We had two key rights in play: to defend our business and to attend the show after having paid the fee. The timing of all this left the impression that Mr. Clay and The ClayGroup were not interested in the business, because we did not attend the show. That clearly was a misrepresentation of our position and desire to be at the show. After all, we did pay to be there. No one knew I had paid to be in the show and then been told I could not attend. Those are the types of tactics that some in government contracting authorities use and that you have to be aware of. Everything is done for a reason. Some things you just know.

Following the show, there would be a Request for Quote (RFQ) for paper towel and toilet paper products we offered and more. I knew our product offering in response to the RFQ was viewed as much stronger, more attractive in appearance. It was also easier to load and use with a five-year warranty. It had a self-locking design and a low-paper indicator trigger to alert the VA staff when it was time to replace with a refill. Most of the complaints an EMS (housekeeping) staff received were about the bathroom running out of towels or toilet paper. With the number of veterans using the bathrooms each day, that could easily happen, so a low-paper indicator trigger was an important feature. The ClayGroup also provided additional dispensers at no charge for emergency replacements and would replace equipment if it broke down or was defective. Often, veterans took out their frustrations on a dispenser if it did not work, so in our RFQ response, we made sure an automated solution stayed within budget.

In fact, we were one of the three SDVOSBs to compose a response. One of the owners we knew had a background in contracting and knew the ins and outs of influencing an RFQ decision by using the evaluation process as well as knowing when to challenge and how to get a favorable decision using specifications. By that time, I was very knowledgeable about the ins and outs of contracting, but did not have the contracting relationships like those of my SDVOSB competitor. It was on, and a line had to be drawn in the sand. I knew if they won the RFQ within VISN 33, the same tactics would be used elsewhere, and the situation would go on and on.

In contracting, there was always a game within the game. In order to flush out what was happening with the specifications of our quote, we had to make the tough decision to question the RFQ and then protest, which we did not want to do. First, we needed to have a good case based on the facts and regulations in play. Second, we needed good lawyers and money to pay the lawyers, betting that we could win. I always considered protesting an award only if I was working to protect current business and I was assured that we were on good footing to protest legally. I essentially used current profits to save the future business we had at risk. This reasoning created a budget for all the legal-related services. In VISN 33, we had important business to protect, so we had to protest at all costs.

Not taking anything for granted, we protested with confidence and won. The game within the game was that the contracting authorities manipulated the weighted averages to favor another bidder in the know. For example, a competitor could inflate certain fees that would have a dollar impact on the total value of your submission but withdraw or reduce those fees without impacting their real pricing and profits later in the award process. It was clever but not honest and up front.

Frankly, I did not know the protest decision would end up being such a big deal in key case law. You can now Google B-406647 and B-406647.2, dated July 30, 2012, to see all the details of how everything played out. Many lawyers now use this case with their clients. Though all of that sounds good, I simply was trying to protect our business and the business of our mutual partners who did not want to touch the protest in any way. Filing a protest is tough business. When you protest, you protest alone, and if you win, it's for all those who mutually enjoy the current business, but you have to pay the legal fees up front. In our case, we got some of those fees back. Not many protests are won, but by the grace of God, The ClayGroup won.

The GAO also agreed with the Clay Group that the record failed to demonstrate a reasonable basis for the low and inconsistent scores assigned to The ClayGroup's quotation under the past performance factors. Although The ClayGroup had submitted past performance evaluations with excellent ratings, the agency had assigned the protestors' scores as "below satisfactory" and "below marginal" with no explanation in the record. I call that blackballing your bid submission. When that happens, you have no choice but to protest to have the situation challenged; however, you can only find this type of information if you protest. The key is, you have to have the money up front to pay the lawyers to get involved and assess the situation before fully committing to the protest. I maintained a budget for legal fees each year, which allowed me to have the money to make the right decision.

The GAO even found that contacting authorities had helped my competition by allowing them to address their shortcomings in their submissions but ignoring The ClayGroup in that regard. That behavior was comparable to restricting me personally from being at a scheduled vendor show. Some might have called that discrimination, but I could not afford to go there. Filing accusations of discrimination makes even lawyers nervous because people get personal and emotional in those types of cases.

I'd rather protest on the facts and let a judgement on the merit produce a final outcome.

At times, the VA and my competition wanted to put a stop to our business model, which was working well for us. For five years, we'd been taking major market share. A win for my competition and non-supporters could not come on the merits of the product offering, quality of representation or the benefits to our veteran so it always had to be another challenge. Sometimes in business, people feel they have to fight dirty. When they played dirty, their actions brought out the Philly or military in me. I just wanted to run a good business and compete cleanly as long as I could. The GAO decision is a must-read for those doing business with the government, as it will open your eyes to how things can go behind the scenes when you are doing your best to make a good-faith response to an RFQ but others have a different agenda of manipulation.

A GAO protest is costly when you use the best lawyers. Reading the GAO's evaluation and conclusion—"We sustain the protest"—was satisfying; however, knowing that The ClayGroup is part of key case law is also rewarding because we have contributed to making life better for other SDVOSBs out there who could not or cannot afford to protest. As a previous legal clerk for the US Army, I took pride in helping to prepare our legal case with our legal team when we submitted our concerns to the GAO.

While we were awaiting that decision, other challenges popped up as The ClayGroup celebrated its fifth year in business. We had beaten all the odds and significantly grown the business to the point that our partners were threatening a move to cancel our independent distributor agreement. Still, going into 2013, despite all those challenges, The

ClayGroup was doing well, and the business was adequately staffed, with my daughter and son-in-law working for me. Their presence had an impact on me. I had my daughter and son-in-law call me "MC"—for Mr. Clay—which was a breakthrough in communication. We kept the office businesslike at all times, and I never discussed company business on weekends, which were designated as family time. I enjoyed my entire staff, but being around and talking with my daughter almost every day was a blessing—something most parents don't get a chance to do. In a way, it made me work harder because I wanted my family to see me working hard and being successful.

Our SDVOSB status had gotten The ClayGroup into the janitorial and sanitation business quickly, and we had diversified and built The ClayGroup on a strong value-added proposition. With our GAO victory, I made a commitment to be in Washington, DC, once every three months to see and hear firsthand what was going on. I was in Washington on July 28, 2011, to hear the witness testimony of the executive director of small and veteran business programs of the Office of Small and Disadvantaged Business Utilization (OSDBU), US Department of Veterans Affairs. Our agreement with our network of independent distributors was stronger than ever now that we had secured the VISN 33 business and been victorious with our GAO protest. In fact, contracting authorities were very much on guard about how they treated SDVOSBs in all their solicitations. However, there were some who resented the fact that The ClayGroup had gotten its way and who paid little regard to the improprieties that were improperly carried out in the VISN 33 solicitation.

Someone told me we were cited in the *Bid Protest Weekly* on July 30, 2012, and I knew this was not over by any means. In fact, another GAO decision, B-405727, favoring an SDVOSB had to go to the Supreme Court. It dealt with the recommendation that the VA again had to conduct market research regarding its procurements. If the results determined there were two or more SDVOSBs, then dismissals would be in order. These would ironically be African American–owned SDVOSBs like The ClayGroup.

Every year, The ClayGroup was improving, making major changes year after year. I first moved the office and then got a new phone system to handle more calls. Then we got better software to process more orders, established better banking relationships, and got new furniture. Now it was time to empower the staff. Tamra, my office manager, was doing many new and dynamic things; however, the one thing we were doing better than anyone was billing on a timely basis and paying our key vendors in twenty days. My favorite person for this was Marlena. She seemed to know the customers well enough to get their payments on a routine basis. On a side note, I learned a lot from Mr. Watson, Marlena's Dad. One day, it was raining and Mr. Watson was in his business best suit. I saw him changing his daughter's flat tire at his elder age. It has stayed with me for life that I need to always be ready to be there for my girls. Fatherhood never stops. Having relationships like I had were priceless. Having a staff and friends like I did was a true blessing to my business and me personally.

CHAPTER 21

Hard to Do without You

It was time to place an employee in charge of sales at The ClayGroup. We needed to put someone in place who would take The ClayGroup to the next level while I would take on a new role. I chose an old Georgia Pacific (GP) employee who lived in Florida and had previous sales experience as a janitorial and sanitary supply distributor, and he knew the workings of corporate America. More importantly, he knew me and my ways. Ken Thomas had my intensity, boldness, and honesty. He knew my partner, Mr. Simms, and all our vendors. I brought him on board and made him my Vice President of sales and he was to report directly to me. In a lot of ways, we were alike, as evidenced by one direct conversation we had during our introduction to each other for his position. Ken was intense and put me on the spot to test me, saying, "You know, I don't need you or the job."

To his surprise, I said quickly, "You know, the job doesn't need you, and I don't need you either. Now that that is out of the way, let's go to work!"

We laughed hard together and got down to business. Ken always said, "Frank, you are doing the right thing. If you keep doing the right thing, everything will work out."

I would say to Ken, "I do not want to keep doing this business if you are not around."

Ken and I became good Christian friends doing business together with all of our strengths and imperfections. One thing was for sure, we were praying for one another all the time.

Ken believed in the vision I had for The ClayGroup, which was to improve all the restrooms in the VA Medical System and other federal agencies. To make them better, we needed to train the housekeeping staff about the emerging supplies and technologies that could make their jobs more efficient. I wanted that vision to extend to all federal agencies, particularly the Department of Defense. We both believed the products, programs, and services we were selling were the best in the industry. I remembered my mother and grandmother in pursuing this mission. Both had been housekeepers, and I saw all the housekeepers in the VA doing their work the old-fashioned way: mopping floors improperly; wasting trash bags; using cheap cleaning materials that streaked; and repeatedly going to towel dispensers that were old, fragile, and they were in frequent need of refilling. This was the situation we were facing in the early days of The ClayGroup. I wanted better for these government workers and our veterans. I knew what commercial hospitals were providing to make their restrooms look amazing. Our goal was to bring the same thing that same array of products to the VA Hospitals and other medical facilities.

Ken took The ClayGroup to another level by leveraging the support of the distributor community, which he knew well—much better than I did. From that perspective, I really did need him. At the same time, Ken knew our mission was an SDVOSB play, and he was not a veteran. He also knew that he needed me to help him chart those waters and that I needed to be in DC, staying on top of the policies and legislation that were impacting our business. Together we were one hell of a team, constantly exchanging ideas and approaches to be successful in business. With Ken in the picture, I was able to work the relationships I had and bring solutions to the VA to solve their problem. Ken would manage the operations and distribution end of the business.

In addition to Ken's help, I had a number of VAs I could call on that would give me honest feedback on any idea I put out there. In commercial-world terminology, I was sampling to gain information and feedback within the targeted market we were focused on. I valued the opinions of EMS chiefs in the VA, such as Mr. Diggs, Ms. Triggs, Mr. Carter, Mr. Lesane, Mr. Hill, Mr. Anderson, Ms. Taylor, Mr. Patton, and Mr. Hayes, Ms. Brewington, and others. I would be forever grateful to each of these professionals for their time and honest feedback. I tactfully approached each of them to assess not only what we were doing but also how we were doing things to make things better; ensuring we were never offending a veteran or violating VA protocols and regulations.

I learned that a silent response was valuable. They knew I would never press for clarity on any concern I had. They could support what we were doing, or they could choose not to support what we were doing; either was okay with me. At the core of what The ClayGroup was doing was a simple desire to make things better for our veterans. I never wanted to promote any product, program, or service that was not supported by this core group. If they were excited, then I knew we were on to something special.

Being in Washington, DC, at the beginning of 2013 paid off because I was made abreast of the last in-person pre-solicitation industry meeting scheduled by the GSA, which was a public forum to say, "Get ready, all you distributors, because you are going to lose your business." As I sat in the meeting, I looked around and said to myself, *This is a setup.* It was an attempt to wipe out the SDVOSB supply and distribution network that supported the VA. What was being discussed strategically was restrictive and eliminating. As an example of the restrictiveness of what was being proposed, to qualify to bid, a contractor needed to be AbilityOne certified, and The ClayGroup was not. I had come to a public meeting in which I was told that we were going to be locked out of doing business in the future. Without an AbilityOne certification, The ClayGroup could not even bid to save all the business I had; yet we were not included in all the discussions. At that moment, I had a chance to say something, but I did not want to do it. The palms of my hands began to sweat as I fought thoughts of reacting to what was being said. I sat at the end of the row taking note of the microphone stand that was right next to me. I took that as a sign from God to stand up and speak out on the injustice being paraded as a small-business-friendly program wherein twenty-one out of a thousand distributors would enjoy all the business, and over 900 businesses would be cut out. I figured that The ClayGroup already had the majority of business in the paper category. This whole strategy was clearly about taking The ClayGroup's business. Some things you just know.

We were told, "The government agencies have committed to the FSSI [Federal Strategic Sourcing Initiative] BPA [blanket purchase agreement] programs, but they're not mandatory." Early in the meeting, they specifically stated, "These BPAs are not mandatory at this time."

The longer I sat there the more I felt that I had to say something. I had to grab the microphone and say how I thought the proposition they were explaining was unfair because my company, The ClayGroup, had most of the paper business and couldn't get certified by AbilityOne, thereby locking us out. After explaining that I had already submitted my application a few times with no response, I finally asked the question, "Why should The ClayGroup be restricted from participating in this FSSI solicitation?" I said more, expressing my feelings about how SDVOSBs would be disenfranchised by what they were doing, sweating nervously the whole time, knowing the meeting was being recorded for public record.

At least I got it out and said my piece; not just for The ClayGroup but also on behalf of all the SDVOSBs that were not in my position. After I spoke, a lady in GSA who was visiting with the AbilityOne representative, who was a veteran, quickly sidelined me and insist that I talk with the AbilityOne representative. We went to lunch in

Washington, DC, right down the street from the meeting, and I paid for the most expensive lunch I had ever had. It was good, though, and before I finished lunch, The ClayGroup was AbilityOne certified. I was silenced because I was certified now and I was authorized to participate in the bid process that was essentially targeting The ClayGroup's SDVOSB business.

After many challenges and requests for clarification, in August 2014, the FSSI BPAs were awarded, and The ClayGroup was not chosen. Though we had staffed up and upgraded our systems in preparation for the good news, it was not to be. We were not alarmed because we were also prepared for that outcome, having made sure the products we were selling were not on the solicitation, nor were they AbilityOne. In fact, we had secured our own BPA which was just awarded, and it covered us through 2018 thanks to the good work of my Vice President, Ken Thomas, on the West Coast.

As 2014 ended, we had surpassed $10 million in sales and were closely approaching our tenth year of excellent service to the VA, despite the multiple threats to our business. I looked at a survey from our industry and saw that only 15 percent of all distributors were national, The ClayGroup being one of them. The average distributor was selling just a little more than $3 million per year in our segment—we were selling more than three times that. We continued to be recertified time and again when enduring multiple inspections announced and unannounced.

The ClayGroup was a well-run machine, and I had the best inside staff money could buy, headed by the young lady I'd met putting the chamber together, Tamra. In fact, The ClayGroup was supporting four single mother families all working hard to take care of their children and put them through school. We had a great work and family policy. We were hitting all our numbers, even with all the ups and downs we all had professional and personally. In the upcoming year, however, things changed.

President John Kennedy's father is credited with the following quote: "When the going gets tough, the tough get going." That is so true if you are going to be successful during challenging times. Going into the new year, I visited with Ken and developed a business strategy to allow him to run The ClayGroup and give him full reign for six months to see how he would work out. The plan was to turn the overall management of the business over to him if all went well.

In February, as I turned sixty, my staff uncovered an email issued to the VHA contracting Officer leadership for the VA hospitals from VA Logistics Headquarters that required all the contract authorities to buy from an FSSI awardee only. These companies were our direct competition. This was an important concern to our business. It signaled that D-day for the rollout of this directive was soon. The Government Services Administration (GSA) and the VA were teaming up to take all decision-making power from our EMS customers. They now had no say in the choice to buy from The ClayGroup. It was an unprecedented act that disregarded the fact that The ClayGroup had a valid GSA schedule. In fact, we had two valid GSA schedules that allowed for a buying authority to use The ClayGroup as a supplier. We also had an active BPA that was good through 2018. Yet, this new logistical directive overrode our legitimate status as a valid GSA holder to take orders.

I was forced to make another bold decision on two fronts by requesting a congressional inquiry and paying my DC lawyers to file an injunction—something I had never heard of before. That was our only recourse because within weeks, we lost more than $300,000 in sales due to this VA logistics directive. My staff was so alarmed that they begged me to do something to put a hold on this activity. What I knew was that we had to demonstrate a major loss to get everyone's attention and to prove a negative impact on The ClayGroup's business. I couldn't believe the way VA Logistics was treating a successful SDVOSB. I was given no notice, and had we not uncovered the email, we would have been put out of business by this miniscule communication from the VA Logistics Headquarters.

It took a lot of work to get our facts together to figure this one out. The ClayGroup was about to find itself in a war with the same organization it was trying to help out: The VA. I was told that pushing the legal agenda by a strong counter response to the unfavorable email would be problematic and that we needed to find another way to work with the VA. I agreed. Going legal in Washington, DC, was like setting a fire near your own home. Whatever you were burning could end up burning your house down too. However, a proper counter response to the action levied upon The ClayGroup surely had merit if The ClayGroup was to continue servicing the VA. One thing was for sure: if we did not act, it was all over. With all the resources we could muster, The ClayGroup successfully filed an injunction to temporarily stop the VA from halting our orders. This allowed our customers to still purchase from The ClayGroup.

LOSING A LIGHT

September 14, 2015 was a day I will never forget. It was on par with 9/11, when the Twin Towers fell. I was in the office early, which was unusual for me. By the time I got there, Tamra had opened the office, and the coffee was ready. She was the one to keep the light on for me when I traveled weekly. It was a Friday, and Tamra and I stayed late that day. She shared how happy she was; her daughter had graduated from high school, and Tamra had just taken her to college that week. Years before, I had assured Tamra she would see a day when she and her daughter would be on the same page and free to express their love and admiration. Like many single mothers, Tamra had struggled and sacrificed quite a bit for her children with the hope that one day everything would work out for the good.

Tamra had many good days coming to her. Tamra was about to walk to receive her own diploma. I'd encouraged her time and again to finish her degree, and now all that encouragement was about to pay off. In fact, she had gotten a raise for showing me her transcript. I was so proud of her in that moment.

On the Monday morning after our one-on-one powwow on Friday, my daughter was on the phone, repeatedly calling Tamra's cell phone, as she hadn't shown up to work. Remarkably, Tamra's baby son answered the phone, and my daughter sensed something was wrong. It was unusual for the staff to talk to Tamra's son for that long. Normally, Tamra would have picked up the phone by now. "Something is wrong," I said. I told my staff to keep him on the phone and use the other line to call 911. I rushed out of the office and headed to Tamra's house. By the time I got there, the police were there and were knocking at the door and looking inside the windows. They were about to leave, when I ran toward them, telling them they had to go inside. I insisted, saying, "I am Tamra's boss, and my office is talking to Tamra's son inside there, and there is something is wrong."

The police found an open window and went inside. They came out with Tamra's son in their arms and gave him to me. It was like a movie scene. How had I gotten into that position? What was I to do, and where was Tamra? Then they pulled out the yellow tape as the ambulance rushed into the driveway, and the EMTs got out with their equipment rushing to the front door. The ambulance staff went inside and came right back out. I wanted to say, "Wait a minute. Tamra is in there—go back." The police came out and told me Tamra had been pronounced dead right as her sister came onto the scene. It was a long morning, as I had to go with the police to tell Tamra's mother the news and go back to the office to comfort my staff. It was tough.

Tamra had been the heart of The ClayGroup, and for days, I drew a heart with a different color on our dry board until there was no room for another one. I had to give remarks at her funeral, and that was tough as well. All our customers had known Tamra well because she'd been cheerful and down to earth. She'd share her concern by doing what she could to make things better for veterans. She showed us all how to take care of the customer. She'd been there with me from the beginning and losing her took a lot out of me and out of the team. It was a challenge for months and every time I look back on this memory, the one-word question that remains is, "why?"

Tamra had been special, but now we had to find a replacement for her. Brianne, my daughter, who had shadowed Tamra for months as a backup, performed two jobs as we interviewed quickly. As the candidates were presented, I turned to Brianne one day and said, "You might do well to find someone who can help us get through this period of grief. Hiring simply the most skilled and experienced candidate might be a waste of time." Tamra had taken much intellectual property with her when she left us. However, at the moment, we just needed a smiling face—someone to answer the phone while we figured things out. By the grace of God, we found the right person, a lady named Tracey. With her presence, we started to rebound from there. Tracey helped us as we helped ourselves recover.

Only two months later after losing Tamra, we took another blow to the back. The injunction we filed against the VA was reversed, and the reinstatement of the mandatory-use memorandum supporting FSSI JanSan was issued on November 2, 2015. My lawyers in Washington, DC, advised me not to appeal because matters were addressed behind the scenes that would somehow allow us to continue doing business for a little while longer. Washington, DC, is funny like that. It was the second time I'd been told I was better off not saying anything and to just let things work themselves out. In retrospect, I realize the judge saved The ClayGroup's business because she took the sting out of the initial rollout of the VA Logistics Directive and gave many people time to consider what was really going on. I took my lawyers' advice because with Tamra gone, we just didn't have it together to fight another battle anytime soon.

However, the Supreme Court decision on the Kingdomware case in February 2016—another must-read for an SDVOSB—gave us additional hope. The decision brought a preference for the mandatory use of an SDVOSB under the rule of two. GSA and the VA were against a favorable ruling, considering the reinstatement of the mandatory-use memorandum supporting FSSI JanSan issued by the VA. What I never understood was why the VA created a program for Veterans to team with larger businesses, made us jump through hoops to have us certified, and then turn around and support an initiative to wipe us all out in the name of this mandatory use program that supported GSA's Federal Strategic Sourcing Initiative and the AbilityOne program. Why would the Veterans Administration be against veteran business like The ClayGroup but be so supportive of AbilityOne—an industry that supported the blind? Both groups were disadvantaged. All this was going on while the federal government was investigating AbilityOne for fraud, which I had experienced firsthand.

With a signal to keep doing business as usual, I sought to meet with the OSDBU from the VA and GSA in February 2016 in Washington, DC, to validate our GSA schedules and our BPA, which was good through 2018. On my birthday, February 23, 2016, I got a birthday present from the OSDBU of GSA: a memo on GSA letterhead that said, "The ClayGroup is in good standing for the following contracts under the MAS program." That meant any federal customer could still buy off our GSA schedule.

We circulated that letter among our buying authorities and alerted our buying customers, which seemed to neutralize the reinstatement of the exclusive mandatory-use memorandum supporting FSSI JanSan BPA. We got more help when, in June 2016, the Supreme Court ruled that the VA had to apply the rule of two in all contracting decisions. That was great news for all SDVOSBs and embarrassed the opposition in the Office of Acquisition and Logistics, causing the OSDBU to reverse their positions to support the FSSI BPAs only.

While the higher-ups in the Office of Logistics and Acquisition were modifying SDVOSB policy, the strategic sourcing program manager at the Department of Veteran Affairs sent an email to all of The ClayGroup's end-user customers in EMS (housekeeping). The email was strategic and intentionally framed a negative impression of the excellent work The ClayGroup had done to work with its manufacturers to create a hands-free environment within the restrooms in all VA facilities. We'd found a way to standardize the restrooms in more than 100 of the 150-plus VA hospitals, which was a goal of the VA.

The end of the memo got personal, and everyone knew it, but no one would call it out. The reference in the communication would be singling out The ClayGroup, which serviced all the equipment and paper towels we had placed for the past ten years. We visited the VA facilities and serviced them. We were not determined to forge a deviation from the FAR; we were committed to helping the VA have cleaner, healthier, safer, and greener restroom facilities. We were not being persuasive in our role as a vendor; we were helpful in allowing the VA to make the best decisions to improve their facilities for veterans. The memo ended by asking the VA to refrain from any additional commitments that did not deal with AbilityOne. Was that a restriction of trade? I thought it was or at least close to it.

On September 20, 2016, I attended a committee hearing with the leaders of the procurement and logistics division for the Veteran Health Administration. Leading the group would be the same contract officer I started out with almost ten years ago who had misled me and established a five-year mandatory and exclusive BPA to my local SDVOSB competitor by issuing a set-aside. There they were, promoting a centralized acquisition system that restricted choice and used limited vendors to support the system. Almost ten years later, we both were in Washington, DC, standing up for what we believed in. I found some joy in knowing his decisions did not prevent me from making my contribution to the VA and in a way, I was wishing him the best at what he was advocating. In retrospect, both of our efforts could prove to help the VA receive the right solution long-term. I was sure of this. He thought what he was doing was best for him and the VA. However, I was also confident that what The ClayGroup was doing was a better way. What's more is that we had proven it to be so.

A few weeks later, on November 6, 2016, The ClayGroup had been in business for ten years. It was hard to celebrate without Tamra there, but we had much to be thankful for. Personally, I had achieved my goal of beating the odds and staying in business for ten years. I reflected back on when I'd started and forecast that an African American business or businesses would generate $50 million in sales in the state of Kansas.

Over the years, The ClayGroup had surpassed that goal. I never had thought a company I would lead would achieve this goal. God was true to his Word, and I gave thanks for all the provisions made possible by The ClayGroup's existence.

As the month ended, The ClayGroup faced another challenge. We were given a med-surg prime vendor (MSPV) BPA for paper and asked to work with all four prime vendors. The ClayGroup incurred the expense of having our legal team craft agreements with each one. I attended our annual conference and was told our MSPV-NG BPA was in good standing. That led me to believe the VA or GSA was attempting to right some wrongs.

When I returned from the convention after watching the FSSI SDVOSBs complain to the director of the Strategic Acquisition Center (SAC) about not getting business, I was told The ClayGroup's MSPV-NG BPA had been canceled without cause. I traveled to Virginia to meet with the SAC director to get an explanation for why our MSPV-NG BPA had been canceled. The excuses were baseless, and it was clear the two FSSI SDVOSBs were being positioned to satisfy the rule of two, and The ClayGroup was apparently not part of the solution.

The ClayGroup, working alongside our Kansas congressman, was able to get report language in the appropriations bill urging the support of all SDVOSBs. However, with all these mandatory sanctions, it was getting difficult to plan for the future without knowing if The ClayGroup was standing on solid ground to make the needed financial commitments for future growth. During the first week in December of 2016, I attended the National Center for Veteran Institute for Procurement (VIP). I took part in their growth curriculum as I had very good ideas about how to enlarge the business. In fact, we had met several potential partners that could help us ramp up our distribution capabilities. The ClayGroup graduated from the program with flying colors. The core business was steady, and our new business was growing. At the first of 2017, The ClayGroup was designated as a certified ethical company after my staff and I were interviewed and our policies were looked at closely.

ANOTHER BIG LOSS

You might say the first ten years were the glory days for The ClayGroup. Though we had our challenges, we always persevered and it was rewarding to run a successful SDVOSB that had grown to generate a little more than a million dollars each month. "When much is given, much is expected," I always said to myself. We were expected to deliver as the best SDVOSB every month to take care of our nation's veterans. At the same time, The ClayGroup also took care of its own. An indication of that was the employee insurance we chose for our staff.

I was glad we made the right decision for the best health care. You just never know what can happen in a small company. Ken's daughter, whom I had just seen when I traveled to Panama City on business to meet with him, was now fighting for her life and needed an immediate operation. The news would come right before it was time for her to attend her senior prom. I was so glad we had the proper insurance in place allowing Ken to get the best treatment for his daughter. As the majority owner, I saw the hits we took in profits to be able to afford good healthcare for our people—but it was well worth it.

While there in Panama City, before that news came, Ken and I were preparing for a business meeting which we prefaced with a memorable fishing excursion. Ken and I had attempted to catch some red snapper just a year ago on a fishing trip there. It was a frustrating outing because we did not catch one fish; we returned home empty-handed. I was tempted to call Jesus jokingly to help us, but I thought I'd save my request for more serious things.

I will never forget when Ken called me with only a week to spare and said, "Frank, you have three days to catch red snapper if you are going to do it this year—come on down now!"

It was the fishing trip of a lifetime, and we pulled in our entire allotment of red snapper. I caught the biggest red snapper—but only after losing three nice ones to my dolphin friends in the water. We caught yellowtail, grouper, and triggerfish—some were nice round, fat ones, but we had to throw them back into the water because they were out of season. I took video of Ken pulling in fish and saw him get some father-son time with his son. Many knew I always had wanted a son. Seeing Ken place his arm around his son as the sun rose was priceless. To witness them spending quality time together out on the water was touching. It would be a great memory that would be etched in my mind forever.

I came home bruised in the rib cage from pulling in the red snapper incorrectly, but it was the best fishing day of my life. Had I not responded to Ken's urgent call and put business aside, I would have missed one of the most enjoyable times on water in my life.

After the fishing trip, we had a meeting at his home and got down to business. It had almost been six months with Ken running the company, and I wanted to know how he felt about running the company for the last few months. Ken simply said to just look at the numbers—which were good. I left Panama City excited about the fact that Ken had a good handle on things and that his vision for the business was on solid footing. We shook hands and I gave him the go ahead to take The ClayGroup to the next level.

Sadly, only three weeks after my meeting with Ken during our June 2 fishing trip, I got a call from Ken's wife on June 24 saying that my good friend and business partner Ken Thomas was dead. She said, "We lost Ken."

I replied, "Lost?" I never had felt such a sense of loss in my life. The feeling was beyond sorrow and sadness; it was too close to my own destruction, and it was close to breaking my heart. Lost? I was lost! The last time I'd seen Ken in person, we had spent a wonderful day in the St. Andrews Bay, going miles into the Gulf of Mexico. It was a memory that would last a lifetime. It was a marker that would signal the importance of living each moment to the fullest. I kept seeing a vivid vision of Ken standing next to his son and reeling in fish after fish. I kept remembering how he had just stood by his daughter during a tough time and now he was gone.

On that trip, we had talked in detail about his running the company and my stepping back. Ken had a doable plan written out. Ken was a special person who knew the Lord. He read his Bible and went to church routinely. I knew he was a changed man, and I stood by him as a Christian friend in every way possible. He had overcome so much in the last two years that I could not understand why the Lord would take him from me at the time when I needed him the most. Being a true friend to Ken was my greatest act of compassion. As a Christian, I believe he made it to heaven, and one day I will see him again. Man, have I missed him since I last saw him.

I was now missing Ken and Tamra; both had helped me build The ClayGroup into the great company it was. I thanked Pastor Joe for his message on perseverance that I had heard him give in November 2016. He'd talked about "stick-to-it-ness" and referenced the slaves and how they'd held on while singing the spiritual "Hold On (Keep Your Hand to the Plow)." He'd talked about having spiritual grit. I'd needed to hear that sermon then, and I was comforted in recalling it after Ken's death.

God's Word kept me strong during that time, as I had to regroup quickly and pick up where Ken had left things. I never had been so proud to see my daughter and son-in-law by my side. Their encouragement was priceless. I was the point man again, and the change took me back five years or more to when I'd been doing a lot of the day-to-day interactions with the inside staff and working late hours with multiple days of travel to visit with our customers.

I used to tell Ken I did not want to do the business without him. My business partner did not participate in the day-to-day business, so Ken had been my active partner in making The ClayGroup work. He was now gone, and so was Tamra. It seemed that with Ken gone, the foes of the company came with their best challenges and devious assaults on our business. It seemed I was left to forge a defense all by myself that time around, or at least it felt as if I were by myself on many key matters. All I could do for weeks was just hold on and tread water. Quickly, I tried hard to replace Ken and Tamra. Much uncertainty faced The

ClayGroup, and in my mind, it was overwhelming. Feeling the way that I was, I would simply have to draw a line in the sand to make good sense of it all. We needed the FSSI RFQ award to be issued to The ClayGroup in order to continue being in the business, and therefore, I needed a replacement for Ken immediately. To be prepared for such an award would require all of us to do so much more to reach our business goals.

CHAPTER 22

Knowing When

Surprisingly, while we were still waiting for a decision on the ever important FSSI RFQ to be awarded, we continued to stay in growth mode and hired an inside person with excellent computer skills. For a small business, I like using the "temp to hire" option to find the right employee when you are in need of specific skills. The local agency we used was excellent in finding qualified candidates to interview. Like in the past, we would quickly find our ideal candidate and bring them on. The new temp-to-hire's orientation period went well until around late October 2017, when she had a challenge with her daughter in school. It was then that her personal problem was exposed. This would be right before the final decision to bring her on full-time. At the time, we were also in negotiation with a perfect replacement for Ken; however, to secure him, we had to offer equity in the company in some way. I commissioned our lawyers to complete an offer, but they required a sit-down with our candidate for potential hire, during which multiple legal concerns surfaced, raising major concerns for all of us. Both of these targeted potential hires had me concerned as a decision to say "yes" to hire either was problematic.

In addition to those final decisions, I was now looking closely at twenty or more factors that were necessary to determine the health of the business, our cash flow projections, and growth objectives. To consummate a deal with Ken's replacement, the numbers had to work out because hitting sales objectives was surely going to be part of the deal.

November 30, 2017, would be "decision day" for me according to my planning. This was my deadline to be fully staffed just in time to give The ClayGroup thirty days to transition our new Vice President so he would be empowered to grow the business going into 2018.

Lurking in the back of my mind, however, was the fact that the worst hurricane season in the country's history was impacting sales in key areas like Houston. In August and September, our distributors had to send products to areas hit by Irma (Florida) and Harvey (Texas), where there were major VA medical centers. We noticed the manufacturers were starting to struggle with back orders as demand for toilet paper and towels bubbled quickly in September. That caused a noticeable slowdown in cash flow. Back orders started to increase and our own distributors were doing end-arounds, selling direct to our mutual customers to meet demands and maximize profits for distributing products, charging higher prices our VAs that were smart enough to stock up to ensure they had supplies.

Hurricane Maria in Puerto Rico also caused a major backup in supplies in October. As we satisfied large orders going into Puerto Rico, I saw the issue surrounding cash flow increase because we could not get confirmations from Puerto Rico for multiple reasons; the main one being that there was no communication with our suppliers and the VA on the island. Without confirmations, we could not bill, and facing the holidays in November and December, during which the VA would be closed for one to two days for the holidays, we were facing a major shortfall in accounts-receivable dollars. In fact, FEMA was inadvertently blocking commercial shipments at a great expense to The ClayGroup, as communications were so poor and the need was so great that our confirmations suffered more.

Going into November, our inside-staff new hire was doing a good job, and she would have helped us tremendously, but the week before

November 30th, she stopped showing up for work. Shame, pride, or both concerning her personal problem prevented her from doing the right thing. Our professional organization employer, who handled HR matters, advised me to fire her, but I personally could not and professionally would not fire her before the Thanksgiving holiday, knowing she was a single mother. I could not add to her concerns, and I believed that being an encouragement to her under the circumstances was the right thing to do. At the same time, I was even willing to gamble on her turnaround because we needed her skills.

All those business concerns came to a head, yet a tough business decision was surfacing with November 30 coming. If I let my temp to hire go, we would be down another employee—making three full-time employees we had lost in one year—not to mention a layoff was pending if we did not get a favorable decision on the pending FSSI RFQ.

Then, the ground shaking news was revealed that our candidate to replace Ken needed surgery and would be down for a few months. His coming on board was key to meeting the obligations of a favorable FSSI RFQ award. He was also the center of our "going forward" business strategy for 2018. He was the perfect replacement for Ken. Disappointingly, having received this news, everything stopped, and we still had no word on the FSSI RFQ, which had been going on ten months by then. With all of that happening as we were ending the fourth quarter, with thirty days to go, I knew we were facing a crisis, and a bad business decision now would make a bad situation worse. I knew it certainly was a business situation that would take a few years to rebound from if I let everything play out and we somehow got back on course with our growth strategy. The question was, how could we do it being down three key people.

I did a lot of praying during that time, when the VA put out another communication that was not only damaging but also personal, as it referenced our socioeconomic status indirectly. The proverbial race card was played, in my opinion, and that was uncalled for. The situation with VA Logistics was getting really personal, and I could not keep a level head with such attacks under the circumstances. I was off my A-game and could not control my emotions. The decision not to go down that personal road of getting back at them was solely in my hands. I would recall the stirring words of Michelle Obama, "When they go low, we go high." Some things you just know. They were going low business-wise, and I was fighting to not go any lower. Making this whole ordeal personal was something I did not want to do at this point in my life.

I now seriously considered getting out of the business and just giving up to be honest. It was a quick shift in paradigm for me, not because I could not go on but, rather, because I was looking at the business situation that required more from me than I was willing to give. A decision to step away from the business appeared it was best for my partners, my employees, my family, and me. We were facing too many risks and too much uncertainty with GSA and the VA. It was getting too personal. Suddenly, it was not a battle I was willing to fight. There was no hope for something better. Only days after Thanksgiving, when I'd been feeling grateful, I had no feelings for what was happening. I had to make a decision now, plain and simple.

To me, our business had always been about the veterans. If the VA did not want us as one of the best SDVOSBs ever, then I did not want to continue with all these business concerns we were facing. As a result of the VA memo, our customers in EMS were silenced and confused. We saw a significant drop in sales around the Thanksgiving holiday and thereafter. Clearly, layoffs were imminent with Christmas and New Year's approaching. A projected drop in cash flow was forecasted. In eleven years, The ClayGroup never had a layoff or even missed a payroll before. Something was different, even with our partners, as new leadership surfaced at the top of those corporations. I did not have to see it; after being in business for most of my life, I could feel it. The business was changing quickly. Customers were retiring abruptly, and respect for truth, laws, and fairness in contracting in the VA was disappearing.

There was one more meeting in Washington, DC, at which I hoped to hear specifics about the med-surg prime vendor program— another mandatory program with no validation worth noting—or an announcement on the FSSI RFQ award. The meeting featured the acting chief procurement and logistics officer for the Veteran Health Administration. He started the meeting by talking about further possible consolidation with various companies, such as Amazon, and wanted to hear our ideas on how we could make that happen. *Really?* I said to myself. I was sitting in the front row of tables, and when I heard that introduction I had instant clarity about was about to happen. There was no microphone near me so I was not compelled to say a word. I just got up, walked out, and went to my favorite restaurant nearby, the Peking Pavilion, and ordered my favorite: Peking duck. That made my day!

The Veterans Administration, under the country's new president, seemed out of control, and the privatization of doing business with the VA seemed to be the major focus of the VA. They had plans to outsource everything and cut out SDVOSBs from doing government business with The VA. We were the same veterans mind you who had put our very lives on the line to defend the country. The VA was adamant about stopping veterans from doing business with them. They were looking at companies like Amazon to handle the distribution of supplies. Nothing was mentioned in the meeting about SDVSOBs. One business partner recently had told me there was "a new sheriff in town." Those types of subtle innuendos were clearly sending a message to me, and I was listening. In the back of my mind were Kenny Rogers's famous lyrics: "You've got to know when to hold 'em, know when to fold 'em, know when to walk away, and know when to run."

Still, the entrepreneur in me was looking for a path forward. I was looking for a sign that would help me see through all the personal and business challenges I was facing as the majority owner of The ClayGroup. I wanted to find a way to stay the course. My daughter Brianne, whom I'd had the pleasure to work beside for many years, had never lost her composure in front of me. She was the calming element in our company. However, when our major manufacturer reversed a major order after she had worked so hard to make it happen—an order mind you that would have helped our cash flow—she went off. Seeing this, I knew we all had different views on what 2018 meant for the business. Too many critical things were happening outside of our control. It was another sign to me that we had peaked with our tolerance of the complicated situation The ClayGroup was in. I knew it because I felt it and my best reasoning confirmed it.

It was crunch time, and I needed to make a firm and final business decision, considering twenty-plus key factors regarding the state of the business. I thought about my staff and, mostly, my wife. Regarding my staff, I was aware that the sign-up period for Obamacare was quickly approaching, and if I was going to have layoffs or shut down the business, I needed to keep in mind the deadline for enrollment that left fourteen days for my staff to act. As for my wife, who was about to announce her retirement just thirty days out, in January 2018, I could not ask her again to put our savings at risk and sign off on the line of credit that we would need to turn everything around. For The ClayGroup to go on, the line of credit would need to be tapped heavily, and both of us were personally liable for that new note.

Many people don't realize that the spouse has to go along with the entrepreneur's vision of success and personally sign a bank note in most cases, waiving his or her rights and other key things to allow the business to be formed properly. I had asked my lovely and supportive wife, Joy, to do that too many times. When I would ask that of her, I firmly believed we had a great chance for success. However, with the FSSI RFQ award undecided and the way the VA was treating The ClayGroup and me at that time, my optimism had waned. My gratitude to Joy for sticking with me all those years was a more prominent factor than the twenty-plus business factors I was evaluating. She was deserving of the right decision, which was to shut The ClayGroup, LLC down. Seeing as Thanksgiving was only two days before the end of the month, I would do just that.

That Thursday night, as I made the final decision, I sat in my chair in my office, struggling with the email I was about to send to my lawyers and others. No one really knew about my concluding thoughts or actions to exit the business. It was after midnight as I prayed in my recliner in my office. Even my dog, Chip, knew something was bothering me, as he jumped into my lap and hugged and licked me until my blood pressure came down and my inner spirit was right. Then a scripture came to my mind: "A time to get, and a time to lose; a time to keep, and a time to cast away" (Ecclesiastes 3:6 KJV).

After reading that scripture, I was okay.

I had started The ClayGroup in November 2006 and would now end it in November 2017. I accepted the fact that there was no easy path to keep going or to close the business down. I could have gone either way. I had documentation from the VA that basically told their buying authorities not to do business with The ClayGroup, though many customers always found a way to make it happen. I did not want my customers to be in a compromising position, even though they had every right to do business with The ClayGroup.

From a legal standpoint, I was not able to say goodbye or even thank you to my many partners. The statutes in the state of Kansas precluded me from favoring one vendor over another. In private consultation with my partner, I was forced to keep a low profile because I was obligated to do so. I could not be seen giving preference to any loyal supporter of mine who had believed in what The ClayGroup was doing. Everything was now in my lawyers' hands, and I had to follow legal counsel to protect my own interests as well as my partner's. Business is tough in this regard. If you are not tough on the details, you can inadvertently hurt yourself and others.

I was aware of many positive and a few negative comments about The ClayGroup and me. I wish I could have responded to each one. No one should have been surprised, in my opinion. I could only take so many rejections and misrepresentations, some of which came close to slander in certain cases.

I found it funny that during my eleven years in business, my foes in the government or elsewhere never had the guts to sit me down and say anything to my face. Recalling all the good things said over those years—all the thank-yous and well-wishes—made me think, *How can just a few foes override the desires of so many?* I think those who knew us and had supported The ClayGroup all those years, just assumed we would live to fight another battle one more time. I conceded that those in the government had won the war they'd started against The ClayGroup and would get their way.

Doing government business is like being in a war you will never win. It is designed to create losers, because the government focuses only on price, preference, and far too often, personal agendas. You just have to enjoy the battles as long as you can, and I was proud of every battle I had won whether it was a legal matter or matter of resilience. There are always challenges at the VA and any other federal agency that will require change in order for success to happen. If you are blessed like The ClayGroup, you get your opportunity to make things better when your time comes. The ClayGroup made a positive impact for eleven years and serviced more than one hundred VA medical centers. We changed the way veterans received their care by improving the health conditions of the restroom areas in our VA medical facilities and doing all we could to promote products that improved hand washing and reduced waste. Two of my employees, Tamra and Ken, gave their all to be the best SDVOSB for the VA before they suddenly lost their lives. For their dedication, I will always owe them my love and gratitude.

What I miss most are the veterans. I miss the professionals who have the awesome task of keeping the VA clean every day and doing all they can to create a healthy environment. I miss the fine corporate partners who went to battle with me. Our network of independent distributors was the best in the industry—simply the best! When the VA needed product, our distributors made sure it was there. I only wish the VA had incorporated our business model.

I also miss not being able to do as much good as The ClayGroup was doing in the community. We employed five single mothers. We helped multiple businesses grow locally. I supported the activities of multiple churches across the country, including my own, and recommended that church leaders and business leaders meet and pray with business owners like myself. A business owner never knows when his or her business will become plentiful and how the extra dollars can be used in the church or the community. If the entrepreneur is made aware of the need, there is a possibility he or she can help. It was a pleasure to send products to a church or home after a vendor show instead of throwing good products away. It was cheaper to give them away versus paying the shipping fee to send them back to the office. Giving products to veteran homes was a great joy for me.

I had a solid partner in Mr. Simms, who understood the predicament we were in. I was in 100 percent control of the business because of the directive from the VA. I had to be the majority owner—a tough position for the minority owner to accept. Mr. Simms accepted that, and he was the type of partner The ClayGroup needed in order to be a success within the VA. I learned a lot from his success as well as his mistakes in the past with Commercial Express, and I benefited from his wise counsel and cooperation as a friend. We never had an argument in our partnership—not one. We did not always agree or like how we positioned things, but we knew each other's ways and worked to make it work on the important issues, such as supporting our families, the business, and each other. Under the circumstances it was truly a successful business relationship.

I also had the best staff. My staff prayed for The ClayGroup daily and worked hard. I firmly believe that God protected us up until the very day that I had to shut it down. They loved our customers and supported me 100 percent. Tamra, Ken, Brianne, Chris, Marlena, Tracey, Nicole, Sterling, and my wife, Joy, were a pleasure to work with. I miss working with them closely each day. The ClayGroup, working with its partners, made a difference, and I was glad to have been the one to start it and end it. Nothing has been more rewarding. It was the business of a lifetime for me, and I hope many, especially veteran owners, will learn from my experiences and take their opportunities to run a successful business and enjoy the greatness of being an owner or entrepreneur in the right season of their lives.

CHAPTER 23

A Lot to Be Thankful For

With the closing of The ClayGroup behind me, I felt I had come full cycle, from the time I was a little boy with my *Philadelphia Bulletin* paper route and all my other little hustles, through corporate American, through consulting small businesses and running a chamber, to the pinnacle of being fully in charge of my own business The ClayGroup for eleven years, one year past my original goal of ten years. I'd done what I had set out to do in life. Clearly, all my academic studies in business at Towson State College and my graduate school days at Central Michigan University had paid off. I even enrolled in a doctorate program in business at Cal University, where I had begun a study in entrepreneurship. I decided after three courses to devote my effort, time, and money to writing my own book on business. It was interesting to read about others who had researched entrepreneurs like me and created papers that I had to study, but I had my own theories, thoughts, and realities that had proven to be very effective not only in my business, but in the businesses and small corporations of others. I wanted to tell my story versus being given a grade for reading and writing about the stories of others.

Life allowed me to have a great management career and serve in a variety of leadership capacities in the military as an Officer to include being a Headquarters Battery Commander. Starting a chamber of commerce was a great way to support and work with small businesses. Consulting, coaching, and doing executive search were all good ways to discover, place, and help young businesspeople with their career goals. I found that work rewarding; however, I enjoyed starting my own business with employees the most. Being in business with the ClayGroup for eleven years while generating more than $10 million in sales was by far one of my greatest achievements in my professional life. And of course, being a SDVOSB was the joy of a lifetime to me— even amid all the ups and downs.

The little boy from Philadelphia had done his thing. My advice to others is this: education has to be number one starting point. A young person is wise if they can understand the importance of college early on. You need to know the fundamentals and basic principles that establish the foundations of any area you desire and wish to achieve. Proverbs 4:7 says, "Wisdom is the principal thing; therefore get wisdom: and with all thy getting get understanding." I say, "Get a good education, and with getting an education, get application!" Learn how, and be willing to apply what you have learned to help others while earning a good living for yourself. You have to do your best to be the best, but it all starts with a good education.

I will always remember Rowan Elementary School's motto: "Keep the light of learning burning." I have done that by establishing a personal library of books that reflected my body of knowledge in the area of business. I still have most of my college and business books, plus all of my Bibles that I have taken notes in from over the years. I have few fiction books because in many ways, I considered my own life was a bundle of unbelievable occurrences to be fiction enough for me. In my opinion, it is important to know how life really is, how it works out and does not work out, and how people cope and succeed. I did not leave one moment to chance. I planned my work and worked my plan, which included a calculated plan for all my fun and folly to keep me in control, because I loved to party and enjoy life once completion or success was in my hands.

Still though, life can have some fiction in it. For example, my mother told me I was Cherokee Indian. I find it odd that the history I was taught excluded the real story of the Native Americans and the true conquering nature of the settlers. I remember seeing my great-grandmother Lawson on her deathbed at my grandmother's house in Philadelphia. She had long silver-gray hair and was short. The census recorded her as "mulatto." However, I did an ancestry test and found out that almost 59 percent of my associations were from West Africa in Benin/Togo, Cameroon/Congo, and Ivory Coast/Ghana. When I first visited Guinea in 2001, I was traveling close to the Cameroon people that my DNA reflects. Was this true or fiction? My search to find the truth would reveal that West Africa was where the European slave trade originated. The DNA testing suggested I was more African and not Native American. Thus, another possible mistruth or fiction was told to me just to help me fit into America culture in some healthy way. Where my ancestors came from is still a mystery but not a myth. I look at the Benin/Togo people, and I think, *That's me.*

For sure, I am a descendant of African slaves who collectively suffered greatly so I could be the living extension of those who survived and were not wiped out, as most of the Native Americans were. That is a blessing from God. I trust that my children and grandchildren will be comfortable in referring to themselves as African Americans because of the contributions their parents, grandparents, and great-grandparents made to this country, which are all factual and documented here in America. There is no mystery or fiction about where I was or who I am. However, they should never forget the connotations of the names associated with being called a slave: *nigger, free Negro, black, Afro-American,* and other derivatives. We were also referenced in the Constitution in 1787, in the phrase "the whole Number of free Persons … and three fifths of all other Persons." African Americans were deemed to be property that was bought and sold on auction blocks in major US port cities where Americans now vacation. This is the history of our ancestry and the United States of America.

Though I was never one to live in the past—because there was too much to be done in the present—I was constantly aware that because of the happenings of the past, I had to be cognizant of certain attitudes and expressions that still lingered from then. The book *Roll, Jordan, Roll: The World the Slaves Made* by Eugene D. Genovese, published in 1972, is a detailed documentary of the world of African slavery and addresses our acceptance of Christianity, which created trust and a sense of love for one another as well as those who controlled and enslaved. *Remembering Slavery*, published in 1998, included comments from former slaves, such as Betty Simmons, who was a slave in Alabama, Texas. She said, "T's satisfy den L los' my people and ain't never goin to see dem no more in dis world." Those words rang true for me. "Done lost my people, and I am not going to ever see them and more in this world" is my translation. What a soul-wrenching statement. *Remembering Slavery* is full of them. It's a touching statement from a touching book. These readings allowed me never to forget that slavery was real.

As I took a moment to peruse my personal library, I observed that it told a story about how my own character had developed over the years. My quiet reading of nonfiction and factual pondering of the past allowed for an appreciation of what was truth in the eyes of all those great authors.

I read Lerone Bennett Jr.'s *What Manner of Man: A Biography of Martin Luther King Jr., 1929–1968*, published in 1976, during my senior year at Towson. The book had just come out. Later, in 2005, my wife, Joy, bought me my own copy.

Ironically, after Dr. King's death, I got more out of reading his *The Measure of a Man*, published in 1968, which depicted just how big he was as a man in my lifetime. He was invaluable to the civil rights movement, yet many African Americans, including me, took what he did for granted. Dr. King is responsible for this country peacefully achieving the Civil Rights Act of 1964. It is crazy to think I was nine years old when that happened. The Voting Rights Act of 1965 was another milestone that came from Dr. King's work.

Though Dr. King was nonviolent, Malcolm X was not, and he preached equality with a contrasting message of "by any means necessary." I studied both in college. Both Dr. King and Malcolm X were working to bring about change. They met during a Senate debate on Capitol Hill on March 26, 1964. It was the only time the two met. That struck me hard because there was a triangle present between them: you, me, and them. How does one get to *we* from those three? The reality is, we all are different, but we breathe the same air and bleed the same blood. Medicine proves our neutrality as human beings. Why don't we save every ounce of blood from being spilled over the sin of hate, which is unfounded in God's purpose for his creation?

I read Elijah Muhammad's *The Fall of America*, published in 1973, which was given to me by a sister of Muhammad's Temple of Islam No. 2 that same year while I was in Washington, DC. I also read Peter Goldman's *The Death and Life of Malcolm X*, published in 1979, after college. I found myself at Muhammad's Temple No. 4 in Washington, DC, listening to Minister Lonnie Shabazz give their full and detailed account of the atrocities of the white man against the so-called Negro in America. It was a call for the black man to be and take care of his own, as other ethnic groups were allowed to. It made sense to have plans to take care of us; however, I was not a Black Muslim, and I was not one of *us*. If I was not a Black Muslim, then I was a so-called Negro, according to Black Muslims, which left me with the following question again: "Who am I?" Every African American will ask him- or herself this question in life and have to come to an individual meaning and answer.

The temptation to join the Nation of Islam was great. In fact, I was vulnerable to many groups in the mid-1970s. I almost joined the Seventh-Day Adventist Church and Jehovah's Witnesses via innocent invitations that also served to help me answer the question "Who am I?" In my adult life, a cousin of 2014 presidential candidate Mitt Romney gave me the Articles of Faith of the Church of Jesus Christ of Latter-Day Saints. All of those religious groups had something positive to offer, but none of them measured up to what my grandmother had instilled in me or what I'd felt when I accepted Jesus Christ into my life back in Philadelphia during the 1960s.

My belief in Jesus Christ had been deeply rooted in His Word. I was a New Testament Christian for the most part and desired to spread the gospel—the good news about Jesus Christ and his love for us. I also desired to love and encourage others, which was a natural gift of mine. Love and forgiveness were anchored inside of me so that I could officially answer the question "Who am I?" "I am a believer in Jesus Christ, the one who saved me, justified me, and made me righteous in his sight." Though I was in the world, trying to figure things out, I knew inside that I was not of the world. All I had to do was acknowledge the Lord and put my trust in him to know where I needed to go in life. The Bible is God's Word, and I believe it is true. Though man has used it to make gains for himself by abusing others, God's Word is the way and the truth for me. It was good enough for my elders, and I know it to be good enough for me. It's the best book I have ever read. I trust it will be good enough for my children, their children, and their children's children yet to come.

A book that is thoughtfully given to you at the right time can have a dramatic impact on your life and your spirit. As a previous legal clerk for the US Army, I was grateful to receive Juan Williams's book *Thurgood Marshall: American Revolutionary*, published in 1998, as a gift from my best friend, roommate, and peer at Spencer and Spencer, Jeff Woodard. After his success as a medical sales representative, Jeff became a lawyer in Baltimore before his premature death at a young age. Thurgood Marshall was at the center of the *Brown v. Board of Education* case in 1954, which outlawed school segregation. Marshall was a Washington, DC, elite, and my friend Jeff was a new lawyer and admired him for his work. Jeff Woodard was someone I could call on anytime and anywhere. He was smart. When I called him, I always said, "Jeff, is that you?"

He always replied with a giggle, "Yes, it's me. Who in the hell do you think this is?"

My friend gave me one more book on January 30, 1995, right before his passing, almost as if he knew it was coming: Nathan McCall's *Makes*

Me Wanna Holler: A Young Black Man in America, published in 1994. This would be another hard for me because the content was raw and made me want to say something and do something to establish a real change in the way African Americans were treated in this country. What made the gift meaningful was what Jeff wrote to me on the inside cover of the book. As you will see, I am honoring his wishes by sharing the following:

> Once I am of this world no more,
> It will matter not what I did for a living.
> How did I treat the people I loved
> And most important did I love the Lord?
> Tell them ...
> I treated them the best I could
> And I loved the Lord.
>
> Jeff Woodard

I knew two pastors who went on to be confirmed as bishops with full ceremonies: Bishop Steve Houpe (Harvest Church International Outreach, Kansas City) and Bishop Jerry Diggs (New Israelite Church of Deliverance, Baltimore). I watched how God used people like them to bless souls and lead many to Jesus Christ. I truly admire both of these men of God for their dedication and support of their communities. My Pastor at First Baptist Church, Mound City, Kansas, encouraged me to write my book on Salvation: Go To The Word. I would always admire him for his dedication to missions around the world. I joined him on a mission to Honduras where we were roommates together. Probably the only time I ever spent rooming with Pastor to watch his discipline to prayer and organization. You learn a lot about another person on a mission trip but more important, I learned a lot about myself.

I always considered myself a Christian businessperson, with all the pluses and minuses like any other Christian. I somehow decided to stand in the gap and take the hits of untruth that came my way when my only intention was to attempt to point others to a better way and more success. I will say that having a moral compass helped me greatly. I knew that if God continued to bless me, I would continue to bless his church and his people, especially by helping those in business. That was my calling. I believe businesspeople and entrepreneurs have that responsibility. The two Bishops I have known have been an inspiration to me, they have been friends, and they have prayed for me over the years.

Bishop Steve Houpe would render me a surprise honor for my community service, and I was in tears by what was said because God knew, and Bishop Steve Houpe knew, some of what I had gone through. Some things you just know. Bishop Jerry Diggs knew too. Though we had a business relationship at the VA in Baltimore, he prayed a covering over me and for me many times before I walked out of his office after doing business. Each time, certain challenges followed me, but I knew I was covered by the blood of Jesus, which allowed me to stand until my work was done. I admired their commitments to their callings in the church as well as the difference they made in the local African American community. It was a blessing to be allowed to speak at each of their churches.

Bishop Jerry Diggs gifted me a book on April 19, 2011, that was timely: James MacDonald's *Lord, Change My Attitude: Before It's Too Late*, published in 2008. My takeaway was found in the title itself. My reading alerted me to the fact that I had to fix some things because my time was running out. I got on it, and I paid attention to chapter 5, which said, "A continuously critical attitude toward those around me will consume all that is healthy and joy producing in my life."

Being given the right book at the right time can be like medicine that helps one to get better or get through a challenge. To this day, I am thankful for all the books gifted to me, because they all were helpful. Though the book *Lord, Change My Attitude* came from Bishop Diggs, I knew it was also a message from God to me. What a blessing! Sometimes you have to know God is trying to get your attention, and he sends those who know him to help you. It is unwise to ignore the prayers and wisdom of a pastor or bishop.

While I was with the chamber of commerce and throughout all my years in a small business with The ClayGroup, I came to realize God had sent me a professional confidante in a lady named Marquita Miller. I had started out as her mentor but then discovered I could use her services to help me manage our internal accounting matters at The ClayGroup. As she grew her accounting business, Five Star Tax, we became close as Christian friends and as business associates. I made sure to always keep our relationship professional and keep our spouses aware of where the line was drawn both professionally and friendship-wise. During our general exchanges, I knew I was going to get a big hug and a wide smile from Mrs. Miller, whom I trusted 100 percent. Sometimes in business, your numbers cannot speak to the integrity of how you conduct business, but the professional accountant checking your numbers can. I always had two accountants involved with the finances of the businesses and organizations I ran, and I took their input and advice to heart.

In fact, I periodically had Mrs. Miller check my staff's work in accounts receivable and accounts payable to make sure we were doing things according to General Accepted Accounting Principles, or GAAP. If I mentioned GAAP when coaching small businesses and got the look of bewilderment, I put up the yellow flag and recommended a consultation with Mrs. Miller of Five Star Tax. I knew from our work with the Kauffman Foundation that she understood small businesses.

Mrs. Miller and I had many coaching sessions over lunch. Then, one day, she wanted to interview me and ask me questions because she was going to write a business book for Christians. Being a Christian, I was all in, and before I knew it, she had published a Christian best seller called *Faithpreneur: God Is Not an Agent for Your Failure but for Your Success*, published in 2010. It even featured me for a business Q & A session. Her book is a must read for Christians going into business.

One other important nugget worth mentioning that came out of my association with Mrs. Miller's book is that too often, we forget to acknowledge those who have helped us. True acknowledgment is not a money thing or something that requires a gift or personal sacrifice. In fact, it is not even required of you, and most times, the person who it is addressed to will minimize the gesture by saying something along the lines of, "You did not have to do that." However, let it be known that giving thanks is important to the process of continually giving to others and receiving from others, particularly in business.

When we give thanks to others who have given to us, we are saying we respect them. I have always said that when we are respected and feel respected, we are more apt to be responsive to the requests of others. It's human nature. Who wants to help someone who does not respect him or her? When a person responds to you, oftentimes he or she gives the resources and results you need or desire. It starts with respect because when we have what we need, there is something there to acknowledge and recognize. I have learned from many years of dealing with people in business that if you do not recognize their efforts, by human nature, they feel disrespected and will be inclined not to respond to your requests in the future. I call the following my five Rs: respect, responsiveness, resources, results, and recognition. If you're in business, make saying thank you a priority out of respect.

> Give, and it will be given to you. Good measure, pressed down, shaken together, running over, will it be put into your lap. For with the measure you use it will be measured back to you. (Luke 6:38 NIV)

> One gives freely, yet grows all the richer; another withholds what he should give, and only suffers want. Whoever brings blessing will be enriched, and one who waters will himself be watered. (Proverbs 11:24–25)

If there ever was someone I wanted to be in life other than myself, it was Tiger Woods—with the exception of his indiscretions. I loved the relationship he had with his father, and somehow, maybe I felt I needed to be him in order to get a hug or sign of affection like that from my own father after a big win. It was touching to me. I have many books and magazines about Tiger, and I loved reading each one because they had to respect him for his achievements. That is the one thing about golf, it's a game of respect among the best. I first saw him play in person at the 2007 Tour Championship in Atlanta. He was the best golfer for a long time but messed up his personal life.

David Owen's little book called *The Chosen One: Tiger Woods and the Dilemma of Greatness*, published in 2001, tells you much of what you need to know about Tiger Woods on paper. You can see most everything else on the golf course—how great he was, is, and is going to be when history adds up his achievements in golf. Tiger has been a joy to watch over the years. Interestingly, for the first time in a long time, Woods almost won again, and his two girls were there to give him a hug, as his father used to do. I might have had a chance of that happening to me. I recently shot a 74 for the first time in my life on July 24, 2018—all pars on the back nine. I have to say, I felt like Tiger that day and was on top of the world. It just goes to show you that anything can happen in life.

A POET...

Outside the business world, I am a poet at heart. I love poetry books. Probably even more than that, I love poets as people and seeing their poems as parts of themselves they were willing to share with others. As a poet myself, I view this vulnerable part of me as the best part of me. My poetry is the inner part of me who is in rhythm, romantically honest, and truthfully raw.

My favorite poet of all time is Langston Hughes; I love his style and write as a shadow of him. I understand where Langston was coming from in most of his poems, and if I could have made a living to support my family by writing poems, I surely would have done so. But that was not in the cards for me.

My first book, *Press On: Truthful Insights into the Lives We Live!*, published in 2004, is an easy read with poems that express how I feel on important key social issues. I wrote "Use What You Have" to point out that you are blessed with the things God has given you. To stress the importance of family, I wrote the poem "Family," and I wrote a poem called "Family Prayer" for families to use around the kitchen table. I loved hearing my grandchildren recite this poem when they were young.

To address how I felt about gay marriages, I wrote "Lifestyles," which allowed me to say that the only problem I have with people with alternative lifestyles is that they do not reproduce as God intended. It hurts me to see a woman miss out on being a mother with children of her own. I pray that my daughters will enjoy motherhood one day.

I got a little sexy with the poem "Move Me," and the lead poem of my book, "Press On," was written to encourage the reader to do just that: press on.

Like Gordon Parks and James Mercer, poet, social activist, and playwright Langston Hughes had his roots in the Midwest, only a few hours from where I lived in Mound City, Kansas. Hughes was born in Joplin, Missouri, in 1902 and stayed in Lawrence, Kansas, with his grandmother until age thirteen. Parks and Mercer were my authors of choice when I lived on the East Coast. I never thought I would end up living near the birthplace of those two insightful writers in the Midwest.

I wrote my second book in a place where I love to write: Saint Thomas, Virgin Islands. I love the water, the fish, the breeze, the sand, and the people. I usually run in circles in the sand before I start writing. I learned to do that when I was in Africa. I observed a man from Guinea running on the water's edge early in the morning. I asked why he ran in circles, and he replied, "When you run in your own footsteps, you are running into your past in a way that can help you see the future more clearly." He was right. It's amazing how things come to your remembrance if you run that way to the point of mental and physical exhaustion. For me, it is a cleansing process and allows my inner thoughts to come out.

Speaking of inspiring poetry, the words of Nikki Giovanni are always luminous and thought-provoking. I met Nikki on July 14, 2002, when she signed her new book, *Quilting the Black-Eyed Pea: Poems and Not Quite Poems*, published in 2002. I have a picture of us together and even have a note she wrote to me after we spent some quality time discussing poetry. She almost had me ready to live my dream and quit my job. Sometimes it is a crazy word love affair when poets get together. We had a good time, and she was so vivacious.

THE MOST IMPORTANT BOOK OF ALL

Books were the big investment that I always made in myself as an adult, and each of my many books had something I needed; otherwise, I would not have taken it to the cashier. Whether I had a budget for self-development or not, I bought books to enlighten and inspire me throughout my career. Unfortunately, in a highly competitive corporate environment, there is a good chance you will not have a mentor nearby to help you advance. Investing in books can keep you relevant in your career, usually on a monthly basis. Many young professionals fail to get ahead because they don't read the available industry journals or papers to grasp the full body of knowledge in their professional lives. I always kept the light of learning burning by buying and reading books. If I could not buy them, I borrowed them from a friend or went to the library. For me, reading was achieving.

So, what is the number-one book I have read? What is the best seller for me? That is an easy question. It is God's Word, the Bible. I have many Bibles in different versions on my shelves. I have read the Bible from cover to cover two times, and I plan to do it one more time, the Lord willing. I have read key scriptures multiple times with much joy, such as the Twenty-Third Psalm. World Bible Publishers published my favorite Bible. It is a white covered Holy Bible replete with a dictionary and study guides that are in print so small I cannot read it unless I have glasses on. I love this Bible because it was presented by me as a gift to New Light Bethel Baptist Church in Olathe on November 3, 1991, in memory of my mother, Geraldine Clay Jones. Each Bible was imprinted with the following words in gold: "In Memory of Bro. Clay's Mom." It was my way of making sure my mom's memory was not lost over time, and I prayed the use of the Bible would help bring someone to the acceptance of Jesus Christ.

I want to share three Bible verses in particular that are foundational pillars of my faith:

> All Scripture is breathed out by God and profitable for teaching, for reproof, for correction, and for training in righteousness. (2 Timothy 3:16)
>
> In the beginning was the Word, and the Word was with God, and the Word was God. (John 1:1)
>
> For the word of God is alive and active. Sharper than any double-edged sword, it penetrates even to dividing soul and spirit, joints and marrow; it judges the thoughts and attitudes of the heart. (Hebrews 4:12 NIV)

When I read the Bible, I am reading so that God, the Creator, can inspire his creation with his Word. His creation would be me and you. Many people don't want to hear it, let alone read it, but they sure could benefit from being inspired by God's Word or The Bible.

When I finally wrote my inspired book called *Salvation: Go to the Word*, published in 2015, this would be my way of fulfilling God's command in Mark 16:15: "And he said unto them, Go ye into all the world, and preach the gospel to every creature." Knowing that many do not read the Bible, I hoped they would read the scriptures directly related to the act of accepting Jesus Christ as their Lord and Savior. Once we brought our house in Kansas, I started a home base Bible study in my for men. We would sight a scripture to study, pose three questions, discuss the responses and then have prayer acknowledging prayer concerns. The Bible study continues to this day and it a firm example of what God can do. I thank God for placing this act service in my heart as it is encouraging to see how the men have carried on in this way over the years.

Numerous books did much to enlighten me and develop my thinking, but none of them gave me the truth about how I could have my sins forgiven. Only the Bible provided that assurance, and for that reason, the Bible will always be the number-one best book of truth to help any of us succeed in life. The Word that gives us life everlasting declares that if we seek the kingdom of God, all the things that concern us will work together for our good—if we believe.

> But seek ye first the kingdom of God, and his righteousness; and all these things shall be added unto you. (Matthew 6:33)
>
> And we know that all things work together for good to them that love God, to them who are the called according to his purpose. (Romans 8:28)

So, I say again, keep the light of learning burning by reading as many books as you can. I have found them to be the objective truth that has helped me gain wisdom and information about all aspects of this life we live. The books I have read have helped make me the person I am today. Each one of them is right on the shelf in my office for those who come behind me to read and know.

PRIVILEGES

Make no mistake about it: I was privileged to be part of so many organizations, attend so many special events, meet so many special people, and have so many special moments and experiences in my life, and I have cherished them all. Some I was given, and many I had to earn. With others, I had no choice; I had to live with them and make the most of them. However, I am grateful for every privilege I have ever had.

My dad, Corporal Francis L. Clay Sr., US Army, is buried in Indiantown Gap National Cemetery, Annville, Pennsylvania (plot 18, O, 140); my uncle Lieutenant Colonel William A. L. Clay Jr. is buried in Arlington National Cemetery, Arlington, Virginia, with full honors (section 28, grave 1335); and my grandfather Lieutenant Colonel William A. L. Clay Sr. is buried in Arlington National Cemetery, Arlington, Virginia, with full honors (section 60, grave 3490). I am privileged to be part of my family's rich military legacy. Bringing this legacy full circle, my nephew William R. Johnson, a chief of police, has the responsibility of securing the grave sites of our military loved ones (his great-grandfather and great-uncle) at Arlington National Cemetery. All in all, I am glad to represent the third generation of offices in the Clay family.

On November 11, 2015, I attended the Veterans Day program at Arlington National Cemetery with my nephew William R. Johnson. My wife and I had a VIP escort to bring us the Memorial Amphitheater to hear the Honorable Barack Obama give the Veterans Day address. Interestingly—and embarrassingly— someone had spelled the president's name wrong in the programs they handed out. They had printed "Barak Obama." Can you believe that? It's true.

I also was privileged to witness both of Barack Obama's swearing-in ceremonies. The colder of the two was the first time the president took his oath of office, which was much like the oath I'd taken to become an Officer in the US Army. Notably, Barack Obama was the first African American President of the United States.

I have been blessed to have children who did well in grade school and college. I was privileged to watch my first daughter, Brianne, play basketball at Lincoln University in Jefferson City. She has the record in her conference for the most blocked shots in a season, and she is a proud member of Delta Sigma Theta, Inc. She graduated in 2003. My younger daughter, Karrah, played basketball at Hampton University but was on an academic scholarship and made the tough decision to drop basketball to work toward graduation in three years. She also played college golf. She ended up at Wake Forest to earn her graduate degree and was out in the workforce within five years. Her last commencement was in 2009. I can proudly say their daddy was there for every single commencement.

It is my prayer that all young people, single or with a family, will put themselves in a position to have the privilege of experiencing everything God would will them to have—the privilege of experiencing the things that will make a difference in their lives and the lives of others. Being part of something special lifts your sprits for a time so that you can see yourself and your circumstances in a different light. You will see what sacrifice and hard work can bring. You will learn how the God who created you can bless you with a better vision of tomorrow so that you can have hope and enough faith to keep on keeping on.

When you are involved with something that has a greater cause than you, your legacy will last forever. If you can keep all your life commitments and lessons learned close enough to you to share with your family and close friends, they too will be blessed from generation to generation. I wish I had all my friends from high school and college around me in my adult life to share all the blessings I have enjoyed over the years.

I feel the same way about the church. There are many good people that I would come to know well, spiritually. Somehow, we get sideways due to misunderstandings or simply get so busy with life that we go our separate leaving our fellowship with one another behind. I wish Christians would have a little more faith in each other and stay more connected and unified throughout time. We should always leave one phase of our lives in such a way that we are able to come back to any relationship that once started out as a good thing. In order for us to do this, forgiveness has to be a requirement. I wish I could say I am sorry to any of my friends I might have wronged unintentionally. That way, one day, before it is too late, we could say hello and smile again. Hopefully that would lead us to do more good for each other.

As I get older, I wish my cousin John Herbert Clay Jr. and my friends Jeff Woodard, Keith Konstantinos, Tamra Beatty, Norm Romney, and Ken Thomas were all still alive. They all were like 5-hour Energy drinks to me, and they all left this earth way too soon. Each one of them dreamed with me, and we dreamed together of many things. They were my true friends, and I could call on them, count on them, and commit all I had to them. It was my privilege to know each of them, and I pray I will see them again in heaven. This is not a wish. This is my hope!

Though I have been privileged to have and experience so much, I realize that anyone can do the same by making him- or herself available and accessible to the many opportunities life brings. I was blessed to have family, friends, and acquaintances who made a difference in my life. I think I was good at believing in myself to seek better and knowing that if I had one time to do anything, it was my chance to make it special and to get it right. No matter how big or small the moment, I'm good for giving it my all.

I was blessed to be born into the extended family with last names of Clay, Whitley, Richardson, Thomas, and Lawson. All, from what I know and have read, were good, hardworking family people who believed in God. Some came from Florence, South Carolina, near where I played golf in Myrtle Beach each year. My people are from Woodbine, New Jersey, where the great railroads used to be outside of Atlantic City in the North. Others are from Marion Junction and Selma, Alabama, where significant civil rights marches took place.

Late in my life, I met my family in Alabama. My parents and grandparents never took my siblings and me there. I don't know why, but I am glad I went. I found out that when I'd had my small business, I'd had customers in the areas the Clays were from. At a reunion there, I walked across Edmund Pettus Bridge from Selma to Montgomery with my brother Sidney and realized how blessed we were to be descendants of the Clay family in that area and to never have experienced anything like the brutal Bloody Sunday beatings of the civil rights marchers during the first march for voting rights.

When the Clay men who'd been there as boys recounted how they'd traveled by moonlight to get where they were going, avoiding danger after dark, their stories paralleled the discussions I'd had with my troops on night maneuvers. We'd moved in such a way as to not be detected by the enemy. The Clay men told me they'd built houses that couldn't be seen from the road, and they'd even used the rivers to escape danger. The images on TV portray a helpless people, but what I heard showed intelligence regarding how to avoid the enemy, fight back when necessary, and by all means know how to survive.

Mount Airy Baptist Church was near the home of my great-great-grandmother Mrs. Lonnie Clay. I saw pictures of the strong African American women who led the church for many years. Their faces had dark reflections of determination and pride that made me feel glad. I wondered, *Where were all the men?* Then I put one and one together: my grandfather left Selma to go to Philadelphia for his own reasons. I am not going to speak for him, but he left with all his boys.

My grandparents met at Selma University, where my grandmother, Mother Clay, earned her teaching degree. She taught in the public schools of Selma in the 1920s. I did not know that until I read her obituary. I only saw her in church or in the kitchen. She had a degree, when my own mother did not have one. My mother was my example; she told me to get my degree, and I did. I regret not knowing all of my family history while growing up. My parents did not talk about the family makeup in the South, and I didn't know what I know today until I was well into my adult days.

It would have done me some good to at least spend a summer down there to learn some things. The reasons why I was sheltered from knowing about those places is a mystery. I was somewhat remorseful that I'd had to learn about Selma, Alabama, in my history classes, when family members could have told me the specifics on their own. I surely would have written a paper based on the conversations with my own family. Perhaps they knew where Dr. Martin Luther King ate lunch, rested, slept, and had dinner and even who brought the food over.

I sincerely hope my life honors all the sacrifices of my elders for every single act that benefitted my family and helped them to survive. *Oh yes, my soul says. Hallelujah! Thank you, Lord, for the victories that were won.* Selma is no Philadelphia, but Selma has the roots of my family… the Clay family—something Philadelphia will never have. Equally important are the roots I have established for my children and grandchildren in Overland Park and Mound City, Kansas. I hope and pray my legacy will inspire generations to come to live productively in America.

The Bible says, "Honor your father and mother and your days will be long." My days have been long. I wish my parents could see my family now and the things we are doing. When each of my parents remarried, I struggled to get on board with what was going down. I walked my mother down the aisle when she married her second husband, but I couldn't get close to him because I just knew too much. Some things you just know, and you have to leave it alone. Inside, I feel a sense of disappointment stemming from the fact that I know nothing about that part of her life; I chose to remain ignorant about her relationship with a man I know little about. I never interfered. I just loved my mom, and I showed her great love before she passed. I said to her, "Mom, enjoy the flowers in life while you can, and let the past be in the past." My mother and I had great conversations about men and women— maybe that was why I knew too much. She expected me to be a good husband and put her granddaughters through high school and college so they could get their diplomas. I accomplished that mission, and I know she would have been proud.

I was my dad's best man when he married Denise Clay, who is my age and had four sons. Knowing how he treated his own three boys, I could not fathom why a man with five children would marry for a second time and become responsible for four more boys. I finally got past my feelings and supported the wedding. I watched my dad treat Denise and her boys much better than he'd treated my mom and me. He took them to an Eagles game and bought them Eagles jackets, when he never had taken me to a professional sporting event of any kind. That alone was a big issue for me.

Denise and I reached out to each other as friends, and later we had an open and honest discussion about what went down. I was able to explain my feelings and concerns. I listened to her, and we left things in a place where I decided to just honor what my dad had done and tried to do for everyone—whether I agreed or not. I will always respect Denise in a special way because I saw her take care of my dad till the end. I think when your second parent dies, you know your emotional umbilical cord to your parents is cut once and for all. When my dad died, I realized I had no more parents. I had Denise, who was in the room when my dad passed, and we cried tears of joy together in that moment. She was my dad's widow, and I had a responsibility to do my best to help encourage her, as she has remained faithful to my dad's memory and legacy. Somehow, we worked it out.

My life in a way has always been about being a better sibling, husband, father, uncle, and grandfather. It's been about saying, "I love you." An old Clay's response might be "God loves you, and so do I" or "God be with you." I have tried to demonstrate a more personal love and create lasting memories by hanging out with loved ones and sharing special experiences. I feel a responsibility as the oldest son to give direction to the family who are descendants of my dad. I feel as if I am his voice and represent all he was attempting to do to make life better for the family. I love my brothers Darryl and Sidney and my sisters Deborah and Tracey. There so many good memories of us I hold dearly and I tried my best to help us all as a family. I guess only time will tell how successful I have been at this endeavor.

My life has been a testimony of many things I wished for and hoped for. It has brought me great substance in embracing the true meaning of life. My life is the evidence of things unseen. No one could have imagined all the things and experiences I have enjoyed over the years.

Know I have kept the faith, for I am the evidence unseen.

> Now faith is the substance of things hoped for, the evidence of things not seen. (Hebrews 11:1)

> Remember my affliction and roaming,
> The wormwood and the gall.
> My soul still remembers

And sinks within me.
This I recall to my mind,
Therefore I have hope.
Through the LORD's mercies we are not consumed,
Because His compassions fail not.
They are new every morning;
Great is Your faithfulness.
"The LORD is my portion," says my soul, "Therefore I hope in Him!" **(**Lamentations 3:19– 24 NKJV)

CHAPTER 24

The Joy of It All

I used to ask myself, "What is this life all about?" I remember a song Dionne Warwick sang called "Alfie," in which she asked, "What's it all about, Alfie?" Her voice sent me on an imaginary life journey in my mind to find out exactly what life was really all about, because at the time, I did not know, nor was I able to figure it all out by merely looking at my surroundings. The way Dionne sang the song back in the day was a little too slow for me; however, each lyric had so much meaning and was ever so touching. I always liked her concluding pause in the song, followed by the words "I believe in love, Alfie." Hearing this song, I knew love had something to do with the answer to my question about life.

Growing up as a young man and witnessing relationship after relationship, everyone seemed to have too many irons in the fire to commit to any one relationship with the target of true love forever. I was always in love with each person I had a relationship with, and I considered myself a true romantic at heart, with my own poetic way of doing things. In college, my focus was on graduating and basketball. Every relationship got a little less time as I juggled all the activities I was involved with while in college, but I still felt like I was in love. Other guys on campus probably did a better job of showing love and providing more quality time for a personal relationship than I did. I seemed to always be on the go; always searching for what true love was.

I would secretly resolve in my heart to be purposeful to find true love with someone. I knew I could love anyone, but I could only be committed to and experience true love with one woman somewhere out there. During and after my college years, I let my heart find its own way. However, when I met this young lady by the name of Joy, I was fortunate to slow down long enough so we could have some quiet time to talk seriously before getting romantically involved. We had a discussion at my apartment on Radecke Avenue in Baltimore. We sat at the dining table and allowed the conversation to gravitate to a discussion about life, what it was about, and what we honestly expected to get out of it. It was our first time alone just sharing with each other, and in that unromantic setting, I loved the beauty I was looking at and how the moment felt. There were no party lights or candles glowing in the dark where we sat. It was a simple get-together during the day, which allowed us to see each other for who we were.

I fixed her some tuna salad and applesauce, and our talk was open, direct, and sincere. I looked clearly through her big eyeglass frames and saw everything I wanted. Joy was laying it on me, saying all the words I'd wanted and needed to hear from a woman without knowing it. Joy listened to all the things I said as well, and our questioning of each other led us closer and closer to a better understanding of each other. Somehow, we leaped to a discussion about marriage and kids. I had just broken off an engagement, and I asked, "What would make you happy?" She replied quickly— too quickly, I felt at the time. I asked the same question many times again later in our relationship, but her response never changed. Joy simply said she wanted a husband, family, house, and job. That was it. Simplicity seemed to be good for me at the time. As for my response to the same question, I told her I wanted to travel and see the world. I wanted to write a book and live near the water. I wanted to go to church with my wife and kids. I wanted to have money and have a nice suit to wear. None of that seemed to impress Joy at the time. She was still trying to finish college at Morgan State College, but I must have impressed her enough to let her know I had a plan and something to look forward to.

Having just ended a serious relationship that hadn't worked out, I felt a relationship with Joy might be a good thing for me. Maybe this time I could find a way to be a good husband if I tried harder. I wanted a family and a house. I needed my wife to work if we were going to have the life I envisioned. As we continued to talk, I knew I was in some kind of true love with Joy, but I felt she should go home that evening. I respected our conversation and did not want to mess things up by having sex and trying to prove my love for her in order for us to go on. Abruptly and surprisingly, I asked her to leave after we had moved to the sofa for a passionate kiss. It was surely time for her to go.

I took her back to her place, and from there, we nurtured a relationship on a firm basis of respect. What we had going was unique to me because she and I agreed to take our time and just enjoy being around each other. In light of our desire to just be together, I suggested I move in with her because I was there all the time if I was not working.

Over time, I finally faced the fact that I had some issues blocking me from truly committing myself to one woman and experiencing true love. In my mind, I was not ready for marriage, because I did not believe I was the marrying type. Having had relationships with way too many women, I thought, *How do I narrow it all down to one woman, and can I even do that?* Somehow, I convinced myself to believe that Joy was the one and that it might be my last chance to have true love in my life and have heaven with the woman I loved right here on earth. "This Must Be Heaven" with LaMont Johnson (Brainstorm) we would dance to on our wedding day. For me, the song was my way of reminding myself not to blow it… don't blow a good thing but trust what you were feeling. The words at the end of the song were an affirmation: "Yes, I'm loving you, put my trust in you."

Without knowing it, Joy and I built a trust that allowed us to have the lives we both wanted and were hoping for. That developed trust allowed us to make a commitment to be there with and for each other. All our moments together became more special day by day. I became more attracted to her physically, emotionally, and mentally and cared for her in many ways that I didn't even realize. I also was honest with her and insisted she finish her degree before we went further and got engaged. I had my degree from Towson, and I did not want to disrupt her senior year at Morgan. I wanted her to have room to change her mind about me after graduation from college, but thank God, she never did—even with my going into the service by that time.

Keeping her word, Joy graduated, and she got a great corporate job with Prudential Insurance while I was in basic training in the military. We had corresponded frequently by phone and arranged for her to visit me in Kentucky, taking her first ever plan ride. While she was there, I made my move toward marriage. I always said real and simple, "I just love you." It got to a point where there was nothing more to say. I knew I loved this woman, and she loved me. Forgoing an extended engagement, we went straight to wanting to be married because that was the one thing we both wanted in order to be happy in life. It took three dollars to make it happen. Joy got the marriage license in Anne Arundel County on August 18, 1978. Our number was 35826, and she got it done and paid for it. To this day, I have no clue how a marriage license is secured, but she made it happen. We were married on September 2, 1978, in Joy's grandparents' backyard just one week before I graduated from legal-clerk training at Fort Benjamin Harrison, Indiana. My legal-clerk class gave me one hell of a send-off. I was driven to the airport the day before the wedding. It was a special day for Joy and me. I was truly happy. It was as if I had made it to the finish line after a long race of looking for someone to be committed to and to enjoy true love with. I was finally going to the chapel, and I was going to be married!

As Joy paraded down the aisle, the reality of being married got more serious by the second. The closer she came to me, the more beautiful she looked. There we were, in front of Reverend Bowman, who asked me to repeat after him. I did; however, I had a problem with repeating "in sickness and in health" and "until death do us part." My mindset was more like *This has to work out, or I am out.* Previously while the two of us were alone, I had given Joy a disclaimer that I'd do my best for five years, and I was committed to doing that, but those vows before God had me thinking, *Can I do it?* I knew I loved Joy, but I was not sure whether she could love me or trust me. To be honest, in the beginning, I trusted my wife to pull me through my issue of doubting the possibility of having a trusting marital relationship because of the things I'd witnessed and experienced with my parents. I knew some of that was on me and in me. I was scared of what was in her past too, and I wondered for a moment, whether we could actually work through our insecurities.

The mental challenges of overcoming our pasts was my biggest obstacle to a lasting marital relationship. We had witnessed much, but through our honesty with one another and a loving perseverance, we knew all the emotions that could interfere with the pure and innocent relationship we had stumbled upon. How do you talk about these things to the one you truly love? We had suffered many things that unintentionally created issues for us: past physical abuse, improper touching, drug and alcohol addiction, overspending, stealing, adultery, lying, and other family secrets that had to be kept sacred until folks went to their graves. Those things made me hesitant to say yes and keep going. For me at the time, marriage seemed like an impossible task I was taking on, but I knew Joy had a good handle on how we could make it work, and she wanted it to work for us and our future family. Her vision was better than mine and coupled with my willingness, we had what we needed to help us find success. In the short first five years of marriage, we worked openly through those issues, knowing we had to just let some things be.

I came to accept the reality that having a good time drinking with my wife did not mean I was an alcoholic, and if my wife got wild for a night, which I loved, that did not mean she was a wayward woman of some kind. If she hugged an old friend, that did not mean she was going to leave me, and if I touched my wife in a certain way to bring pleasure, that did not mean I was a pervert doing something inappropriate.

I struggled with perceptions. I did not want to be an unlikeable husband who ran around disrespecting my wife. Even though I enjoyed a good time when I was partying, I did not want to be seen as a wayward man if I happened to hug a female family member or my children, whom I loved. For too long, I was not true to myself because I did not want misperceptions to follow me when I was just being me.

Joy, though not always perfect either, which, of course, no one is, had a better grasp on all the personal issues I was struggling with. Knowing I was struggling, she would say, "People are going to do what they are going to do." She was really saying, "Let them do what they do. We just need to do what we do and be us!" She did not want to waste any time with my misconceptions. My wife helped me find a healthy and proper perspective on all my mental hang-ups, predispositions, and perceptions.

We were united in making sure we did not pass our concerns on to our children if possible. We did not drink or smoke around our children, day or night. They saw us party at our home in healthy ways. There were no adulterous activities around my girls. I was adamant about that when we moved to Kansas. As small as the city was, I would not be seen in a nightclub or gentlemen's club there. That's not to say I never have been to a club or gentlemen's club in my life; I surely have attended my share, but I never went to one near where I lived, not even a nightclub. It was important to me to never have misperceptions that would be a concern for my children. Papa was NOT a rolling stone—Papa would be a man who was found in his home!

In fact, concerning misperceptions, my privacy settings on my computer are set for a child. It's not that I can't handle adult material; I just don't want the misperception or the labeling of one who looks at porn on the computer, and if my wife picks up my laptop or cell phone, I wanted to explain anything I was looking at without a concern. Although I'm proud of this personal standard, you can bet my wife was checking all the time. But alas, she would not find anything to call me out on, not even a pop-up—knock on wood. Be careful, those pop-ups can bring up some unwanted sites even if you're doing an innocent search on any of your devices. Such are the times we live in. That is why I have taken steps to provide a clean and trusting living environment for my wife and my children. However, if I go to Vegas, well, we know what they say: "What happens in Vegas stays in Vegas." Right? My wife would probably say, "And what happens in Vegas had better stay there without you."

Many factors in business, especially for a person traveling like I was, can put you in a compromising situation. Your spouse simply has to find a way to trust you when you are at conventions and have a room alone or find yourself working late with a peer of the opposite sex. You should be free to ask questions to keep each other in check, but at the same time, you want to enjoy and live your life with your business associates. Joy and I found ways to do that by calling at the right time or taking advantage of FaceTime on our iPhones, which we bought for that purpose.

Early in our marriage, giving proper attention to each other was important, but equally important was having space when we were having a good time with our friends apart from our spouse. I sometimes caught the wrong parts of conversations between my wife and her friends. I had a problem with my timing on too many occasions. Some things you just don't need to know. I am so terrible at keeping secrets that I am probably not the right kind of friend she would want around, and I accept that. I have gotten better at not repeating certain things, as my memory is slipping with age, but I was too judgmental in the early years.

I worked out compromises with my wife if we were going out. I would say, for example, "If you want me to hold your hand and be with you at this event, let me know, and I am right there with you the whole time." However, if we both were in partying mode, I'd say, "You do your thing, and I will do mine." She would counter, "Let's party, and when I am ready to hold hands, I will come get you."

I always say at least one person has to keep the relationship's foundation solid and make sure the money is right, even if the other person is a little unwilling, uncooperative, or preoccupied. One person also has to keep it together, show the love, pray for the family, and focus on the making-a-house-a-home sort of thing. It is great if both partners are doing both. However, if no one is keeping it going and no one wants to keep it together, that is not good.

We also had the eleven-o'clock rule at night. In the early days, I hung out on Fridays with the guys, drinking and playing cards for the most part. Surely, I was doing life the wrong way, but if I had too much, I would stay where I was. I stayed out one time and did not call home, and boy, did I hear about it. I explained, but it did no good. We finally discussed the issue, and my wife shared that she didn't like worrying about me. I could do my thing, but I should not make her worry. I understood, and I agreed and committed to call her before eleven o'clock to explain where I was and whom I was with. If she wanted me home and I had been drinking, she could come get me, and I would come home. From that day on, whether I was doing business, hanging out, or spending time with family, I made a point to call and check in. It's a habit now.

My wife has been there with me and for me every step of the way. I could not have asked God for a better woman to be beside me. We have worked hard to establish a good Christian home and a sound financial foundation for our family. We have happily traveled all around the world together. We have made a commitment to make our faith a priority, and we have learned to pray together when neither of us knows what to do. She wanted a husband, and she got one. Her children know their father, who has been in their lives since they were born. Joy never knew her father, so she's happy I have been the type of father she never knew. Joy has made for a wonderful family for children and grandchildren. She has been the best mom a child could want, and her grandchildren love her all the more.

Not only did she raise our girls, but for many years, Joy mothered nurtured my niece for many years. This was a big sacrifice for the family as my niece was the same age as my youngest daughter. My greatest fear was my daughter grades would drop under these family circumstances. However, God blessed us to see both my daughter and niece achieving as straight A's / Honor Role students. My wife had so much to do with this outcome and I will always thank her for demonstrating agape love to my niece.

If you were to ask her today, "What makes you happy?" she would say that having me as her husband all these years has made her happy. Her two daughters, Brianne and Karrah, with their spouses and our grandchildren, all have made her happy. Every home or place we have lived in—except for one hotel—has made her happy. In 2012, when the housing market hit an all-time low, so did housing materials. Workers were looking for work, and I was playing with the idea of building a lake property. I had been going to Sugar Valley Lake for years to go camping, when one day, the opportunity to buy two lots came our way. One afternoon, my wife and I played house and laid out the floor plan, using string, empty Coke cans, and a measuring tape. We started building in late summer 2012, and we moved in during late spring 2013. I had the privilege of being my own architect and general contractor in building our lake home and working closely with my friend Jason. Together we got 'er done!

At this age, as a man in my mid-60s, I love the fact that I have made my wife happy in her lifetime. I have loved Joy Annette Holland Clay, and I have kept my vows to her, trust in her, and commitment to her. We have been married for forty plus wonderful years as of September 2, 2022, and we give God all the glory for all the things he has done in our relationship—not that we have done anything special. We keep trying harder to show the true love that drives us to each other both day and night. I call her Honey because she is so sweet, and when she is not, I still call her Honey!

I am grateful to have been part of her happiness in our forty-year plus journey through this life. I asked her to share with me in her own words how she feels about us at this milestone in our lives. Her thoughts follow:

Over forty years ago, I met my soul mate in you. You have set the foundation for our relationship and charted the direction and path for our life together. I would not be the person I am today without your love and understanding. I recall you saying that I had potential. You believed in me when I may not have believed in myself. You have been and continue to be my mentor, friend, partner, confidant, and spiritual partner and the best husband ever.

Over the years, I have witnessed your love for others and how you have shared your wisdom, talents, support, time, and money without seeking anything in return. To truly know you is to love you.

I pray that others will get to know and appreciate your love of life as they read this autobiography.

Love you, honey!

Wow. That's coming from my wife after forty years. I am grateful for all we have done together. I hope I have helped her to be the phenomenal and virtuous woman I know she is. I know God sent me a woman called Joy so I would know what true joy really is. Few people get a chance to have a true love that lasts. Too often, we forsake what is good for us during the difficult times. We get that way, I believe, because we don't accept the challenge of sitting down and being open and honest. We do not work hard to understand what is really hindering the relationship and the two people in the relationship. A relationship does not get better unless the people in the relationship get better. Joy and I learned how to sit down and talk early on, and it has helped us to be open and honest.

Yes, I achieved and accomplished many things in my life but not because I was particularly smart or even wealthy. Almost everything in my life happened because of my faith in God – my Lord Jesus Christ. Only by faith could I even have hoped to live this long and do so much. And with all that I have accomplish I still believe there is more to come.

Through faith, I could see better for myself, my family, and my friends. I did not know in the beginning what the word *faith* was all about, but now I do and I "press on!" I've said many times in my life, "Lord, give me more faith" more than anything else. Never let me lose hope. Don't give me more money, favor or help… just give me more faith.

I often realized after everything has been said and done that with my faith, I had everything I needed to be successful in life. Yet all the while, I know something was missing inside me. I just needed a little more faith because faith is the substance of things hoped for and the evidence of things Unseen. When you are walking by faith, having faith is essential. You have to have the faith to keep believing in yourself, your circumstance and those around you. Why? Because one day, like me, you will look back and see that you have in fact become evidence of all the things you, your parents, grandparents, family, and friends have hoped for. More importantly, you are evidence what God destined for you to become. At that moment, you will then realize that like me, **you are ultimately the *EVIDENCE UNSEEN* and *you have lived a life no one could imagine!***

CHAPTER 25

Monticello

I could never have imagined that on July 12, 2021, on the Mountaintop Tour at 2:10PM, I would be visiting the former President Thomas Jefferson's historically famed house (mansion) at Monticello's plantation grounds. Most of my life had been on a grand journey of uncovering the details behind my origin, and I was about to be exposed to more "evidence" that would enlighten me about my family roots that were directly linked to the great President, Thomas Jefferson. What I discovered in amazement would unfold vividly before my eyes. Touring Monticello multiple times, I would hear from many tour guides who were aware of the details about the historical nature of my enslaved family roots.

My Monticello ticket costs us nothing; due to my wife validating that I was, in fact, a descendant of former President Thomas Jefferson's enslaved population through her research on the ANCESTRY(A common DNA discovery site) app. Right there in Charlottesville, Virginia, I was located only miles from where a mob of white nationalists, with burning torches, once rallied at the University of Virginia over plans to remove a Confederate statue. Clearly, it cost my ancestors their lives, as well as their freedom on this earth to exist at Monticello as the house "slaves" of Thomas Jefferson. The commercial attempts to humanize the deplorable and oppressive living conditions that my ancestors were forced to endure, constantly forced me to blindly rejoice in their survival and suffering as slaves, and as the human beings they were. I have started to realize how impactful and courageous my bloodline had to have been back in those days.

The day had come where I made the decision to return to Monticello in reverence to their legacy. I had now come to the realization that all the time I spent at Monticello was a celebration of my ancestor's greatness. It would serve as confirmation that surviving a life of enslavement in order for their children's children to one day be free and prosperous, was enough for me to come back singing inside… "free at last, free at last." As a direct descendant, I was able to return to Monticello, free in mind and body. Thank God that I, nor my children have ever been enslaved. The fact that Monticello still stands today significantly proud in the nation's eyes for all to see, for me it was a sad commentary for what it stood for as a plantation of the enslaved.

While visiting the plantation's grounds, there was a chilling reminder in my soul that what Monticello represented could in fact happen again in this country. It is hard to overlook the blatant symbolism that can readily be found on the back of U.S. currency- the nickel. Monticello is listed as a United Nations Educational Scientific and Cultural Organization (UNESCO) site known for its original purpose of being a plantation. Though the recognition of Monticello can decidedly be for the honoring of our 3rd President for his architectural design of his mansion as well as for being the author of the Declaration of Independence, it was still the place that enslaved my ancestors. No recognition of Monticello should be highlighted without disclosing that it was indeed a plantation that had over 600 enslaved people; that were directly owned by Thomas Jefferson. It is this fact of life that I could not ignore having learned all that I know now.

JUST A REMINDER

My Charlottesville hotel was within walking distance from where, on August 11, 2017 Heather Heyer, a Caucasian (White) woman, died when she was struck by a car that had rammed into a crowd of counter protestors who had formed on a very narrow Charlottesville street. Here I was in July of 2021, walking in the very place where my understanding of the past and present were converging in a very historic sense. I could not have imagined that we would be in the area where there was a "Unite the Right" rally of white supremacist that was held on August 12, 2017. It was one thing to watch it on T.V. but quite another walk where so much hatred was on blast. I was at ground zero where Neo-Confederates who believe in slavery where marching down the streets with fire-lite torches along with Klansmen displaying crosses, flags and anti-Semitic slogans. No one could imagine that this would be happening in America again. But there I was envisioning what had happen in real time before my own very eyes.

In this moment, I was quickly reminded of Charleston, VA when there was the June 17, 2015 mass shooting of 9 African American (black) people attending Bible Study at the historic Mother Emanuel African Methodist Episcopal Church. The shooting itself was discriminately carried out by a white nationalist by the name of Dylan Roof. This memory of mind also left a chilling reminder to my soul that what America had experienced could happen again in this country because it happened right there in Charleston. We want to forget but it is better to be aware and be on guard. I recall having a family reunion in Myrtle Beach, S.C. A group of family members from various religious backgrounds such as Ministers, Deacons, and myself on my dad's side of the family all decided to travel to support the congregation and offer our prayers. I never would have imagined we would be sitting on the Mother Emanuel African Methodist Episcopal Church grounds where this heinous and brutal crime took place. It was a vivid remembrance that there are those who would rather see us dead… even as we worship the God of love and peace… who had "brought us thus far on our way."

Being there to tour Monticello and walking around in the beautiful scenery of Charlottesville, Virginia was almost surreal. I was boiling over with frustrating - reflective thoughts, and emotions that ran so deep within that it was hard to imagine what I was actually discovering about my own roots. I was now dealing with a higher sense of recognition about the facts that surrounded my family history. I struggled with reconciling with the many incidences of injustice in my own life that equally had many deep truths and their disappointing realities. The culminating questions were: "Has it gotten better? Is there any real change?" The unemotional answer to both questions is "yes." I think I was really saying, " considering all the suffering my people had gone through and fighting over the issue of slavery and the Civil War, why are there still signs and symbols that signal a desire to return to the past?

I was just so disappointed, and concerned that race relations were not getting better in America despite the arduous struggles my people went through. It was like wanting something to go away that you know never will. Monticello would be confirmation this might be so because of its glorifying existence. I concluded, there will always be an ideology that specific groups of people will promote that will them to feel that they are much better than others and that they are entitled to rule over others. My time at Monticello, would force me to look in the mirror, and somehow see that I lived a life where I have never been beaten or lynched. I am not a slave nor am I the "master" with such a desire to enslave other people either. Somehow, I was blessed to make it through life to find good, better and best in America. I felt a need to reassure myself that I was okay, and I would remain that way despite how I was feeling. However, the current events of recent years that I would witness since publishing the 1st Edition of my memoir in 2019 would certainly challenge my faith, and cause me to pause and recall the many sensational moments of awareness that I would experience at Monticello that would both bewilder and enlighten me each day.

MY MONTICELLO FAMILY TREE

My birth name is Francis Leander Clay, Jr. (1955 - present) and my mother, whom I deeply love, is Geraldine Marcel Thomas (1933 - 1991) ... the daughter of my grandmother, whom I hold in high regard called: Marion Virginia Lawson (1916 - 1991). Her mother was Sidney Louise Fleming Lawson (1888 - 1960), who I remembered clearly standing by her side at her death in my grandmother's house. My little brother Sidney would take on her first name as he was born right around the time of her death. My great grandmother, Sidney Louise Fleming Lawson was the daughter of Mariah Hughes (1857-1923) and Lewis Fleming (1853 - 1935), my great, great grandparents.

When I fully absorbed these connections, I found myself engulfed in this distant reality that I was in fact related to the Hughes family and sought to find out more about the fifth generation of Hughes. My great, great, great grandfather would now be none other than Rev. Robert Hughes (1821-1895), who was the son of Wormley Hughes (1781-1858…born. At Monticello… the grandson of Elizabeth Hemings) my great, great, great, great grandfather. Wormley Hughes would be a notable connection to Thomas Jefferson's Monticello because he dug Thomas Jefferson's grave and Robert Hughes, his son, would establish my family's path, and legacy towards freedom. This calculation of my family history had my blood pressure rising, and my curiosity at its peak because now the name Hughes was prominently featured in the historical recordings of Monticello. I recalled during the tour of the Burial Grounds for Enslaved People, there was a plaque that read:

"Robert Hughes, a minister who was born into slavery at Monticello, led mourners in prayers and hymns as the grave was filled and then covered by tree boughs."

During a tour at Monticello, anyone could see that my relative Rev. Robert Hughes was born a slave on Jefferson's plantation. Sadly, I just didn't get this connection for a long time. The education in our schools and in college that we are given about slavery taught many of us that slaves where brought here to America from Africa which is true. However, somewhere I missed the fact that there were many slaves born right here in America… enslaved from birth. Knowing this truth, Monticello, to me, was gravely more than a national landmark now… Monticello was where my ancestors were born right here in America as "American slaves," so to speak. I had to think: "was there a difference between an African slave brought to America versus a slave born in America?"

No one could have imagined that this revelation would come upon me in a way that would prompt me to reconcile these feelings of what I knew before to what I now know. From some place inside me, I welcomed everything I would learn and experience at Monticello. However, I had no idea about how I would get myself to accept these historical truths without asking a few simple questions. My simple questions were: "Why? And How?" Why did my people become enslaved in the first place and how did "they" manage to survive and break through slavery, racism, discrimination, and more? "They" meaning my family whose first names were... Wormley, Robert, Mariah, Sidney, Marion, and Geraldine. Six generations of survivors and thrivers in life!

At Monticello, Wormley Hughes (1781 - 1858) was the head gardener at the estate. It was first hand common knowledge that my grandmother, Marion Virginia Lawson, was an immaculate gardener too. I knew this first hand. During the summer months, she had me work in her beautiful and spectacular garden. Her garden of colorful flowers of all types was the whole length of an entire city block in Philadelphia. I wondered with confidence, and began to ask myself: "Did she inherit her pristine gardening skills from her family... her mother or grandmother Mariah Hughes (1857-1923) whose grandfather was Wormley Hughes? The tour guide at Monticello said to me that every group of descendants he had ever spoken to always state that someone in the family was a successful gardener. As I glazed over the immaculate flower gardens on the Monticello tour, I could only think of my grandmother's particulars to attending a garden that she taught us.

Wormley Hughes is said to have worked in the Monticello mansion and was one of the most trusted enslaved servants. He and his wife, Ursula Granger, the niece of Issac Granger Jefferson, had 12 children. Wormley is recorded as being freed by Jefferson's daughter Martha Randolph. What was more interesting about all this to me... was the fact that Wormley Hughes was the oldest son of Betty Brown Hemings

(1759-1831), who was the daughter of Elizabeth Betsy Hemings (1735 - 1807) Elizabeth arrived at Monticello in 1774 as a part of President Thomas Jefferson's inheritance.

For too long, no one in my family could have or even wanted to try to imagine this connection to Thomas Jefferson to be our truth. That the man so many admired from our history lessons of the past for having so much character, not only enslaved but had sexually adulterous relationships with his female slaves. Yes, the rumor and accusations of such behaviors at Monticello had more truths than anyone could imagine. In my Monticello reflections, it was all getting personal now. To be directly associated with Jefferson's plantation via the Hughes was a personal and anticlimactic experience. Clearly my roots are undeniably buried deep in many places on and around the Monticello plantation.

UNBELIEVABLE EVENTS

On March 13, 2020, the President of the United States declared a national emergency over the outbreak of the coronavirus (2019 COVID 19) epidemic. It would be plain for anyone to see that we had a national problem on our hands. Everyone saw the power of government leaders around the world to attempt to control our daily lives. For months, we were restricted from moving around in group settings and there were places we could not go. We were required and in some places forced to wear masks and take vaccines that had new approval protocols. We were essentially "enslaved" by these health directives to protect our own health and others for all the right reasons. Still, many of us resented that fact that we were being told what to do. Surely my enslaved ancestors at Monticello knew these feelings of corporate control and selected rationing of needed resources.

I knew, as the National Planning Manager for Spencer & Spencer Medical in the mid 1980's, that the company always kept a 10% reserve for medical supplies in case of a war and for national emergencies. I knew capacity that could be generated if needed by maximizing production shifts and using automation. And as a previous Headquarters

Commander in the U. S. Army, who had the responsibility of keeping an inventory of medical masks in our reserve stockpiles, there were always plans in place to have masks and other medical supplies available in case of a nuclear, biological or chemical attack. So I was somewhat perplexed to see how we handled protecting medical personnel at the beginning of the pandemic. Successful leaders have the responsibility to protect their people in a crisis or when faced with a major challenge.

In fact in the Army, we were trained on the "buddy system" of fitting your mask and we knew how to social distance from someone who was contaminated. All these past experiences of preparation deeply alarmed me that at some level of leadership the priority of planning for the unexpected was intentionally removed for short term profitable gains or just in neglect. I concluded America was now going to pay a big price for a major leadership mistake in contingency planning and crisis decision making. Not having an adequate reserve in medical masks and supplies would make all the government mandates and restrictions difficult. During the 2019 Covid 19 pandemic, I would ask: Why were we not prepared to have needed masks on hand when they were needed most? I would think similarly about Monticello having some correlating thoughts: Where were the plans to profitably manage the Jefferson plantation? Why were there no plans to keep the enslaved families at Monticello together upon Jefferson's death? Why did so many suffer because of the desires of a few? I somehow expected more from the great Thomas Jefferson who was President and spoke against slavery continuing... who knew he was responsible for my ancestors' plight upon his death.

As I examined the Presidency of Thomas Jefferson in his time of office, there were noble acts of statesmanship that proved to be a potential benefit to my enslaved ancestors. Giving credit where credit is due, it appears that Monticello's Thomas Jefferson opposed slavery even though he had approximately 600 or more slaves. In 1778, he drafts a Virginia law that prohibits the importing of slaves from Africa. In 1784 he proposed legislation that would band slavery in the Northwest Territories. Then there were the 1782 "Notes on the State of Virginia," that highlighted Jefferson's plans for the emancipation of all slaves and his honest account of our differences as human beings... clearly showed "evidence" of Jefferson's humanity. My conclusion was that Thomas Jefferson wanted the stopping of the trading of slaves because he felt there were enough slaves reproducing to sustain the need for slaves here in America. He was not on board with doing away with all slaves in America to the point where he would direct the freeing of all his own slaves. And, Jefferson had a different definition of equality for his slaves.

On the other side of this observation were Jefferson's own words that **"slavery was like holding a wolf by the ear, and we can neither hold onto him , nor safely let him go."** The preservation of these words alone, by those who managed Monticello, felt like a hidden political "dog whistle" of some sort to always say to "white America" that you can never hold back a "black American" who is determined to be free. The caution brought by this quote was designed to instill fear amongst slave owners. It fostered the thought that to let the "black American" taste and embrace some sense of freedom would seemingly not be a safe endeavor for "white America" due to a possible retaliation for the way one might have treated as a slave in the past. So in essence, the charge given to those who lived and upheld the "Monticello life" was to "keep holding the wolf by the ear... keep control of the black American!" This charge essentially continues as long as this Monticello slavery mantra remains.

Conclusively, I couldn't help but to believe that Monticello for "white America" was a serious historical symbol of the way life used to be with all the wonderful glory days of a fully functioning plantation... preserved especially for the purpose of letting generations to see just how good the master had it with all his slave hands working hard 24/7. In fact, I believe that there are those who still believe in the "Monticello life" who felt like they still had the right to enslave "black Americans - the wolves" and demanded a return to their good old days where the master and their overseers ruled by threats, intimidation and hurtful acts. Then too, there was the reality that the "house slaves" had it better than the field slaves who seemingly worked hard to protect their preferred slave status on the plantation. This was not a fictional assumption on my part, this would actually prove to be an American reality that we all live with each day.

FAST FORWARD

January 6, 2021 would be a vivid example of the deep revolutionary intentions of the "Alt-Right" to manipulate lawful elections. We all were in shock watching the "live election news" televised in every way. An actual revolutionary insurrection happened in and around our nation's capitol conducted by mostly "white American" citizens who were labeled patriots. No one could imagine that they would see a time when our own citizens would over take the Capitol while Congress was in session to conduct the peaceful transfer of power from one President to another. This mob even threatened with tolerable resistance to hang a sitting Vice President while the current President looked on and did nothing to call off or stop the insurgency which was clearly being instigated by his rhetoric, prevocational acts and intentional silence. No one could ever imagine a day like this would be recorded in the history books. We should have known though… there is "evidence" that on August 24th, 1814, as the War of 1812 was in motion, there were British Troops who had marched into Washington and set the U.S. Capitol - the President's Mansion on fire… only three years after Jefferson had left office as President.

The treatment of slaves by the President Jefferson who lived at Monticello cause me to think and compare the response of law enforcement under a sitting President to the Black Lives Matter protest on May 29, 2020 with the January 6th, 2021 protest and insurrection at the Capitol grounds. One was met with an increased level of law enforcement and preparation as participants faced a wall of law enforcement with shields and guns pointed at them. The other response we know "the powers that be" allowed the advancement of insurrectionists and did not prepare properly for the potential threat that was emanate. The treatment of "black American" protests, going back to Bloody Sunday in my family hometown of Selma, Alabama, seemed to always be more physical, well anticipated and deadly. The quote from Thomas Jefferson would characterize the law enforcement response in the Black Lives Matter protest… clearly someone must "pull the ear of the wolf and hold it tightly."

I thought to myself that there were some comparable behavior by our country's governmental leaders, specifically the President, looking at January 6, 2021. Thomas Jefferson knew that slavery was wrong but did not have what it took to stop the unbelievable acts of injustice… and he preferred to allow the status quo to continue to be as is and just let history take its course. The President on January 6, 2021 did the same by tweeting "Be there… it will be wild." Monticello was a vivid reminder of how fragile our freedoms are in America in part because of it leaders and how they act or fail to act. If a leader dies or the transfer of power does not happen like it should, we could all find ourselves in a Monticello reality. Government leaders have the ability to empower others to use force anyway they choose in order to establish what they think is right or to turn a blind eye to unlawful and inhumane acts to facilitate what they think is right.

Then I thought further, how Jefferson handled slavery was just an impulsive strategy that many leader might employ to go against the grain and bring about a desired change. I remembered Malcom X would say about affecting change…"by any means necessary." Then I thought of the late John Robert Lewis who died July 17th, 2020. Congressman Lewis who made history in the Civil Rights movement in the city of Selma, Alabama where my grandparents on my father's side had their roots. In 1965, when I was ten years old, Lewis would be on the front line of the Edmund Pettus Bridge on the day that is known as Bloody Sunday (March 7, 1965 600 African Americans marched 54 miles). On this day Lewis was brutally attacked, beaten by police and bit by police dogs during the freed march from Selma to Montgomery to bring about change. The "evidence" was all there captured by news cameras and reporters that day. Ironically, at Monticello, all the evidence that slaves were there and all they did is on full display for all to see.

One of John Lewis' last quotes made me ponder the negative aspects of his leadership style to bring about real change. He would say, **"Do not get lost in the sea of despair, be hopeful, be optimistic. Our struggle is not the struggle of a day, a week, a month, or a year, it is the struggle of a lifetime. Never, ever be afraid to make some noise and get in good trouble, necessary trouble."** The quote caused me to articulate the thought that Monticello would be a vivid symbol of the lifetime struggle for freedom here in America and I was certainly not going to be silent about it now that I know what I know. I concluded, "Good trouble must confront bad trouble to avoid being in trouble."

All these unbelievable events were circulating within my mind to grasp the true meaning of what I was feeling as I toured Monticello again specifically to discover the "right questions" to be asked that fit the answers that were so evident in the facts I had gathered about each of these events circulating in my mind. My ancestors knew the meaning of John Lewis' words… "Never be afraid" to seek the change that is necessary to make change. In other words, you have to get messy to clean up what is messy. What happened at Monticello was a reminder that things in America could get messy again if we don't keep the struggle to be free going. When a leader attempts to "make America great again," one question that fits the facts would be: "make America great again for who?" Keeping Monticello for all its beauty appears to be a good thing. The question is: " It's a good thing for who?" And if there was still a question in anyone's mind about what the struggle is… the answer is simply to stay informed and to vote in numbers.

Even my favorite poet, Langston Hughes would pop in my mind on this thought. Could it be that he too was related to Monticello being a Hughes? He would write a poem called: "Let America Be America Again (1935)." Some of the words of this poem would resinate as I ponder the question again: "make America great again for who?"

> The millions who have nothing for our pay?
> For all the dreams we've dreamed

And all the songs we've sung
And all the hopes we've held
And all the flags we've hung
The millions have nothing for our pay -
Except the dreams that's almost dead today
O, let America be America again -

AN IMAGINARY ESCAPE

Where I stood before the tour guide came, on the North side terrace of Monticello, I could only imagine that my ancestors were just as aware as I was. By instinct, you would know that freedom would not be found by escaping to the west where there were more high mountains to climb in the heat of the day. The shadows of the eastern morning sun were cooler and perfect for escaping into the early morning. Between Monticello and the high mountains to the west was this vast valley of green trees that were rooted in a beautiful green landscape. Anyone could smell the moisture fermenting from the Virginia valley on a clear perfect sunny day. The water found in the valley had to be a faithful friend of slaves trying to escape north because the dogs would have to lose their scent at some point.

I knew this from first hand experience, when I was viciously attacked by dogs running through the woods in Woodlawn, Maryland by Glenridge Jr. High on my way home. The body of water that I would end up struggling through made it difficult for the dogs to stay with me as they were attacking. Monticello brought back that vivid youthful memory and it was the answer to the question I posed to myself if I was a slave escaping: "where would I go if I could escape these Monticello grounds?" The flowing clear waters would surely be a source of energy and food from the plants and animals found near its banks. Anything found there would be delicious to eat while in survival mode. I naturally concluded that if I were a slave planning to escape Monticello, I would never travel south. I would probably have figured out the direction where most slaves who had been purchased were being taken. An assumption would be that the south, where more plantations were, would not be a good direction to go and risk being beaten or killed.

Thus I concluded from the "mountaintop" of Monticello where I stood while awaiting the next tour of Thomas Jefferson mansion... that the best escape route had to be to travel north, a little after sunset, when the shadows of the sun would be in your left eye. An escaping slave would have followed the deep valley ways through the night and kept a rising easterly sun hitting your right shoulder walking alertly in the shadow of tall trees and high grass. For some reason, I imagined how I would one day have navigated to escape successfully if I was enslaved here at the Monticello plantation. I could not imagine that I would be standing there alone, with the only thought on my mind being: "how do I escape?" The ironic and noticeable thing at Monticello was that there were no descriptions or any mention of successful slaves escaping the plantation. Nor were there any recordings of slaves who had died trying to escape. There was no one to mention the "underground railroad" that some of my ancestors might have taken. The tour at Monticello gave you the feeling that those that did live on the best plantation, were there happy doing the day to day "slave workings" of Thomas Jefferson and his family.

Inside Jefferson's mansion were indeed very impressive collectables that I am sure some slaves admired and enjoyed to the point they did not want to leave the "best slave environment" around. The tour gave you the feeling that each of the 600 or so of Jefferson's slaves were very satisfied "pieces of property" and they were most comfortable with their status in life, particularly if they were born on Monticello grounds. If this speculation were true, my thoughts about escaping would be pointless and unfounded. However, my inner instincts told me that there had to be those who felt like me... who made the same observations as me when they set foot on the Monticello grounds. I know there were those who took a risk to find freedom somehow. Some made it and I am sure many did not. Some were loyal and stayed until Thomas Jefferson died, and then received their freedom. I concluded that there was something very special about my ancestors who trusted and stayed hoping their freedom would one day be granted by their master. I believe they had the vision of being free human beings like master Jefferson and his family one day. They believed if they worked hard enough for it, good would come.

Slaves like Robert Hughes, my great, great, great, grandfather had learned the wisdom, wit and ways of his master Thomas Jefferson; and lived in such a way to enjoy what he had which would include embracing one's faith in God. Born at Monticello in America, the question might be where does a slave then escape to? What would be a better plight than to live a "Monticello life" like the Jeffersons back in those days? I reasoned that the only thing better than being a slave to Thomas Jefferson in those days would be to be like Thomas Jefferson destined to be a master of one's own life. Then I surmised reflectively, who would then be "the wolf" if that were to be?

FIRST FLOOR LEVEL

Thomas Jefferson's Monticello house, as it is referred to in the marketing materials, was really a mansion by any standards. It looked like a miniature Capital of the United States. The old brick structure with its wooden framed architecture that still has its original construction in certain areas… had 35 rooms according to the Monticello guide I had. The information shared about Monticello the mansion gave the appearance that it took some time to build it and the slaves who built it would work on it from 1784 to 1796 while Jefferson kept planning its alterations and expansions after returning from trips abroad. My initial tour took me through the entry hall, south square room, library, cabinet, bed chamber, Tea room, Madison room, dining room, greenhouse, cabinet and parlor. Monticello was bigger that your normal house… it was a huge mansion back then and it is still huge today.

On the first floor, as I entered the mansion from the east portico or porch, my eyes were glued to the blue and white settings for coffee or tea that were centered near the large windows. My grandmother Marion had a set of these types of tea cups and she would have tea every morning for my grandfather with toast. The large fireplaces in each room with the wooden chairs, which had a red velvet type of material, clearly required someone to manage each fireplace to keep these rooms warm in the winter. There was a second and third floor for Jefferson's family of 40 including his Aunt and grandchildren. I knew who would be doing the work around Monticello servicing all the family back in the slavery days.

During the tour, I clearly remembered the wooden chess set facing the west lawn because I said to myself… I might have been able to play chess with the master himself, if I were a slave. To have the opportunity to win a game or two with President Thomas Jefferson, was improbable maybe! I then recalled my child's experience of beating my Jewish neighbor's son at chess. I never played another chess game in their house again. I knew from experience, it was possible to learn the game from watching. This was how I learned to play chess and checkers. No one had formally taught me how to play these games… maybe it was in my genes to pick up a game of chess without ever playing someone directly. No doubt, I believed I could have beaten the master if I were to have had the opportunity to do so at Monticello.

Now the beds I saw were very small to me, and Jefferson's tiny "alcove" bed that he would eventually die in seemed to be positioned between two walls like a closet. Me being taller than 6 feet, getting in his bed might have been a big problem for me at Monticello… I was too tall for the sleeping accommodations there in Jefferson's "house." Having a good place to sleep would be one of the reasons I joined the Army and not the Navy. I knew there were tight quarters on a Navy ship, and that was definitely not for me. Being "for real" about this, there would never be a "first level" bed for me at Monticello. Slaves that look like me did not sleep in the master's nice plush bed. The Monticello mansion would have many beds for family and guests to sleep or to do other things.

Toward the end of the tour, there was a wooden piano and harpsichord that was clearly there for entertainment and the pleasure of his family. Seeing these items and others made me think about my father, Francis

L. Clay, Sr., who as a pianist. My dad always had a piano in the home. I had one too in my house and like Thomas Jefferson, I first brought our family piano for the entertainment and musical education of my wife and daughters. If I could just get past the "slavery thing," Monticello with its wooden floors seemed to be a place you could dance, sing, laugh and have so much fun. If I could have lived on the first floor, I certainly would have called Monticello "my home."

Being a writer myself, I admired original documents with Thomas Jefferson and John Hancock signatures. One document, on display behind a clear glass exhibit window, mentioned the "Independent States" which was framed inside Thomas Jefferson's private office and library that had over 200 hard cover bound books of various languages. I would have a private office too with a library in my lake home in Kansas that I had built and designed like Jefferson. It was only two stories and it had 12 living areas but I would call it "my Monticello" jokingly as I looked at it setting up on the top of the hill when I returned home. There were no slaves there but I was indeed the "master."

The first floor level was an amazing museum to show how our 3rd President… a man of great influence; or to say it differently, a man who was a plantation owner of hundreds of slaves… could live amazingly well in America. Jefferson did live lavishly at Monticello in this beautiful state of Virginia. Who would not want to live like that without understanding the untold human price of forced labor that was required to make the "first level" happen on a day to day basis. Though this was reality at one time, no one today could ever imagine there being enslaved African Americans (not workers) laboring against their own will just for a few privileged people to live a elite and royal life at the expense of 600 or so enslaved people's freedom.

THE BASEMENT LEVEL

As soon as I entered the basement level which had "dependencies" throughout and around the foundation of the Monticello mansion that was connected by a long walkway of carved stones found on the top and both sides of the walls. My senses, as a descendent of those who were enslaved in this environment, went into a totally different gear of fight or flight. The old formation of aging stones made all this feel so real and it let you concede that this place was an authentic plantation of hard work. Because the stones were original in some places, you knew slavery was as real as the giant stone construction that formed Monticello's foundation. I distinctly viewed, that where I was walking deserved my upmost respect and full attention. As a direct descendant of the people who did the all the hard slave work beneath the first floor of privilege above, I felt I was walking in their shoes. I would be taking the same footsteps as a free man, as they did as slaves many years ago.

The eastern bright sunlight from the large blocked caged windows provided adequate light for anyone to see where they were going during the day. It felt like I was being put in a deeply trenched bunker during wartime that was designed to protect you from a nuclear bomb. I began to have a "historical seizure" and got claustrophobic by an intimate sense of being a worked to death every day as a slave to keep Monticello's master or overseers happy. I just did not envision glorifying these slave conditions as a noble exhibit knowing how good life was for others that did not look like me back in those days. There were no smiles of admiration from any of the visitors during this part of the tour, just glazes of amazement. Regardless of race or color, no one could ever imagine that slaves did all the things that were mentioned during the tour gracefully against their own free will.

As you walked down the hall there were clearly working stations that the master's slaves worked in. The basement wine cellar clearly showed Thomas Jefferson loved his drink and if you matched this exhibit with the well manicured grapevines in the vineyard on the Monticello grounds toward south… bingo, the 3rd President had one hell of a wine cellar of the finest bottles of wine and this was truly the place to party! I am sure the slaves that worked there had the skills to produce wine if given the chance to so. They probably sipped a little here or there. I know I would have under those conditions.On a red brick floor there was the first kitchen and clearly there would be slaves doing all the cooking at Monticello. I reasoned that James Hemings (brother of Sally Hemings) did some cooking because Monticello had a list of kitchen items on display that dated back to 1796. We know he joined Thomas Jefferson on a trip in 1784 to learn about French cooking and upon his return became the "chef de cuisine" at Monticello.

Monticello had its own smoke house, ice house and carving station for its meats. There was a fishing pond to catch fresh fish. There were carriage bays, privies, and a dairy. There was also a storehouse to iron clothes and a joinery… Monticello basement level was a 24/7 production operation with everything flowing in and out of the basement to be made everything and anything available for Thomas Jefferson, his family and guests. Fruits that were grown in the plentiful orchards of Monticello… vegetables that were picked fresh daily from the south side garden on the hill, were all funneled into the basement level for processing and cooking. This would also include tobacco and flowers of Thomas Jefferson's preference.

To be honest, I did not buy the tour guide's stories that Jefferson's slaves worked for food and got a "small pay" for all the forced labor they provided. Slaves were said to have been given two sets of clothing and a blanket every three years. What was not mentioned was the brutality of the "overseer" during the enslaved times of Monticello. I said to myself, "though I might have accepted the fact that I had to be enslaved and make do while I was there at Monticello; I never ever would have said, it would be my own choice to be enslaved and express that I would be happy to stay there at Monticello forever. No… I could never have imagined accepting Monticello as my home.

FREED AT LAST… MAYBE NOT

One of the biggest disappointments for me walking away from the Monticello grounds, from the east side of the Monticello mansion, was the fact that my ancestors, particularly the Hughes clan, turned out that they would all lose everything they had and be sold when Thomas Jefferson died. It was hard for me to reconcile within myself that human beings were merely property and had no entitlements. I said to myself, "you mean to tell me that my people that were enslaved here - all those many years... having built this place and they ended up being split apart and sold with nothing." It hit me too hard toward the end the tour... simply asking: what was all this slavery for if Thomas Jefferson ended up dying broke and was not able not protect his personal human property that had been loyal to him and his family?

You had 130 -200 people who were enslaved at Monticello from the mid 1700's, all through Thomas Jefferson's presidency until his death in 1826... my beloved ancestors all were sold at an estate sale after Thomas Jefferson's death because Thomas Jefferson's estate could not pay his debts. Mr. Jefferson would die on July 4th, 1826 at the age of 83 the same day President James Monroe died. Now my mind keenly focuses on the significance of July 4th and what this date would mean to me going forward. July 4th would be a day that would take me back to my youth because it was Independence Day! Monticello would clearly beg the question: "Independence Day for who?" Surely, not for my enslaved ancestors who would realize their trauma over being enslaved would start all over with another master at another plantation. I would remember these words I was taught in grade school:

> **"We hold these truths to be self-evident, that all men are created equal, that they are endowed by their Creator with certain unalienable (absolute) Rights, that among these are Life, Liberty and the pursuit of Happiness." - Preamble, Declaration of Independence, 1776.**

Thomas Jefferson was the primary author of these words in a document called "The Declaration of Independence " which was signed on July 4th in my home town of Philadelphia, Pennsylvania where the Liberty Bell, the symbol of American Independence... proclaiming LIBERTY throughout all the land unto all the inhabitants thereof. Though Thomas Jefferson is on record for speaking out against the international slave trade; again, I believed he would take this position only when he knew a new generation of his slaves were beginning to be born on his Monticello grounds. Sadly by establishing and talking about his anti-slavery position, Jefferson would only end up freeing just two of his 600 slaves during his lifetime and seven would be freed during his death.

Another question that the facts about Jefferson would answer would be: Is saying you are against slavery and having slaves a version of hypocrisy of some sort? My answer will always be " yes" within the context of shedding light on Thomas Jefferson thinking of wanting to do good and actually doing bad. Pondering this point, I recall in reading my Bible some words from Paul who said in Romans 7:15-20... **"I do not understand what I do. For what I want to do I do not do, but what I hate I do. And if I do what I do not want to do, I agree that the law is good. As it is, it is no longer myself who do it, but it is sin living in me. For I know that good itself does not dwell in me, that is, in my sinful nature. For I have the desire to do what is good , but I cannot carry it out. For I do not do the good I want to do, but the evil I do not want to do - this I keep on doing. Now if I do what I do not want to do it is no longer I who do it, but it is is living in me that does it."**

I reasoned, that against the background of deadly slave revolts like the one in Haiti in 1791 where slaves took bloody revenge on their captive and masters, Thomas Jefferson was scared to free his slaves that had been held in captivity all these years. This would be certainly be reflective of his quote about holding the wolf's ear... there was a danger in letting a wolf go. This was the reason he continued to do what he did not want to do, sin or not - lawful or not. As a slave, you had four options to be freed from slavery... freedom was granted, you purchased your freedom, you waited for the establishment of the Thirteenth Amendment in 1865 (almost 40 years after Thomas Jefferson died and after the Civil War) or you gained freedom by escaping successfully. The irony of it all was that though a slave might find freedom, many who enslaved their slaves never could imagine slaves being gainfully free human beings.

Wormley Hughes, Rev. Robert Hughes father was one of Jefferson's slaves that was emancipated (freed from any legal commitments) and given his freedom by Thomas Jefferson's family. His son Robert Hughes would still remain a slave until his emancipation. Through a family gesture of favor, Thomas Jefferson's grandson would give an acre of land to Rev. Hughes congregation to build a church that Robert Hughes would become one of its founders. Monticello had me pondering about why I, as an African American man, would now want to celebrate anything about July 4th... a day that specifically symbolized the re-enslavement of my ancestors... some of President Thomas Jefferson's most favored, trusted and loyal slaves. The very man who authored the Declaration of Independence for all men, sadly was not man enough to freed his own slaves when he was alive and did not protect them so that they would remain at Monticello (their home of many years) upon his death. I found this to be quite repulsive.

Near the time I visited Monticello for the 3rd time, it would be timely for me to learn that a U.S. President finally signed Bill S. 475 on Thursday, June 17th, 2021. This legislation supported "Juneteenth National Independence Day Act" as a holiday just 30 days before my last visit to Monticello. This bill made June 19th... the day General Order No. 3 by the Union Army General Gordon Granger came down 1865 which declared "freedom" for slaves in Texas, an official Federal holiday for all Americans. During slavery days, June 19th would come after President Lincoln issued the Emancipation Proclamation on January 1, 1863 freeing all slaves in Texas. The Thirteenth Amendment to the constitution abolishing chattel slavery nationwide on December 6, 1865, at the end of the Civil War, appeared to be the more appropriate day for a slave to celebrate their freedom. Then again, December 6th probably would be too cold to cook out and have a July 4th fun-like celebration outside in winter weather. June 19th had be the better day to celebrate when school was out and the weather was much better.

It made sense to me more than ever that on June 19th (1865) it would be completely appropriate to celebrate what happened on January 1, 1863 along with July 4th which represented our country's independence.

Though many of my ancestors were not freed prior to 1865, it was clear to me I was blessed because Wormley Hughes was free and because he was freed by Jefferson himself. Somehow his son, my great, great, great, grandfather, Robert Hughes would soon be freed. Monticello, if it is to be celebrated for anything, it would not be for the freedoms it afforded to its slaves. Rather, this place should be shamed and condemned unofficially in a reflective conversation for the enslavement of my people for 60 years and for the re-enslavement of my ancestors upon Thomas Jefferson's death. All this history got very personal during my last visit at Monticello and I couldn't help but to feel this way knowing all that I know now. In my mind, there could be no celebration of July 4th without acknowledging June 19th and my remembering what happen to my ancestors around that time.

REV. ROBERT HUGHES

When I went to Monticello this last time solely for the purpose of seeing the burial place of my ancestors, of which none of them would I be able to identify when I got to the exhibit, it felt like someone just said, "bury the slave over the hill by the big tree." As I walked from the parking lot to the "Burial Grounds For Enslaved People" - a private area surrounded by a roadside wired fence was nothing like the tall black erected royal fenced area of the Jefferson's family cemetery only a few minutes walk away. This would be another vivid example of the difference in the treatment of the slave and his master even in death at Monticello. Commentary: "I did not like it at all."

At this exhibit with its rusty sign, I was forced to believe that a few stones facing the east, the direction back to Africa(home), were actually the tombstones of those that died there. Someone placed an arrangement of plastic flowers out of respect near one of the larger stones that had no name or marking of any kind. I recall there was a sign at the burial grounds that said many of the graves belonged to the children enslaved at Monticello. I thought, if this were so, where were the adults buried? And then exhibit signs listed family names which included the Hemings. Bang - it hit me, again… those buried would be from my family line. The "evidence" was clear. Elizabeth Betsy Hemings, my 6th great grandmother, would be our matriarch At Monticello. More "evidence" to provide answers to the hidden questions I had.

At the "Burial Grounds For Enslaved People" exhibit, I would go on to take the time to read the last description of this burial ground memorial. For all that it was worth, I am so glad I did. There were way too many unknown facts about those slaves who had died at Monticello and I was overwhelmed in amazement while reading the inscriptions for this exhibit. The more I read, I immediately became deeply connected to the words. The last sentence which read:

> **"After a procession to a burial ground in a grove, Robert Hughes, a minister who was born into slavery at Monticello, led mourners in prayer and hymns as the grave was filled and then covered by tree boughs."**

This one sentence grounded me into the history of Monticello and it was the key "evidence" I needed to see before leaving the plantation grounds. All the tour guides there and all the verbal information shared and read, along with my wife Joy's tireless detailed research within ancestry.com and other genealogical sites... they all brought me to this truth that I could not deny. I was directly related to Rev. Robert Hughes and my Monticello roots... It was factually documented for me to know about and see the fruits of some of Robert Hughes' labor, his faith and his freedom. A connection forged by faith was being made and that was all I could focus on at the moment.

I believe it was from listening to a YouTube presentation about Monticello's "Getting Word" project, I heard the melody of an old slave song "Beyond the hill we will be free some day" - words of hope that lead me to believe that "true freedom" for a slave was achieved without question at death. Dying was now one more valid way for a slave to be free and many would exercise their right to die this way by trying to escape or resisting to be a slave anymore. Only now, would the old spiritual hymn "Oh Freedom" that use to be sung during the Civil Rights movement in the 60's gain its true meaning in my remembrance:

Oh, freedom
Oh, freedom
Oh, freedom over me!
And before I'd be a slave
I'll be buried in my grave
And go home to my Lord and be free.

This was my own assumption but it was the first thing that came into my spirit when I walked on the grounds of Monticello, "How do I get the hell out of here?" And if I could not, I would be willing to die trying. Thank God I did not have to make that choice in life. I could not believe that when I came to Monticello on my 2nd visit, my wife and I would visit the very church grounds of the church that my great, great, great grandfather built some 200 years ago. It would be Founders Day and we would attend his church. After emancipation, the Hughes were taken to the Edgehill plantation near Monticello. Apparently, to reunify the family and community of those who were enslaved at Monticello, an acre of land was given by Thomas J Randolph to establish Union Run Baptist Church in 1865… the same church I would attend that day.

Rev. Robert Hughes, Union Run Baptist Church founding minister, would pastor this church for 30 years. I could not have imagined on our 2nd visit to Monticello, we would arrive just days from the church discovering the large tombstone of Rev. Hughes on the church grounds. More "evidence" to questions that were bubbling inside me. It would be Sunday, July 11, 2021 and I would sit there in pews weeping in tears as the spirituals were sung. All I could think about was my grandmother as the choir sang the words, **"this is my story, this is my song… praising my Saviour all the day long, this is my story, this my song.. praying my Saviour all the day long."**

I would remember that my grandmother, Marion, was a "housekeeper" at one of the big mansions in Philadelphia, she would wear a white uniform with an apron to work. She taught us how to walk properly with your head and chin up while balancing the thick "yellow pages" as we walked across the room. My grandmother showed us the exercises she did against the wall to strengthen her back. She would say a server or worker had to have a strong back as she stood in her old age completely against the wall and could bend down and touch her toes coming right back up in one motion. No one could do what she did, but it was obvious that she learned all this from somewhere… along with all her professional gardening skills and techniques for cleaning silver.

I looked firmly at one lady at church thinking of my grandmother and her avid love for the Lord. At one time with so much passion, she would declare boldly… "you can't take away my Jesus… you can't take away my Jesus." She taught me to remember and memorize the 23 Psalms. She guided me to reading "Proverbs" during our summer visits. Where did her sense of faith come from? What caused her to be so committed to the church, and the Lord? As I glanced at the lady way too often, she looked so much like my grandmother, I just had to approach her. I introduced myself before leaving for my brother's wedding that was 30 minutes away that day. It turned out this beautiful lady was a direct descendant of Rev. Robert Hughes with full knowledge of her connection to Monticello. More "evidence" I could not deny that was cementing me into this historical paradox called Monticello. The same faith… the same God that Rev. Robert Hughes devoted his life to was the same faith I had all throughout my own life. This family icon believed in the same God I have been worshiping all my life. "Wow… wow… Amen… Amen…" was all I could say within myself.

At Union Run Baptist Church, 3220 Keswick Road, Keswick, Virginia - Rev. Dr. Rickey White would be the Senior Pastor on my 3rd visit to Monticello. August 7th, 2022 was Founders Day again and there was now a historical sign to be unveiled that stood wrapped up in front of the church. Rev. Robert Hughes was the Founding Pastor and served August 5, 1821 to 1895. I asked if there were any written sermons that I could see and the disappointing answer was "no," along with an explanation of a church fire which destroyed everything. For me, the answer blocked out the light of the celebration we were having. Yes... the answer did spark another thought provoking question that was unanswered, but I thank the current Pastor for continuing to honor my great, great, great grandfather Rev. Rober Hughes all these years.

On this day there would be a representative from the Getting Word African American Oral History Project from Monticello, and a representative from the Albemarle County Community Remembrance Project to unveil the official historical marker in front of the church Rev Robert Hughes founded. As an acknowledged descendant, I would be blessed to have helped out with the unveiling of the official historic marker which was a proud moment. I believe my mother and grandmother would have loved it. Who could imagine one of his descendants having such an honor. A map was shared that showed how the church was moved to its current location years ago. The historical market reads:

> **"Soon after the Civil War, the Rev. Robert Hughes (1821 -1895) and other freedmen organized Union Branch Church, later known as Union Run Baptist Church. Spiritual life was vital to formerly enslaved African Americans, and establishing churches and creating communities were of primary importance. Thomas Jefferson Randolf of Edgehill deeded one acre to the church's deacons in 1867. The congregation purchased the Limestone Church building and re-erected it on this site, where it also served as a school. The church became a cornerstone of the community. The Rev. Hughes, pastor for three decades, was inferred into the church yard, the resting place of hundreds of its members. - Department of Historical Records 2021.**

There you have it... more "evidence" that no one could have imagined existed. In the first sentence of the marker, the inscription read "..., the Rev. Robert Hughes (1821 -1895) and other freedmen...." This part of the historical journey extending from Monticello that I would witness first hand and be a part of was surreal. I was so grateful for such an enlightening experience that addresses the multiple complexities of uncovering one's family history. It is like putting together a 5,000 piece puzzle and you just finished connecting the edges. Because of Rev. Hughes, I ultimately concluded... "I am here today." If there was no Rev. Robert Hughes and his wife Sidney Evans, there would be no Mariah Hughes or Sidney Louise Fleming who birthed my grandmother... who birthed my mother... who birthed me. This is the "evidence" - no one I know could have ever imagined I would be a part of to carry on the legacy of a remarkable people. The journey continues but who would ever have imagined I would be related and historically connected to all this.

NEVER IMAGINED

Ironically, two days after my father-in-law's 90th birthday on September 10th, 2022, Her Majesty Queen Elizabeth II would die at the age of 96. I was mindful of the Colonies that were established under the Royal family and their roll in the Trans Atlantic Slave Trading that brought slaves to Thomas Jefferson's Monticello plantation. Here were two people who have lived through some difficult times as the world transitioned from enslaving people for economic gain. Even my high school math teacher Mr. Warrick Samuel Hill, whom I loved and called my friend for over 50 years, would die 30 days before the Queen at the age of 94. He would author the book, "Before Us Lies The Timber" where I would learn about the segregation that took place in the Maryland county where I grew up. He too would have seen the world grappling with its legacy of human slavery, injustice and racial discrimination. At my father-in-law's 90th birthday party, we had over 90 people, mostly family, who celebrated for the man I would have known for over 44 years who I called, "Pop Jones." The timing of all these elders passing forced me to reflect on the meaning of their lives.

I looked at how each had lived. Having been to England and Buckingham Palace, Queen Elizabeth's death would remind me of Jefferson's death at Monticello. The Queen clearly lived a privileged life like Thomas Jefferson. Her castle and Jefferson's mansion seemed to merely be living symbols of privilege and a monarchy. Each building they had lived in would be preserved to remind generations of the "old way of life" and to communicate a feeling of royalty, imperialism and domination over others. Then there were others like my enslaved ancestors who might have lived a "privileged enslaved life" in a small one room log cabin 12' x14' on what is known as Mulberry Row. I reflected again back on my days at Monticello during my father-in-law's 90th celebration and a pointed question surfaced within me: "What life deserved, celebrating and the playing of Sir Edward Elgar's Pomp and Circumstance March No. 1" as we sang Stevie Wonder's version of "Happy Birthday during Pop Jones' celebration?"

A similar question I would ask of myself watching the pageantry of Queen Elizabeth II departure: "At Monticello, what life style would deserve a national tribute… the lifestyles of the enslaved who served their master faithfully or the life of the master who lived royally because of the forced labor performed by their slaves or even because of the selling and trading of slaves for over 400 years?" My ancestors were forced to pay the price for the great achievements of others in America and around the world. But now, a new awareness would be emerging as the truth would finally emerge within me. It would be a few weeks later, that I would have completed reading the book called: The Love Songs of W.E.B. Du Bois (2021)… a fictional novel by the American Poet Honoree Fanonne Jeffers. This 800 page bible size read brought some critical context to the true impact of slavery on the African American culture and attitudes today. Jeffers book carried through the emotions associated with the plantation owner and the enslaved African giving a voice to what was lost and gained over time.

On September 25, 2022, I would sit and watch the film "Woman King." The fictional movie is based on true facts that took place in the early 1800's in the kingdom called Dahomey, where African people were bartered by other Africans and then traded to the Europeans. There was an all-African woman elite army called Agojie (1818 -1889) that fought against this abuse. As I watched the film, I realized it provided more "evidence" that my ancestors might have come from the counties of Benin where the city of Dahomey resides or Togo during the Transatlantic Slave Trading in that region. As the movie went on, I would recount my Ancestry Ethnicity DNA estimates that 17% of my DNA comes from these countries and 25% from Nigeria. Putting these observations all together, could it be that the slaves that came to Monticello did so by way of the Transatlantic SlaveTrading that Thomas Jefferson would one day oppose. And as we celebrate the late Queen Elizabeth ll, who would distance her reputation from the "The Royal African Company" and the slave voyages marked "DY" or Duke of York that transported millions of African people away from their home land to be enslaved... should their be a pause to realize their greatness came impart because of the forced labor and trading of my ancestors.

It just seemed like the world was in a rush culturally to find the real truth about slavery and all the hidden details about the past. As our elders died, we were now free to have a discussion about what was once taboo. It seemed like the "wolf" Thomas Jefferson was alluding to in his quote could not be held back. In fact, we all are feeling a little unsafe because this truth was being communicated and embedded into the minds and souls of a "woke" generation of skeptics and those who were just not aware. It seems like the more evidence people like me uncovered, the more all of us are coming to realize that the truth we own now is somehow just ours alone to be brutally honest with. Some in "white America" appear to be losing grip on the hidden secrets they once knew. For others like me, it is truly a matter of coping with the realities that we could never imagine would be factually and verifiably true.

Still, there is no changing the past when the forces that created the past still exist. This is the reality we now struggle with. An example of this paradox was made clear in The Love Songs of W.E.B. Du Bois (2021)... a fictional novel where its author clearly felt obligated to tell a fictional story with all the "evidence" of what our "real" story is all about. There is an obligation not to cut corners in getting to the truth whether or not you have room for foul language to be said to turn a bad situation around for future generations to come. I was given all the opportunities I could want to see and examine all the "evidence" that I could have never imagined was there about my family.

AN ENDING THOUGHT

I want my children, their children, and the world to know the stories about where my people have seemingly come from based on the facts I have uncovered. We should appreciate the historical journey of all enslaved people to fully appreciate who we have become as African Americans today. All Americans should recognize the enslavement and suffering endured by the slaves at Monticello against their will. I want everyone to know that we are all born free with the God given right to live free and to enjoy this life which is eloquently echoed in the Declaration of Independence authored by Monticello's creator President Thomas Jefferson. The world where my ancestors were enslaved never destroyed their will for freedom. Each had to make their own decision about making the most of the situation they were in. Many in my family line hoped for and dreamed that we, as a people and family, would one day be free.

Looking back to times where people like me were enslaved at Monticello and when we marched in Selma for voting rights and equality, who could ever imagine that those days of struggling to survive would be behind us? "They did… " They will never know the successes of their descendants like myself, who offer a gratitude of thanks for keeping their will to be free alive through their steadfast faith in God and each other. And it is true, I too faced many challenges and took many risks to find better in my free-life. I believe my ancestors imagined one day things would change, if they kept their will to live to find what was good, better, and best. I would tell them they were right! Like a baby eagle trying to get out of its nest which can be messy, scary and hurtful at times, we all have to learn how to spread our wings and how to fly freely in this life and go wherever our wings take us. It's a wonderful thing to be free!

Knowing that there are those who would seek to entrap us by creating toils and snares, we still must march on until victory is won. Survival is our victory! Our quest is to avoid and defend ourselves against the negative intentions of our foes ….to embrace our right to be free, to vote our way to better and to seek our own paths of true happiness for ourselves and others by working hard. We must collectively, as Americans, keep this hope alive by being vigilant and well aware of the doings of our national and world leaders. We only need to take heed to the recent actions of the Russian leader who invaded the sovereign country of Ukraine to see that our freedoms can be put at peril by the leader's decision to conquer a people's homeland without provocation. Who could have imagined that on February 24th, 2022, Russia would take military action to invade Ukraine as the world watched not realizing that this action alone jeopardized all freedoms that the world enjoys. This is the world we live in today. Some things will never change… we must learn to imagine the unimaginable!

This memoir gives all the "evidence" I could come up with that no one could ever imagine would be the truth for someone like me. As I look at my life, I can say by the grace of God and the hopes of my ancestors, I am free! I have found much joy, success and happiness along the way. I am not bitter about Monticello at all; I am better because of Monticello. I wanted my children, their children, and the world to know about this "evidence" I could have never imagine was here for me to find.

Yearbook photo of
Frank Clay playing
soccer in high school.

Yearbook photo of
Frank Clay playing
basketball in high school.

Frank Clay's senior high school photo, 1972.

The founding members of the Rho chapter of Iota Phi Theta fraternity (with Frank Clay pictured on the far right).

Francis L. Clay Sr. enlisted photo.

Three seniors who came to Towson as freshmen and graduated in four years (left).

More than forty years later, the three remain good friends (right).

My official *Who's Who among Students in American Universities and Colleges* certificate.

Francis L. Clay Jr.,
enlisted photo.

Officer Candidate Clay on the
cover of the September 1979
issue of Soldier magazine.

Me as the guidon bearer during
OCS graduation, 1979.

My official swearing-in for service as an Officer in the US Army.

Joy and I anticipating the arrival of our first child, 1979.

Frank in his Army days, burning the midnight oil.

Frank is standing with his Line Brothers who chartered the first Greek fraternity on Towson University's campus (Iota Phi Theta, Inc.). Frank is standing with the Honorable Founder Lonnie Spruill Jr. (October, 2022 NPHC Tribute)

With my late business mentor and friend, Mr Tombs, during one of the chamber's events.

My corporate photo.

With colleagues of the minority chamber's sister chapter in China.

Me with the secretary of Veterans Affairs.

Me at the rear of my veteran grandfather's casket during his funeral services at Arlington National Cemetery.

Me representing the ClayGroup as a corporate sponsor at a golf tournament.

The headquarters of the ClayGroup in Overland Park, Kansas.

With my late business partner, Ken Thomas, in Panama City.

At an Iota Phi Theta fraternity
leadership conference, 2017.

The late and beautiful, Tamra Beatty—one of The ClayGroup's beloved team members and my dear friend.

With my nephew, who is the chief of police at Fort Meyer, on Veterans' Day.

At the Miami book fair featuring
the release of my third book.

My father, Francis L. Clay Sr., playing the piano.

My mother, Geraldine Clay.

My lovely wife, Joy, over the years.

My grandfather and my daughter Brianne.

Standing among the beauty of our lake house as it was being built.

Frank is standing in front of Union Run Baptist Church that was pastored by its founder Rev. Robert Hughes… who was born as a slave on Thomas Jefferson's Monticello plantation and he is Frank's great, great, great grandfather.

Frank help unveil the historical sign marking the founding of Union Run Baptist church by his ancestors who were enslaved at Monticello (August 7, 2022).

My beautiful family.

APPENDIX

"Balm in Gilead" | Harry Thacker Burleigh
https://www.loc.gov/item/ihas.200185367/
Black Wallstreet | What happen...
https://www.theringer.com/2018/6/28/17511818/black-wall-street-oklahoma-greenwood-destruction-tulsa

Barack Obama | First African American President
https://en.wikipedia.org/wiki/Barack_Obama

Benin Togo | My ancestry
https://www.ancestry.com/dna/ethnicity/benin-togo

Bill Lester | Only African American on NSACAR circuit
https://en.wikipedia.org/wiki/Bill_Lester

Bill Zirger | Banner Creek
https://www.cjonline.com/article/20121208/NEWS/312089901

Black Expo USA
http://articles.baltimoresun.com/1991-05-11/business/1991131050_1_expo-roebuck-businesses

CLAYGROUP LLC | Injunction
https://www.leagle.com/decision/infdco20150901839

ClayGroup LLC | Successful Protest
https://www.bloomberg.com/profile/company/0076899D:US
https://www.gao.gov/products/B-406647,B-406647.2

http://www.cordatislaw.com/resources/legal-cases/the-clay-group-llc-b-406647-b-406647-2-jul-30-2012-2012-cpd-%C2%B6-214
https://www.gao.gov/products/D02752
https://www.bidprotestweekly.com/the-clay-group-llc-b-406647-b-406647-2-july-30-2012/
https://catalog.princeton.edu/catalog/7218993
https://vabusinesslaw.wordpress.com/category/government-contracts/page/6/
http://link.library.missouri.edu/portal/The-Clay-Group-LLC-electronic/xl6T9YPBzvk/
http://legal1280.rssing.com/browser.php?indx=1451012&item=332
http://publiccontractinginstitute.com/the-toilet-paper-case-the-clay-group-decision-serves-as-lesson-in-what-not-to-do/
https://www.bidprotestweekly.com/the-clay-group-llc-b-406647-b-406647-2-july-30-2012/
https://www.gsaadvantage.gov/ref_text/GS07F0003V/0SEOH1.3KR84_V_GS-07F-0003V_GS07F0003V.PDF

Corporate Mastery | Dr. Ramon Corrales:
http://www.integralmasterycenter.com/corporate_mastery.cfm

Credit Card Processor | Brad Oddo
http://destinationraycounty.com/Apr_2011/ImagesandArticles/40UnderForty/forty6.php Oddo
https://basyspro.com/our-team/ Oddo

Dream Team | Olymic basketball
https://en.wikipedia.org/wiki/1992_United_States_men%27s_Olympic_basketball_team

East Germantown Recreation Center | Lonnie Young (now)
https://www.google.com/maps/place/Lonnie+Young+Recreation+Cen ter/@40.0500324,-75.1591241,117m/data=!3m1!1e3!4m6!3m5!1s0x0:0xe3eeab13f1023730!4b1!8m2!3d40.0499977!4d-75.1592808

FORT IRWIN, California | Four paratroopers died and more than 100

were injured 1982
https://www.upi.com/Archives/1982/03/30/Four-paratroopers-died-and-more-than-100-were-injured/9997386312400/

Fort Knox | Basic Training
https://en.wikipedia.org/wiki/Fort_Knox
https://www.google.com/search?q=misery+heartbreak+ft+knox&tbm=isch&source=iu&ictx=1&fir=NDsCeOnrkAtOoM%253A%252CA6k9vvE74l4scM%252C_&vet=1&usg=AI4_-kQ7m8RbTeTwm6b6gLI8ld7fouOtdw&sa=X&ved=2ahUKEwjczZmhg73iAhUqgK0KHcRBAlgQ9QEwBXoECAgQCA#imgrc=NDsCeOnrkAtOoM:

Frank Clay | Salvation: Go to the Word
https://catalog.loc.gov/vwebv/holdingsInfo?searchId=17148&recCount=25&recPointer=0&bibId=20250898

Francis Clay | Right To The Point Seminars Copyright
https://cocatalog.loc.gov/cgi-bin/Pwebrecon.cgi?Search_Arg=Right+to+the+point+seminars&Search_Code=TALL&PID=PjDbrol1vvke_nYJp9jE7YeSlh&SEQ=20180707092045&CNT=25&HIST=1

Gang Life |
https://www.youtube.com/watch?v=dODPu3tYhRM
https://www.youtube.com/watch?v=Jn6Z5sZZMqk

Hoagie | Origin
https://en.wikipedia.org/wiki/Hog_Island,_Philadelphia Hog Island

Homestead Acts |
https://en.wikipedia.org/wiki/Homestead_Acts

HURRICANE | Imra, Maria, Harvey
https://weather.com/storms/hurricane/news/2017-11-11-moments-hurricane-season-atlantic-irma-maria-harvey

If - | RUDYARD KIPLING
https://www.poetryfoundation.org/poems/46473/if---

Iota Phi Theta Inc.
https://www.iotaphitheta.org/reminder/82-last

IOTA PHI THETA - The Founding and Ascendancy
https://www.amazon.com/IOTA-PHI-THETA-Founding-Ascendancy/dp/B003VGCXMS

Joe Fraizer| Gym
https://savingplaces.org/places/joe-frazier-s-gym#.XOyCM9NKh8c

Junius Groves | The Potato King Of The World
https://en.wikipedia.org/wiki/Junius_George_Groves
http://www.bonnersprings.com/news/2007/aug/15/crowd_honors_potato/
http://www.communityvoiceks.com/junius-groves-the-potato-king-of-the-world/article_ca35df48-cd3c-11e5-8cf7-fbb2ece98fdb.html

Kauffman | Kansas City
https://en.wikipedia.org/wiki/Marion_Merrell_Dow

KEN THOMAS|
https://www.kentforestlawn.com/tributes/Kenneth-Thomas

Kenny Rodger | You Got To Know When To Hold Them
https://www.youtube.com/watch?v=6X7Sx62plCw

KINGDOMWARE TECHNOLOGIES, INC (SDVOSB) | Supreme Court
https://www.supremecourt.gov/opinions/15pdf/14-916_6j37.pdf

Leroy Tombs |
http://www.bonnersprings.com/news/2006/may/18/leroy_tombs_de_ad/

Michelle Obama | When They Go Low, We Go High
https://www.youtube.com/watch?v=mu_hCThhzWU Mrs. Obama

Mulatto | Definition
https://en.wikipedia.org/wiki/Mulatto

NAMD | African American Marketing
https://blacksuccessfoundation.org/african-american-organizations/name/national-alliance-of-market-developers/

OCS | Officer Candidate School
https://www.benning.army.mil/Infantry/199th/OCS/

Peary High School | 1972 Year Book (My Senior Year)
http://repearyhs.org/yearbooks/1972-yearbook/

Philadelphia Boys Choir & Chorale |
https://en.wikipedia.org/wiki/Philadelphia_Boys_Choir_%26_Chorale

Senator Pat Roberts |
https://www.cjonline.com/news/20190104/us-sen-pat-roberts-to-retire-wont-seek-re-election-in-2020

Service Disabled Veteran Owned Small Business (SDVOSB)| GSA
https://www.gsa.gov/acquisition/assistance-for-small-businesses/find-and-pursue-government-contracts/seek-opportunities/setasides-special-interest-groups/for-servicedisabled-veteranowned-small-businesses 51% owner - 100% control

Skillpath Seminar |
https://skillpath.com/?se=gs0003&utm_source=google&utm_medium=search&utm_campaign=brand&utm_topic=all&utm_stareq=gs0003&gclid=EAIaIQobChMIn5Lv8fi84gIVSZ7ACh2vRgfrEAAYASAAEgJ8Q_D_BwE

TAMRA BEATTY |
https://www.legacy.com/obituaries/kansascity/obituary.aspx?n=tamra-l-beatty&pid=175855934&fhid=14669

Three Fifths Clause in the Constitution |
http://www.blackpast.org/aah/three-fifths-clause-united-states-constitution-1787

TOWSON STATE COLLEGE | TOWSON UNIVERSITY
https://www.baltimoresun.com/bal-towson0701-pic-photo.html

TOWSON TOWERLIGHT | Black fraternal groups expanding at Towson (Francis Clay) –
http://library.towson.edu/digital/collection/stunews/id/4059
http://library.towson.edu/digital/collection/stunews/id/3950/rec/4
http://library.towson.edu/digital/collection/stunews/id/2110/rec/1
http://library.towson.edu/digital/collection/stunews/id/2141/rec/5★★★

TUSKEGEE AIRMEN | Discriminated against
https://www.c-span.org/video/?c4515007/freeman-mutiny

VA Hospital Directory |
https://www.va.gov/directory/guide/rpt_fac_list.cfm

Warrick Hill | His Book –Before Lies Timber
http://bartlebythepublisher.com/featured/before-us-lies-the-timber/

Wayne Schelle |Celluar Phones
https://www.rcrwireless.com/20050314/carriers/wayne-schelle-pioneer-in-cellular-pcs
https://www.baltimoresun.com/news/bs-xpm-1990-10-08-1990281031-story.html
https://www.legacy.com/obituaries/baltimoresun/obituary.aspx?n=wayne-schelle&pid=183573446&fhid=4134

William Rowen School | My Elementary School
https://en.wikipedia.org/wiki/William_Rowen_School

2-110 FA MDARNG | Headquarter Battery Commander
https://en.wikipedia.org/wiki/110th_Information_Operations_Battalion

ABOUT THE AUTHOR

Frank Clay is the author of five books. His previous release is a book on leadership called: SUCCESSFUL LEADERS | BIG BELIEVERS - How to Lead During Challenging Times. Frank is a member of the National Speakers Association (NSA) and he enjoys speaking to groups and businesses about leadership, business and professional development.

Frank has owned a multimillion dollar small business for 11 years. He spent 10 years in the US Army working his way from being a Private to a Commander. Frank has worked with three Fortune 50 companies, spending 13 years with Johnson & Johnson (Medical) as a representative, manager, executive (National Sales Planning Manager). Frank was the first African American to sell cellular telephones in the early 1980's and has been a certified instructor for SkillPath Seminars (Management & Leadership Skills). Frank has a Bachelors and Master (MBA) Degree in Business Administration and he has a love for music, poetry, golf, and basketball.

Frank's mission in life is to help people prepare themselves to lead during challenging times. He uses his own personal and professional life experiences to give authentic advice on how to prepare yourself and others to lead when their leadership moment comes. He believes the best leader is the one who is prepared to lead!

To book Frank Clay for a speaking engagement or workshop, visit www.frankclayjr.com. You can reach out to Mr. Clay on social media by using any of the following handles:

LinkedIn: Frank Clay Jr.
Facebook: Frank Clay Jr.
Instagram: @FrankClayJr
YouTube: Frank Clay Jr.
Twitter: FrankClayJr

EMAIL: Callhere4me@gmail.com

www.ingramcontent.com/pod-product-compliance
Lightning Source LLC
LaVergne TN
LVHW010306070526
838199LV00065B/5462